Pro JavaFX 9: A Definitive Guide to Building Desktop, Mobile, and Embedded Java Clients

Johan Vos
Leuven, Belgium

Stephen Chin
BELMONT, California, USA

Weiqi Gao
Ballwin, Missouri, USA

James Weaver
Marion, Indiana, USA

Dean Iverson
Fort Collins, Colorado, USA

ISBN-13 (pbk): 978-1-4842-3041-1
https://doi.org/10.1007/978-1-4842-3042-8

ISBN-13 (electronic): 978-1-4842-3042-8

Library of Congress Control Number: 2017963349

Cover image by Freepik (`www.freepik.com`)

Managing Director: Welmoed Spahr
Editorial Director: Todd Green
Acquisitions Editor: Steve Anglin
Development Editor: Matthew Moodie
Technical Reviewers: Mark Heckler and Jonathan Giles
Coordinating Editor: Mark Powers
Copy Editor: Kimberly Burton-Weisman

Distributed to the book trade worldwide by Springer Science+Business Media New York, 233 Spring Street, 6th Floor, New York, NY 10013. Phone 1-800-SPRINGER, fax (201) 348-4505, e-mail orders-ny@springer-sbm.com, or visit `www.springeronline.com`. Apress Media, LLC is a California LLC and the sole member (owner) is Springer Science + Business Media Finance Inc (SSBM Finance Inc). SSBM Finance Inc is a **Delaware** corporation.

For information on translations, please e-mail rights@apress.com, or visit `http://www.apress.com/rights-permissions`.

Apress titles may be purchased in bulk for academic, corporate, or promotional use. eBook versions and licenses are also available for most titles. For more information, reference our Print and eBook Bulk Sales web page at `http://www.apress.com/bulk-sales`.

Any source code or other supplementary material referenced by the author in this book is available to readers on GitHub via the book's product page, located at `www.apress.com/9781484230411`. For more detailed information, please visit `http://www.apress.com/source-code`.

Printed on acid-free paper

Pro JavaFX 9

A Definitive Guide to Building Desktop, Mobile, and Embedded Java Clients

Fourth Edition

Johan Vos
Stephen Chin
Weiqi Gao
James Weaver
Dean Iverson

Apress®

Contents

About the Authors

Johan Vos is a Java Champion who started to work with Java in 1995. As part of the Blackdown team, he helped port Java to Linux. With LodgON, the company he cofounded, he has been mainly working on Java-based solutions for social networking software. His main focus is on end-to-end Java, combining the strengths of back-end systems and embedded devices. His favorite technologies are currently Java EE/ Glassfish at the back end and JavaFX at the front end. He contributes to a number of open source projects, including DataFX and the Android port of JavaFX. Johan's blog can be followed at `http://blogs.lodgon.com/johan`, he tweets at `http://twitter.com/johanvos`, and can be reached at `johan@lodgon.com`.

Stephen Chin is a Java Ambassador at Oracle specializing in embedded and user interface technology and the JavaOne Content Chair. He has been featured at Java conferences around the world including Devoxx, JFokus, OSCON, JFall, GeeCON, JustJava, and JavaOne, where he three times received a Rock Star Award. Stephen is an avid motorcyclist who has done several Pan-European evangelism tours, interviewing hackers in their natural habitat and posting the videos on `http://nighthacking.com`. When he is not traveling, he enjoys teaching kids how to do embedded and robot programming together with his 11-year-old daughter.

Weiqi Gao is a principal software engineer with Object Computing, Inc. in St. Louis, Missouri. He has decades of software development experience and has been using Java technology since 1998. He is interested in programming languages, object-oriented systems, distributed computing, and graphical user interfaces. He is a member of the steering committee of the St. Louis Java Users Group. Weiqi holds a PhD in mathematics.

James Weaver is an author, a speaker, a teacher, and a developer in rich Internet application technologies such as JavaFX. He is also an Oracle engineer. He may be contacted at `jim.weaver@javafxpert.com`.

Dean Iverson has been writing software professionally for more than 15 years. He is employed by the Virginia Tech Transportation Institute, where he is a senior researcher and rich client application developer. He also has a small software consultancy called Pleasing Software Solutions, which he cofounded with his wife.

About the Technical Reviewers

Mark Heckler is a Java software architect/engineer with development experience in numerous environments. He has worked for and with key players in the manufacturing, emerging markets, retail, medical, telecom, and financial industries to develop and deliver critical capabilities on time and on budget. Currently, he works primarily with enterprise customers using Java throughout the stack. He also participates in open source development at every opportunity, being a JFXtras project committer, developer of DialogFX and MonologFX, co-developer of Autonomous4j, and more. When Mark isn't working with Java, he enjoys sharing his experiences at conferences and via the Java Jungle web site (`https://blogs.oracle.com/javajungle`), his personal web site (`www.thehecklers.org`), and Twitter (`@MkHeck`). Mark lives with his very understanding wife, three kids, and dog in St. Louis, Missouri.

Jonathan Giles is a software engineer who has worked with Java and JavaFX for a very long time. He has been responsible for large sections of the JavaFX toolkit stack since 2009, and as such, is intimately familiar with it. He is a JavaOne Rockstar speaker and track lead, an initiator of many open source projects (such as ControlsFX and Scenic View—both referenced in this book), and a technical reviewer of many Java-related books. He blogs at `jonathangiles.net`, and can be found on Twitter `@JonathanGiles`.

Acknowledgments

Writing a book is often done in spare time. I want to thank my wife, Kathleen, and our children, Merlijn and Linde, for allowing me to spend evening and weekend time in front of my computer. I want to thank authors Jim Weaver, Weiqi Gao, Stephen Chin, and Dean Iverson; technical reviewer Mark Heckler; and the Apress team for their trust in me. A special thanks to my LodgON colleagues Joeri Sykora and Erwin Morrhey for helping me with the examples. The JavaFX team at Oracle did a great job releasing JavaFX 8. The combination of their efforts and those of the Java community makes JavaFX an excellent platform for an increasing number of clients.

—Johan Vos

To my wife, Justine, and daughters, Cassandra and Priscilla, who supported me in writing this book on top of all my other responsibilities. Also, a huge thanks to the entire author team, including our newest members, Johan Vos and Mark Heckler, who both went above and beyond in their contributions to this title. Finally, a great debt of gratitude to the JavaFX team and JVM language designers who have produced technology that will profoundly change the way we design and code user interfaces going forward.

—Stephen Chin

I would like to thank my wife, Youhong Gong, for her support, understanding, and encouragement during the writing process. My thanks also go to the author and technical review team: Johan Vos, Jim Weaver, Stephen Chin, Dean Iverson, and Mark Heckler for making this book a fun project. I share with my coauthors the appreciation for the JavaFX team at Oracle and the editorial team at Apress.

—Weiqi Gao

I would like to thank my family, Sondra, Alex, and Matt, for their support and understanding during yet another writing project. You guys make this possible. I would also like to thank the writing and review team of Jim Weaver, Stephen Chin, Weiqi Gao, Johan Vos, and Mark Heckler for their dedication and their patience. The editorial team at Apress was, as usual, first rate and utterly professional. And, of course, none of this would be possible without the hard work of an extremely talented team of engineers on the JavaFX team at Oracle.

—Dean Iverson

To my wife Julie, daughters, Lori and Kelli, son, Marty, and grandchildren, Kaleb and Jillian. Thanks Merrill and Barbara Bishir, Ken and Marilyn Prater, and Walter Weaver for being such wonderful examples. My contributions to this book are dedicated to the memory of Merrill Bishir and Ken Prater. *"I have told you these things, so that in me you may have peace. In this world you will have trouble. But take heart! I have overcome the world."* (John 16:33)

—James Weaver

Foreword

I remember it distinctly, like it was yesterday: standing center stage at Moscone Center when we launched JavaFX at JavaOne 2007. We promised to build a world-class client platform for Java. With the world watching with skeptical eyes and in a crowded client arena, we set out to build the dream. In hindsight, it was a rather ambitious goal.

Fast-forward seven years, with the release of Java SE 8, we have taken a huge leap forward in fulfilling that promise. As the vision unfolded, our product plans have shifted to match the evolving RIA market and what developers and the Java community told us they were looking for. As someone who was there at the inception of JavaFX and who has watched it mature over the last seven years to this current release, my feelings are akin to a parent watching a toddler blossom.

James Weaver and Stephen Chin have been traveling through the evolution of JavaFX with me. They have both presented on JavaFX at numerous international conferences and have been developing with and blogging about JavaFX since 2007. James is a 30-year software veteran who has authored several books on Java, as well as articles for *Java Magazine* and the Oracle Technology Network. He has also developed numerous JavaFX applications for a wide variety of customers.

Stephen is passionate about open source technologies and is the founder of WidgetFX and JFXtras. He also has a deep passion for improving development technologies and processes, as well as agile development methodologies.

Johan Vos is cofounder of LodgON. He holds a PhD in applied physics and he has been a very prolific member of the JavaFX community. His interest lies in the enterprise communication aspects of JavaFX, combining the world of large servers with end-user devices. Johan's analogy to physics: The grand unified theory combines quantum mechanics (small) with relativity theory (large); similarly, in software, Java combines JavaFX with Java EE.

Dean Iverson is a longtime client developer with a great eye for creating elegant user interfaces. He develops GroovyFX libraries and is a contributor to the JFXtras project. He has been developing and blogging about JavaFX since 2007. Weiqi Gao holds a PhD in mathematics. His expertise is in the language aspects of JavaFX, as reflected in the chapters on properties and bindings, and collections and concurrency.

Today, the core JavaFX team at Oracle still has several of the developers who were part of the early versions of JavaFX and we also have new engineers who have joined us. As we move ahead and open source JavaFX, we are looking forward to having more developers and experts from the extended Java community join us in making JavaFX the number one choice for client development.

I am proud and honored to be part of this key software technology. Given their length of experience and depth of expertise in all aspects of JavaFX and across the Java platform, I cannot think of a better group of authors to bring you JavaFX 8. I hope you will enjoy this book and find JavaFX as satisfying as I have found it over the years. I hope it piques your interest sufficiently to join the JavaFX community in making JavaFX the platform of choice for clients.

—Nandini Ramani
Vice President, Java Client Development
Oracle Corporation

Introduction

As a developer, author, speaker, and advocate for JavaFX since its inception in 2007, I am very excited about JavaFX 8. It was released in March 2014 as an integral part of Java SE 8, and is the successor to Java Swing. As you'll read in the pages of this book, JavaFX runs on desktops (Mac, Windows, Linux), as well as embedded devices such as the Raspberry Pi. As the Internet of things (IoT) is increasingly realized, JavaFX is well positioned to enable the user interface of IoT. Also, because of community projects led by folks such as Johan Vos and Niklas Therning, developers are deploying JavaFX apps on Android and iOS devices.

The JavaFX community has many talented, passionate, and cordial developers, and I count it a privilege to call them my colleagues. One such colleague, Johan Vos, is a coauthor of our *Pro JavaFX 2* book, and is the lead author of *Pro JavaFX 8*. It has been my pleasure to continue working with Johan on this book under his leadership. Please join me in welcoming and congratulating him in this role, perhaps by tweeting him at @JohanVos or posting a review of this book on Amazon. It is my hope that you'll find this book both enjoyable and instrumental in helping you learn JavaFX!

—James L. Weaver
Java Technology Ambassador
Oracle Corporation

CHAPTER 1

■ ■ ■

Getting a Jump-Start in JavaFX

Don't ask what the world needs. Ask what makes you come alive, and go do it. Because what the world needs is people who have come alive.

—Howard Thurman

At the annual JavaOne conference in May 2007, Sun Microsystems announced a new product family named JavaFX. Its stated purpose includes enabling the development and deployment of content-rich applications on consumer devices such as cell phones, televisions, in-dash car systems, and browsers. Josh Marinacci, a software engineer at Sun, made the following statement, very appropriately, in a Java Posse interview: "JavaFX is sort of a code word for reinventing client Java and fixing the sins of the past." He was referring to the fact that Java Swing and Java 2D have lots of capability, but are also very complex. Furthermore, technologies have evolved a lot since Swing and Java 2D were created. Today's client systems (desktops as well as mobile and embedded devices) are equipped with powerful graphical processors—the GPU. JavaFX takes advantage of the new features and performance increases offered by GPUs. By using FXML, JavaFX allows us to simply and elegantly express user interfaces (UIs) with a declarative programming style. It also leverages the full power of Java, because you can instantiate and use the millions of Java classes that exist today. Add features such as binding the UI to properties in a model and change listeners that reduce the need for setter methods, and you have a combination that will help restore Java to the client-side Internet applications.

In this chapter, we give you a jump-start in developing JavaFX applications. After bringing you up to date on the brief history of JavaFX, we show you how to get the required tools. We also explore some great JavaFX resources and walk you through the process of compiling and running JavaFX applications. In the process, you'll learn a lot about the JavaFX *application programming interface* (API) as we walk through application code together.

A Brief History of JavaFX

JavaFX started life as the brainchild of Chris Oliver when he worked for a company named SeeBeyond. They had a need for richer user interfaces, so Chris created a language that he dubbed F3 (Form Follows Function) for that purpose. In the article "Mind-Bendingly Cool Innovation" (cited in the "Resources" section at the end of this chapter), Chris is quoted as follows: "When it comes to integrating people into business processes, you need graphical user interfaces for them to interact with, so there was a use case for graphics in the enterprise application space, and there was an interest at SeeBeyond in having richer user interfaces."

SeeBeyond was acquired by Sun, who subsequently changed the name of F3 to JavaFX, and announced it at JavaOne 2007. Chris Oliver joined Sun during the acquisition and continued to lead the development of JavaFX.

© Johan Vos, Stephen Chin, Weiqi Gao, James Weaver, and Dean Iverson 2018
J. Vos et al., *Pro JavaFX 9*, https://doi.org/10.1007/978-1-4842-3042-8_1

The first version of JavaFX Script was an interpreted language, and was considered a prototype of the compiled JavaFX Script language that was to come later. Interpreted JavaFX Script was very robust, and there were two JavaFX books published in the latter part of 2007 based on that version. One was written in Japanese, and the other was written in English (*JavaFX Script: Dynamic Java Scripting for Rich Internet/Client-Side Applications* by Jim Weaver (Apress, 2007)).

While developers were experimenting with JavaFX and providing feedback for improvement, the JavaFX Script compiler team at Sun was busy creating a compiled version of the language. This included a new set of runtime API libraries. The JavaFX Script compiler project reached a tipping point in early December 2007, which was commemorated in a blog post entitled "Congratulations to the JavaFX Script Compiler Team—The Elephant Is Through the Door." That phrase came from the JavaFX Script compiler project leader Tom Ball in a blog post, which contained the following excerpt.

> *An elephant analogy came to me when I was recently grilled about exactly when the JavaFX Script compiler team will deliver our first milestone release. "I can't give you an accurate date," I said. "It's like pushing an elephant through a door; until a critical mass makes it past the threshold you just don't know when you'll be finished. Once you pass that threshold, though, the rest happens quickly and in a manner that can be more accurately predicted."*

A screenshot of the silly, compiled JavaFX application written by one of the authors, Jim Weaver, for that post is shown in Figure 1-1, demonstrating that the project had in fact reached the critical mass to which Tom Ball referred.

Figure 1-1. *Screenshot for the "Elephant Is Through the Door" program*

Much progress continued to be made on JavaFX in 2008:

- The NetBeans JavaFX plug-in became available for the compiled version in March 2008.

- Many of the JavaFX runtime libraries (mostly focusing on the UI aspects of JavaFX) were rewritten by a team that included some very talented developers from the Java Swing team.

- In July 2008, the JavaFX Preview Software Development Kit (SDK) was released, and at JavaOne 2008, Sun announced that the JavaFX 1.0 SDK would be released in fall 2008.

- On December 4, 2008, the JavaFX 1.0 SDK was released. This event increased the adoption rate of JavaFX by developers and IT managers because it represented a stable codebase.

- In April 2009, Oracle and Sun announced that Oracle would be acquiring Sun. The JavaFX 1.2 SDK was released at JavaOne 2009.

- In January 2010, Oracle completed its acquisition of Sun. The JavaFX 1.3 SDK was released in April 2010, with JavaFX 1.3.1 being the last of the 1.3 releases.

At JavaOne 2010, JavaFX 2.0 was announced. The JavaFX 2.0 roadmap was published by Oracle and included items such as the following.

- Deprecate the JavaFX Script language in favor of using Java and the JavaFX 2.0 API. This brings JavaFX into the mainstream by making it available to any language (e.g., Java, Groovy, and JRuby) that runs on the Java Virtual Machine (JVM). As a consequence, existing developers do not need to learn a new language, but they can use existing skills and start developing JavaFX applications.

- Make the compelling features of JavaFX Script, including binding to expressions, available in the JavaFX 2.0 API.

- Offer an increasingly rich set of UI components, building on the components already available in JavaFX 1.3.

- Provide a Web component for embedding HTML and JavaScript content into JavaFX applications.

- Enable JavaFX interoperability with Swing.

- Rewrite the media stack from the ground up.

JavaFX 2.0 was released at JavaOne 2011, and has enjoyed a greatly increased adoption rate due to the innovative features articulated previously.

JavaFX 8 marked another important milestone. JavaFX is now an integral part of the Java Platform, Standard Edition.

- This is a clear indication that JavaFX is considered mature enough, and that it is the future of Java on the client.

- This greatly benefits developers, as they don't have to download two SDKs and tool suites.

- The new technologies in Java 8, in particular the lambda expressions, Stream API, and default interface methods, are very usable in JavaFX.

- Many new features have been added, including native 3D support, a printing API, and some new controls including a datepicker.

- Since the release of JavaFX 8, the JavaFX platform follows the same version and release procedures as the Java Platform, Standard Edition. As a consequence, when Java 9 was released, JavaFX 9 was released as well.

- The main focus for Java 9 is modularity. The Java Platform, Standard Edition, has become bigger and bigger, and not all applications require all classes to be available. By modularizing the Java Platform, it is easier to create subsets of the Java platform that combine a number of modules that are sufficient to run a particular application. This modularization effort was huge, and it took many years before it was complete. All parts of the Java Platform, Standard Edition have been refactored into modules, including the JavaFX 9 Platform APIs.

- One of the consequences of the modularization is that it is now not allowed anymore for code to depend on internal APIs of another module. This has far-reaching consequences. Before JavaFX 9, Controls were often created by implementing undocumented internal APIs. Those APIs were public, because they were used internally by other JavaFX classes, in different packages. As a consequence, developer could use them as well.

- Since those internal APIs are now in modules that by default do not expose this functionality, a new approach was needed for developers who want to create custom controls. Hence, the JavaFX team was not only faced with moving all the JavaFX public APIs into a number of modules, it also had to provide public APIs for functionality that was previously accessed via internal APIs.

In Java 9, the JavaFX platform provides the following modules:

- javafx.base
- javafx.controls
- javafx.fxml
- javafx.graphics
- javafx.jmx
- javafx.media
- javafx.swing
- javafx.swt
- javafx.web
- jdk.packager
- jdk.packager.services

Now that you've had the obligatory history lesson in JavaFX, let's get one step closer to writing code by showing you where some examples, tools, and other resources are.

Prepare Your JavaFX Journey

Required Tools

Because JavaFX is part of Java 9, you don't have to download a separate JavaFX SDK. The whole JavaFX API and implementation is part of the Java 9 SE SDK that can be downloaded from www.oracle.com/technetwork/java/javase/downloads/index.html.

This SDK contains everything you need to develop, run, and package JavaFX applications. You can compile JavaFX applications using command-line tools contained in the Java 9 SE SDK.

Most developers, however, prefer an *integrated development environment* (IDE) for increased productivity. By definition, an IDE that supports Java 9 also supports JavaFX 9. Hence, you can use your favorite IDE and develop JavaFX applications. In this book, we mainly use the NetBeans IDE, but other

IDE's, such as IntelliJ or Eclipse, can be used as well. The NetBeans IDE can be downloaded from `https://netbeans.org/downloads`.

Many JavaFX developers, especially those working on user interfaces, prefer a WYSIWYG tool for creating interfaces. Scene Builder is a stand-alone tool that allows you to design JavaFX interfaces rather than coding them. We discuss Scene Builder in Chapter 4. Although Scene Builder produces FXML—and we discuss FXML in Chapter 3 as well—that can be used in any IDE, NetBeans provides a tight integration with Scene Builder. The Scene Builder tool can be downloaded at `http://gluonhq.com/products/scene-builder/`.

JavaFX, the Community

JavaFX is not a closed-source project, developed in a secret bunker. To the contrary, JavaFX is being developed in an open spirit, with an open source code base, open mailing lists, and an open and active community sharing knowledge.

The source code is developed in the OpenJFX project, which is a subproject of the OpenJDK project in which Java SE is being developed. If you want to examine the source code or the architecture, or if you want to read the technical discussions on the mailing list, have a look at `http://openjdk.java.net/projects/openjfx`.

The developer community is very active, both in OpenJFX as well as in application-specific areas. Many JavaFX developers regularly blog about their JavaFX activities, and many non-Oracle products and projects related to JavaFX are being created and maintained by this community.

In addition, blogs maintained by JavaFX engineers and developers are great resources for up-to-the-minute technical information on JavaFX. For example, Oracle JavaFX Engineer Jonathan Giles keep the developer community apprised of the latest JavaFX innovations at `http://fxexperience.com`. The "Resources" section at the end of this chapter contains the URLs of the blogs that the authors of this book use to engage the JavaFX developer community.

Two important characteristics of the JavaFX Community are its own creativity and the desire to share. There are a number of open-source efforts bringing added value to the JavaFX Platform. Because of good cooperation between the JavaFX platform engineers and the external JavaFX developers, these open-source projects fit very well with the official JavaFX platform.

Some of the most interesting efforts are listed here:

- Gluon allows you to create iOS and Android applications using Java and JavaFX. As a consequence, your JavaFX application can be used to create an app for Android devices and for the iPhone or the iPad.

This mobile port of JavaFX is discussed in more detail in Chapter 12.

- ControlsFX is a project working on adding high-quality controls and add-ons to the JavaFX platform.

- JFXtras.org is another project working on adding high-quality controls and add-ons to the JavaFX platform.

It is worth mentioning that the JavaFX team is closely watching the efforts in both JFXtras.org and ControlsFX, and ideas that start in one of those projects might make it into one of the next releases of JavaFX.

Take a few minutes to explore these sites. Next, we point out some valuable resources.

Use the Official Specifications

While developing JavaFX applications, it is very useful to have access to the API Javadoc documentation, which is available at `http://download.java.net/jdk9/jfxdocs/index.html` and shown in Figure 1-2.

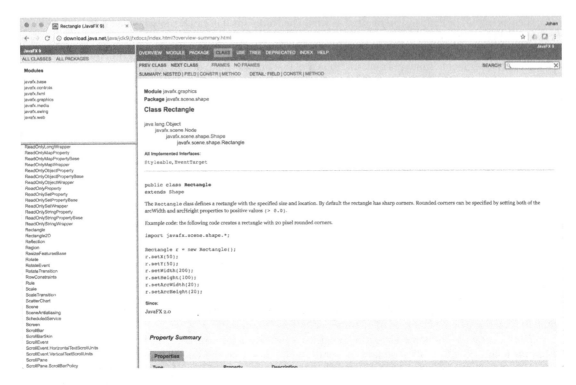

Figure 1-2. *JavaFX SDK API Javadoc*

The API documentation in Figure 1-2, for example, shows how to use the `Rectangle` class, located in the `javafx.scene.shape` package. Scrolling down this web page shows the properties, constructors, methods, and other helpful information about the `Rectangle` class. By the way, this API documentation is available in the Java 8 SE SDK that you downloaded, but we wanted you to know how to find it online as well.

Apart from the Javadoc, it is very useful to have the Cascading Style Sheets (CSS) style reference at hand as well. This document explains all the style classes that can be applied to a particular JavaFX element. You can find this document at `http://download.java.net/jdk9/jfxdocs/javafx/scene/doc-files/cssref.html`.

Scenic View

You already downloaded Scene Builder, which is the tool that allows you to create UIs by designing them, rather than writing code. We expect that there will be more tools developed by companies and individuals that help you create JavaFX applications. One of the first tools that was made available for free and that is very helpful when debugging JavaFX applications is ScenicView, originally created by Amy Fowler at Oracle, and later maintained by Jonathan Giles. You can download ScenicView at `http://scenic-view.org/`.

ScenicView is particularly helpful because it provides a convenient UI that allows developers to inspect properties of nodes (i.e., dimensions, translations, CSS) at runtime.

Packaging and Distribution

The techniques used for delivering software to the end user are always changing. In the past, the preferred way for delivering Java applications was via the Java Network Launch Protocol (JNLP). Doing so, both applets and stand-alone applications can be installed on a client. However, there are a number of issues with this technique. The idea only works if the end user has a JVM installed that is capable of executing the application. This is not always true. Even in the desktop world, where a system can be delivered preinstalled with a JVM, there are issues with versioning and security. Indeed, some applications are hard-coded against a specific version of the JVM. Although vulnerabilities in the JVM are in most cases fixed very fast, this still requires the end user to always install the latest version of the JVM, which can be pretty frustrating.

On top of that, browser manufacturers are increasingly reluctant to support alternative embedded platforms. In summary, relying on a browser and on a local, preinstalled JVM does not provide the best end-user experience.

The client software industry is shifting more and more toward the so-called app stores. In this concept, applications can be downloaded and installed that are self-containing. They do not rely on preinstalled execution environments. The principles originated in the mobile space, where Apple's AppStore and Android's Play Store are leading the market. Especially in these markets, single-click installs have a huge advantage over local downloads, unpacking, manual configuration, and more nightmares.

In Java terminology, a self-contained application means that the application is bundled together with a JVM that is capable of running the application. In the past, this idea was often rejected because it made the application bundle too big. However, with increasing memory and storage capacities, and with decreasing costs of sending bytes over the Internet, this disadvantage is becoming less relevant.

There are a number of technologies being developed currently that help you bundle your application with the correct JVM version and package it.

The standard technology for bundling Java applications with a Java Virtual Machine runtime is the JavaPackager, which is developed inside the OpenJFX project area. JavaFXPackager contains an API for creating self-contained bundles. This tool is used by NetBeans, and it can be used to generate self-contained bundles with just a few clicks.

Now that you have the tools installed, we show you how to create a simple JavaFX program, and then we walk through it in detail. The first program that we've chosen for you is called "Hello Earthrise," which demonstrates more features than the typical beginning "Hello World" program.

Developing Your First JavaFX Program: Hello Earthrise

On Christmas Eve in 1968, the crew of *Apollo 8* entered lunar orbit for the first time in history. They were the first humans to witness an "Earthrise," taking the magnificent picture shown in Figure 1-3. This image is dynamically loaded from this book's web site when the program starts, so you'll need to be connected to the Internet to view it.

Figure 1-3. *The Hello Earthrise program*

In addition to demonstrating how to dynamically load images over the Internet, this example shows you how to use animation in JavaFX. Now it's time for you to compile and run the program. We show you two ways to do this: from the command line and using NetBeans.

Compiling and Running from the Command Line

We usually use an IDE to build and run JavaFX programs, but to take all of the mystery out of the process we use the command-line tools first.

■ **Note** For this exercise, as with most others in the book, you need the source code. If you prefer not to type the source code into a text editor, you can obtain the source code for all of the examples in this book from the code download site. See the "Resources" section at the end of this chapter for the location of this site.

Assuming that you've downloaded and extracted the source code for this book into a directory, follow the directions in this exercise, performing all of the steps as instructed. We dissect the source code after the exercise.

COMPILING AND RUNNING THE HELLO EARTHRISE PROGRAM FROM THE COMMAND LINE

You'll use the javac and java command-line tools to compile and run the program in this exercise. From the command-line prompt on your machine:

1. Navigate to the Chapter01/Hello directory.

2. Execute the following command to compile the HelloEarthRiseMain.java file.

    ```
    javac -d . HelloEarthRiseMain.java
    ```

3. Because the –d option was used in this command, the class files generated are placed in directories matching the package statements in the source files. The roots of those directories are specified by the argument given for the –d option, in this case the current directory.

4. To run the program, execute the following command. Note that we use the fully qualified name of the class that will be executed, which entails specifying the nodes of the path name and the name of the class, all separated by periods.

    ```
    java projavafx.helloearthrise.ui.HelloEarthRiseMain
    ```

The program should appear as shown in Figure 1-4, with the text scrolling slowly upward, reminiscent of the *Star Wars* opening crawls.

Congratulations on completing your first exercise as you explore JavaFX!

Understanding the Hello Earthrise Program

Now that you've run the application, let's walk through the program listing together. The code for the Hello Earthrise application is shown in Listing 1-1.

Listing 1-1. The HelloEarthRiseMain.java Program

```java
package projavafx.helloearthrise.ui;

import javafx.animation.Interpolator;
import javafx.animation.Timeline;
import javafx.animation.TranslateTransition;
import javafx.application.Application;
import javafx.geometry.VPos;
import javafx.scene.Group;
import javafx.scene.Scene;
import javafx.scene.image.Image;
import javafx.scene.image.ImageView;
import javafx.scene.paint.Color;
import javafx.scene.shape.Rectangle;
import javafx.scene.text.Font;
import javafx.scene.text.FontWeight;
import javafx.scene.text.Text;
```

9

```java
import javafx.scene.text.TextAlignment;
import javafx.stage.Stage;
import javafx.util.Duration;

/**
 * Main class for the "Hello World" style example
 */
public class HelloEarthRiseMain extends Application {

    /**
     * @param args the command line arguments
     */
    public static void main(String[] args) {
        Application.launch(args);
    }

    @Override
    public void start(Stage stage) {

        String message
                = "Earthrise at Christmas: "
                + "[Forty] years ago this Christmas, a turbulent world "
                + "looked to the heavens for a unique view of our home "
                + "planet. This photo of Earthrise over the lunar horizon "
                + "was taken by the Apollo 8 crew in December 1968, showing "
                + "Earth for the first time as it appears from deep space. "
                + "Astronauts Frank Borman, Jim Lovell and William Anders "
                + "had become the first humans to leave Earth orbit, "
                + "entering lunar orbit on Christmas Eve. In a historic live "
                + "broadcast that night, the crew took turns reading from "
                + "the Book of Genesis, closing with a holiday wish from "
                + "Commander Borman: \"We close with good night, good luck, "
                + "a Merry Christmas, and God bless all of you -- all of "
                + "you on the good Earth.\"";

        // Reference to the Text
        Text textRef = new Text(message);
        textRef.setLayoutY(100);
        textRef.setTextOrigin(VPos.TOP);
        textRef.setTextAlignment(TextAlignment.JUSTIFY);
        textRef.setWrappingWidth(400);
        textRef.setFill(Color.rgb(187, 195, 107));
        textRef.setFont(Font.font("SansSerif", FontWeight.BOLD, 24));

        // Provides the animated scrolling behavior for the text
        TranslateTransition transTransition = new TranslateTransition(new Duration(75000),
        textRef);
        transTransition.setToY(-820);
        transTransition.setInterpolator(Interpolator.LINEAR);
        transTransition.setCycleCount(Timeline.INDEFINITE);
```

```
        // Create an ImageView containing the Image
        Image image = new Image ("http://projavafx.com/images/earthrise.jpg");
        ImageView imageView = new ImageView(image);

        // Create a Group containing the text
        Group textGroup = new Group(textRef);
        textGroup.setLayoutX(50);
        textGroup.setLayoutY(180);
        textGroup.setClip(new Rectangle(430, 85));

        // Combine ImageView and Group
        Group root = new Group(imageView, textGroup);
        Scene scene = new Scene(root, 516, 387);

        stage.setScene(scene);
        stage.setTitle("Hello Earthrise");
        stage.show();

        // Start the text animation
        transTransition.play();
    }
}
```

Now that you've seen the code, let's take a look at its constructs and concepts in some more detail.

What Happened to the Builders?

If you were using JavaFX 2 before, you are probably familiar with the so-called builder pattern. Builders provide a declarative style of programming. Rather than calling set() methods on a class instance to specify its fields, the builder pattern uses an instance of a Builder class to define how the target class should be composed.

Builders were very popular in JavaFX. However, it turned out that there were major technical hurdles with keeping them in the platform. As a consequence, the decision was made to phase out builders. In Java 8, Builder classes were still usable, but they are deprecated. In Java 9, Builder classes have been removed entirely.

More information on the reason why Builder classes are not preferred anymore can be found in a mailing list entry by JavaFX Client Architect Richard Bair at http://mail.openjdk.java.net/pipermail/openjfx-dev/2013-March/006725.html. The bottom of this entry contains a very important statement: "I believe that FXML or lambda's or alternative languages all provide other avenues for achieving the same goals as builders but without the additional cost in byte codes or classes."

This is what we will show throughout this book. Near the end of this chapter, we show a first example of a lambda expression in our code. In Chapter 3, we show how Scene Builder and FXML allow you to use a declarative way of defining a UI.

In the current example, we programmatically define the different components of the UI, and we glue them together. In Chapter 3, we show the same example using a declarative FXML-based approach.

The JavaFX Application

Let's have a look at the class declaration in our first example:

```
public class HelloEarthRiseMain extends Application
```

This declaration states that our application extends the `javafx.application.Application` class. This class has one abstract method that we should implement:

```
public void start(Stage stage) {}
```

This method will be called by the environment that executes our JavaFX application.

Depending on the environment, JavaFX applications will be launched in a different way. As a developer, you don't have to worry about how your application is launched, and where the connection to a physical screen is made. You have to implement the "start" method and use the provided `Stage` parameter to create your UI, as discussed in the next paragraph.

In our command-line example, we launched the applications by executing the main method of the application class. The implementation of the main method is very simple:

```
public static void main(String[] args) {
    Application.launch(args);
}
```

The only instruction in this main method is a call to the static launch method of the application, which will launch the application.

■ **Tip** A JavaFX application always has to extend the `javafx.application.Application` class.

A Stage and a Scene

A `Stage` contains the UI of a JavaFX app, whether it is deployed on the desktop, on an embedded system, or on other devices. On the desktop, for example, a `Stage` has its own top-level window, which typically includes a border and title bar.

The initial stage is created by the JavaFX runtime, and passed to you via the `start()` method, as described in the previous paragraph. The `Stage` class has a set of properties and methods. Some of these properties and methods, as shown in the following code snippet from the listing, are as follows.

- A scene that contains the graphical nodes in the UI

- A title that appears in the title bar of the window (when deployed on the desktop)

- The visibility of the Stage

```
stage.setScene(scene);
stage.setTitle("Hello Earthrise");
stage.show();
```

A `Scene` is the top container in the JavaFX scene graph. A `Scene` holds the graphical elements that are displayed on the Stage. Every element in a `Scene` is a graphical node, which is any class that extends `javafx.scene.Node`. The scene graph is a hierarchical representation of the Scene. Elements in the scene graph may contain child elements, and all of them are instances of the Node class.

The Scene class contains a number of properties, such as its width and height. A Scene also has a property named root that holds the graphical elements that are displayed in the Scene, in this case a Group instance that contains an ImageView instance (which displays an image) and a Group instance. Nested within the latter Group is a Text instance (which is a graphical element, usually called a graphical node, or simply node).

Notice that the root property of the Scene contains an instance of the Group class. The root property may contain an instance of any subclass of javafx.scene.Node, and typically contains one capable of holding its own set of Node instances. Take a look at the JavaFX API documentation that we showed you how to access in the "Use the Official Specifications" section and check out the Node class to see the properties and methods available to any graphical node. Also, take a look at the ImageView class in the javafx.scene.image package and the Group class in the javafx.scene package. In both cases, they inherit from the Node class.

■ **Tip** We can't emphasize enough the importance of having the JavaFX API documentation handy while reading this book. As classes, variables, and functions are mentioned, it's a good idea to look at the documentation to get more information. In addition, this habit helps you become more familiar with what is available to you in the API.

Displaying Images

As shown in the following code, displaying an image entails using an ImageView instance in conjunction with an Image instance.

```
Image image = new Image ("http://projavafx.com/images/earthrise.jpg");
ImageView imageView = new ImageView(image);
```

The Image instance identifies the image resource and loads it from the URL assigned to its URL variable. Both of these classes are located in the javafx.scene.image package.

Displaying Text

In the example, we created a Text Node as follows:

```
Text textRef = new Text(message);
```

If you consult the JavaFX API documentation, you will notice that a Text instance, contained in package javafx.scene.text, extends a Shape that extends a Node. As a consequence, a Text instance is a Node as well, and all the properties on Node apply on Text as well. Moreover, Text instances can be used in the scene graph the same way other nodes are used.

As you can detect from the example, a Text instance contains a number of properties that can be modified. Most of the properties are self-explanatory, but again, it is always useful to consult the JavaFX API documentation when manipulating objects.

Because all graphical elements in JavaFX directly or indirectly extend the Node class, and because the Node class already contains many useful properties, the amount of properties on a specific graphical element such as Text can be rather high.

In our example, we set a limited number of properties that are briefly explained next.

The textRef.setLayoutY(100) method applies a vertical translation of 100 pixels to the Text content. The fill method is used to specify the color of the text.

While you're looking at the `javafx.scene.text` package in the API documentation, take a look at the font function of the `Font` class, which is used to define the font family, weight, and size of the `Text`.

The `textOrigin` property specifies how the text is aligned with its area.

Referring again to the JavaFX API documentation, notice that the VPos enum (in the `javafx.geometry` package) has fields that serve as constants, for example, BASELINE, BOTTOM, and TOP. These control the origin of the text with respect to vertical locations on the displayed `Text`:

- The TOP origin, as we're using it in the previous code snippet, places the top of the text (including ascenders) at the layoutY position, relative to the coordinate space in which the `Text` is located.

- The BOTTOM origin would place the bottom of the text, including descenders (located in a lowercase g, for example) at the layoutY position.

- The BASELINE origin would place the baseline of the text (excluding descenders) at the layoutY position. This is the default value for the `textOrigin` property of a `Text` instance.

The `wrappingWidth` property enables you to specify at what number of pixels the text will wrap.

The `textAlignment` property enables you to control how the text will be justified. In our example, `TextAlignment.JUSTIFY` aligns the text on both the left and right sides, expanding the space between words to achieve that.

The text that we're displaying is sufficiently long enough to wrap and be drawn on the Earth, so we need to define a rectangular region, outside of which the text cannot be seen.

■ **Tip**   We recommend you modify some of the values, recompile the example, and run it again. This will help you understanding how the different properties work. Alternatively, by using `ScenicView` you can inspect and modify the different properties at runtime.

Working with Graphical Nodes as a Group

One powerful graphical feature of JavaFX is the ability to create scene graphs, which consist of a tree of graphical nodes. You can then assign values to properties of a `Group` located in the hierarchy, and the nodes contained in the `Group` will be affected. In our current example from Listing 1-1, we're using a `Group` to contain a `Text` node and to clip a specific rectangular region within the `Group` so that the text doesn't appear on the moon or the Earth as it animates upward. Here's the relevant code snippet:

```
Group textGroup = new Group(textRef);
textGroup.setLayoutX(50);
textGroup.setLayoutY(180);
textGroup.setClip(new Rectangle(430, 85));
```

Notice that the `Group` is located 50 pixels to the right and 180 pixels down from where it would have been located by default. This is due to the values assigned to the `layoutX` and `layoutY` variables of the `Group` instance. Because this `Group` is contained directly by the `Scene`, its upper-left corner's location is 50 pixels to the right and 180 pixels down from the upper-left corner of the `Scene`. Take a look at Figure 1-4 to see this example illustrated as you read the rest of the explanation.

Figure 1-4. *The Scene, Group, Text, and clip illustrated*

A Group instance contains instances of Node subclasses by assigning a collection of them to itself via the children() method. In the previous code snippet, the Group contains a Text instance that has a value assigned to its layoutY property. Because this Text is contained by a Group, it assumes the two-dimensional space (also called the coordinate space) of the Group, with the origin of the Text node (0,0) coincident with the top-left corner of the Group. Assigning a value of 100 to the layoutY property causes the Text to be located 100 pixels down from the top of the Group, which is just below the bottom of the clip region, thus causing it to be out of view until the animation begins. Because a value isn't assigned to the layoutX variable, its value is 0 (the default).

The layoutX and layoutY properties of the Group just described are examples of our earlier statement that nodes contained in a Group will be affected by values assigned to properties of the Group. Another example is setting the opacity property of a Group instance to 0.5, which causes all of the nodes contained in that Group to become translucent. If the JavaFX API documentation is handy, look at the properties available in the javafx.scene.Group class. Then look at the properties available in the javafx.scene.Node class properties, which is where you'll find the layoutX, layoutY, and opacity variables that are inherited by the Group class.

Clipping Graphical Areas

To define a clipping area, we assign a Node subclass to the clip property that defines the clipping shape, in this case a Rectangle that is 430 pixels wide and 85 pixels high. In addition to keeping the Text from covering the moon, when the Text scrolls up as a result of animation, the clipping area keeps the Text from covering the earth.

Animating the Text to Make It Scroll Up

When the HelloEarthriseMain program is invoked, the Text begins scrolling up slowly. To achieve this animation, we're using the TranslateTransition class located in the javafx.animation package, as shown in the following snippet from Listing 1-1.

```
TranslateTransition transTransition = new TranslateTransition(new Duration(75000), textRef);
transTransition.setToY(-820);
transTransition.setInterpolator(Interpolator.LINEAR);
transTransition.setCycleCount(Timeline.INDEFINITE);
...code omitted...
// Start the text animation
transTransition.play();
```

The javafx.animation package contains convenience classes for animating nodes. This TranslateTransition instance translates the Text node referenced by the textRef variable from its original Y position of 100 pixels to a Y position of –820 pixels, over a duration of 75 seconds. The Interpolator. LINEAR constant is assigned to the interpolator property, which causes the animation to proceed in a linear fashion. A look at the API docs for the Interpolator class in the javafx.animation package reveals that there are other forms of interpolation available, one of which is EASE_OUT, which slows down the animation toward the end of the specified duration.

■ **Note**   Interpolation in this context is the process of calculating the value at any point in time, given a beginning value, an ending value, and a duration.

The last line in the previous snippet begins executing the play method of the TranslateTransition instance created earlier in the program. This makes the Text begin scrolling upward. Because of the value assigned to the cycleCount variable, this transition will repeat indefinitely.

Now that you've compiled and run this example using the command-line tools and we've walked through the code together, it is time to begin using the NetBeans IDE to make the development and deployment process faster and easier.

Building and Running the Program with NetBeans

Assuming that you've downloaded and extracted the source code for this book into a directory, follow the directions in this exercise to build and run the Hello Earthrise program in NetBeans. If you haven't yet downloaded the Java SDK and NetBeans, please do so from the site listed in the "Resources" section at the end of this chapter.

BUILDING AND RUNNING HELLO EARTHRISE WITH NETBEANS

To build and run the Hello Earthrise program, perform the following steps.

1. Start NetBeans.

2. Choose File ➤ New Project from the menu bar. The first window of the New Project Wizard will appear. Select the JavaFX category, and you will see wizard shown in Figure 1-5.

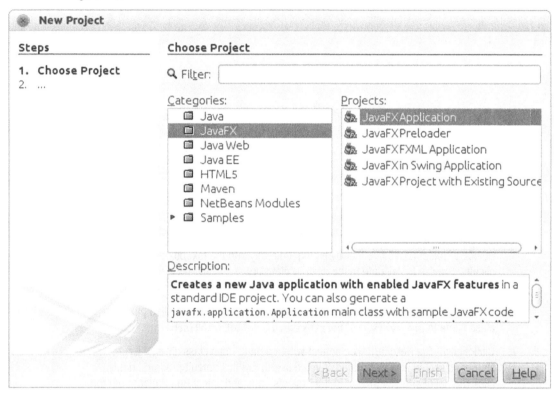

Figure 1-5. *New Project Wizard*

3. Choose JavaFX Application in the Projects pane, and then click Next. The next page in the New Project Wizard, shown in Figure 1-6, should appear.

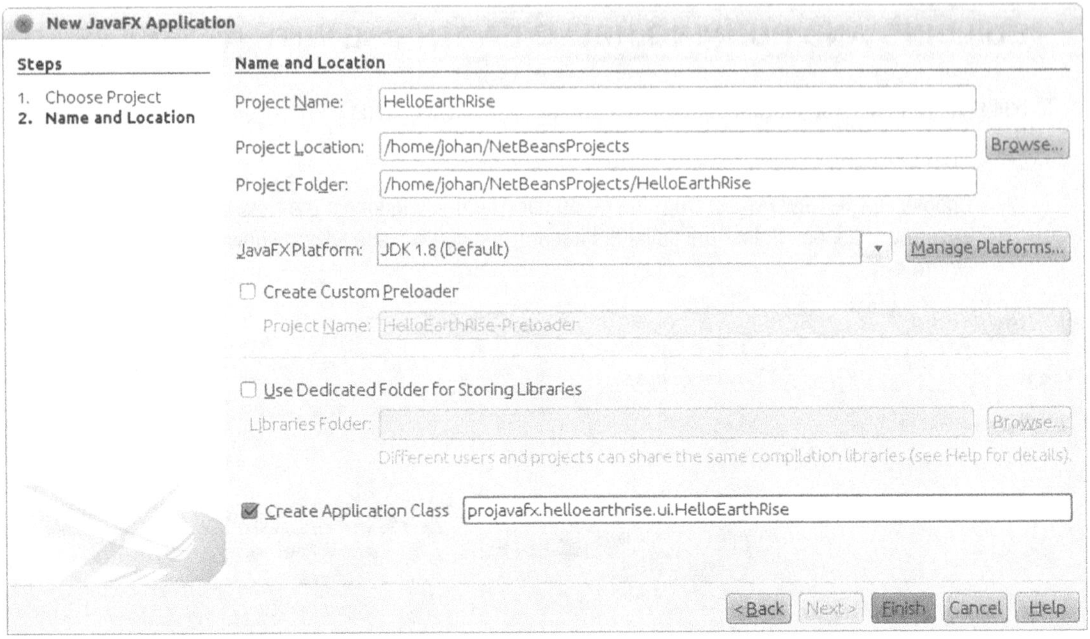

Figure 1-6. *The next page of the New Project Wizard*

4. On this screen, type the project name (we used HelloEarthRise) and click Browse.

5. Select a Project Location either by typing it directly into the text box or by clicking Browse to navigate to the desired directory (we used /home/johan/ NetBeansProjects).

6. Select the Create Application Class check box, and change the supplied package/ class name to projavafx.helloearthrise.ui.HelloEarthRiseMain

7. Click Finish. The HelloEarthRise project with a default main class created by NetBeans should now be created. If you'd like to run this default program, right-click the HelloEarthRise project in the Projects pane and select Run Project from the shortcut menu.

8. Enter the code from Listing 1-1 into the HelloEarthRiseMain.java code window. You can type it in, or cut and paste it from the HelloEarthRiseMain.java file located in the Chapter01/HelloEarthRise/src/projavafx/helloearthrise/ui directory of this book's source code download.

9. Right-click the HelloEarthRise project in the Projects pane and select Run Project from the shortcut menu.

The HelloEarthRise program should begin executing, as you saw in Figure 1-3 earlier in the chapter.

At this point, you've built and run the "Hello Earthrise" program application, both from the command line and using NetBeans. Before leaving this example, we show you another way to achieve the scrolling Text node. There is a class in the javafx.scene.control package named ScrollPane whose purpose is to provide a scrollable view of a node that is typically larger than the view. In addition, the user can drag the node being viewed within the scrollable area. Figure 1-7 shows the Hello Earthrise program after being modified to use the ScrollPane control.

Figure 1-7. *Using the* ScrollPane *control to provide a scrollable view of the* Text *node*

Notice that the move cursor is visible, signifying that the user can drag the node around the clipped area. Note that the screenshot in Figure 1-7 is of the program running on macOS X, and the move cursor has a different appearance on other platforms. Listing 1-2 contains the relevant portion of code for this example, named HelloScrollPaneMain.java.

Listing 1-2. The HelloScrollPaneMain.java Program

```
...code omitted...
    // Create a ScrollPane containing the text
        ScrollPane scrollPane = new ScrollPane();
        scrollPane.setLayoutX(50);
        scrollPane.setLayoutY(180);
        scrollPane.setPrefWidth(400);
        scrollPane.setPrefHeight(85);
        scrollPane.setHbarPolicy(ScrollPane.ScrollBarPolicy.NEVER);
        scrollPane.setVbarPolicy(ScrollPane.ScrollBarPolicy.NEVER);
        scrollPane.setPannable(true);
        scrollPane.setContent(textRef);
        scrollPane.setStyle("-fx-background-color: transparent;");
```

```
// Combine ImageView and ScrollPane
Group root = new Group(imageView, scrollPane);
Scene scene = new Scene(root, 516, 387);
```

Now that you've learned some of the basics of JavaFX application development, let's examine another sample application to help you learn more JavaFX concepts and constructs.

Developing Your Second JavaFX Program: "More Cowbell!"

If you're familiar with the *Saturday Night Live* television show, you may have seen the "More Cowbell" sketch, in which Christopher Walken's character keeps asking for "more cowbell" during a Blue Oyster Cult recording session. The following JavaFX example program covers some of the simple but powerful concepts of JavaFX in the context of an imaginary application that lets you select a music genre and control the volume. Of course, "Cowbell Metal," shortened to "Cowbell," is one of the available genres. Figure 1-8 shows a screenshot of this application, which has a sort of retro iPhone application look.

Figure 1-8. *The Audio Configuration "More Cowbell" program*

Building and Running the Audio Configuration Program

Earlier in the chapter, we showed you how to create a new JavaFX project in NetBeans. For this example (and the rest of the examples in the book), we take advantage of the fact that the code download bundle for the book contains both NetBeans and Eclipse project files for each example. Follow the instructions in this exercise to build and run the Audio Configuration application.

BUILDING AND RUNNING THE AUDIO CONFIGURATION PROGRAM USING NETBEANS

To build and execute this program using NetBeans, perform the following steps.

1. From the File menu, select the Open Project menu item. In the Open Project dialog box, navigate to the Chapter01 directory where you extracted the book's code download bundle, as shown in Figure 1-9.

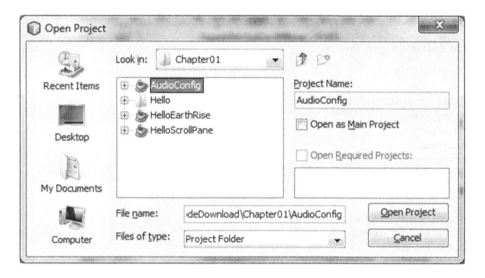

Figure 1-9. *The Chapter 01 directory in the Open Project dialog box*

2. Select the AudioConfig project in the pane on the left, and click Open Project.

3. Run the project as discussed previously.

The application should appear as shown in Figure 1-8.

The Behavior of the Audio Configuration Program

When you run the application, notice that adjusting the volume slider changes the associated decibel (dB) level displayed. Also, selecting the Muting check box disables the slider, and selecting various genres changes the volume slider. This behavior is enabled by concepts that are shown in the code that follows, such as the following:

- Binding to a class that contains a model

- Using change listeners

- Creating observable lists

Understanding the Audio Configuration Program

The Audio Configuration program contains two source code files, shown in Listing 1-3 and Listing 1-4:

- The AudioConfigMain.java file in Listing 1-3 contains the main class, and expresses the UI in a manner that you are familiar with from the Hello Earthrise example in Listing 1-1.

- The AudioConfigModel.java file in Listing 1-4 contains a model for this program, which holds the state of the application, to which the UI is bound.

Take a look at the AudioConfigMain.java source code in Listing 1-3, after which we examine it together, focusing on concepts not covered in the previous example.

Listing 1-3. The AudioConfigMain.java Program

```
package projavafx.audioconfig.ui;

import javafx.application.Application;
import javafx.geometry.VPos;
import javafx.scene.Group;
import javafx.scene.Scene;
import javafx.scene.control.CheckBox;
import javafx.scene.control.ChoiceBox;
import javafx.scene.control.Slider;
import javafx.scene.paint.Color;
import javafx.scene.paint.CycleMethod;
import javafx.scene.paint.LinearGradient;
import javafx.scene.paint.Stop;
import javafx.scene.shape.Line;
import javafx.scene.shape.Rectangle;
import javafx.scene.text.Font;
import javafx.scene.text.FontWeight;
import javafx.scene.text.Text;
import javafx.stage.Stage;
import projavafx.audioconfig.model.AudioConfigModel;

public class AudioConfigMain extends Application {

    // A reference to the model
    AudioConfigModel acModel = new AudioConfigModel();

    Text textDb;
    Slider slider;
    CheckBox mutingCheckBox;
    ChoiceBox genreChoiceBox;
    Color color = Color.color(0.66, 0.67, 0.69);

    public static void main(String[] args) {
        Application.launch(args);
    }
```

```java
@Override
public void start(Stage stage) {
    Text title = new Text(65,12, "Audio Configuration");
    title.setTextOrigin(VPos.TOP);
    title.setFill(Color.WHITE);
    title.setFont(Font.font("SansSerif", FontWeight.BOLD, 20));

    Text textDb = new Text();
    textDb.setLayoutX(18);
    textDb.setLayoutY(69);
    textDb.setTextOrigin(VPos.TOP);
    textDb.setFill(Color.web("#131021"));
    textDb.setFont(Font.font("SansSerif", FontWeight.BOLD, 18));

    Text mutingText = new Text(18, 113, "Muting");
    mutingText.setTextOrigin(VPos.TOP);
    mutingText.setFont(Font.font("SanSerif", FontWeight.BOLD, 18));
    mutingText.setFill(Color.web("#131021"));

    Text genreText = new Text(18,154,"Genre");
    genreText.setTextOrigin(VPos.TOP);
    genreText.setFill(Color.web("#131021"));
    genreText.setFont(Font.font("SanSerif", FontWeight.BOLD, 18));

    slider = new Slider();
    slider.setLayoutX(135);
    slider.setLayoutY(69);
    slider.setPrefWidth(162);
    slider.setMin(acModel.minDecibels);
    slider.setMax(acModel.maxDecibels);

    mutingCheckBox = new CheckBox();
    mutingCheckBox.setLayoutX(280);
    mutingCheckBox.setLayoutY(113);

    genreChoiceBox = new ChoiceBox();
    genreChoiceBox.setLayoutX(204);
    genreChoiceBox.setLayoutY(154);
    genreChoiceBox.setPrefWidth(93);
    genreChoiceBox.setItems(acModel.genres);
    Stop[] stops = new Stop[]{new Stop(0, Color.web("0xAEBBCC")), new Stop(1, Color.
    web("0x6D84A3"))};

    LinearGradient linearGradient = new LinearGradient(0, 0, 0, 1, true, CycleMethod.
    NO_CYCLE, stops);
    Rectangle rectangle = new Rectangle(0, 0, 320, 45);
    rectangle.setFill(linearGradient);

    Rectangle rectangle2 = new Rectangle(0, 43, 320, 300);
    rectangle2.setFill(Color.rgb(199, 206, 213));
```

```
Rectangle rectangle3 = new Rectangle(8, 54, 300, 130);
rectangle3.setArcHeight(20);
rectangle3.setArcWidth(20);
rectangle3.setFill(Color.WHITE);
rectangle3.setStroke(color);

Line line1 = new Line(9, 97, 309, 97);
line1.setStroke(color);

Line line2 = new Line(9, 141, 309, 141);
line2.setFill(color);

Group group = new Group(rectangle, title, rectangle2, rectangle3,
        textDb,
        slider,
        line1,
        mutingText,
        mutingCheckBox, line2, genreText,
        genreChoiceBox);
Scene scene = new Scene(group, 320, 343);

textDb.textProperty().bind(acModel.selectedDBs.asString().concat(" dB"));
slider.valueProperty().bindBidirectional(acModel.selectedDBs);
slider.disableProperty().bind(acModel.muting);
mutingCheckBox.selectedProperty().bindBidirectional(acModel.muting);
acModel.genreSelectionModel = genreChoiceBox.getSelectionModel();
acModel.addListenerToGenreSelectionModel();
acModel.genreSelectionModel.selectFirst();

stage.setScene(scene);
stage.setTitle("Audio Configuration");
stage.show();
    }
}
```

Now that you've seen the main class in this application, let's walk through the new concepts.

The Magic of Binding

One of the most powerful aspects of JavaFX is binding, which enables the application's UI to easily stay in sync with the state, or model, of the application. The model for a JavaFX application is typically held in one or more classes, in this case the AudioConfigModel class. Look at the following snippet, taken from Listing 1-3, in which we create an instance of this model class.

```
AudioConfigModel acModel = new AudioConfigModel();
```

There are several graphical node instances in the scene of this UI (recall that a scene consists of a sequence of nodes). Skipping past several of them, we come to the graphical nodes shown in the following snippet that have a property bound to the selectedDBs property in the model.

```
textDb = new Text();
... code omitted
slider = new Slider();
...code omitted...
textDb.textProperty().bind(acModel.selectedDBs.asString().concat(" dB"));
slider.valueProperty().bindBidirectional(acModel.selectedDBs);
```

As shown in this code, the text property of the Text object is bound to an expression. The bind function contains an expression (that includes the selectedDBs property), which is evaluated and becomes the value of the text property. Look at Figure 1-9 (or check the running application) to see the content value of the Text node displayed to the left of the slider.

Notice also in the code that the value property of the Slider node is bound to the selectedDBs property in the model as well, but that it uses the bindBidirectional() method. This causes the bind to be bidirectional, so in this case when the slider is moved, the selectedDBs property in the model changes. Conversely, when the selectedDBs property changes (as a result of changing the genre), the slider moves.

Go ahead and move the slider to demonstrate the effects of the bind expressions in the snippet. The number of decibels displayed at the left of the slider should change as the slider is adjusted.

There are other bound properties in Listing 1-3 that we point out when we walk through the model class. Before leaving the UI, we point out some color-related concepts in this example.

Colors and Gradients

The following snippet from Listing 1-3 contains an example of defining a color gradient pattern, as well as defining colors.

```
Stop[] stops = new Stop[]{new Stop(0, Color.web("0xAEBBCC")), new Stop(1, Color.
web("0x6D84A3"))};
LinearGradient linearGradient = new LinearGradient(0, 0, 0, 1, true, CycleMethod.NO_CYCLE,
stops);
Rectangle rectangle = new Rectangle(0, 0, 320, 45);
rectangle.setFill(linearGradient);
```

If the JavaFX API docs are handy, first take a look at the javafx.scene.shape.Rectangle class and notice that it inherits a property named fill that is of type javafx.scene.paint.Paint. Looking at the JavaFX API docs for the Paint class, you'll see that the Color, ImagePattern, LinearGradient, and RadialGradient classes are subclasses of Paint. This means that the fill of any shape can be assigned a color, pattern, or gradient.

To create a LinearGradient, as shown in the code, you need to define at least two stops, which define the location and color at that location. In this example, the offset value of the first stop is 0.0, and the offset value of the second stop is 1.0. These are the values at both extremes of the unit square, the result being that the gradient will span the entire node (in this case a Rectangle). The direction of the LinearGradient is controlled by its startX, startY, endX, and endY values, which we pass via the constructor. In this case, the direction is only vertical because the startY value is 0.0 and the endY value is 1.0, whereas the startX and endX values are both 0.0.

Note that in the Hello Earthrise example in Listing 1-1, the constant named Color.WHITE was used to represent the color white. In the previous snippet, the web function of the Color class is used to define a color from a hexadecimal value.

The Model Class for the Audio Configuration Example

Take a look at the source code for the AudioConfigModel class in Listing 1-4.

Listing 1-4. The Source Code for AudioConfigModel.java

```java
package projavafx.audioconfig.model;

import javafx.beans.Observable;
import javafx.beans.property.BooleanProperty;
import javafx.beans.property.IntegerProperty;
import javafx.beans.property.SimpleBooleanProperty;
import javafx.beans.property.SimpleIntegerProperty;
import javafx.collections.FXCollections;
import javafx.collections.ObservableList;
import javafx.scene.control.SingleSelectionModel;

/**
 * The model class that the AudioConfigMain class uses
 */
public class AudioConfigModel {
  /**
   * The minimum audio volume in decibels
   */
  public double minDecibels = 0.0;

  /**
   * The maximum audio volume in decibels
   */
  public double maxDecibels = 160.0;

  /**
   * The selected audio volume in decibels
   */
  public IntegerProperty selectedDBs = new SimpleIntegerProperty(0);

  /**
   * Indicates whether audio is muted
   */
  public BooleanProperty muting = new SimpleBooleanProperty(false);

  /**
   * List of some musical genres
   */
  public ObservableList genres = FXCollections.observableArrayList(
    "Chamber",
    "Country",
    "Cowbell",
    "Metal",
    "Polka",
    "Rock"
  );
```

```
    /**
     * A reference to the selection model used by the Slider
     */
    public SingleSelectionModel genreSelectionModel;

    /**
     * Adds a change listener to the selection model of the ChoiceBox, and contains
     * code that executes when the selection in the ChoiceBox changes.
     */
public void addListenerToGenreSelectionModel() {
    genreSelectionModel.selectedIndexProperty().addListener((Observable o) -> {
        int selectedIndex = genreSelectionModel.selectedIndexProperty().getValue();
        switch(selectedIndex) {
            case 0: selectedDBs.setValue(80);
            break;
            case 1: selectedDBs.setValue(100);
            break;
            case 2: selectedDBs.setValue(150);
            break;
            case 3: selectedDBs.setValue(140);
            break;
            case 4: selectedDBs.setValue(120);
            break;
            case 5: selectedDBs.setValue(130);
        }
    });

  }
}
```

Using InvalidationListeners and Lambda Expressions

In the "The Magic of Binding" section, we showed how you can use property binding for dynamically changing parameters. There is another, more low-level but also more flexible way of achieving this, using ChangeListeners and InvalidationListeners. These concepts are discussed in more detail in Chapter 4.

In our example, we add an InvalidationListener to the selectedIndexProperty of the genreSelectionModel. When the value of the selectedIndexProperty changes, and when we didn't retrieve it yet, the invalidated(Observable) method on the added InvalidationListener will be called. In the implementation of this method, we retrieve the value of the selectedIndexProperty, and based on its value, the value of the selectedDBs property is changed. This is achieved with the following code:

```
public void addListenerToGenreSelectionModel() {
    genreSelectionModel.selectedIndexProperty().addListener((Observable o) -> {
        int selectedIndex = genreSelectionModel.selectedIndexProperty().getValue();
        switch(selectedIndex) {
            case 0: selectedDBs.setValue(80);
            break;
            case 1: selectedDBs.setValue(100);
            break;
            case 2: selectedDBs.setValue(150);
            break;
```

```
            case 3: selectedDBs.setValue(140);
            break;
            case 4: selectedDBs.setValue(120);
            break;
            case 5: selectedDBs.setValue(130);
        }
    });

}
```

Note that we are using a lambda expression here rather than creating a new instance of the InvalidationListener and implementing its single abstract method invalidated.

■ **Tip**   One of the major enhancements in JavaFX 8 is the fact that it is using Java 8. As a consequence, abstract classes with a single abstract method can easily be replaced by lambda expressions, which clearly enhance the readability of the code.

What causes selectedIndexProperty of the genreSelectionModel to change? To see the answer to this, we have to revisit some code in Listing 1-3. In the following code snippet, the setItems method of ChoiceBox is used to populate the ChoiceBox with items that each contain a genre.

```
genreChoiceBox = new ChoiceBox();
genreChoiceBox.setLayoutX(204);
genreChoiceBox.setLayoutY(154);
genreChoiceBox.setPrefWidth(93);
genreChoiceBox.setItems(acModel.genres);
```

This snippet from the model code in Listing 1-4 contains the collection to which the ComboBox items are bound:

```
/**
 * List of some musical genres
 */
public ObservableList genres = FXCollections.observableArrayList(
  "Chamber",
  "Country",
  "Cowbell",
  "Metal",
  "Polka",
  "Rock"
);
```

When the user chooses a different item in the ChoiceBox, the invalidationListener is invoked. Looking again at the code in the invalidationListener, you'll see that the value of the selectedDBs property changes, which as you may recall, is bidirectionally bound to the slider. This is why the slider moves when you select a genre in the combo box. Go ahead and test this by running the Audio Config program.

■ **Note**   Associating the items property of the ChoiceBox with an ObservableList causes the items in the ChoiceBox to be automatically updated when the elements in the underlying collection are modified.

Surveying JavaFX Features

We close this chapter by surveying many of the features of JavaFX, some of which are a review for you. We do this by describing several of the more commonly used packages and classes in the Java SDK API.

The javafx.stage package contains the following:

- The Stage class, which is the top level of the UI containment hierarchy for any JavaFX application, regardless of where it is deployed (e.g., the desktop, a browser, or a cell phone).

- The Screen class, which represents the displays on the machine in which a JavaFX program is running. This enables you to get information about the screens, such as size and resolution.

The javafx.scene package contains some classes that you'll use often:

- The Scene class is the second level of the UI containment hierarchy for JavaFX applications. It includes all of the UI elements contained in the application. These elements are called graphical nodes, or simply nodes.

- The Node class is the base class of all of the graphical nodes in JavaFX. UI elements such as text, images, media, shapes, and controls (e.g., text boxes and buttons) are all subclasses of Node. Take a moment to look at the variables and functions in the Node class to appreciate the capabilities provided to all of its subclasses, including bounds calculation and mouse and keyboard event handling.

- The Group class is a subclass of the Node class. Its purpose includes grouping nodes together into a single coordinate space and allowing transforms (e.g., rotate) to be applied to the whole group. Also, attributes of the group that are changed (e.g., opacity) apply to all of the nodes contained within the group.

Several packages begin with javafx.scene that contain subclasses of Node of various types. Examples include the following:

- The javafx.scene.image package contains the Image and ImageView classes, which enable images to be displayed in the Scene. The ImageView class is a subclass of Node.

- The javafx.scene.shape package contains several classes for drawing shapes such as Circle, Rectangle, Line, Polygon, and Arc. The base class of the shapes, named Shape, contains an attribute named fill that enables you to specify a color, pattern, or gradient with which to fill the shape.

- The javafx.scene.text package contains the Text class for drawing text in the scene. The Font class enables you to specify the font name and size of the text.

- The javafx.scene.media package has classes that enable you to play media. The MediaView class is a subclass of Node that displays the media.

- The javafx.scene.chart package has classes that help you easily create area, bar, bubble, line, pie, and scatter charts. The corresponding UI classes in this package are AreaChart, BarChart, BubbleChart, LineChart, PieChart, and ScatterChart.

Here are some other packages in the JavaFX 8 API.

- The `javafx.scene.control` package contains several UI controls, each one having the ability to be skinned and styled via CSS.

- The `javafx.scene.transform` package enables you to transform nodes (scale, rotate, translate, shear, and affine).

- The `javafx.scene.input` package contains classes such as `MouseEvent` and `KeyEvent` that provide information about these events from within an event handler function such as the `Node` class's `onMouseClicked` event.

- The `javafx.scene.layout` package contains several layout containers, including `HBox`, `VBox`, `BorderPane`, `FlowPane`, `StackPane`, and `TilePane`.

- The `javafx.scene.effect` package contains easy-to-use effects such as `Reflection`, `Glow`, `Shadow`, `BoxBlur`, and `Lighting`.

- The `javafx.scene.web` package contains classes for easily embedding a web browser in your JavaFX applications.

- The `javafx.animation` package contains time-based interpolations typically used for animation and convenience classes for common transitions.

- The `javafx.beans`, `javafx.beans.binding`, `javafx.beans.property`, and `javafx.beans.value` packages contain classes that implement properties and binding.

- The `javafx.fxml` package contains classes that implement a very powerful facility known as FXML, a markup language for expressing JavaFX UIs in XML.

- The `javafx.util` package contains utility classes such as the `Duration` class used in the HelloEarthRise example.

- The `javafx.print` package contains utilities for printing (parts of) the layout of a JavaFX application.

- The `javafx.embed.swing` package contains the required functionality for embedded JavaFX applications in a Swing application.

- The `javafx.embed.swt` package contains the required functionality for embedding JavaFX applications in an SWT application.

Take a look at the JavaFX API docs again in light of this information to get a deeper sense of how you can use its capabilities.

Summary

Congratulations! You learned a lot about JavaFX in this chapter, including

- JavaFX is rich-client Java, and is needed by the software development industry.

- Since the Java 9 release, the JavaFX APIs are split in a number of modules that follow the Java 9 conventions and rules.

- Some of the high points of the history of JavaFX.

- Where to find JavaFX resources, including the Java SDK, NetBeans, Scene Builder, ScenicView, and the API documentation.

- How to compile and run a JavaFX program from the command line.

- How to build and run a JavaFX program using NetBeans.

- How to use several of the classes in the JavaFX API.

- How to create a class in JavaFX and use it as a model that contains the state of a JavaFX application.

- How to use property binding to keep the UI easily in sync with the model.

We also looked at many of the available API packages and classes, and you learned how you can leverage their capabilities. Now that you have a jump-start in JavaFX, you can begin examining the details of JavaFX in Chapter 2.

Resources

For some background information on JavaFX, you can consult the following resources.

- This book's code examples: The Source Code/Download section on the Apress web site (www.apress.com).

- Java Posse #163: Newscast for February 8, 2008: This is a podcast of a Java Posse interview with Josh Marinacci and Richard Bair on the subject of JavaFX. (http://javaposse.com/java_posse_163_newscast_for_feb_8th_2008).

- "Congratulations to the JavaFX Script Compiler Team—The Elephant Is Through the Door": A blog post by one of this book's authors, Jim Weaver, that congratulated the JavaFX compiler team for reaching a tipping point in the project. (http://learnjavafx.typepad.com/weblog/2007/12/congratulations.html).

- Oracle's JavaFX.com site: The home page for JavaFX where you can download the JavaFX SDK and other resource for JavaFX. (www.javafx.com)

- FX Experience: A blog maintained by Oracle JavaFX Engineers Richard Bair, Jasper Potts, and Jonathan Giles. (http://fxexperience.com)

- Jim Weaver's JavaFX Blog: A blog, started in October 2007, the stated purpose of which is to help the reader become a "JavaFXpert." (http://javafxpert.com)

- Weiqi Gao's Observation: A blog in which Weiqi Gao shares his experience in software development. (http://weiqigao.blogspot.com)

- Dean Iverson's Pleasing Software Blog: A blog in which Dean Iverson shares his innovations in JavaFX and GroovyFX. (http://pleasingsoftware.blogspot.com)

- Steve on Java: A blog in which Stephen Chin keeps the world updated on his tireless exploits in the areas of JavaFX, Java, and Agile development. (http://steveonjava.com)

- Johan's blog: A blog in which Johan Vos discusses JavaFX and Java Enterprise. (http://blogs.lodgon.com/johan)

- JavaFX Eclipse Plugin: Eclipse tooling for JavaFX 2.0, developed by Tom Shindl. (http://tomsondev.bestsolution.at/2011/06/24/introducing-efxclipse/)

- Scenic View: An application for inspecting the scenegraph of your JavaFX applications. (http://scenic-view.org)

- Gluon web site: (http://gluonhq.com)

- ControlsFX, high-quality custom JavaFX controls. (http://controlsfx.org)

- JFXtras.org, high-quality custom JavaFX controls. (http://jfxtras.org)

CHAPTER 2

Creating a User Interface in JavaFX

Life is the art of drawing without an eraser.

—John W. Gardner

Chapter 1 gave you a jump start using JavaFX by covering the basics in developing and executing JavaFX programs. Now we cover many of the details about creating a UI in JavaFX that were glossed over in Chapter 1. First on the agenda is to get you acquainted with the *theater* metaphor used by JavaFX to express UIs and to cover the significance of what we call a *node-centric UI*.

Programmatic vs. Declarative Creation of the User Interface

The JavaFX platform provides two complementary ways for creating a UI. In this chapter, we discuss how you can use the Java API to create and populate a UI. This is a convenient way for Java developers who are used to writing code to leverage APIs.

Designers often use graphical tools that allow them to declare rather than program a UI. The JavaFX platform defines FXML, which is an XML-based markup language that can be used to declaratively describe a UI. Furthermore, a graphical tool called Scene Builder is made available by Gluon, and this tool is capable of working with FXML files. The use of Scene Builder is demonstrated in Chapter 4.

Note that parts of a UI can be created using the API, where other parts can be created using Scene Builder. The FXML APIs provide the bridge and the integration glue between the two approaches.

Introduction to Node-Centric UIs

Creating a UI in JavaFX is like creating a theater play, in that it typically consists of these very simple steps:

1. *Create a stage on which your program will perform.* The realization of your stage will depend on the platform on which it is deployed (e.g., a desktop, a tablet, or an embedded system).

2. *Create a scene in which the actors and props (nodes) will visually interact with each other and the audience (the users of your program).* Like any good set designer in the theater business, good JavaFX developers endeavor to make their scenes visually appealing. To this end, it is often a good idea to collaborate with a graphic designer on your "theater play."

© Johan Vos, Stephen Chin, Weiqi Gao, James Weaver, and Dean Iverson 2018
J. Vos et al., *Pro JavaFX 9*, https://doi.org/10.1007/978-1-4842-3042-8_2

3. *Create nodes in the scene.* These nodes are subclasses of the `javafx.scene.Node` class, which include UI controls, shapes, Text (a type of shape), images, media players, embedded browsers, and custom UI components that you create. Nodes can also be containers for other nodes, often providing cross-platform layout capabilities. A scene has a scene graph that contains a directed graph of nodes. Individual nodes and groups of nodes can be manipulated in many ways (e.g., moving, scaling, and setting opacity) by changing the values of a very rich set of Node properties.

4. *Create variables and classes that represent the model for the nodes in the scene.* As discussed in Chapter 1, one of the very powerful aspects of JavaFX is binding, which enables the application's UI to stay in sync easily with the state, or model, of the application.

■ **Note** Most of the examples in this chapter are small programs intended to demonstrate UI concepts. For this reason, the model in many of these examples consists of variables appearing in the main program, rather than being contained by separate Java classes (e.g., the `AudioConfigModel` class in Chapter 1).

---

5. *Create event handlers, such as* `onMousePressed`*, that allow the user to interact with your program.* Often these event handlers manipulate instance variables in the model. Many of these handlers require a single abstract method to be implemented, and as a consequence provide a perfect opportunity to use lambda expressions.

6. *Create timelines and transitions that animate your scene.* For example, you might want the thumbnail images of a list of books to move smoothly across the scene or a page in the UI to fade into view. You might simply want a ping-pong ball to move across the scene, bouncing off walls and paddles; this is demonstrated later in this chapter in the "The Zen of Node Collision Detection" section.

Let's get started with a closer look at step 1, in which we examine the capabilities of the stage.

Setting the Stage

The appearance and functionality of your stage will depend on the platform on which it is deployed. For example, if deployed in a mobile device, or an embedded device with a touch screen, your stage might be the whole touch screen. The stage for a JavaFX program deployed in an X11 system will be a window.

Understanding the Stage Class

The Stage class is the top-level container for any JavaFX program that has a graphical UI. It has several properties and methods that allow it, for example, to be positioned, sized, given a title, made invisible, or given some degree of opacity. The two best ways that we know of to learn the capabilities of a class are to study the JavaFX API documentation and to examine (and write) programs that use it. In this section, we ask you to do both, beginning with looking at the API docs.

The JavaFX API docs, just like the other Java API docs, are available online at the http://download.java.net/java/jdk9/docs/api/overview-summary. Open the index.html file in your browser, navigate to the javafx.stage package in the javafx.graphics module, and select the Stage class. That page should contain tables of Properties, Constructors, and Methods, including select ones shown in the excerpt in Figure 2-1.

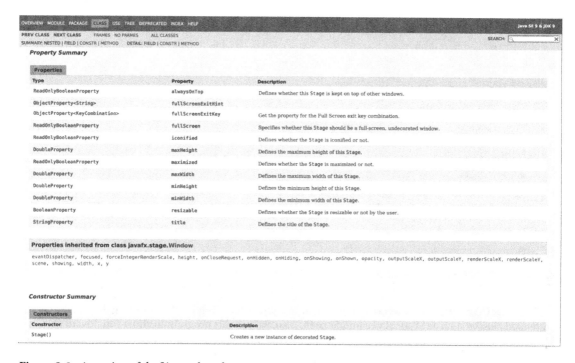

Figure 2-1. *A portion of the* Stage *class documentation in the JavaFX API*

Go ahead and explore the documentation for each of the properties and methods in the Stage class, remembering to click the links to reveal more detailed information. When you're finished, come back and we'll show you a program that demonstrates many of the properties and methods available in the Stage class.

Using the Stage Class: The StageCoach Example

A screenshot of the unassuming, purposely ill-fitting StageCoach example program is shown in Figure 2-2.

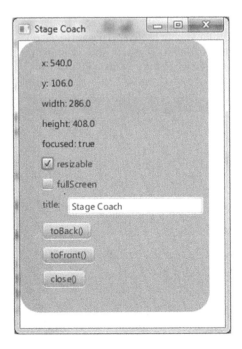

Figure 2-2. *A screenshot of the StageCoach example*

The StageCoach program was created to coach you through the finer points of using the Stage class and related classes such as StageStyle and Screen. Also, we use this program to show you how to get arguments passed into the program. Before walking through the behavior of the program, go ahead and open the project. Follow the instructions for building and executing the Audio-Config project in Chapter 1. The project file is located in the Chapter02 directory subordinate to where you extracted the book's code download bundle.

EXAMINING THE BEHAVIOR OF THE STAGECOACH PROGRAM

When the program starts, its appearance should be similar to the screenshot in Figure 2-2. To fully examine its behavior, perform the following steps. Note that for instructional purposes, the property and method names on the UI correspond to the properties and methods in the Stage instance.

Notice that the StageCoach program's window is initially displayed near the top of the screen, with its horizontal position in the center of the screen. Drag the program's window and observe that the x and y values near the top of the UI are dynamically updated to reflect its position on the screen.

Resize the program's window and observe that the width and height values change to reflect the width and height of the Stage. Note that this size includes the decorations (title bar and borders) of the window.

Click the program (or cause it to be in focus some other way) and notice that the focused value is true. Cause the window to lose focus, perhaps by clicking somewhere else on the screen, and notice that the focused value becomes false.

Clear the resizable check box and then notice that the resizable value becomes false. Then try to resize the window and note that it is not permitted. Select the resizable check box again to make the window resizable.

Select the fullScreen check box. Notice that the program occupies the full screen and that the window decorations are not visible. Clear the fullScreen check box to restore the program to its former size.

Edit the text in the text field beside the title label, noticing that the text in the window's title bar is changed to reflect the new value.

Drag the window to partially cover another window, and click toBack(). Notice that this places the program behind the other window, therefore causing the z-order to change.

With a portion of the program's window behind another window, but with the toFront() button visible, click that button. Notice that the program's window is placed in front of the other window.

Click close(), noticing that the program exits.

Invoke the program again, passing in the string "undecorated". If invoking from NetBeans, use the Project Properties dialog box to pass this argument as shown in Figure 2-3. The "undecorated" string is passed as a parameter without a value.

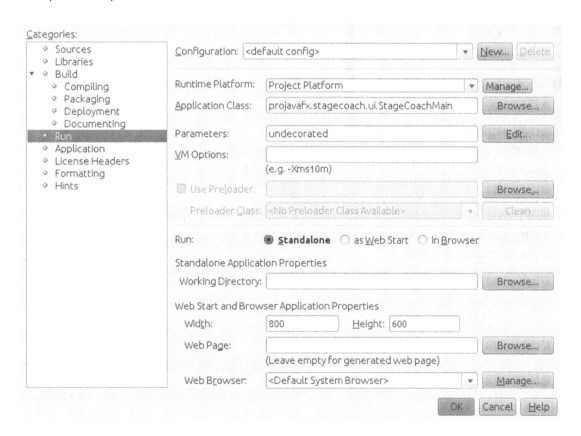

Figure 2-3. *Using NetBeans' Project Properties dialog box to pass an argument into the program*

Notice that this time the program appears without any window decorations, but the white background of the program includes the background of the window. The black outline in the screenshot shown in Figure 2-4 is part of the desktop background.

Exit the program again by clicking close(), and then run the program again, passing in the string "transparent" as the argument. Notice that the program appears in the shape of a rounded rectangle, as shown in Figure 2-5.

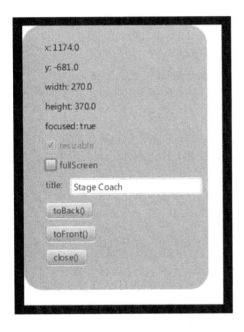

Figure 2-4. The StageCoach program after being invoked with the undecorated argument

■ **Note**   You might have noticed that the screenshots in Figures 2-4 and 2-5 have y values that are negative. This is because the application was positioned on the secondary monitor, logically above the primary monitor, when the screenshots were taken.

Figure 2-5. *The StageCoach program after being invoked with the transparent argument*

Click the application's UI, drag it around the screen, and click close()when finished. Congratulations on sticking with this 13-step exercise! Performing this exercise has prepared you to relate to the code behind it, which we now walk through together.

Understanding the StageCoach Program

Take a look at the code for the StageCoach program in Listing 2-1 before we point out new and relevant concepts.

Listing 2-1. StageCoachMain.java

```
package projavafx.stagecoach.ui;
import java.util.List;
import javafx.application.Application;
import javafx.beans.property.SimpleStringProperty;
import javafx.beans.property.StringProperty;
import javafx.geometry.Rectangle2D;
import javafx.geometry.VPos;
import javafx.scene.Group;
import javafx.scene.Scene;
import javafx.scene.control.Button;
import javafx.scene.control.CheckBox;
import javafx.scene.control.Label;
import javafx.scene.control.TextField;
import javafx.scene.input.MouseEvent;
import javafx.scene.layout.HBox;
import javafx.scene.layout.VBox;
```

```java
import javafx.scene.paint.Color;
import javafx.scene.shape.Rectangle;
import javafx.scene.text.Text;
import javafx.stage.Screen;
import javafx.stage.Stage;
import javafx.stage.StageStyle;
import javafx.stage.WindowEvent;

public class StageCoachMain extends Application {

    StringProperty title = new SimpleStringProperty();

    Text textStageX;
    Text textStageY;
    Text textStageW;
    Text textStageH;
    Text textStageF;
    CheckBox checkBoxResizable;
    CheckBox checkBoxFullScreen;

    double dragAnchorX;
    double dragAnchorY;

    public static void main(String[] args) {
        Application.launch(args);
    }

    @Override
    public void start(Stage stage) {
        StageStyle stageStyle = StageStyle.DECORATED;
        List<String> unnamedParams = getParameters().getUnnamed();
        if (unnamedParams.size() > 0) {
            String stageStyleParam = unnamedParams.get(0);
            if (stageStyleParam.equalsIgnoreCase("transparent")) {
                stageStyle = StageStyle.TRANSPARENT;
            } else if (stageStyleParam.equalsIgnoreCase("undecorated")) {
                stageStyle = StageStyle.UNDECORATED;
            } else if (stageStyleParam.equalsIgnoreCase("utility")) {
                stageStyle = StageStyle.UTILITY;
            }
        }
        final Stage stageRef = stage;
        Group rootGroup;
        TextField titleTextField;
        Button toBackButton = new Button("toBack()");
        toBackButton.setOnAction(e -> stageRef.toBack());
        Button toFrontButton = new Button("toFront()");
        toFrontButton.setOnAction(e -> stageRef.toFront());
        Button closeButton = new Button("close()");
        closeButton.setOnAction(e -> stageRef.close());
        Rectangle blue = new Rectangle(250, 350, Color.SKYBLUE);
```

```
blue.setArcHeight(50);
blue.setArcWidth(50);
textStageX = new Text();
textStageX.setTextOrigin(VPos.TOP);
textStageY = new Text();
textStageY.setTextOrigin(VPos.TOP);
textStageH = new Text();
textStageH.setTextOrigin(VPos.TOP);
textStageW = new Text();
textStageW.setTextOrigin(VPos.TOP);
textStageF = new Text();
textStageF.setTextOrigin(VPos.TOP);
checkBoxResizable = new CheckBox("resizable");
checkBoxResizable.setDisable(stageStyle == StageStyle.TRANSPARENT
        || stageStyle == StageStyle.UNDECORATED);
checkBoxFullScreen = new CheckBox("fullScreen");
titleTextField = new TextField("Stage Coach");
Label titleLabel = new Label("title");
HBox titleBox = new HBox(titleLabel, titleTextField);
VBox contentBox = new VBox(
        textStageX, textStageY, textStageW, textStageH, textStageF,
        checkBoxResizable, checkBoxFullScreen,
        titleBox, toBackButton, toFrontButton, closeButton);
contentBox.setLayoutX(30);
contentBox.setLayoutY(20);
contentBox.setSpacing(10);
rootGroup = new Group(blue, contentBox);

Scene scene = new Scene(rootGroup, 270, 370);
scene.setFill(Color.TRANSPARENT);

//when mouse button is pressed, save the initial position of screen
rootGroup.setOnMousePressed((MouseEvent me) -> {
    dragAnchorX = me.getScreenX() - stageRef.getX();
    dragAnchorY = me.getScreenY() - stageRef.getY();
});

//when screen is dragged, translate it accordingly
rootGroup.setOnMouseDragged((MouseEvent me) -> {
    stageRef.setX(me.getScreenX() - dragAnchorX);
    stageRef.setY(me.getScreenY() - dragAnchorY);
});

textStageX.textProperty().bind(new SimpleStringProperty("x: ")
        .concat(stageRef.xProperty().asString()));
textStageY.textProperty().bind(new SimpleStringProperty("y: ")
        .concat(stageRef.yProperty().asString()));
textStageW.textProperty().bind(new SimpleStringProperty("width: ")
        .concat(stageRef.widthProperty().asString()));
textStageH.textProperty().bind(new SimpleStringProperty("height: ")
        .concat(stageRef.heightProperty().asString()));
```

41

```
        textStageF.textProperty().bind(new SimpleStringProperty("focused: ")
                .concat(stageRef.focusedProperty().asString())));
        stage.setResizable(true);
        checkBoxResizable.selectedProperty()
                .bindBidirectional(stage.resizableProperty());
        checkBoxFullScreen.selectedProperty().addListener((ov, oldValue, newValue) -> {
            stageRef.setFullScreen(checkBoxFullScreen.selectedProperty().getValue());
        });
        title.bind(titleTextField.textProperty());

        stage.setScene(scene);
        stage.titleProperty().bind(title);
        stage.initStyle(stageStyle);
        stage.setOnCloseRequest((WindowEvent we) -> {
            System.out.println("Stage is closing");
        });
        stage.show();
        Rectangle2D primScreenBounds = Screen.getPrimary().getVisualBounds();
        stage.setX((primScreenBounds.getWidth() - stage.getWidth()) / 2);
        stage.setY((primScreenBounds.getHeight() - stage.getHeight()) / 4);
    }
}
```

Obtaining Program Arguments

The first new concept introduced by this program is the ability to read the arguments passed into a JavaFX program. The javafx.application package includes a class named Application that has application life cycle-related methods such as launch(), init(), start(), and stop(). Another method in the Application class is getParameters(), which gives the application access to the arguments passed on the command line, as well as unnamed parameters and <name,value> pairs specified in a JNLP file. Here's the relevant code snippet from Listing 2-1 for your convenience:

```
StageStyle stageStyle = StageStyle.DECORATED;
List<String> unnamedParams = getParameters().getUnnamed();
if (unnamedParams.size() > 0) {
  String stageStyleParam = unnamedParams.get(0);
  if (stageStyleParam.equalsIgnoreCase("transparent")) {
    stageStyle = StageStyle.TRANSPARENT;
  }
  else if (stageStyleParam.equalsIgnoreCase("undecorated")) {
    stageStyle = StageStyle.UNDECORATED;
  }
  else if (stageStyleParam.equalsIgnoreCase("utility")) {
    stageStyle = StageStyle.UTILITY;
  }
}
...code omitted...
stage.initStyle(stageStyle);
```

Setting the Style of the Stage

We're using the getParameters() method described previously to get an argument that tells us whether the stage style of the Stage instance should be its default (StageStyle.DECORATED), StageStyle.UNDECORATED, or StageStyle.TRANSPARENT. You saw the effects of each in the preceding exercise, specifically in Figures 2-2, 2-4, and 2-5.

Controlling Whether a Stage Is Resizable

As shown in the following excerpt from Listing 2-1, to make this application's window initially resizable we're calling the setResizable() method of the Stage instance. To keep the resizable property of the Stage and the state of the resizable check box synchronized, the check box is bidirectionally bound to the resizable property of the Stage instance.

```
stage.setResizable(true);
checkBoxResizable.selectedProperty()
        .bindBidirectional(stage.resizableProperty());
```

■ **Tip**   A property that is bound cannot be explicitly set. In the code preceding the snippet, the resizable property is set with the setResizable() method *before* the property is bound in the next line.

Making a Stage Full Screen

Making the Stage show in full-screen mode is done by setting the fullScreen property of the Stage instance to true. As shown in the following snippet from Listing 2-1, to keep the fullScreen property of the Stage and the state of the fullScreen check box synchronized, the fullScreen property of the Stage instance is updated whenever the selected property of the checkBox changes.

```
checkBoxFullScreen.selectedProperty().addListener((ov, oldValue, newValue) -> {
    stageRef.setFullScreen(checkBoxFullScreen.selectedProperty().getValue());
});
```

Note that the full-screen mode doesn't have an impact on some platforms. On mobile, for example, the JavaFX applications will by default be in full-screen mode, and the distribution for JavaFX on Mobile does not allow a non-full-screen option because that does not make sense in the world of mobile apps on devices.

Working with the Bounds of the Stage

The bounds of the Stage are represented by its x, y, width, and height properties, the values of which can be changed at will. This is demonstrated in the following snippet from Listing 2-1 where the Stage is placed near the top and centered horizontally on the primary screen after the Stage has been initialized.

```
Rectangle2D primScreenBounds = Screen.getPrimary().getVisualBounds();
stage.setX((primScreenBounds.getWidth() - stage.getWidth()) / 2);
stage.setY((primScreenBounds.getHeight() - stage.getHeight()) / 4);
```

We're using the Screen class of the javafx.stage package to get the dimensions of the primary screen so that the desired position may be calculated.

■ **Note**   We intentionally made the Stage in Figure 2-2 larger than the Scene contained within to make the following point. The width and height of a Stage include its decorations (title bar and border), which vary on different platforms. It is therefore usually better to control the width and height of the Scene (we show you how in a bit) and let the Stage conform to that size.

Drawing Rounded Rectangles

As pointed out in Chapter 1, you can put rounded corners on a Rectangle by specifying the arcWidth and arcHeight for the corners. The following snippet from Listing 2-1 draws the sky-blue rounded rectangle that becomes the background for the transparent window example in Figure 2-5.

```
Rectangle blue = new Rectangle(250, 350, Color.SKYBLUE);
blue.setArcHeight(50);
blue.setArcWidth(50);
```

In this snippet, we use the three-argument constructor of Rectangle, in which the first two parameters specify the width and the height of the Rectangle. The third parameter defines the fill color of the Rectangle.

As you can detect from this code snippet, rounded rectangles are easily created using the arcWidth(double v) and arcHeight(double v) methods, where the parameter v defines the diameter of the arc.

Dragging the Stage on the Desktop When a Title Bar Isn't Available

The Stage may be dragged on the desktop using its title bar, but in the case where its StageStyle is UNDECORATED or TRANSPARENT, the title bar isn't available. To allow dragging in this circumstance, we added the code shown in the following code snippet from Listing 2-1.

```
//when mouse button is pressed, save the initial position of screen
rootGroup.setOnMousePressed((MouseEvent me) -> {
    dragAnchorX = me.getScreenX() - stageRef.getX();
    dragAnchorY = me.getScreenY() - stageRef.getY();
});

//when screen is dragged, translate it accordingly
rootGroup.setOnMouseDragged((MouseEvent me) -> {
    stageRef.setX(me.getScreenX() - dragAnchorX);
    stageRef.setY(me.getScreenY() - dragAnchorY);
});
```

Event handlers are covered a little later in the chapter, but as a preview, the lambda expression that is supplied to the onMouseDragged() method is called when the mouse is dragged. As a result, the values of the x and y properties are altered by the number of pixels that the mouse was dragged, which moves the Stage as the mouse is dragged.

Using UI Layout Containers

When developing applications that will be deployed in a cross-platform environment or are internationalized, it is good to use *layout containers*. One advantage of using layout containers is that when the node sizes change, their visual relationships with each other are predictable. Another advantage is that you don't have to calculate the location of each node that you place in the UI.

The following snippet from Listing 2-1 shows how the VBox layout class, located in the `javafx.scene.layout` package, is used to arrange the Text, CheckBox, HBox, and Button nodes in a column. This snippet also shows that layout containers may be nested, as demonstrated by the HBox with the name `titleBox` that arranges the Label and TextField nodes horizontally. Note that several lines of code are omitted from this snippet to show the layout nesting clearly:

```
HBox titleBox = new HBox(titleLabel, titleTextField);
VBox contentBox = new VBox(
        textStageX, textStageY, textStageW, textStageH, textStageF,
        checkBoxResizable, checkBoxFullScreen,
        titleBox, toBackButton, toFrontButton, closeButton);
```

The VBox layout class is similar to the Group class discussed in the Hello Earthrise example in Chapter 1, in that it contains a collection of nodes within it. Unlike the Group class, the VBox class arranges its contained nodes vertically, spacing them apart from each other by the number of pixels specified in the spacing property.

Ascertaining Whether the Stage Is in Focus

To know whether your JavaFX application is the one that currently is in focus (e.g., keys pressed are delivered to the application), simply consult the `focused` property of the Stage instance. The following snippet from Listing 2-1 demonstrates this.

```
textStageF.textProperty().bind(new SimpleStringProperty("focused: ")
        .concat(stageRef.focusedProperty().asString()));
```

Controlling the Z-Order of the Stage

In the event that you want your JavaFX application to appear on top of other windows or behind other windows onscreen, you can use the `toFront()` and `toBack()` methods, respectively. The following snippet from Listing 2-1 shows how this is accomplished.

```
Button toBackButton = new Button("toBack()");
toBackButton.setOnAction(e -> stageRef.toBack());
Button toFrontButton = new Button("toFront()");
toFrontButton.setOnAction(e -> stageRef.toFront());
```

Once again, note how using lambda expressions enhances the readability of the code. It is clear from the first line of the snippet that a Button named toBackButton is created with a text "toBack()" being displayed on the button. The second line defines that when an action is performed on the button (i.e., the button is clicked), the stage is sent to the back.

Without using a lambda expression, the second line would be replaced by a call to an anonymous inner class as follows:

```
toBackButton.setOnAction(new EventHandler<javafx.event.ActionEvent>() {
  @Override public void handle(javafx.event.ActionEvent e) {
    stageRef.toBack();
  }
})
```

This approach not only requires more code, it doesn't allow the Java runtime to optimize calls and it is much less readable.

Closing the Stage and Detecting When It Is Closed

As shown in the following code snippet from Listing 2-1, you can programmatically close the Stage with its close() method. This is important when the stageStyle is undecorated or transparent, because the close button supplied by the windowing system is not present.

```
Button closeButton = new Button("close()");
closeButton.setOnAction(e -> stageRef.close());
```

By the way, you can detect when there is an external request to close the Stage by using the onCloseRequest event handler as shown in the following code snippet from Listing 2-1.

```
stage.setOnCloseRequest((WindowEvent we) -> {
        System.out.println("Stage is closing");
});
```

To see this in action, run the application without any arguments so that it has the appearance of Figure 2-2 shown previously, and then click the close button on the decoration of the window.

■ **Tip** The onCloseRequest event handler is only called when there is an external request to close the window. This is why the "Stage is closing" message doesn't appear in this example when you click the button labeled "close()".

Making a Scene

Continuing on with our theater metaphor for creating JavaFX applications, we now discuss putting a Scene on the Stage. The Scene, as you recall, is the place in which the actors and props (nodes) visually interact with each other and the audience (the users of your program).

Using the Scene Class: The OnTheScene Example

As with the Stage class, we're going to use a contrived example application to demonstrate and teach the details of the available capabilities in the Scene class. See Figure 2-6 for a screenshot of the OnTheScene program.

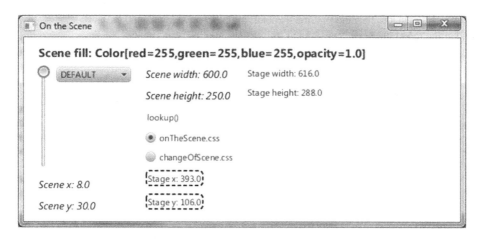

Figure 2-6. *The OnTheScene program when first invoked*

Go ahead and run the OnTheScene program, putting it through its paces as instructed in the following exercise. We follow up with a walkthrough of the code so that you can associate the behavior with the code behind it.

EXAMINING THE BEHAVIOR OF THE ONTHESCENE PROGRAM

When the OnTheScene program starts, its appearance should be similar to the screenshot in Figure 2-6. To fully examine its behavior, perform the following steps. Note that the property and method names on the UI correspond to the property and methods in the Scene, Stage, and Cursor classes, as well as Cascading Style Sheets (CSS) file names.

1. Drag the application around, noticing that although the Stage x and y values are relative to the screen, the Scene's x and y values are relative to the upper-left corner of the exterior of the Stage (including decorations). Similarly, the width and height of the Scene are the dimensions of the interior of the Stage (which doesn't include decorations). As noted earlier, it is best to set the Scene width and height explicitly (or let them be set implicitly by assuming the size of the contained nodes), rather than setting the width and height of a decorated Stage.

2. Resize the program's window and observe that the width and height values change to reflect the width and height of the Scene. Also notice that the position of much of the content in the scene changes as you change the height of the window.

3. Click the lookup() hyperlink and notice that the string "Scene height: XXX.X" prints in the console, where XXX.X is the Scene's height.

4. Hover the mouse over the choice box drop-down list and notice that it becomes slightly larger. Click the choice box and choose a cursor style in the list, noticing that the cursor changes to that style. Be careful about choosing NONE, as the cursor might disappear, and you'll need to use the keyboard (or psychic powers while moving the mouse) to make it visible.

5. Drag the slider on the left, noticing that the fill color of the Scene changes and that the string at the top of the Scene reflects the red-green-blue (RGB) and opacity values of the current fill color.

6. Notice the appearance and content of the text on the Scene. Then click changeOfScene.css, noticing that the color and font and content characteristics for some of the text on the Scene changes as shown in the screenshot in Figure 2-7.

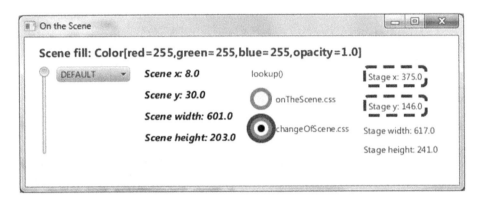

Figure 2-7. *The OnTheScene program with the changeOfScene CSS style sheet applied*

7. Click OnTheScene.css, noticing that the color and font characteristics return to their previous state.

Now that you've explored this example program that demonstrates features of the Scene, let's walk through the code!

Understanding the OnTheScene Program

Take a look at the code for the OnTheScene program in Listing 2-2, before we point out new and relevant concepts.

Listing 2-2. OnTheSceneMain.java

```
import javafx.application.Application;
import javafx.beans.property.DoubleProperty;
import javafx.beans.property.SimpleDoubleProperty;
import javafx.beans.property.SimpleStringProperty;
import javafx.collections.FXCollections;
import javafx.collections.ObservableList;
import javafx.geometry.HPos;
import javafx.geometry.Insets;
import javafx.geometry.Orientation;
import javafx.geometry.VPos;
import javafx.scene.Cursor;
import javafx.scene.Scene;
import javafx.scene.control.ChoiceBox;
```

```java
import javafx.scene.control.Hyperlink;
import javafx.scene.control.Label;
import javafx.scene.control.RadioButton;
import javafx.scene.control.Slider;
import javafx.scene.control.ToggleGroup;
import javafx.scene.layout.FlowPane;
import javafx.scene.layout.HBox;
import javafx.scene.paint.Color;
import javafx.scene.text.Font;
import javafx.scene.text.FontWeight;
import javafx.scene.text.Text;
import javafx.stage.Stage;

public class OnTheSceneMain extends Application {

    DoubleProperty fillVals = new SimpleDoubleProperty(255.0);

    Scene sceneRef;

    ObservableList cursors = FXCollections.observableArrayList(
            Cursor.DEFAULT,
            Cursor.CROSSHAIR,
            Cursor.WAIT,
            Cursor.TEXT,
            Cursor.HAND,
            Cursor.MOVE,
            Cursor.N_RESIZE,
            Cursor.NE_RESIZE,
            Cursor.E_RESIZE,
            Cursor.SE_RESIZE,
            Cursor.S_RESIZE,
            Cursor.SW_RESIZE,
            Cursor.W_RESIZE,
            Cursor.NW_RESIZE,
            Cursor.NONE
    );

    public static void main(String[] args) {
        Application.launch(args);
    }

    @Override
    public void start(Stage stage) {
        Slider sliderRef;
        ChoiceBox choiceBoxRef;
        Text textSceneX;
        Text textSceneY;
        Text textSceneW;
        Text textSceneH;
        Label labelStageX;
        Label labelStageY;
```

```java
Label labelStageW;
Label labelStageH;

final ToggleGroup toggleGrp = new ToggleGroup();
sliderRef = new Slider(0, 255, 255);
sliderRef.setOrientation(Orientation.VERTICAL);
choiceBoxRef = new ChoiceBox(cursors);
HBox hbox = new HBox(sliderRef, choiceBoxRef);
hbox.setSpacing(10);
textSceneX = new Text();
textSceneX.getStyleClass().add("emphasized-text");
textSceneY = new Text();
textSceneY.getStyleClass().add("emphasized-text");
textSceneW = new Text();
textSceneW.getStyleClass().add("emphasized-text");
textSceneH = new Text();
textSceneH.getStyleClass().add("emphasized-text");
textSceneH.setId("sceneHeightText");
Hyperlink hyperlink = new Hyperlink("lookup");
hyperlink.setOnAction((javafx.event.ActionEvent e) -> {
    System.out.println("sceneRef:" + sceneRef);
    Text textRef = (Text) sceneRef.lookup("#sceneHeightText");
    System.out.println(textRef.getText());
});
RadioButton radio1 = new RadioButton("onTheScene.css");
radio1.setSelected(true);
radio1.setToggleGroup(toggleGrp);
RadioButton radio2 = new RadioButton("changeOfScene.css");
radio2.setToggleGroup(toggleGrp);
labelStageX = new Label();
labelStageX.setId("stageX");
labelStageY = new Label();
labelStageY.setId("stageY");
labelStageW = new Label();
labelStageH = new Label();

FlowPane sceneRoot = new FlowPane(Orientation.VERTICAL, 20, 10, hbox,
        textSceneX, textSceneY, textSceneW, textSceneH, hyperlink,
        radio1, radio2,
        labelStageX, labelStageY,
        labelStageW,
        labelStageH);
sceneRoot.setPadding(new Insets(0, 20, 40, 0));
sceneRoot.setColumnHalignment(HPos.LEFT);
sceneRoot.setLayoutX(20);
sceneRoot.setLayoutY(40);

sceneRef = new Scene(sceneRoot, 600, 250);

sceneRef.getStylesheets().add("onTheScene.css");
stage.setScene(sceneRef);
```

```java
choiceBoxRef.getSelectionModel().selectFirst();

// Setup various property binding
textSceneX.textProperty().bind(new SimpleStringProperty("Scene x: ")
        .concat(sceneRef.xProperty().asString()));
textSceneY.textProperty().bind(new SimpleStringProperty("Scene y: ")
        .concat(sceneRef.yProperty().asString()));
textSceneW.textProperty().bind(new SimpleStringProperty("Scene width: ")
        .concat(sceneRef.widthProperty().asString()));
textSceneH.textProperty().bind(new SimpleStringProperty("Scene height: ")
        .concat(sceneRef.heightProperty().asString()));
labelStageX.textProperty().bind(new SimpleStringProperty("Stage x: ")
        .concat(sceneRef.getWindow().xProperty().asString()));
labelStageY.textProperty().bind(new SimpleStringProperty("Stage y: ")
        .concat(sceneRef.getWindow().yProperty().asString()));
labelStageW.textProperty().bind(new SimpleStringProperty("Stage width: ")
        .concat(sceneRef.getWindow().widthProperty().asString()));
labelStageH.textProperty().bind(new SimpleStringProperty("Stage height: ")
        .concat(sceneRef.getWindow().heightProperty().asString()));
sceneRef.cursorProperty().bind(choiceBoxRef.getSelectionModel()
        .selectedItemProperty());
fillVals.bind(sliderRef.valueProperty());

// When fillVals changes, use that value as the RGB to fill the scene
fillVals.addListener((ov, oldValue, newValue) -> {
    Double fillValue = fillVals.getValue() / 256.0;
    sceneRef.setFill(new Color(fillValue, fillValue, fillValue, 1.0));
});

// When the selected radio button changes, set the appropriate style sheet
toggleGrp.selectedToggleProperty().addListener((ov, oldValue, newValue) -> {
    String radioButtonText = ((RadioButton) toggleGrp.getSelectedToggle())
            .getText();
    sceneRef.getStylesheets().clear();
    sceneRef.getStylesheets().addAll(radioButtonText);
});

stage.setTitle("On the Scene");
stage.show();

// Define an unmanaged node that will display Text
Text addedTextRef = new Text(0, -30, "");
addedTextRef.setTextOrigin(VPos.TOP);
addedTextRef.setFill(Color.BLUE);
addedTextRef.setFont(Font.font("Sans Serif", FontWeight.BOLD, 16));
addedTextRef.setManaged(false);

// Bind the text of the added Text node to the fill property of the Scene
addedTextRef.textProperty().bind(new SimpleStringProperty("Scene fill: ").
        concat(sceneRef.fillProperty()));
```

```
        // Add to the Text node to the FlowPane
        ((FlowPane) sceneRef.getRoot()).getChildren().add(addedTextRef);
    }
}
```

Setting the Cursor for the Scene

The cursor can be set for a given node, for the entire scene, or for both. To do the latter, set the cursor property of the Scene instance to one of the constant values in the Cursor class, as shown in the following snippet from Listing 2-2.

```
sceneRef.cursorProperty().bind(choiceBoxRef.getSelectionModel()
        .selectedItemProperty());
```

These cursor values can be seen by looking at the javafx.scene.Cursor class in the JavaFX API docs; we've created a collection of these constants in Listing 2-2.

Painting the Scene's Background

The Scene class has a fill property of type javafx.scene.paint.Paint. Looking at the JavaFX API will reveal that the known subclasses of Paint are Color, ImagePattern, LinearGradient, and RadialGradient. Therefore, a Scene's background can be filled with solid colors, patterns, and gradients. If you don't set the fill property of the Scene, the default color (white) will be used.

■ **Tip**   One of the Color constants is Color.TRANSPARENT, so you may make the Scene's background completely transparent if desired. In fact, the reason that the Scene behind the rounded-cornered rectangle in the StageCoach screenshot in Figure 2-5 isn't white is that its fill property is set to Color.TRANSPARENT (see Listing 2-1).

To set the fill property in the OnTheScene example, instead of using one of the constants in the Color class (e.g., Color.BLUE), we're using an RGB formula to create the color. Take a look at the javafx.scene.paint.Color class in the JavaFX API docs and scroll down past the constants such as ALICEBLUE and WHITESMOKE to see the constructors and methods. We're using a constructor of the Color class, setting the fill property to it, as shown in the following snippet from Listing 2-2.

```
sceneRef.setFill(new Color(fillValue, fillValue, fillValue, 1.0));
```

As you move the Slider, to which the fillVals property is bound, each of the arguments to the Color() constructor is set to a value from 0 to 255, as indicated in the following code snippet from Listing 2-2.

```
fillVals.bind(sliderRef.valueProperty());
```

Populating the Scene with Nodes

As covered in Chapter 1, you can populate a Scene with nodes by instantiating them and adding them to container nodes (e.g., Group and VBox) that can contain other nodes. These capabilities enable you to construct complex *scene graphs* containing nodes. In the example here, the root property of the Scene contains a Flow layout container, which causes its contents to flow either vertically or horizontally, wrapping as necessary. The Flow container in our example contains an HBox (which contains a Slider and a ChoiceBox) and several other nodes (instances of Text, Hyperlink, and RadioButton classes).

Finding a Scene Node by ID

Each node in a Scene can be assigned an ID in the id property of the node. For example, in the following snippet from Listing 2-2, the id property of a Text node is assigned the String "sceneHeightText". When the action event handler in the Hyperlink control is called, the lookup() method of the Scene instance is used to obtain a reference to the node with the id of "sceneHeightText". The event handler then prints the content of the Text node to the console.

▪ **Note**   The Hyperlink control is essentially a button that has the appearance of hyperlink text. It has an action event handler in which you could place code that opens a browser page or any other desired functionality.

```
textSceneH = new Text();
textSceneH.getStyleClass().add("emphasized-text");
textSceneH.setId("sceneHeightText");
Hyperlink hyperlink = new Hyperlink("lookup");
hyperlink.setOnAction((javafx.event.ActionEvent e) -> {
    System.out.println("sceneRef:" + sceneRef);
    Text textRef = (Text) sceneRef.lookup("#sceneHeightText");
    System.out.println(textRef.getText());
});
```

A close examination of the action event handler reveals that the lookup() method returns a Node, but the actual type of object returned in this snippet is a Text object. Because we need to access a property of the Text class (text) that isn't in the Node class, it is necessary to coerce the compiler into trusting that at runtime the object will be an instance of the Text class.

Accessing the Stage from the Scene

To obtain a reference to the Stage instance from the Scene, we use a property in the Scene class named window. The accessor method for this property appears in the following snippet from Listing 2-2 to get the x and y co-ordinates of the Stage on the screen.

```
labelStageX.textProperty().bind(new SimpleStringProperty("Stage x: ")
        .concat(sceneRef.getWindow().xProperty().asString()));
labelStageY.textProperty().bind(new SimpleStringProperty("Stage y: ")
        .concat(sceneRef.getWindow().yProperty().asString()));
```

Inserting a Node into the Scene's Content Sequence

Sometimes it is useful to add a node dynamically to the children of a UI container class. The code snippet from Listing 2-2 that follows demonstrates how this may be accomplished by dynamically adding a Text node to the children of the FlowPane instance:

```
// Define an unmanaged node that will display Text
Text addedTextRef = new Text(0, -30, "");
addedTextRef.setTextOrigin(VPos.TOP);
addedTextRef.setFill(Color.BLUE);
addedTextRef.setFont(Font.font("Sans Serif", FontWeight.BOLD, 16));
addedTextRef.setManaged(false);

// Bind the text of the added Text node to the fill property of the Scene
addedTextRef.textProperty().bind(new SimpleStringProperty("Scene fill: ").
        concat(sceneRef.fillProperty()));

// Add the Text node to the FlowPane
((FlowPane) sceneRef.getRoot()).getChildren().add(addedTextRef);
```

This particular Text node is the one at the top of the Scene shown in Figures 2-6 and 2-7, in which the value of the Scene's fill property is displayed. Note that in this example the managed property of the addedTextRef instance is set to false, so its position isn't governed by the FlowPane. By default, nodes are "managed," which means that their parent (the container to which this node is added) is responsible for the layout of the node. By setting the managed property to false, the developer is assumed to be responsible for laying out the node.

CSS Styling the Nodes in a Scene

A very powerful aspect of JavaFX is the ability to use CSS to style the nodes in a Scene dynamically. You used this capability in step 6 of the previous exercise when you clicked changeOfScene.css to change the appearance of the UI from what you saw in Figure 2-6 to what was shown in Figure 2-7. Also, in step 7 of the exercise, the appearance of the UI changed back to what was shown in Figure 2-6 when you selected the onTheScene.css radio button. The relevant code snippet from Listing 2-2 is shown here:

```
sceneRef.getStylesheets().add("onTheScene.css");
...code omitted...
// When the selected radio button changes, set the appropriate stylesheet
        toggleGrp.selectedToggleProperty().addListener((ov, oldValue, newValue) -> {
        String radioButtonText = ((RadioButton) toggleGrp.getSelectedToggle())
                .getText();
        sceneRef.getStylesheets().clear();
        sceneRef.getStylesheets().addAll("/"+radioButtonText);
});
```

In this snippet, the stylesheets property of the Scene is initialized to the location of the onTheScene. css file, which in this case is the root directory. Also shown in the snippet is the assignment of the CSS files to the Scene as the appropriate buttons are clicked. The text of the RadioButton instances is equal to the names of the style sheets, hence we can easily set the corresponding style sheet to the scene. Take a look at Listing 2-3 to see the style sheet that corresponds to the screenshot in Figure 2-6. Some of the CSS *selectors* in this style sheet represent the nodes whose id property is either "stageX" or "stageY". There is also a selector in this style sheet that represents nodes whose styleClass property is "emphasized-text". In addition, there is a selector in this style sheet that maps to the ChoiceBox UI control by substituting the camel-case name of the control to a lowercase hyphenated name (choice-box). The *properties* in this style sheet begin with "-fx", and correspond to the type of node with which they are associated. The *values* in this style sheet (e.g., black, italic, and 14pt) are expressed as standard CSS values.

Listing 2-3. onTheScene.css

```css
#stageX, #stageY {
  -fx-padding: 1;
  -fx-border-color: black;
  -fx-border-style: dashed;
  -fx-border-width: 2;
  -fx-border-radius: 5;
}

.emphasized-text {
  -fx-font-size: 14pt;
  -fx-font-weight: normal;
  -fx-font-style: italic;
}

.choice-box:hover {
    -fx-scale-x: 1.1;
    -fx-scale-y: 1.1;
}

.radio-button .radio  {
  -fx-background-color: -fx-shadow-highlight-color, -fx-outer-border,
                        -fx-inner-border, -fx-body-color;
  -fx-background-insets: 0 0 -1 0,  0,  1,  2;
  -fx-background-radius: 1.0em;
  -fx-padding: 0.333333em;
}

.radio-button:focused .radio {
    -fx-background-color: -fx-focus-color, -fx-outer-border,
                          -fx-inner-border, -fx-body-color;
    -fx-background-radius: 1.0em;
    -fx-background-insets: -1.4, 0, 1, 2;
}
```

Listing 2-4 is the style sheet that corresponds to the screenshot in Figure 2-7. For more information on CSS style sheets, see the "Resources" section at the end of this chapter.

Listing 2-4. changeOfScene.css

```css
#stageX, #stageY {
  -fx-padding: 3;
  -fx-border-color: blue;
  -fx-stroke-dash-array: 12 2 4 2;
  -fx-border-width: 4;
```

```
  -fx-border-radius: 5;
}

.emphasized-text {
  -fx-font-size: 14pt;
  -fx-font-weight: bold;
  -fx-font-style: normal;
}

.radio-button *.radio  {
    -fx-padding: 10;
    -fx-background-color: red, yellow;
    -fx-background-insets: 0, 5;
    -fx-background-radius: 30, 20;
}

.radio-button:focused *.radio {
    -fx-background-color: blue, red, yellow;
    -fx-background-insets: -5, 0, 5;
    -fx-background-radius: 40, 30, 20;
}
```

Now that you've had some experience with using the Stage and Scene classes, several of the Node subclasses, and CSS styling, we show you how to handle events that can occur when your JavaFX program is running.

Handling Input Events

So far we've shown you a couple of examples of event handling. For example, we used the onAction event handler to execute code when a button is clicked. We also used the onCloseRequest event handler of the Stage class to execute code when the Stage has been requested externally to close. In this section, we explore more of the event handlers available in JavaFX.

Surveying Mouse, Keyboard, Touch, and Gesture Events and Handlers

Most of the events that occur in JavaFX programs are related to the user manipulating input devices such as a mouse, a keyboard, or a multitouch screen. To see the available event handlers and their associated event objects, we take yet another look at the JavaFX API documentation. First, navigate to the javafx.scene. Node class and look for the properties that begin with the letters "on". These properties represent the event handlers common to all nodes in JavaFX. Here is a list of these event handlers in the JavaFX 8 API:

- Key event handlers: onKeyPressed, onKeyReleased, onKeyTyped

- Mouse event handlers: onMouseClicked, onMouseDragEntered, onMouseDragExited, onMouseDragged, onMouseDragOver, onMouseDragReleased, onMouseEntered, onMouseExited, onMouseMoved, onMousePressed, onMouseReleased

- Drag-and-drop handlers: onDragDetected, onDragDone, onDragDropped, onDragEntered, onDragExited, onDragOver

- Touch handlers: onTouchMoved, onTouchPressed, onTouchReleased, onTouchStationary

- Gesture handlers: onRotate, onRotationFinished, onRotationStarted, onScroll, onScrollStarted, onScrollFinished, onSwipeLeft, onSwipeRight, onSwipeUp, onSwipeDown, onZoom, onZoomStarted, onZoomFinished

Each of these is a property that defines a method to be called when particular input events occur. In the case of the key event handlers, as shown in the JavaFX API docs, the method's parameter is a javafx. scene.input.KeyEvent instance. The method's parameter for the mouse event handlers is a javafx.scene. input.MouseEvent. Touch handlers consume a javafx.scene.input.TouchEvent instance, and when a gesture event occurs, the method's parameter for the handle event is an instance of javax.scene.input. GestureInput.

Understanding the KeyEvent Class

Take a look at the JavaFX API docs for the KeyEvent class, and you'll see that it contains several methods, a commonly used one being getCode(). The getCode() method returns a KeyCode instance representing the key that caused the event when pressed. Looking at the javafx.scene.input.KeyCode class in the JavaFX API docs reveals that a multitude of constants exist that represent keys on an international set of keyboards. Another way to find out what key was pressed is to call the getCharacter() method, which returns a string that represents the Unicode character associated with the key pressed.

The KeyEvent class also enables you to see whether the Alt, Ctrl, Meta, and/or Shift keys were down at the time of the event by calling the isAltDown(), isControlDown(), isMetaDown(), or isShiftDown() methods, respectively.

Understanding the MouseEvent Class

Take a look at the MouseEvent class in the JavaFX API docs, and you see that significantly more methods are available than in KeyEvent. Like KeyEvent, MouseEvent has the isAltDown(), isControlDown(), isMetaDown(), and isShiftDown() methods, as well as the source field, which is a reference to the object in which the event originated. In addition, it has several methods that pinpoint various coordinate spaces where the mouse event occurred, all expressed in pixels:

- getX() and getY() return the horizontal and vertical position of the mouse event, relative to the origin of the node in which the mouse event occurred.

- getSceneX() and getSceneY() return the horizontal and vertical position of the mouse event, relative to the Scene.

- getScreenX() and getScreenY() return the horizontal and vertical position of the mouse event, relative to the screen.

Here are a few other commonly useful methods:

- isDragDetect() returns true if a drag event is detected.

- getButton(), isPrimaryButtonDown(), isSecondaryButtonDown(), isMiddleButtonDown(), and getClickCount() contain information about what button was clicked, and how many times it was clicked.

A little later in this chapter you get some experience with creating key and mouse event handlers in the ZenPong example program. To continue preparing you for the ZenPong example, we now give you a look at how you can animate the nodes that you put in your scene.

Understanding the TouchEvent Class

With more and more devices being equipped with a touch screen, built-in support for touch events makes JavaFX a state-of-the art platform for creating applications that leverage multitouch capabilities, by which we mean that the platform is able to track more than one touchpoint in a single set of events.

The TouchEvent class provides the getTouchPoint() method, which returns a specific touch point. The methods on this TouchPoint are similar to the methods on a MouseEvent, for example, you can retrieve the relative and absolute positions by calling getX() and getY(), or getSceneX() and getSceneY(), or getScreenX() and getScreenY().

The TouchEvent class also allows the developer to get information about the other touch points that belong to the same set. By calling getEventSetId(), you get the unique identifier of the set of TouchEvent instances, and the list of all touch points in the set can be obtained by calling getTouchPoints(), which returns a list of TouchPoint instances.

Understanding the GestureEvent Class

Besides handling multitouch events, JavaFX also supports the creation and dispatching of gesture events. Gestures are increasingly used on smartphones, tablets, touch screens, and other input devices. They provide an intuitive way of performing an action, for example, by having the user swipe his or her finger. The GestureEvent class currently has four subclasses, each representing a specific gesture: RotateEvent, ScrollEvent, SwipeEvent, and ZoomEvent. All of these events have methods comparable to the MouseEvent for retrieving the position of the action—the getX() and getY(), getSceneX() and getSceneY(), and the getScreenX() and getScreenY() methods.

The specific subclasses all allow for retrieving a more detailed type of the event. A SwipeEvent, for example can be a swipe to the right or the left, to the top or the bottom. This information is obtained by calling the getEventType() method on the GestureEvent.

Animating Nodes in the Scene

One of the strengths of JavaFX is the ease with which you can create graphically rich UIs. Part of that richness is the ability to animate nodes that live in the Scene. At its core, animating a node involves changing the value of its properties over a period of time. Examples of animating a node include the following.

- Gradually increasing the size of a node when the mouse enters its bounds, and gradually decreasing the size when the mouse exits its bounds. Note that this requires scaling the node, which is referred to as a transform.

- Gradually increasing or decreasing the opacity of a node to provide a fade-in or fade-out effect, respectively.

- Gradually altering values of properties in a node that change its location, causing it to move from one location to another. This is useful, for example, when creating a game such as Pong. A related capability is detecting when a node has collided with another node.

Animating a node involves the use of the Timeline class, located in the javafx.animation package. Depending on the requirements of an animation and personal preference, use one of two general techniques:

- Create an instance of the Timeline class directly and supply key frames that specify values and actions at specific points in time.

- Use the javafx.animation.Transition subclasses to define and associate specific transitions with a node. Examples of transitions include causing a node to move along a defined path over a period of time, and rotating a node over a period of time. Each of these transition classes extends the Timeline class.

We now cover these techniques, showing examples of each, beginning with the first one listed.

Using a Timeline for Animation

Take a look at the `javafx.animation` package in the JavaFX API docs, and you see three of the classes that are used when directly creating a timeline: `Timeline`, `KeyFrame`, and `Interpolator`. Peruse the docs for these classes, and then come back so we can show you some examples of using them.

■ **Tip**   Remember to consult the JavaFX API docs for any new packages, classes, properties, and methods that you encounter.

The Metronome1 Example

We use a simple metronome example to demonstrate how to create a timeline.

As the screenshot in Figure 2-8 shows, the Metronome1 program has a pendulum as well as four buttons that start, pause, resume, and stop the animation. The pendulum in this example is a `Line` node, and we're going to animate that node by *interpolating* its `startX` property over the period of one second. Go ahead and take this example for a spin by doing the following exercise.

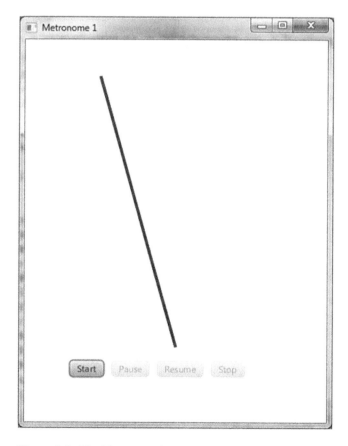

Figure 2-8. *The Metronome1 program*

EXAMINING THE BEHAVIOR OF THE METRONOME1 PROGRAM

When the Metronome1 program starts, its appearance should be similar to the screenshot in Figure 2-8. To fully examine its behavior, perform the following steps.

1. Observe that of the four buttons on the scene, only the Start button is enabled.

2. Click Start. Notice that the top of the line moves back and forth, taking one second to travel each direction. Also, observe that the Start and Resume buttons are disabled and that the Pause and Stop buttons are enabled.

3. Click Pause, noticing that the animation pauses. Also, observe that the Start and Pause buttons are disabled and that the Resume and Stop buttons are enabled.

4. Click Resume, noticing that the animation resumes from where it was paused.

5. Click Stop, noticing that the animation stops and that the button states are the same as they were when the program was first started (see step 1).

6. Click Start again, noticing that the line jumps back to its starting point before beginning the animation (rather than simply resuming as it did in step 4).

7. Click Stop.

Now that you've experienced the behavior of the Metronome1 program, let's walk through the code behind it.

Understanding the Metronome1 Program

Take a look at the code for the Metronome1 program in Listing 2-5, before we discuss relevant concepts.

Listing 2-5. Metronome1Main.java

```java
package projavafx.metronome1.ui;

import javafx.animation.Animation;
import javafx.animation.Interpolator;
import javafx.animation.KeyFrame;
import javafx.animation.KeyValue;
import javafx.animation.Timeline;
import javafx.application.Application;
import javafx.beans.property.DoubleProperty;
import javafx.beans.property.SimpleDoubleProperty;
import javafx.scene.Group;
import javafx.scene.Scene;
import javafx.scene.control.Button;
import javafx.scene.layout.HBox;
import javafx.scene.paint.Color;
import javafx.scene.shape.Line;
import javafx.stage.Stage;
import javafx.util.Duration;
```

```java
public class Metronome1Main extends Application {

    DoubleProperty startXVal = new SimpleDoubleProperty(100.0);

    Button startButton;
    Button pauseButton;
    Button resumeButton;
    Button stopButton;
    Line line;
    Timeline anim;

    public static void main(String[] args) {
        Application.launch(args);
    }

    @Override
    public void start(Stage stage) {
        anim = new Timeline(
                new KeyFrame(new Duration(0.0), new KeyValue(startXVal, 100.)),
                new KeyFrame(new Duration(1000.0), new KeyValue(startXVal, 300.,
                Interpolator.LINEAR))
        );
        anim.setAutoReverse(true);
        anim.setCycleCount(Animation.INDEFINITE);
        line = new Line(0, 50, 200, 400);
        line.setStrokeWidth(4);
        line.setStroke(Color.BLUE);
        startButton = new Button("start");
        startButton.setOnAction(e -> anim.playFromStart());
        pauseButton = new Button("pause");
        pauseButton.setOnAction(e -> anim.pause());
        resumeButton = new Button("resume");
        resumeButton.setOnAction(e -> anim.play());
        stopButton = new Button("stop");
        stopButton.setOnAction(e -> anim.stop());
        HBox commands = new HBox(10,
                startButton,
                pauseButton,
                resumeButton,
                stopButton);
        commands.setLayoutX(60);
        commands.setLayoutY(420);
        Group group = new Group(line, commands);
        Scene scene = new Scene(group, 400, 500);

        line.startXProperty().bind(startXVal);
        startButton.disableProperty().bind(anim.statusProperty()
                .isNotEqualTo(Animation.Status.STOPPED));
        pauseButton.disableProperty().bind(anim.statusProperty()
                .isNotEqualTo(Animation.Status.RUNNING));
        resumeButton.disableProperty().bind(anim.statusProperty()
```

```
                    .isNotEqualTo(Animation.Status.PAUSED)));
        stopButton.disableProperty().bind(anim.statusProperty()
                    .isEqualTo(Animation.Status.STOPPED));

        stage.setScene(scene);
        stage.setTitle("Metronome 1");
        stage.show();
    }
}
```

Understanding the Timeline Class

The main purpose of the Timeline class is to provide the ability to change the values of properties in a gradual fashion over given periods of time. Take a look at the following snippet from Listing 2-5 to see the timeline being created, along with some of its commonly used properties.

```
DoubleProperty startXVal = new SimpleDoubleProperty(100.0);

    ...code omitted...

Timeline anim = new Timeline(
                new KeyFrame(new Duration(0.0), new KeyValue(startXVal, 100.)),
                new KeyFrame(new Duration(1000.0), new KeyValue(startXVal, 300.,
                Interpolator.LINEAR))
        );
anim.setAutoReverse(true);
        anim.setCycleCount(Animation.INDEFINITE);

    ...code omitted...

line = new Line(0, 50, 200, 400);
        line.setStrokeWidth(4);
        line.setStroke(Color.BLUE);

    ...code omitted...

    line.startXProperty().bind(startXVal);
```

■ **Note**   In JavaFX 2, it was recommended to use the builder pattern for creating Nodes. As a consequence, creating a Line would be done as follows:

```
line = LineBuilder.create()

.startY(50)

.endX(200)
```

```
.endY(400)
```

```
.strokeWidth(4)
```

```
.stroke(Color.BLUE)
```

```
.build();
```

The advantage of this approach is that it is clear what the parameter "50" in the second line means: The line has a start-coordinate of 50 in the vertical position. The same readability can be achieved by calling setter methods, for example

```
line.setStartY(50);
```

In practice, however, many parameters are passed via the constructor of the Node. In the case of a Line instance, the second parameter is the startY parameter. This approach leads to fewer lines of code, but the developer should be careful about the order and the meaning of the parameters in the constructor. Once again, we strongly recommend having the Javadoc available while writing JavaFX applications.

Inserting Key Frames into the Timeline

Our timeline contains a collection of two KeyFrame instances. Using the KeyValue constructor, one of these instances assigns 100 to the startXVal property at the beginning of the timeline, and the other assigns 300 to the startXVal property when the timeline has been running for one second. Because the startX property of the Line is bound to the value of the startXVal property, the net result is that the top of the line moves 200 pixels horizontally over the course of one second.

In the second KeyFrame of the timeline, the KeyValue constructor is passed a third argument that specifies that the interpolation from 100 to 300 will occur in a linear fashion over the one-second duration. Other Interpolation constants include EASE_IN, EASE_OUT, and EASE_BOTH. These cause the interpolation in a KeyFrame to be slower in the beginning, ending, or both, respectively.

The following are the other Timeline properties, inherited from the Animation class, used in this example:

- autoReverse, which we're initializing to true. This causes the timeline to automatically reverse when it reaches the last KeyFrame. When reversed, the interpolation goes from 300 to 100 over the course of one second.

- cycleCount, which we're initializing to Animation.INDEFINITE. This causes the timeline to repeat indefinitely until stopped by the stop() method of the Timeline class.

Speaking of the methods of the Timeline class, now is a good time to show you how to control the timeline and monitor its state.

Controlling and Monitoring the Timeline

As you observed when using the Metronome1 program, clicking the buttons causes the animation to start, pause, resume, and stop. This in turn has an effect on the states of the animation (running, paused, or stopped). Those states are reflected in the buttons in the form of being enabled or disabled. The following snippet from Listing 2-5 shows how to start, pause, resume, and stop the timeline, as well as how to tell whether the timeline is running or paused.

```
startButton = new Button("start");
startButton.setOnAction(e -> anim.playFromStart());
pauseButton = new Button("pause");
pauseButton.setOnAction(e -> anim.pause());
resumeButton = new Button("resume");
resumeButton.setOnAction(e -> anim.play());
stopButton = new Button("stop");
stopButton.setOnAction(e -> anim.stop());
```

...code omitted...

```
startButton.disableProperty().bind(anim.statusProperty()
        .isNotEqualTo(Animation.Status.STOPPED));
pauseButton.disableProperty().bind(anim.statusProperty()
        .isNotEqualTo(Animation.Status.RUNNING));
resumeButton.disableProperty().bind(anim.statusProperty()
        .isNotEqualTo(Animation.Status.PAUSED));
stopButton.disableProperty().bind(anim.statusProperty()
        .isEqualTo(Animation.Status.STOPPED));
```

As shown here in the action event handler of the Start button, the playFromStart() method of the Timeline instance is called, which begins playing the timeline from the beginning. In addition, the disable property of that Button is bound to an expression that evaluates whether the status property of the timeline is not equal to Animation.Status.STOPPED. This causes the button to be disabled when the timeline is not stopped (in which case it must be either running or paused).

When the user clicks the Pause button, the action event handler calls the timeline's pause() method, which pauses the animation. The disable property of that Button is bound to an expression that evaluates whether the timeline is not running.

The Resume button is only disabled when the timeline is not paused. To resume the timeline from where it was paused, the action event handler calls the play() method of the timeline.

Finally, the Stop button is disabled when the timeline is stopped. To stop the timeline, the action event handler calls the stop() method of the timeline.

Now that you know how to animate nodes by creating a Timeline class and creating KeyFrame instances, it's time to learn how to use the transition classes to animate nodes.

Using the Transition Classes for Animation

Using a TimeLine allows very flexible animations. There are a number of common animations facilitating the translation from one state to another that are out-of-the box supported by JavaFX. The javafx.animation package contains several classes whose purpose is to provide convenient ways to do these commonly used animation tasks. Both TimeLine and Transition (the abstract root class for all concrete transitions) extend the Animation class.

Table 2-1 contains a list of transition classes in that package.

Table 2-1. *Transition Classes in the* `javafx.animation` *Package for Animating Nodes*

Transition Class Name	Description
TranslateTransition	Translates (moves) a node from one location to another over a given period of time. This was employed in the Hello Earthrise example program in Chapter 1.
PathTransition	Moves a node along a specified path.
RotateTransition	Rotates a node over a given period of time.
ScaleTransition	Scales (increases or decreases the size of) a node over a given period of time.
FadeTransition	Fades (increases or decreases the opacity of) a node over a given period of time.
FillTransition	Changes the fill of a shape over a given period of time.
StrokeTransition	Changes the stroke color of a shape over a given period of time.
PauseTransition	Executes an action at the end of its duration; designed mainly to be used in a SequentialTransition as a means to wait for a period of time.
SequentialTransition	Allows you to define a series of transitions that execute sequentially.
ParallelTransition	Allows you to define a series of transitions that execute in parallel.

Let's take a look at a variation on the metronome theme in which we create a metronome using TranslateTransition for the animation.

The MetronomeTransition Example

When using the transition classes, we take a different approach toward animation than when using the Timeline class directly:

- In the timeline-based Metronome1 program, we bound a property of a node (specifically, startX) to a property in the model (startXVal), and then used the timeline to interpolate the value of the property in the model.

- When using a transition class, however, we assign values to the properties of the Transition subclass, one of which is a node. The net result is that the node itself is affected, rather than just a bound attribute of the node being affected.

The distinction between these two approaches becomes clear as we walk through the MetronomeTransition example. Figure 2-9 shows a screenshot of this program when it is first invoked.

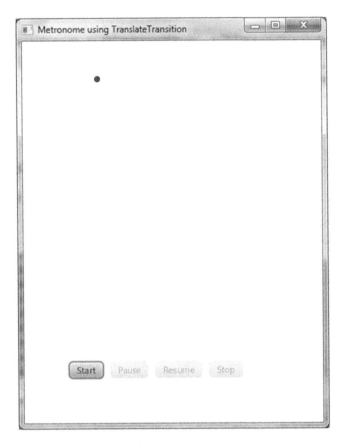

Figure 2-9. *The MetronomeTransition program*

The first noticeable difference between this example and the previous (Metronome1) example is that instead of one end of a line moving back and forth, we're going to make a Circle node move back and forth.

The Behavior of the MetronomeTransition Program

Go ahead and run the program, and perform the same steps that you did in the previous exercise with Metronome1. Everything should function the same, except for the visual difference pointed out previously.

Understanding the MetronomeTransition Program

Take a look at the code for the MetronomeTransition program in Listing 2-6, before we point out relevant concepts.

Listing 2-6. MetronomeTransitionMain.fx

```
package projavafx.metronometransition.ui;

import javafx.animation.Animation;
import javafx.animation.Interpolator;
import javafx.animation.TranslateTransition;
```

```java
import javafx.application.Application;
import javafx.scene.Group;
import javafx.scene.Scene;
import javafx.scene.control.Button;
import javafx.scene.layout.HBox;
import javafx.scene.paint.Color;
import javafx.scene.shape.Circle;
import javafx.stage.Stage;
import javafx.util.Duration;

public class MetronomeTransitionMain extends Application {

    Button startButton;
    Button pauseButton;
    Button resumeButton;
    Button stopButton;
    Circle circle;

    public static void main(String[] args) {
        Application.launch(args);
    }

    @Override
    public void start(Stage stage) {
        circle = new Circle(100, 50, 4, Color.BLUE);
        TranslateTransition anim = new TranslateTransition(new Duration(1000.0), circle);
        anim.setFromX(0);
        anim.setToX(200);
        anim.setAutoReverse(true);
        anim.setCycleCount(Animation.INDEFINITE);
        anim.setInterpolator(Interpolator.LINEAR);
        startButton = new Button("start");
        startButton.setOnAction(e -> anim.playFromStart());
        pauseButton = new Button("pause");
        pauseButton.setOnAction(e -> anim.pause());
        resumeButton = new Button("resume");
        resumeButton.setOnAction(e -> anim.play());
        stopButton = new Button("stop");
        stopButton.setOnAction(e -> anim.stop());
        HBox commands = new HBox(10, startButton,
                pauseButton,
                resumeButton,
                stopButton);
        commands.setLayoutX(60);
        commands.setLayoutY(420);
        Group group = new Group(circle, commands);
        Scene scene = new Scene(group, 400, 500);
        startButton.disableProperty().bind(anim.statusProperty()
                .isNotEqualTo(Animation.Status.STOPPED));
        pauseButton.disableProperty().bind(anim.statusProperty()
                .isNotEqualTo(Animation.Status.RUNNING));
```

```
        resumeButton.disableProperty().bind(anim.statusProperty()
                .isNotEqualTo(Animation.Status.PAUSED));
        stopButton.disableProperty().bind(anim.statusProperty()
                .isEqualTo(Animation.Status.STOPPED));

        stage.setScene(scene);
        stage.setTitle("Metronome using TranslateTransition");
        stage.show();
    }
}
```

Using the TranslateTransition Class

As shown in the following snippet from Listing 2-6, to create a TranslateTransition we're supplying values that are reminiscent of the values that we used when creating a timeline in the previous example. For example, we're setting autoReverse to true and cycleCount to Animation.INDEFINITE. Also, just as when creating a KeyFrame for a timeline, we're supplying a duration and an interpolation type here as well.

In addition, we're supplying some values to properties that are specific to a TranslateTransition, namely fromX and toX. These values are interpolated over the requested duration and assigned to the layoutX property of the node controlled by the transition (in this case, the circle). If we also wanted to cause vertical movement, assigning values to fromY and toY would cause interpolated values between them to be assigned to the layoutY property.

An alternative to supplying toX and toY values is to provide values to the byX and byY properties, which enables you to specify the distance to travel in each direction rather than start and end points. Also, if you don't supply a value for fromX, the interpolation will begin with the current value of the node's layoutX property. The same holds true for fromY (if not supplied, the interpolation will begin with the value of layoutY).

```
circle = new Circle(100, 50, 4, Color.BLUE);
TranslateTransition anim = new TranslateTransition(new Duration(1000.0), circle);
anim.setFromX(0);
anim.setToX(200);
anim.setAutoReverse(true);
anim.setCycleCount(Animation.INDEFINITE);
anim.setInterpolator(Interpolator.LINEAR);
```

Controlling and Monitoring the Transition

The TranslateTransition class, as do all of the classes in Table 2-1, extends the javafx.animation. Transition class, which in turn extends the Animation class. Because the Timeline class extends the Animation class, as you can see by comparing Listings 2-5 and 2-6, all of the code for the buttons in this example is identical to that in the previous example. Indeed, the functionality required to start, pause, resume, and stop an animation is defined on the Animation class itself, and inherited by both the Translation classes as well as the Timeline class.

The MetronomePathTransition Example

As shown in Table 2-1, PathTransition is a transition class that enables you to move a node along a defined geometric path. Figure 2-10 shows a screenshot of a version of the metronome example, named MetronomePathTransition, that demonstrates how to use the PathTransition class.

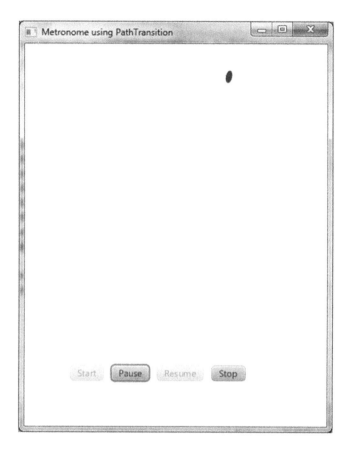

Figure 2-10. *The MetronomePathTransition program*

The Behavior of the MetronomePathTransition Program

Go ahead and run the program, performing once again the same steps that you did for the Metronome1 exercise. Everything should function the same as it did in the MetronomeTransition example, except that the node is an ellipse instead of a circle, and the node moves along the path of an arc.

Understanding the MetronomePathTransition Program

Listing 2-7 contains code snippets from the MetronomePathTransition program that highlight the differences from the preceding (MetronomeTransition) program. Take a look at the code, and then we review relevant concepts.

Listing 2-7. Portions of MetronomePathTransitionMain.java

```java
package projavafx.metronomepathtransition.ui;
```

...imports omitted...

```java
public class MetronomePathTransitionMain extends Application {

    Button startButton;
    Button pauseButton;
    Button resumeButton;
    Button stopButton;
    Ellipse ellipse;

    Path path;

    public static void main(String[] args) {
        Application.launch(args);
    }

    @Override
    public void start(Stage stage) {
        ellipse = new Ellipse(100, 50, 4, 8);
        ellipse.setFill(Color.BLUE);
        path = new Path(
                new MoveTo(100, 50),
                new ArcTo(350, 350, 0, 300, 50, false, true)
        );
        PathTransition anim = new PathTransition(new Duration(1000.0), path, ellipse);
        anim.setOrientation(OrientationType.ORTHOGONAL_TO_TANGENT);
        anim.setInterpolator(Interpolator.LINEAR);
        anim.setAutoReverse(true);
        anim.setCycleCount(Timeline.INDEFINITE);
        startButton = new Button("start");
        startButton.setOnAction(e -> anim.playFromStart());
        pauseButton = new Button("pause");
        pauseButton.setOnAction(e -> anim.pause());
        resumeButton = new Button("resume");
        resumeButton.setOnAction(e -> anim.play());
        stopButton = new Button("stop");
        stopButton.setOnAction(e -> anim.stop());
        HBox commands = new HBox(10, startButton,
                pauseButton,
                resumeButton,
                stopButton);
        commands.setLayoutX(60);
        commands.setLayoutY(420);
        Group group = new Group(ellipse, commands);
        Scene scene = new Scene(group, 400, 500);

        startButton.disableProperty().bind(anim.statusProperty()
                .isNotEqualTo(Animation.Status.STOPPED));
```

```
        pauseButton.disableProperty().bind(anim.statusProperty()
                .isNotEqualTo(Animation.Status.RUNNING));
        resumeButton.disableProperty().bind(anim.statusProperty()
                .isNotEqualTo(Animation.Status.PAUSED));
        stopButton.disableProperty().bind(anim.statusProperty()
                .isEqualTo(Animation.Status.STOPPED));

        stage.setScene(scene);
        stage.setTitle("Metronome using PathTransition");
        stage.show();
    }
}
```

Using the PathTransition Class

As shown in Listing 2-7, defining a PathTransition includes supplying an instance of type Path to the path property that represents the geometric path that the node is to travel. Here we're creating a Path instance that defines an arc beginning at 100 pixels on the x axis and 50 pixels on the y axis, ending at 300 pixels on the x axis and 50 pixels on the y axis, with 350 pixel horizontal and vertical radii. This is accomplished by creating a Path that contains the MoveTo and ArcTo path elements. Take a look at the javafx.scene.shape package in the JavaFX API docs for more information on the PathElement class and its subclasses, which are used for creating a path.

■ **Tip**   The properties in the ArcTo class are fairly intuitive except for sweepFlag. If sweepFlag is true, the line joining the center of the arc to the arc itself sweeps through increasing angles; otherwise, it sweeps through decreasing angles.

Another property of the PathTransition class is orientation, which controls whether the node's orientation remains unchanged or stays perpendicular to the path's tangent as it moves along the path. Listing 2-7 uses the OrientationType.ORTHOGONAL_TO_TANGENT constant to accomplish the latter, as the former is the default.

Drawing an Ellipse

As shown in Listing 2-7, drawing an Ellipse is similar to drawing a Circle, the difference being that an additional radius is required (radiusX and radiusY instead of just radius).

Now that you've learned how to animate nodes by creating a timeline and by creating transitions, we create a very simple Pong-style game that requires animating a ping-pong ball. In the process, you learn how to detect when the ball has hit a paddle or wall in the game.

The Zen of Node Collision Detection

When animating a node, you sometimes need to know when the node has collided with another node. To demonstrate this capability, our colleague Chris Wright developed a simple version of the Pong-style game that we call ZenPong. Originally, we asked him to build the game with only one paddle, which brought the famous Zen koan (philosophical riddle) "What is the sound of one hand clapping?" to mind. Chris had so much fun developing the game that he snuck a second paddle in, but we're still calling this example ZenPong. Figure 2-11 shows this very simple form of the game when first invoked.

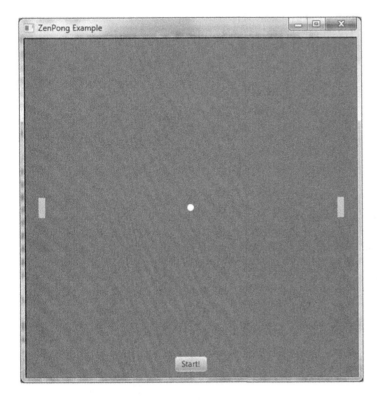

Figure 2-11. *The initial state of the ZenPong game*

Try out the game by following the instructions in the upcoming exercise, remembering that you control both paddles (unless you can get a colleague to share your keyboard and play).

EXAMINING THE BEHAVIOR OF THE ZENPONG GAME

When the program starts, its appearance should be similar to the screenshot in Figure 2-11. To fully examine its behavior, perform the following steps.

1. Before clicking Start, drag each of the paddles vertically to other positions. One game cheat is to drag the left paddle up and the right paddle down, which will put them in good positions to respond to the ball after being served.

2. Practice using the A key to move the left paddle up, the Z key to move the left paddle down, the L key to move the right paddle up, and the comma (,) key to move the right paddle down.

3. Click Start to begin playing the game. Notice that the Start button disappears and the ball begins moving at a 45° angle, bouncing off paddles and the top and bottom walls. The screen should look similar to Figure 2-12.

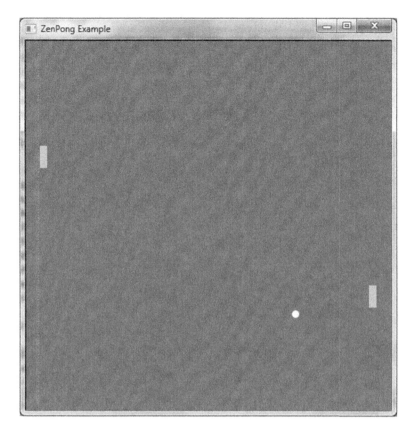

Figure 2-12. *The ZenPong game in action*

4. If the ball hits the left or right wall, one of your hands has lost the game. Notice that
    the game resets, looking again like the screenshot in Figure 2-11.

Now that you've experienced the behavior of the ZenPong program, let's review the code behind it.

Understanding the ZenPong Program

Examine the code for the ZenPong program in Listing 2-8, before we highlight some concepts demonstrated
within.

Listing 2-8. ZenPongMain.java

```
package projavafx.zenpong.ui;
...imports omitted...
public class ZenPongMain extends Application {

    /**
     * The center points of the moving ball
     */
```

```
DoubleProperty centerX = new SimpleDoubleProperty();
DoubleProperty centerY = new SimpleDoubleProperty();

/**
 * The Y coordinate of the left paddle
 */
DoubleProperty leftPaddleY = new SimpleDoubleProperty();

/**
 * The Y coordinate of the right paddle
 */
DoubleProperty rightPaddleY = new SimpleDoubleProperty();

/**
 * The drag anchor for left and right paddles
 */
double leftPaddleDragAnchorY;
double rightPaddleDragAnchorY;

/**
 * The initial translateY property for the left and right paddles
 */
double initLeftPaddleTranslateY;
double initRightPaddleTranslateY;

/**
 * The moving ball
 */
Circle ball;

/**
 * The Group containing all of the walls, paddles, and ball. This also
 * allows us to requestFocus for KeyEvents on the Group
 */
Group pongComponents;

/**
 * The left and right paddles
 */
Rectangle leftPaddle;
Rectangle rightPaddle;

/**
 * The walls
 */
Rectangle topWall;
Rectangle rightWall;
Rectangle leftWall;
Rectangle bottomWall;

Button startButton;
```

```java
/**
 * Controls whether the startButton is visible
 */
BooleanProperty startVisible = new SimpleBooleanProperty(true);

/**
 * The animation of the ball
 */
Timeline pongAnimation;

/**
 * Controls whether the ball is moving right
 */
boolean movingRight = true;

/**
 * Controls whether the ball is moving down
 */
boolean movingDown = true;

/**
 * Sets the initial starting positions of the ball and paddles
 */
void initialize() {
    centerX.setValue(250);
    centerY.setValue(250);
    leftPaddleY.setValue(235);
    rightPaddleY.setValue(235);
    startVisible.set(true);
    pongComponents.requestFocus();
}

/**
 * Checks whether or not the ball has collided with either the paddles,
 * topWall, or bottomWall. If the ball hits the wall behind the paddles, the
 * game is over.
 */
void checkForCollision() {
    if (ball.intersects(rightWall.getBoundsInLocal())
            || ball.intersects(leftWall.getBoundsInLocal())) {
        pongAnimation.stop();
        initialize();
    } else if (ball.intersects(bottomWall.getBoundsInLocal())
            || ball.intersects(topWall.getBoundsInLocal())) {
        movingDown = !movingDown;
    } else if (ball.intersects(leftPaddle.getBoundsInParent()) && !movingRight) {
        movingRight = !movingRight;
    } else if (ball.intersects(rightPaddle.getBoundsInParent()) && movingRight) {
        movingRight = !movingRight;
    }
}
```

```java
/**
 * @param args the command line arguments
 */
public static void main(String[] args) {
    Application.launch(args);
}

@Override
public void start(Stage stage) {
    pongAnimation = new Timeline(
            new KeyFrame(new Duration(10.0), t -> {
                checkForCollision();
                int horzPixels = movingRight ? 1 : -1;
                int vertPixels = movingDown ? 1 : -1;
                centerX.setValue(centerX.getValue() + horzPixels);
                centerY.setValue(centerY.getValue() + vertPixels);
            })
    );
    pongAnimation.setCycleCount(Timeline.INDEFINITE);
    ball = new Circle(0, 0, 5, Color.WHITE);
    topWall = new Rectangle(0, 0, 500, 1);
    leftWall = new Rectangle(0, 0, 1, 500);
    rightWall = new Rectangle(500, 0, 1, 500);
    bottomWall = new Rectangle(0, 500, 500, 1);
    leftPaddle = new Rectangle(20, 0, 10, 30);
    leftPaddle.setFill(Color.LIGHTBLUE);
    leftPaddle.setCursor(Cursor.HAND);
    leftPaddle.setOnMousePressed(me -> {
        initLeftPaddleTranslateY = leftPaddle.getTranslateY();
        leftPaddleDragAnchorY = me.getSceneY();
    });
    leftPaddle.setOnMouseDragged(me -> {
        double dragY = me.getSceneY() - leftPaddleDragAnchorY;
        leftPaddleY.setValue(initLeftPaddleTranslateY + dragY);
    });
    rightPaddle = new Rectangle(470, 0, 10, 30);
    rightPaddle.setFill(Color.LIGHTBLUE);
    rightPaddle.setCursor(Cursor.CLOSED_HAND);
    rightPaddle.setOnMousePressed(me -> {
        initRightPaddleTranslateY = rightPaddle.getTranslateY();
        rightPaddleDragAnchorY = me.getSceneY();
    });
    rightPaddle.setOnMouseDragged(me -> {
        double dragY = me.getSceneY() - rightPaddleDragAnchorY;
        rightPaddleY.setValue(initRightPaddleTranslateY + dragY);
    });
    startButton = new Button("Start!");
    startButton.setLayoutX(225);
    startButton.setLayoutY(470);
    startButton.setOnAction(e -> {
        startVisible.set(false);
```

```
        pongAnimation.playFromStart();
        pongComponents.requestFocus();
    });
    pongComponents = new Group(ball,
            topWall,
            leftWall,
            rightWall,
            bottomWall,
            leftPaddle,
            rightPaddle,
            startButton);
    pongComponents.setFocusTraversable(true);
    pongComponents.setOnKeyPressed(k -> {
        if (k.getCode() == KeyCode.SPACE
                && pongAnimation.statusProperty()
                .equals(Animation.Status.STOPPED)) {
            rightPaddleY.setValue(rightPaddleY.getValue() - 6);
        } else if (k.getCode() == KeyCode.L
                && !rightPaddle.getBoundsInParent().intersects(topWall.
                getBoundsInLocal())) {
            rightPaddleY.setValue(rightPaddleY.getValue() - 6);
        } else if (k.getCode() == KeyCode.COMMA
                && !rightPaddle.getBoundsInParent().intersects(bottomWall.
                getBoundsInLocal())) {
            rightPaddleY.setValue(rightPaddleY.getValue() + 6);
        } else if (k.getCode() == KeyCode.A
                && !leftPaddle.getBoundsInParent().intersects(topWall.
                getBoundsInLocal())) {
            leftPaddleY.setValue(leftPaddleY.getValue() - 6);
        } else if (k.getCode() == KeyCode.Z
                && !leftPaddle.getBoundsInParent().intersects(bottomWall.
                getBoundsInLocal())) {
            leftPaddleY.setValue(leftPaddleY.getValue() + 6);
        }
    });
    Scene scene = new Scene(pongComponents, 500, 500);
    scene.setFill(Color.GRAY);

    ball.centerXProperty().bind(centerX);
    ball.centerYProperty().bind(centerY);
    leftPaddle.translateYProperty().bind(leftPaddleY);
    rightPaddle.translateYProperty().bind(rightPaddleY);
    startButton.visibleProperty().bind(startVisible);

    stage.setScene(scene);
    initialize();
    stage.setTitle("ZenPong Example");
    stage.show();
    }
}
```

Using the KeyFrame Action Event Handler

We're using a different technique in the timeline than demonstrated in the Metronome1 program earlier in the chapter (see Figure 2-8 and Listing 2-5). Instead of interpolating two values over a period of time, we're using the action event handler of the KeyFrame instance in our timeline. Take a look at the following snippet from Listing 2-8 to see this technique in use.

```
pongAnimation = new Timeline(
                new KeyFrame(new Duration(10.0), t -> {
                    checkForCollision();
                    int horzPixels = movingRight ? 1 : -1;
                    int vertPixels = movingDown ? 1 : -1;
                    centerX.setValue(centerX.getValue() + horzPixels);
                    centerY.setValue(centerY.getValue() + vertPixels);
                })
);
pongAnimation.setCycleCount(Timeline.INDEFINITE);
```

As shown in the snippet, we use only one KeyFrame, and it has a very short time (10 milliseconds). When a KeyFrame has an action event handler, the code in that handler—which in this case is once again a lambda expression—is executed when the time for that KeyFrame is reached. Because the cycleCount of this timeline is indefinite, the action event handler will be executed every 10 milliseconds. The code in this event handler does two things:

- Calls a method named checkForCollision(), which is defined in this program, the purpose of which is to see whether the ball has collided with either paddle or any of the walls

- Updates the properties in the model to which the position of the ball is bound, taking into account the direction in which the ball is already moving

Using the Node intersects() Method to Detect Collisions

Take a look inside the checkForCollision() method in the following snippet from Listing 2-8 to see how we check for collisions by detecting when two nodes intersect (share any of the same pixels).

```
void checkForCollision() {
  if (ball.intersects(rightWall.getBoundsInLocal()) ||
      ball.intersects(leftWall.getBoundsInLocal())) {
    pongAnimation.stop();
    initialize();
  }
  else if (ball.intersects(bottomWall.getBoundsInLocal()) ||
          ball.intersects(topWall.getBoundsInLocal())) {
    movingDown = !movingDown;
  }
  else if (ball.intersects(leftPaddle.getBoundsInParent()) && !movingRight) {
    movingRight = !movingRight;
  }
  else if (ball.intersects(rightPaddle.getBoundsInParent()) && movingRight) {
    movingRight = !movingRight;
  }
}
```

The intersects() method of the Node class shown here takes an argument of type Bounds, located in the javafx.geometry package. It represents the rectangular bounds of a node, for example, the leftPaddle node shown in the preceding code snippet. Notice that to get the position of the left paddle in the Group that contains it, we're using the boundsInParent property that the leftPaddle (a Rectangle) inherited from the Node class.

The net results of the intersect method invocations in the preceding snippet are as follows.

- If the ball intersects with the bounds of the rightWall or leftWall, the pongAnimation Timeline is stopped and the game is initialized for the next play. Note that the rightWall and left Wall nodes are one-pixel-wide rectangles on the left and right sides of the Scene. Take a peek at Listing 2-8 to see where these are defined.

- If the ball intersects with the bounds of the bottomWall or topWall, the vertical direction of the ball will be changed by negating the program's Boolean movingDown variable.

- If the ball intersects with the bounds of the leftPaddle or rightPaddle, the horizontal direction of the ball will be changed by negating the program's Boolean movingRight variable.

■ **Tip** For more information on boundsInParent and its related properties, layoutBounds and boundsInLocal, see the "Bounding Rectangles" discussion at the beginning of the javafx.scene.Node class in the JavaFX API docs. For example, it is a common practice to find out the width or height of a node by using the expression myNode.getLayoutBounds().getWidth() or myNode.getLayoutBounds().getHeight().

Dragging a Node

As you experienced previously, the paddles of the ZenPong application may be dragged with the mouse. The following snippet from Listing 2-8 shows how this capability is implemented in ZenPong for dragging the right paddle.

```
  DoupleProperty rightPaddleY = new SimpleDoubleProperty();
  ...code omitted...
  double rightPaddleDragStartY;
  double rightPaddleDragAnchorY;
  ...code omitted...
  void initialize() {
...code omitted...
    rightPaddleY.setValue(235);

  }
  ...code omitted...
rightPaddle = new Rectangle(470, 0, 10, 30);
rightPaddle.setFill(Color.LIGHTBLUE);
rightPaddle.setCursor(Cursor.CLOSED_HAND);
rightPaddle.setOnMousePressed(me -> {
    initRightPaddleTranslateY = rightPaddle.getTranslateY();
    rightPaddleDragAnchorY = me.getSceneY();
});
```

```
rightPaddle.setOnMouseDragged(me -> {
    double dragY = me.getSceneY() - rightPaddleDragAnchorY;
    rightPaddleY.setValue(initRightPaddleTranslateY + dragY);
});
...code omitted...
rightPaddle.translateYProperty().bind(rightPaddleY);
```

Note that in this ZenPong example, we're dragging the paddles only vertically, not horizontally Therefore, the code snippet only deals with dragging on the y axis. After creating the paddle at the initial location, we register event handlers for MousePressed and MouseDragged events. The latter manipulates the rightPaddleY property, which is used for translating the paddle along the y axis. Properties and bindings will be explained in detail in Chapter 3.

Giving Keyboard Input Focus to a Node

For a node to receive key events, it has to have keyboard focus. This is accomplished in the ZenPong example by doing these two things, as shown in the snippet that follows from Listing 2-8:

- Assigning true to the focusTraversable property of the Group node. This allows the node to accept keyboard focus.

- Calling the requestFocus() method of the Group node (referred to by the pongComponents variable). This requests that the node obtain focus.

■ **Tip**   You cannot directly set the value of the focused property of a Stage. Consulting the API docs also reveals that you cannot set the value of the focused property of a Node (e.g., the Group that we're discussing now). However, as discussed in the second point just mentioned, you can call requestFocus() on the node, which if granted (and focusTraversable is true) sets the focused property to true. By the way, Stage doesn't have a requestFocus() method, but it does have a toFront() method, which should give it keyboard focus.

```
...code omitted...
pongComponents.setFocusTraversable(true);
pongComponents.setOnKeyPressed(k -> {
    if (k.getCode() == KeyCode.SPACE
            && pongAnimation.statusProperty()
            .equals(Animation.Status.STOPPED)) {
        rightPaddleY.setValue(rightPaddleY.getValue() - 6);
    } else if (k.getCode() == KeyCode.L
            && !rightPaddle.getBoundsInParent().intersects(topWall.getBoundsInLocal())) {
        rightPaddleY.setValue(rightPaddleY.getValue() - 6);
    } else if (k.getCode() == KeyCode.COMMA
            && !rightPaddle.getBoundsInParent().intersects(bottomWall.getBoundsInLocal())) {
        rightPaddleY.setValue(rightPaddleY.getValue() + 6);
    } else if (k.getCode() == KeyCode.A
            && !leftPaddle.getBoundsInParent().intersects(topWall.getBoundsInLocal())) {
        leftPaddleY.setValue(leftPaddleY.getValue() - 6);
    } else if (k.getCode() == KeyCode.Z
```

```
                && !leftPaddle.getBoundsInParent().intersects(bottomWall.getBoundsInLocal())) {
        leftPaddleY.setValue(leftPaddleY.getValue() + 6);
    }
});
```

Now that the node has focus, when the user interacts with the keyboard, the appropriate event handlers will be invoked. In this example, we're interested in whenever certain keys are pressed, as discussed next.

Using the onKeyPressed Event Handler

When the user presses a key, the lambda expression supplied to the onKeyPressed method is invoked, passing a KeyEvent instance that contains information about the event. The method body of this expression, shown in the preceding snippet from Listing 2-8, compares the getCode() method of the KeyEvent instance to the KeyCode constants that represent the arrow keys to ascertain which key was pressed.

Summary

Congratulations! You have learned a lot in this chapter about creating UIs in JavaFX, including the following.

- Creating a UI in JavaFX, which we loosely based on the metaphor of creating a theater play, and typically consists of creating a stage, a scene, nodes, a model, and event handlers, and animating some of the nodes

- The details about using most of the properties and methods of the Stage class, including how to create a Stage that is transparent with no window decorations

- How to use the HBox and VBox layout containers to organize nodes horizontally and vertically, respectively

- The details about using many of the properties and methods of the Scene class

- How to create and apply CSS styles to nodes in your program by associating one or more style sheets with the Scene

- How to handle keyboard and mouse input events

- How to animate nodes in the scene, both with the Timeline class and the transition classes

- How to detect when nodes in the scene have collided

In Chapter 3, we will discuss the alternative approach for creating UIs, this time with Scene Builder. Then, in Chapter 4, we take a deeper dive into the areas of properties and binding.

Resources

For some additional information on creating JavaFX UIs, you can consult the following resources.

- JavaFX 9 SDK documentation online: http://download.java.net/jdk9/jfxdocs/

- JavaFX 9 CSS Reference Guide: http://docs.oracle.com/javase/9/docs/api/javafx/scene/doc-files/cssref.html

- The w3schools.com CSS Tutorial: www.w3schools.com/css

CHAPTER 3

■ ■ ■

Properties and Bindings

Heaven acts with vitality and persistence.

In correspondence with this

The superior person keeps himself vital without ceasing.

—I Ching

In Chapters 1 and 2, we introduced you to the JavaFX 9 platform that is part of Oracle JDK 9. You set up your development environment with your favorite IDE: Eclipse, NetBeans, or IntelliJ IDEA. You wrote and ran your first JavaFX GUI programs. You learned the fundamental building blocks of JavaFX: the Stage and Scene classes, and the Nodes that go into the Scene. You have no doubt noticed the use of user-defined model classes to represent the application state and have that state communicated to the UI through properties and bindings.

In this chapter, we give you a guided tour of the JavaFX properties and bindings framework. After recalling a little bit of history and presenting a motivating example that shows various ways that a JavaFX Property can be used, we cover key concepts of the framework: Observable, ObservableValue, WritableValue, ReadOnlyProperty, Property, and Binding. We show you the capabilities offered by these fundamental interfaces of the framework. We then show you how Property objects are bound together, how Binding objects are built out of properties and other bindings—using the factory methods in the Bindings utility class, the fluent interface API, or going low level by directly extending abstract classes that implement the Binding interface—and how they are used to easily propagate changes in one part of a program to other parts of the program without too much coding. We then introduce the JavaFX Beans naming convention, an extension of the original JavaBeans naming convention that makes organizing your data into encapsulated components an orderly affair. We finish this chapter by showing how to adapt old-style JavaBeans properties into JavaFX properties.

Because the JavaFX properties and bindings framework is a nonvisual part of the JavaFX platform, the example programs in this chapter are also nonvisual in nature. We deal with Boolean, Integer, Long, Float, Double, String, and Object type properties and bindings as these are the types in which the JavaFX binding framework specializes. Your GUI building fun resumes in the next and further chapters.

Forerunners of JavaFX Binding

The need for exposing attributes of Java components directly to client code, allowing them to observe and to manipulate such attributes, and to take action when their values change, was recognized early in Java's life. The JavaBeans framework in Java 1.1 provided support for properties through the now familiar getter and setter convention. It also supported the propagations of property changes through its PropertyChangeEvent and PropertyChangeListener mechanism. Although the JavaBeans framework is used in many Swing applications, its use is quite cumbersome and requires quite a bit of boilerplate code. Several higher-level data binding frameworks were created over the years with various levels of success. The heritage of the JavaBeans in the JavaFX properties and bindings framework lies mainly in the JavaFX Beans getter, setter, and property getter naming convention when defining JavaFX components. We talk about the JavaFX Beans getter, setter, and property getter naming convention later in this chapter, after we have covered the key concepts and interfaces of the JavaFX properties and bindings framework.

Another strand of heritage of the JavaFX properties and bindings framework comes from the JavaFX Script language that was part of the JavaFX 1.x platform. Although the JavaFX Script language was deprecated in the JavaFX platform in favor of a Java-based API, one of the goals of the transition was to preserve most of the powers of the JavaFX Script's bind keyword, the expressive power of which has delighted many JavaFX enthusiasts. As an example, JavaFX Script supports the binding to complex expressions:

```
var a = 1;
var b = 10;
var m = 4;
def c = bind for (x in [a..b] where x < m) { x * x };
```

This code will automatically recalculate the value of c whenever the values of a, b, or m are changed.

Although the JavaFX properties and bindings framework does not support all of the binding constructs of JavaFX Script, it supports the binding of many useful expressions. We talk more about constructing compound binding expressions after we cover the key concepts and interfaces of the framework.

A Motivating Example

Let's start with an example in Listing 3-1 that shows off the capabilities of the Property interface through the use of a couple of instances of the SimpleIntegerProperty class.

Listing 3-1. MotivatingExample.java

```java
import javafx.beans.InvalidationListener;
import javafx.beans.property.IntegerProperty;
import javafx.beans.property.SimpleIntegerProperty;
import javafx.beans.value.ChangeListener;
import javafx.beans.value.ObservableValue;

public class MotivatingExample {
    private static IntegerProperty intProperty;

    public static void main(String[] args) {
        createProperty();
        addAndRemoveInvalidationListener();
        addAndRemoveChangeListener();
        bindAndUnbindOnePropertyToAnother();
    }

    private static void createProperty() {
        System.out.println();
        intProperty = new SimpleIntegerProperty(1024);
        System.out.println("intProperty = " + intProperty);
        System.out.println("intProperty.get() = " + intProperty.get());
```

```java
        System.out.println("intProperty.getValue() = " + intProperty.getValue().intValue());
}

private static void addAndRemoveInvalidationListener() {
    System.out.println();
    final InvalidationListener invalidationListener = observable ->
        System.out.println("The observable has been invalidated: " + observable + ".");

    intProperty.addListener(invalidationListener);
    System.out.println("Added invalidation listener.");

    System.out.println("Calling intProperty.set(2048).");
    intProperty.set(2048);

    System.out.println("Calling intProperty.setValue(3072).");
    intProperty.setValue(Integer.valueOf(3072));

    intProperty.removeListener(invalidationListener);
    System.out.println("Removed invalidation listener.");

    System.out.println("Calling intProperty.set(4096).");
    intProperty.set(4096);
}

private static void addAndRemoveChangeListener() {
    System.out.println();
    final ChangeListener changeListener = (ObservableValue observableValue, Object
    oldValue, Object newValue) ->
        System.out.println("The observableValue has changed: oldValue = " + oldValue + ",
        newValue = " + newValue);
    intProperty.addListener(changeListener);
    System.out.println("Added change listener.");

    System.out.println("Calling intProperty.set(5120).");
    intProperty.set(5120);

    intProperty.removeListener(changeListener);
    System.out.println("Removed change listener.");

    System.out.println("Calling intProperty.set(6144).");
    intProperty.set(6144);
}

private static void bindAndUnbindOnePropertyToAnother() {
    System.out.println();
    IntegerProperty otherProperty = new SimpleIntegerProperty(0);
    System.out.println("otherProperty.get() = " + otherProperty.get());

    System.out.println("Binding otherProperty to intProperty.");
    otherProperty.bind(intProperty);
    System.out.println("otherProperty.get() = " + otherProperty.get());
```

```
        System.out.println("Calling intProperty.set(7168).");
        intProperty.set(7168);
        System.out.println("otherProperty.get() = " + otherProperty.get());

        System.out.println("Unbinding otherProperty from intProperty.");
        otherProperty.unbind();
        System.out.println("otherProperty.get() = " + otherProperty.get());

        System.out.println("Calling intProperty.set(8192).");
        intProperty.set(8192);
        System.out.println("otherProperty.get() = " + otherProperty.get());
    }
}
```

In this example we created a SimpleIntegerProperty object called intProperty with an initial value of 1024. We then updated its value through a series of different integers while we added and then removed an InvalidationListener, added and then removed a ChangeListener, and finally, created another SimpleIntegerProperty named otherProperty, bound it to, and then unbound it from the intProperty. We have taken advantage of the Java 8 lambda syntax in defining our listeners. The sample program used a generous amount of println calls to show what is happening inside the program.

When we run the program in Listing 3-1, the following output is printed to the console:

```
intProperty = IntegerProperty [value: 1024]
intProperty.get() = 1024
intProperty.getValue() = 1024

Added invalidation listener.
Calling intProperty.set(2048).
The observable has been invalidated: IntegerProperty [value: 2048].
Calling intProperty.setValue(3072).
The observable has been invalidated: IntegerProperty [value: 3072].
Removed invalidation listener.
Calling intProperty.set(4096).

Added change listener.
Calling intProperty.set(5120).
The observableValue has changed: oldValue = 4096, newValue = 5120
Removed change listener.
Calling intProperty.set(6144).

otherProperty.get() = 0
Binding otherProperty to intProperty.
otherProperty.get() = 6144
Calling intProperty.set(7168).
otherProperty.get() = 7168
Unbinding otherProperty from intProperty.
otherProperty.get() = 7168
Calling intProperty.set(8192).
otherProperty.get() = 7168
```

By correlating the output lines with the program source code (or by stepping through the code in the debugger of your favorite IDE), we can draw the following conclusions.

- A SimpleIntegerProperty object such as intProperty and otherProperty holds an int value. The value can be manipulated with the get(), set(), getValue(), and setValue() methods. The get() and set() methods perform their operation with the primitive int type. The getValue() and setValue() methods use the Integer wrapper type.

- You can add and remove InvalidationListener objects to and from intProperty.

- You can add and remove ChangeListener objects to and from intProperty.

- Another Property object such as otherProperty can bind itself to intProperty. When that happens, otherProperty receives the value of intProperty.

- When a new value is set on intProperty, whatever object that is attached to it is notified. The notification is not sent if the object is removed.

- When notified, InvalidationListener objects are only informed of which object is sending out the notification and that object is only known as an Observable.

- When notified, ChangeListener objects are informed on two more pieces of information—the oldValue and the newValue—in addition to the object sending the notification. The sending object is known as an ObservableValue.

- In the case of a binding property such as otherProperty, we cannot tell from the output when or how it is notified of the change of value in intProperty. However, we can infer that it must have known of the change because when we asked otherProperty for its value we got back the latest value of intProperty.

■ **Note** Even though this motivating example uses an Integer property, similar examples can be made to use properties based on the Boolean, Long, Float, Double, String, and Object types. In the JavaFX properties and bindings framework, when interfaces are extended or implemented for concrete types, they are always done for the Boolean, Integer, Long, Float, Double, String, and Object types.

This example brings to our attention some of the key interfaces and concepts of the JavaFX properties and bindings framework: including the Observable and the associated InvalidationListener interfaces, the ObservableValue and the associated ChangeListener interfaces, the get(), set(), getValue(), and setValue() methods that allow us to manipulate the values of a SimpleIntegerProperty object directly, and the bind() method that allows us to relinquish direct manipulation of the value of a SimpleIntegerProperty object by subordinating it to another SimpleIntegerProperty object.

In the next section, we show you these and some other key interfaces and concepts of the JavaFX properties and bindings framework in more detail.

Understanding Key Interfaces and Concepts

Figure 3-1 is a UML diagram showing the key interfaces of the JavaFX properties and bindings framework. It includes some interfaces that you saw in the last section, and some that you haven't yet seen.

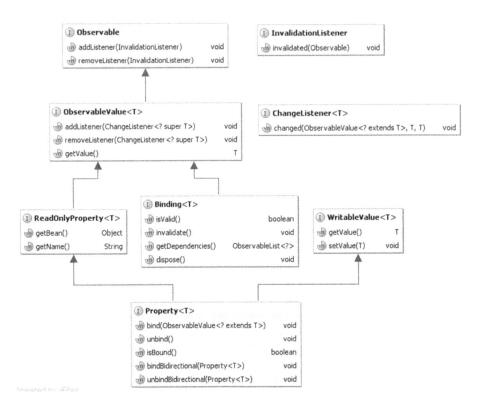

Figure 3-1. *Key interfaces of the JavaFX properties and bindings framework*

■ **Note**   We did not show you the fully qualified names of the interfaces in the UML diagram. These interfaces are spread out in four packages: `javafx.beans`, `javafx.beans.binding`, `javafx.beans.property`, and `javafx.beans.value`. You can easily figure out which interface belongs to which package by examining the JavaFX API documentation or by the "find class" feature of your favorite IDE.

Understanding the Observable Interface

At the root of the hierarchy is the `Observable` interface. You can register `InvalidationListener` objects to an `Observable` object to receive *invalidation* events. You have already seen invalidation events fired from one kind of `Observable` object, the `SimpleIntegerProperty` object `intProperty` in the motivating example in the last section. It is fired when the `set()` or `setValue()` methods are called to change the underlying value from one `int` to a different `int`.

■ **Note**   An invalidation event is fired only once by any of the implementations of the `Property` interface in the JavaFX properties and bindings framework if you call the setter with the same value several times in a row.

Another place where invalidation events are fired is from `Binding` objects. You haven't seen an example of a `Binding` object yet, but there are plenty of `Binding` objects in the second half of this chapter. For now we just note that a `Binding` object may become invalid, for example, when its `invalidate()` method is called, or as we show later in this chapter, when one of its dependencies fires an invalidation event.

■ **Note**   An invalidation event is fired only once by any of the implementations of the `Binding` interface in the JavaFX properties and bindings framework if it becomes invalid several times in a row.

Understanding the ObservableValue Interface

Next up in the hierarchy is the `ObservableValue` interface. It's simply an `Observable` that has a value. Its `getValue()` method returns its value. The `getValue()` method that we called on the `SimpleIntegerProperty` objects in the motivating example can be considered to have come from this interface. You can register `ChangeListener` objects to an `ObservableValue` object to receive *change* events.

You saw change events being fired in the motivating example in the last section. When the change event fires, the `ChangeListener` receives two more pieces of information: the old value and the new value of the `ObservableValue` object.

■ **Note**   A change event is fired only once by any of the implementations of the `ObservableValue` interface in the JavaFX properties and bindings framework if you call the setter with the same value several times in a row.

The distinction between an invalidation event and a change event is made so that the JavaFX properties and bindings framework may support *lazy evaluations*. We show an example of this by looking at three lines of code from the motivating example:

```
otherProperty.bind(intProperty);
intProperty.set(7168);
System.out.println("otherProperty.get() = " + otherProperty.get());
```

When `intProperty.set(7168)` is called, it fires an invalidation event to `otherProperty`. On receiving this invalidation event, `otherProperty` simply makes a note of the fact that its value is no longer valid. It does not immediately perform a recalculation of its value by querying `intProperty` for its value. The recalculation is performed later when `otherProperty.get()` is called. Imagine if instead of calling `intProperty.set()` only once as in the preceding code we call `intProperty.set()` multiple times; `otherProperty` still recalculates its value only once.

■ **Note**   The `ObservableValue` interface is not the only direct subinterface of `Observable`. There are four other direct subinterfaces of `Observable` that live in the `javafx.collections` package: `ObservableList`, `ObservableMap`, `ObservableSet`, and `ObservableArray` with corresponding `ListChangeListener`, `MapChangeListener`, `SetChangeListener`, and `ArrayChangeListener` as callback mechanisms. These JavaFX observable collections are covered in Chapter 7.

Understanding the WritableValue Interface

This might be the simplest subsection in the entire chapter, for the WritableValue interface is truly as simple as it looks. Its purpose is to inject the getValue() and setValue() methods into implementations of this interface. All implementation classes of WritableValue in the JavaFX properties and bindings framework also implement ObservableValue; therefore, you can make an argument that the value of WritableValue is only to provide the setValue() method.

You have seen the setValue() method at work in the motivating example.

Understanding the ReadOnlyProperty Interface

The ReadOnlyProperty interface injects two methods into its implementations. The getBean() method should return the Object that contains the ReadOnlyRroperty or null if it is not contained in an Object. The getName() method should return the name of the ReadOnlyProperty or the empty string if the ReadOnlyProperty does not have a name.

The containing object and the name provide *contextual* information about a ReadOnlyProperty. The contextual information of a property does not play any direct role in the propagation of invalidation events or the recalculation of values. However, if provided, it will be taken into account in some peripheral calculations.

In our motivating example, the intProperty is constructed without any contextual information. Had we used the full constructor to supply it a name,

```
intProperty = new SimpleIntegerProperty(null, "intProperty", 1024);
```

the output would have contained the property name:

```
intProperty = IntegerProperty [name: intProperty, value: 1024]
```

Understanding the Property Interface

Now we come to the bottom of our key interfaces hierarchy. The Property interface has as its superinterfaces all four interfaces we have examined thus far: Observable, ObservableValue, ReadOnlyProperty, and WritableValue. Therefore, it inherits all the methods from these interfaces. It also provides five methods of its own:

```
void bind(ObservableValue<? extends T> observableValue);
void unbind();
boolean isBound();
void bindBidirectional(Property<T> tProperty);
void unbindBidirectional(Property<T> tProperty);
```

You have seen two of the methods at work in the motivating example in the last section: bind() and unbind().

Calling bind() creates a *unidirectional binding* or a dependency between the Property object and the ObservableValue argument. Once they enter this relationship, calling the set() or setValue() methods on the Property object will cause a RuntimeException to be thrown. Calling the get() or getValue() methods on the Property object will return the value of the ObservableValue object. And, of course, changing the value of the ObservableValue object will invalidate the Property object. Calling unbind() releases any existing unidirectional binding the Property object may have. If a unidirectional binding is in effect, the isBound() method returns true; otherwise, it returns false.

Calling `bindBidirectional()` creates a *bidirectional binding* between the `Property` caller and the `Property` argument. Notice that unlike the `bind()` method, which takes an `ObservableValue` argument, the `bindBidirectional()` method takes a `Property` argument. Only two `Property` objects can be bound together bidirectionally. Once they enter this relationship, calling the `set()` or `setValue()` methods on either `Property` object will cause both objects' values to be updated. Calling `unbindBidirectional()` releases any existing bidirectional binding the caller and the argument may have. The program in Listing 3-2 shows a simple bidirectional binding at work.

Listing 3-2. `BidirectionalBindingExample.java`

```java
import javafx.beans.property.SimpleStringProperty;
import javafx.beans.property.StringProperty;

public class BidirectionalBindingExample {
    public static void main(String[] args) {
        System.out.println("Constructing two StringProperty objects.");
        StringProperty prop1 = new SimpleStringProperty("");
        StringProperty prop2 = new SimpleStringProperty("");

        System.out.println("Calling bindBidirectional.");
        prop2.bindBidirectional(prop1);

        System.out.println("prop1.isBound() = " + prop1.isBound());
        System.out.println("prop2.isBound() = " + prop2.isBound());

        System.out.println("Calling prop1.set(\"prop1 says: Hi!\")");
        prop1.set("prop1 says: Hi!");
        System.out.println("prop2.get() returned:");
        System.out.println(prop2.get());

        System.out.println("Calling prop2.set(prop2.get() + \"\\nprop2 says: Bye!\")");
        prop2.set(prop2.get() + "\nprop2 says: Bye!");
        System.out.println("prop1.get() returned:");
        System.out.println(prop1.get());
    }
}
```

In this example we created two `SimpleStringProperty` objects called `prop1` and `prop2`, created a bidirectional binding between them, and then called `set()` and `get()` on both properties.

When we run the program in Listing 3-2, the following output is printed to the console:

```
Constructing two StringProperty objects.
Calling bindBidirectional.
prop1.isBound() = false
prop2.isBound() = false
Calling prop1.set("prop1 says: Hi!")
prop2.get() returned:
prop1 says: Hi!
Calling prop2.set(prop2.get() + "\nprop2 says: Bye!")
prop1.get() returned:
prop1 says: Hi!
prop2 says: Bye!
```

■ **Caution**   Each Property object may have at most one active unidirectional binding at a time. It may have as many bidirectional bindings as you want. The isBound() method pertains only to unidirectional bindings. Calling bind() a second time with a different ObservableValue argument while a unidirectional binding is already in effect will unbind the existing one and replace it with the new one.

Understanding the Binding Interface

The Binding interface defines four methods that reveal the intentions of the interface. A Binding object is an ObservableValue whose validity can be queried with the isValid() method and set with the invalidate() method. It has a list of dependencies that can be obtained with the getDependencies() method. And finally a dispose() method signals that the binding will not be used anymore and resources used by it can be cleaned up.

From this brief description of the Binding interface, we can infer that it represents a *unidirectional binding with multiple dependencies*. Each dependency, we imagine, could be an ObservableValue to which the Binding is registered to receive invalidation events. When the get() or getValue() method is called, if the binding is invalidated, its value is recalculated.

The JavaFX properties and bindings framework does not provide any concrete classes that implement the Binding interface. However, it provides multiple ways to create your own Binding objects easily: You can extend the abstract base classes in the framework; you can use a set of static methods in the utility class Bindings to create new bindings out of existing regular Java values (i.e., unobservable values), properties, and bindings; you can also use a set of methods that are provided in the various properties and bindings classes and form a fluent interface API to create new bindings. We go through the utility methods and the fluent interface API in the "Creating Bindings" section later in this chapter. For now, we show you the first example of a binding by extending the DoubleBinding abstract class. The program in Listing 3-3 uses a binding to calculate the area of a rectangle.

Listing 3-3. RectangleAreaExample.java

```java
import javafx.beans.binding.DoubleBinding;
import javafx.beans.property.DoubleProperty;
import javafx.beans.property.SimpleDoubleProperty;

public class RectangleAreaExample {
    public static void main(String[] args) {
        System.out.println("Constructing x with initial value of 2.0.");
        final DoubleProperty x = new SimpleDoubleProperty(null, "x", 2.0);
        System.out.println("Constructing y with initial value of 3.0.");
        final DoubleProperty y = new SimpleDoubleProperty(null, "y", 3.0);
        System.out.println("Creating binding area with dependencies x and y.");
        DoubleBinding area = new DoubleBinding() {
            private double value;

            {
                super.bind(x, y);
            }

            @Override
            protected double computeValue() {
                System.out.println("computeValue() is called.");
```

```
                return x.get() * y.get();
            }
        };
        System.out.println("area.get() = " + area.get());
        System.out.println("area.get() = " + area.get());
        System.out.println("Setting x to 5");
        x.set(5);
        System.out.println("Setting y to 7");
        y.set(7);
        System.out.println("area.get() = " + area.get());
    }
}
```

In the anonymous inner class, we called the protected bind() method in the superclass DoubleBinding, informing the superclass that we would like to listen to invalidation events from the DoubleProperty objects x and y. We finally implemented the protected abstract computeValue() method in the superclass DoubleBinding to do the actual calculation when a recalculation is needed.

When we run the program in Listing 3-3, the following output is printed to the console:

```
Constructing x with initial value of 2.0.
Constructing y with initial value of 3.0.
Creating binding area with dependencies x and y.
computeValue() is called.
area.get() = 6.0
area.get() = 6.0
Setting x to 5
Setting y to 7
computeValue() is called.
area.get() = 35.0
```

Notice that computeValue() is called only once when we call area.get() twice in a row.

▦ **Caution**   The DoubleBinding abstract class contains a default implementation of dispose() that is empty and a default implementation of getDependencies() that returns an empty list. To make this example a correct Binding implementation, we should override these two methods to behave correctly.

Now that you have a firm grasp of the key interfaces and concepts of the JavaFX properties and bindings framework, we show you how these generic interfaces are specialized to type-specific interfaces and implemented in type-specific abstract and concrete classes.

Type-Specific Specializations of Key Interfaces

We did not emphasize this fact in the last section because we believe its omission does not hurt the explanations there, but except for Observable and InvalidationListener, the rest of the interfaces are generic interfaces with a type parameter <T>. In this section, we examine how these generic interfaces are specialized to the specific types of interest: Boolean, Integer, Long, Float, Double, String, and Object. We also examine some of the abstract and concrete classes of the framework and explore typical usage scenarios of each class.

■ **Note**　Specializations of these interfaces also exist for List, Map, and Set. They are designed for working with observable collections. We cover observable collections in Chapter 7.

A Common Theme for Type-Specific Interfaces

Although the generic interfaces are not all specialized in exactly the same way, a common theme exists:

- The Boolean type is specialized directly.
- The Integer, Long, Float, and Double types are specialized through the Number supertype.
- The String type is specialized through the Object type.

This theme exists in the type-specific specializations of all the key interfaces. As an example, we examine the subinterfaces of the ObservableValue<T> interface:

- ObservableBooleanValue extends ObservableValue<Boolean>, and it offers one additional method.
    - boolean get();
- ObservableNumberValue extends ObservableValue<Number>, and it offers four additional methods.
    - int intValue();
    - long longValue();
    - float floatValue();
    - double doubleValue();
- ObservableObjectValue<T> extends ObservableValue<T>, and it offers one additional method.
    - T get();
- ObservableIntegerValue, ObservableLongValue, ObservableFloatValue, and ObservableDoubleValue extend ObservableNumberValue and each offers an additional get() method that returns the appropriate primitive type value.
- ObservableStringValue extends ObservableObjectValue<String> and inherits its get() method that returns String.

Notice that the get() method that we have been using in the examples is defined in the type-specific ObservableValue subinterfaces. A similar examination reveals that the set() method that we have been using in the examples is defined in the type-specific WritableValue subinterfaces.

A practical consequence of this derivation hierarchy is that any numerical property can call bind()
on any other numerical property or binding. Indeed, the signature of the bind() method on any numerical
property is as follows:

```
void bind(ObservableValue<? extends Number>  observable);
```

And any numerical property and binding is assignable to the generic parameter type. The program in
Listing 3-4 shows that any numerical properties of different specific types can be bound to each other.

Listing 3-4. NumericPropertiesExample.java

```
import javafx.beans.property.DoubleProperty;
import javafx.beans.property.FloatProperty;
import javafx.beans.property.IntegerProperty;
import javafx.beans.property.LongProperty;
import javafx.beans.property.SimpleDoubleProperty;
import javafx.beans.property.SimpleFloatProperty;
import javafx.beans.property.SimpleIntegerProperty;
import javafx.beans.property.SimpleLongProperty;

public class NumericPropertiesExample {
    public static void main(String[] args) {
        IntegerProperty i = new SimpleIntegerProperty(null, "i", 1024);
        LongProperty l = new SimpleLongProperty(null, "l", 0L);
        FloatProperty f = new SimpleFloatProperty(null, "f", 0.0F);
        DoubleProperty d = new SimpleDoubleProperty(null, "d", 0.0);
        System.out.println("Constructed numerical properties i, l, f, d.");

        System.out.println("i.get() = " + i.get());
        System.out.println("l.get() = " + l.get());
        System.out.println("f.get() = " + f.get());
        System.out.println("d.get() = " + d.get());

        l.bind(i);
        f.bind(l);
        d.bind(f);
        System.out.println("Bound l to i, f to l, d to f.");

        System.out.println("i.get() = " + i.get());
        System.out.println("l.get() = " + l.get());
        System.out.println("f.get() = " + f.get());
        System.out.println("d.get() = " + d.get());

        System.out.println("Calling i.set(2048).");
        i.set(2048);

        System.out.println("i.get() = " + i.get());
        System.out.println("l.get() = " + l.get());
        System.out.println("f.get() = " + f.get());
        System.out.println("d.get() = " + d.get());
```

```
        d.unbind();
        f.unbind();
        l.unbind();
        System.out.println("Unbound l to i, f to l, d to f.");

        f.bind(d);
        l.bind(f);
        i.bind(l);
        System.out.println("Bound f to d, l to f, i to l.");

        System.out.println("Calling d.set(10000000000L).");
        d.set(10000000000L);

        System.out.println("d.get() = " + d.get());
        System.out.println("f.get() = " + f.get());
        System.out.println("l.get() = " + l.get());
        System.out.println("i.get() = " + i.get());
    }
}
```

In this example we created four numeric properties and bound them into a chain in decreasing size to demonstrate that the bindings work as expected. We then reversed the order of the chain and set the double property's value to a number that would overflow the integer property to highlight the fact that even though you can bind different sizes of numeric properties together, when the value of the dependent property is outside the range of the binding property, normal Java numeric conversion applies.

When we run the program in Listing 3-4, the following is printed to the console:

```
Constructed numerical properties i, l, f, d.
i.get() = 1024
l.get() = 0
f.get() = 0.0
d.get() = 0.0
Bound l to i, f to l, d to f.
i.get() = 1024
l.get() = 1024
f.get() = 1024.0
d.get() = 1024.0
Calling i.set(2048).
i.get() = 2048
l.get() = 2048
f.get() = 2048.0
d.get() = 2048.0
Unbound l to i, f to l, d to f.
Bound f to d, l to f, i to l.
Calling d.set(10000000000L).
d.get() = 1.0E10
f.get() = 1.0E10
l.get() = 10000000000
i.get() = 1410065408
```

Commonly Used Classes

We now give a survey of the content of the four packages javafx.beans, javafx.beans.binding, javafx. beans.property, and javafx.beans.value. In this section, the SimpleIntegerProperty series of classes refers to the classes extrapolated over the Boolean, Integer, Long, Float, Double, String, and Object types. Therefore, what is said also applies to SimpleBooleanProperty, and so on.

- The most often used classes in the JavaFX properties and bindings framework are the SimpleIntegerProperty series of classes. They provide all the functionalities of the Property interface including lazy evaluation. They are used in all the examples of this chapter up to this point.

- Another set of concrete classes in the JavaFX properties and bindings framework is the ReadOnlyIntegerWrapper series of classes. These classes implement the Property interface but also have a getReadOnlyProperty() method that returns a ReadOnlyProperty that is synchronized with the main Property. They are very handy to use when you need a full-blown Property for the implementation of a component but you only want to hand out a ReadOnlyProperty to the client of the component.

- The IntegerPropertyBase series of abstract classes can be extended to provide implementations of full Property classes, although in practice the SimpleIntegerProperty series of classes is easier to use. The only abstract methods in the IntegerPropertyBase series of classes are getBean() and getName().

- The ReadOnlyIntegerPropertyBase series of abstract classes can be extended to provide implementations of ReadOnlyProperty classes. This is rarely necessary. The only abstract methods in the ReadOnlyIntegerPropertyBase series of classes are get(), getBean(), and getName().

- The WeakInvalidationListener and WeakChangeListener classes can be used to wrap InvalidationListener and ChangeListener instances before addListener() is called. They hold weak references of the wrapped listener instances. As long as you hold a reference to the wrapped listener on your side, the weak references will be kept alive and you will receive events. When you are done with the wrapped listener and have unreferenced it from your side, the weak references will be eligible for garbage collection, and then later garbage collected. All the JavaFX properties and bindings framework Observable objects know how to clean up a weak listener after its weak reference has been garbage collected. This prevents memory leaks when the listeners are not removed after use. The WeakInvalidationListener and WeakListener classes implement the WeakListener interface, whose wasGarbageCollected() method will return true if the wrapped listener instance was garbage collected.

That covers all the JavaFX properties and bindings APIs that reside in the javafx.beans, javafx.beans. property, and javafx.beans.value packages and some but not all of the APIs in the javafx.beans.binding package. The javafx.beans.property.adapters package provides adapters between old-style JavaBeans properties and JavaFX properties. We will cover these adapters in the "Adapting JavaBeans Properties to JavaFX Properties" section. The remaining classes of the javafx.beans.binding package are APIs that help you to create new bindings out of existing properties and bindings. That is the focus of the next section.

Creating Bindings

We now turn our focus to the creation of new bindings out of existing properties and bindings. You learned in the "Understanding Key Interfaces and Concepts" section earlier in this chapter that a binding is an observable value that has a list of dependencies that are also observable values.

The JavaFX properties and bindings framework offers three ways of creating new bindings:

- Extending the IntegerBinding series of abstract classes.

- Using the bindings-creating static methods in the utilities class Bindings.

- Using the fluent interface API provided by the IntegerExpression series of abstract classes.

You saw the direct extension approach in the "Understanding the Binding Interface" section. We explore the Bindings utility class next.

Understanding the Bindings Utility Class

The Bindings class contains 236 factory methods that make new bindings out of existing observable values and regular values. Most of the methods are overloaded to take into account that both observable values and regular Java (unobservable) values can be used to build new bindings. At least one of the parameters must be an observable value. Here are the signatures of the nine overloaded add() methods:

```
public static NumberBinding add(ObservableNumberValue n1, ObservableNumberValue n2)
public static DoubleBinding add(ObservableNumberValue n, double d)
public static DoubleBinding add(double d, ObservableNumberValue n)
public static NumberBinding add(ObservableNumberValue n, float f)
public static NumberBinding add(float f, ObservableNumberValue n)
public static NumberBinding add(ObservableNumberValue n, long l)
public static NumberBinding add(long l, ObservableNumberValue n)
public static NumberBinding add(ObservableNumberValue n, int i)
public static NumberBinding add(int i, ObservableNumberValue n)
```

When the add() method is called, it returns a NumberBinding with dependencies that include all the observable value parameters, and whose value is the sum of the value of its two parameters. Similarly overloaded methods exist for subtract(), multiply(), and divide().

■ **Note**   Recall from the last section that ObservableIntegerValue, ObservableLongValue, ObservableFloatValue, and ObservableDoubleValue are subclasses of ObservableNumberValue. Therefore, the four arithmetic methods just mentioned can take any combinations of these observable numeric values as well as any unobservable values.

The program in Listing 3-5 uses the arithmetic methods in Bindings to calculate the area of a triangle in the Cartesian plane with vertices (x1, y1), (x2, y2), (x3, y3) using this formula:

```
Area = (x1*y2 + x2*y3 + x3*y1 - x1*y3 - x2*y1 - x3*y2) / 2
```

Listing 3-5. TriangleAreaExample.java

```java
import javafx.beans.binding.Bindings;
import javafx.beans.binding.NumberBinding;
import javafx.beans.property.IntegerProperty;
import javafx.beans.property.SimpleIntegerProperty;

public class TriangleAreaExample {
    public static void main(String[] args) {
        IntegerProperty x1 = new SimpleIntegerProperty(0);
        IntegerProperty y1 = new SimpleIntegerProperty(0);
        IntegerProperty x2 = new SimpleIntegerProperty(0);
        IntegerProperty y2 = new SimpleIntegerProperty(0);
        IntegerProperty x3 = new SimpleIntegerProperty(0);
        IntegerProperty y3 = new SimpleIntegerProperty(0);

        final NumberBinding x1y2 = Bindings.multiply(x1, y2);
        final NumberBinding x2y3 = Bindings.multiply(x2, y3);
        final NumberBinding x3y1 = Bindings.multiply(x3, y1);
        final NumberBinding x1y3 = Bindings.multiply(x1, y3);
        final NumberBinding x2y1 = Bindings.multiply(x2, y1);
        final NumberBinding x3y2 = Bindings.multiply(x3, y2);

        final NumberBinding sum1 = Bindings.add(x1y2, x2y3);
        final NumberBinding sum2 = Bindings.add(sum1, x3y1);
        final NumberBinding sum3 = Bindings.add(sum2, x3y1);
        final NumberBinding diff1 = Bindings.subtract(sum3, x1y3);
        final NumberBinding diff2 = Bindings.subtract(diff1, x2y1);
        final NumberBinding determinant = Bindings.subtract(diff2, x3y2);
        final NumberBinding area = Bindings.divide(determinant, 2.0D);

        x1.set(0); y1.set(0);
        x2.set(6); y2.set(0);
        x3.set(4); y3.set(3);

        printResult(x1, y1, x2, y2, x3, y3, area);

        x1.set(1); y1.set(0);
        x2.set(2); y2.set(2);
        x3.set(0); y3.set(1);

        printResult(x1, y1, x2, y2, x3, y3, area);
    }

    private static void printResult(IntegerProperty x1, IntegerProperty y1,
                                    IntegerProperty x2, IntegerProperty y2,
                                    IntegerProperty x3, IntegerProperty y3,
                                    NumberBinding area) {
        System.out.println("For A(" +
```

```
            x1.get() + "," + y1.get() + "), B(" +
            x2.get() + "," + y2.get() + "), C(" +
            x3.get() + "," + y3.get() + "), the area of triangle ABC is " + area.
            getValue());
    }
}
```

We used IntegerProperty to represent the coordinates. The building up of the NumberBinding area uses all four arithmetic factory methods of Bindings. Because we started with IntegerProperty objects, even though the return type from the arithmetic factory methods of Bindings is NumberBinding, the actual objects that are returned, up to determinant, are IntegerBinding objects. We used 2.0D rather than a mere 2 in the divide() call to force the division to be done as a double division, not as int division. All the properties and bindings that we build up form a tree structure with area as the root, the intermediate bindings as internal nodes, and the properties x1, y1, x2, y2, x3, y3 as leaves. This tree is similar to the parse tree we will get if we parse the mathematical expression for the area formula using grammar for the regular arithmetic expressions.

When we run the program in Listing 3-5, the following output is printed to the console:

```
For A(0,0), B(6,0), C(4,3), the area of triangle ABC is 9.0
For A(1,0), B(2,2), C(0,1), the area of triangle ABC is 1.5
```

Aside from the arithmetic methods, the Bindings class also has the following factory methods.

- Logical operators: and, or, not

- Numeric operators: min, max, negate

- Object operators: isNull, isNotNull

- String operators: length, isEmpty, isNotEmpty

- Relational operators:

  - equal

  - equalIgnoreCase

  - greaterThan

  - greaterThanOrEqual

  - lessThan

  - lessThanOrEqual

  - notEqual

  - notEqualIgnoreCase

- Creation operators:

  - createBooleanBinding

  - createIntegerBinding

  - createLongBinding

  - createFloatBinding

- • `createDoubleBinding`
- • `createStringBinding`
- • `createObjectBinding`
- • Selection operators:
  - • `select`
  - • `selectBoolean`
  - • `selectInteger`
  - • `selectLong`
  - • `selectFloat`
  - • `selectDouble`
  - • `selectString`

Except for the creation operators and the selection operators, the preceding operators all do what you think they will do. The object operators are meaningful only for observable string values and observable object values. The string operators are meaningful only for observable string values. All relational operators except for the `IgnoreCase` ones apply to numeric values. There are versions of the `equal` and `notEqual` operators for numeric values that have a third `double` parameter for the tolerance when comparing `float` or `double` values. The `equal` and `notEqual` operators also apply to `boolean`, string, and object values. For string and object values, the `equal` and `notEqual` operator compares their values using the `equals()` method.

The creation operators provide a convenient way of creating a binding without directly extending the abstract base class. It takes a `Callable` and any number of dependencies as an argument. The area double binding in Listing 3-3 can be rewritten using a lambda expression as the `Callable`, as follows,:

```
DoubleBinding area = Bindings.createDoubleBinding(() -> {
    return x.get() * y.get();
}, x, y);
```

The selection operators operate on what are called *JavaFX Beans,* Java classes constructed according to the JavaFX Beans specification. We talk about JavaFX Beans in the "Understanding JavaFX Beans Convention" section later in this chapter.

There are a number of methods in `Bindings` that deal with observable collections. We cover them in Chapter 7.

That covers all methods in `Bindings` that return a binding object. There are 18 methods in `Bindings` that do not return a binding object. The various `bindBidirectional()` and `unbindBidirectional()` methods create bidirectional bindings. As a matter of fact, the `bindBidirectional()` and `unbindBidirectional()` methods in the various properties classes simply call the corresponding ones in the `Bindings` class. The `bindContent()` and `unbindContent()` methods bind an ordinary collection to an observable collection. The `convert()`, `concat()`, and a pair of overloaded `format()` methods return `StringExpression` objects. And finally, the `when()` method returns a `When` object.

The `When` and the `StringExpression` classes are part of the fluent interface API for creating bindings, which we cover in the next subsection.

Understanding the Fluent Interface API

If you asked, "Why would anybody name a method when()?" and "What kind of information would the When class encapsulate?"—welcome to the club. While you were not looking, the object-oriented programming community invented a brand-new method of API design that totally disregards the decades-old principles of object-oriented practices. Instead of encapsulating data and distributing business logic into relevant domain objects, this new methodology produces a style of API that encourages method chaining and uses the return type of one method to determine what methods are available for the next car of the choo-choo train. Method names are chosen not to convey complete meaning, but to make the entire method chain read like a fluent sentence. This style is called a *fluent interface API*.

■ **Note**　You can find a more thorough exposition of fluent interfaces on Martin Fowler's web site, referenced at the end of this chapter.

The fluent interface APIs for creating bindings are defined in the IntegerExpression series of classes. IntegerExpression is a superclass of both IntegerProperty and IntegerBinding, making the methods of IntegerExpression also available in the IntegerProperty and IntegerBinding classes. The four numeric expression classes share a common superinterface NumberExpression, where all the methods are defined. The type-specific expression classes override some of the methods that yield a NumberBinding to return a more appropriate type of binding.

The methods thus made available for the seven kinds of properties and bindings are listed here:

- For BooleanProperty and BooleanBindingBooleanBinding and(ObservableBooleanValue b)

- BooleanBinding or(ObservableBooleanValue b)

- BooleanBinding not()

- BooleanBinding isEqualTo(ObservableBooleanValue b)

- BooleanBinding isNotEqualTo(ObservableBooleanValue b)

- StringBinding asString()

- Common for all numeric properties and bindings

  - BooleanBinding isEqualTo(ObservableNumberValue m)

  - BooleanBinding isEqualTo(ObservableNumberValue m, double err)

  - BooleanBinding isEqualTo(double d, double err)

  - BooleanBinding isEqualTo(float f, double err)

  - BooleanBinding isEqualTo(long l)

  - BooleanBinding isEqualTo(long l, double err)

  - BooleanBinding isEqualTo(int i)

  - BooleanBinding isEqualTo(int i, double err)

  - BooleanBinding isNotEqualTo(ObservableNumberValue m)

  - BooleanBinding isNotEqualTo(ObservableNumberValue m, double err)

- BooleanBinding isNotEqualTo(double d, double err)

- BooleanBinding isNotEqualTo(float f, double err)

- BooleanBinding isNotEqualTo(long l)

- BooleanBinding isNotEqualTo(long l, double err)

- BooleanBinding isNotEqualTo(int i)

- BooleanBinding isNotEqualTo(int i, double err)

- BooleanBinding greaterThan(ObservableNumberValue m)

- BooleanBinding greaterThan(double d)

- BooleanBinding greaterThan(float f)

- BooleanBinding greaterThan(long l)

- BooleanBinding greaterThan(int i)

- BooleanBinding lessThan(ObservableNumberValue m)

- BooleanBinding lessThan(double d)

- BooleanBinding lessThan(float f)

- BooleanBinding lessThan(long l)

- BooleanBinding lessThan(int i)

- BooleanBinding greaterThanOrEqualTo(ObservableNumberValue m)

- BooleanBinding greaterThanOrEqualTo(double d)

- BooleanBinding greaterThanOrEqualTo(float f)

- BooleanBinding greaterThanOrEqualTo(long l)

- BooleanBinding greaterThanOrEqualTo(int i)

- BooleanBinding lessThanOrEqualTo(ObservableNumberValue m)

- BooleanBinding lessThanOrEqualTo(double d)

- BooleanBinding lessThanOrEqualTo(float f)

- BooleanBinding lessThanOrEqualTo(long l)

- BooleanBinding lessThanOrEqualTo(int i)

- StringBinding asString()

- StringBinding asString(String str)

- StringBinding asString(Locale locale, String str)

- For IntegerProperty and IntegerBinding

    - IntegerBinding negate()

    - NumberBinding add(ObservableNumberValue n)

    - DoubleBinding add(double d)

103

- FloatBinding add(float f)
- LongBinding add(long l)
- IntegerBinding add(int i)
- NumberBinding subtract(ObservableNumberValue n)
- DoubleBinding subtract(double d)
- FloatBinding subtract(float f)
- LongBinding subtract(long l)
- IntegerBinding subtract(int i)
- NumberBinding multiply(ObservableNumberValue n)
- DoubleBinding multiply(double d)
- FloatBinding multiply(float f)
- LongBinding multiply(long l)
- IntegerBinding multiply(int i)
- NumberBinding divide(ObservableNumberValue n)
- DoubleBinding divide(double d)
- FloatBinding divide(float f)
- LongBinding divide(long l)
- IntegerBinding divide(int i)

- For LongProperty and LongBinding

  - LongBinding negate()
  - NumberBinding add(ObservableNumberValue n)
  - DoubleBinding add(double d)
  - FloatBinding add(float f)
  - LongBinding add(long l)
  - LongBinding add(int i)
  - NumberBinding subtract(ObservableNumberValue n)
  - DoubleBinding subtract(double d)
  - FloatBinding subtract(float f)
  - LongBinding subtract(long l)
  - LongBinding subtract(int i)
  - NumberBinding multiply(ObservableNumberValue n)
  - DoubleBinding multiply(double d)
  - FloatBinding multiply(float f)

- LongBinding multiply(long l)
- LongBinding multiply(int i)
- NumberBinding divide(ObservableNumberValue n)
- DoubleBinding divide(double d)
- FloatBinding divide(float f)
- LongBinding divide(long l)
- LongBinding divide(int i)

- For FloatProperty and FloatBinding
    - FloatBinding negate()
    - NumberBinding add(ObservableNumberValue n)
    - DoubleBinding add(double d)
    - FloatBinding add(float g)
    - FloatBinding add(long l)
    - FloatBinding add(int i)
    - NumberBinding subtract(ObservableNumberValue n)
    - DoubleBinding subtract(double d)
    - FloatBinding subtract(float g)
    - FloatBinding subtract(long l)
    - FloatBinding subtract(int i)
    - NumberBinding multiply(ObservableNumberValue n)
    - DoubleBinding multiply(double d)
    - FloatBinding multiply(float g)
    - FloatBinding multiply(long l)
    - FloatBinding multiply(int i)
    - NumberBinding divide(ObservableNumberValue n)
    - DoubleBinding divide(double d)
    - FloatBinding divide(float g)
    - FloatBinding divide(long l)
    - FloatBinding divide(int i)

- For DoubleProperty and DoubleBinding
    - DoubleBinding negate()
    - DoubleBinding add(ObservableNumberValue n)
    - DoubleBinding add(double d)

- DoubleBinding add(float f)
- DoubleBinding add(long l)
- DoubleBinding add(int i)
- DoubleBinding subtract(ObservableNumberValue n)
- DoubleBinding subtract(double d)
- DoubleBinding subtract(float f)
- DoubleBinding subtract(long l)
- DoubleBinding subtract(int i)
- DoubleBinding multiply(ObservableNumberValue n)
- DoubleBinding multiply(double d)
- DoubleBinding multiply(float f)
- DoubleBinding multiply(long l)
- DoubleBinding multiply(int i)
- DoubleBinding divide(ObservableNumberValue n)
- DoubleBinding divide(double d)
- DoubleBinding divide(float f)
- DoubleBinding divide(long l)
- DoubleBinding divide(int i)
- For StringProperty and StringBinding
  - StringExpression concat(Object obj)
  - BooleanBinding isEqualTo(ObservableStringValue str)
  - BooleanBinding isEqualTo(String str)
  - BooleanBinding isNotEqualTo(ObservableStringValue str)
  - BooleanBinding isNotEqualTo(String str)
  - BooleanBinding isEqualToIgnoreCase(ObservableStringValue str)
  - BooleanBinding isEqualToIgnoreCase(String str)
  - BooleanBinding isNotEqualToIgnoreCase(ObservableStringValue str)
  - BooleanBinding isNotEqualToIgnoreCase(String str)
  - BooleanBinding greaterThan(ObservableStringValue str)
  - BooleanBinding greaterThan(String str)
  - BooleanBinding lessThan(ObservableStringValue str)
  - BooleanBinding lessThan(String str)
  - BooleanBinding greaterThanOrEqualTo(ObservableStringValue str)

- • BooleanBinding greaterThanOrEqualTo(String str)

- • BooleanBinding lessThanOrEqualTo(ObservableStringValue str)

- • BooleanBinding lessThanOrEqualTo(String str)

- • BooleanBinding isNull()

- • BooleanBinding isNotNull()

- • IntegerBinding length()

- • BooleanExpression isEmpty()

- • BooleanExpression isNotEmpty()

- • For ObjectProperty and ObjectBinding

  - • BooleanBinding isEqualTo(ObservableObjectValue<?> obj)

  - • BooleanBinding isEqualTo(Object obj)

  - • BooleanBinding isNotEqualTo(ObservableObjectValue<?> obj)

  - • BooleanBinding isNotEqualTo(Object obj)

  - • BooleanBinding isNull()

  - • BooleanBinding isNotNull()

With these methods, you can create an infinite variety of bindings by starting with a property and calling one of the methods that is appropriate for the type of the property to get a binding, and calling one of the methods that is appropriate for the type of the binding to get another binding, and so on. One fact that is worth pointing out here is that all the methods for the type-specific numeric expressions are defined in the NumberExpression base interface with a return type of NumberBinding, and are overridden in the type-specific expression classes with an identical parameter signature but a more specific return type. This way of overriding a method in a subclass with an identical parameter signature but a more specific return type is called *covariant return-type overriding*, and has been a Java language feature since Java 5. One of the consequences of this fact is that numeric bindings built with the fluent interface API have more specific types than those built with factory methods in the Bindings class.

Sometimes it is necessary to convert a type-specific expression into an object expression holding the same type of value. This can be done with the asObject() method in the type-specific expression class. The conversion back can be done using static methods in the expressions class. For IntegerExpression, these static methods are as follows:

```
static IntegerExpression integerExpression(ObservableIntegerValue value)
static <T extends java.lang.Number> IntegerExpression integerExpression(ObservableValue<T> value)
```

The program in Listing 3-6 is a modification of the triangle area example in Listing 3-5 that uses the fluent interface API instead of calling factory methods in the Bindings class.

Listing 3-6. TriangleAreaFluentExample.java

```
import javafx.beans.binding.Bindings;
import javafx.beans.binding.NumberBinding;
import javafx.beans.binding.StringExpression;
import javafx.beans.property.IntegerProperty;
import javafx.beans.property.SimpleIntegerProperty;
```

```java
public class TriangleAreaFluentExample {
    public static void main(String[] args) {
        IntegerProperty x1 = new SimpleIntegerProperty(0);
        IntegerProperty y1 = new SimpleIntegerProperty(0);
        IntegerProperty x2 = new SimpleIntegerProperty(0);
        IntegerProperty y2 = new SimpleIntegerProperty(0);
        IntegerProperty x3 = new SimpleIntegerProperty(0);
        IntegerProperty y3 = new SimpleIntegerProperty(0);

        final NumberBinding area = x1.multiply(y2)
                .add(x2.multiply(y3))
                .add(x3.multiply(y1))
                .subtract(x1.multiply(y3))
                .subtract(x2.multiply(y1))
                .subtract(x3.multiply(y2))
                .divide(2.0D);

        StringExpression output = Bindings.format(
                "For A(%d,%d), B(%d,%d), C(%d,%d), the area of triangle ABC is %3.1f",
                x1, y1, x2, y2, x3, y3, area);

        x1.set(0); y1.set(0);
        x2.set(6); y2.set(0);
        x3.set(4); y3.set(3);

        System.out.println(output.get());

        x1.set(1); y1.set(0);
        x2.set(2); y2.set(2);
        x3.set(0); y3.set(1);

        System.out.println(output.get());
    }
}
```

Notice how the 13 lines of code and 12 intermediate variables used in Listing 3-5 to build up the area binding are reduced to the 7 lines of code with no intermediate variables used in Listing 3-6. We also used the Bindings.format() method to build up a StringExpression object called output. There are two overloaded Bindings.format() methods with signatures:

```
StringExpression format(Locale locale, String format, Object... args)
StringExpression format(String format, Object... args)
```

They work similarly to the corresponding String.format() methods in that they format the values args according to the format specification format and the Locale locale, or the default Locale. If any of the args is an ObservableValue, its change is reflected in the StringExpression.

When we run the program in Listing 3-6, the following output is printed to the console:

```
For A(0,0), B(6,0), C(4,3), the area of triangle ABC is 9.0
For A(1,0), B(2,2), C(0,1), the area of triangle ABC is 1.5
```

Next we unravel the mystery of the When class and the role it plays in constructing bindings that are essentially if/then/else expressions. The When class has a constructor that takes an ObservableBooleanValue argument:

```
public When(ObservableBooleanValue b)
```

It has the following 11 overloaded then() methods.

```
When.NumberConditionBuilder then(ObservableNumberValue n)
When.NumberConditionBuilder then(double d)
When.NumberConditionBuilder then(float f)
When.NumberConditionBuilder then(long l)
When.NumberConditionBuilder then(int i)
When.BooleanConditionBuilder then(ObservableBooleanValue b)
When.BooleanConditionBuilder then(boolean b)
When.StringConditionBuilder then(ObservableStringValue str)
When.StringConditionBuilder then(String str)
When.ObjectConditionBuilder<T> then(ObservableObjectValue<T> obj)
When.ObjectConditionBuilder<T> then(T obj)
```

The type of object returned from the then() method depends on the type of the argument. If the argument is a numeric type, either observable or unobservable, the return type is a nested class When.NumberConditionBuilder. Similarly, for Boolean arguments, the return type is When. BooleanConditionBuilder; for string arguments, When.StringConditionBuilder; and for object arguments, When.ObjectConditionBuilder.

These condition builders in turn have the following otherwise() methods.

- For When.NumberConditionBuilder

  - NumberBinding otherwise(ObservableNumberValue n)

  - DoubleBinding otherwise(double d)

  - NumberBinding otherwise(float f)

  - NumberBinding otherwise(long l)

  - NumberBinding otherwise(int i)

- For When.BooleanConditionBuilder

  - BooleanBinding otherwise(ObservableBooleanValue b)

  - BooleanBinding otherwise(boolean b)

- For When.StringConditionBuilder

  - StringBinding otherwise(ObservableStringValue str)

  - StringBinding otherwise(String str)

- For When.ObjectConditionBuilder

  - ObjectBinding<T> otherwise(ObservableObjectValue<T> obj)

  - ObjectBinding<T> otherwise(T obj)

The net effect of these method signatures is that you can build up a binding that resembles an if/then/
else expression this way:

```
new When(b).then(x).otherwise(y)
```

b is an ObservableBooleanValue, and x and y are of similar types and can be either observable or
unobservable. The resulting binding will be of a type similar to that of x and y.

The program in Listing 3-7 uses the fluent interface API from the When class to calculate the area of a
triangle with given sides a, b, and c. Recall that to form a triangle, the three sides must satisfy the following
conditions:

```
a + b > c, b + c > a, c + a > b.
```

When the preceding conditions are satisfied, the area of the triangle can be calculated using Heron's
formula:

```
Area = sqrt(s * (s - a) * (s - b) * (s - c))
```

where s is the semiperimeter:

```
s = (a + b + c) / 2.
```

Listing 3-7. HeronsFormulaExample.java

```java
import javafx.beans.binding.DoubleBinding;
import javafx.beans.binding.When;
import javafx.beans.property.DoubleProperty;
import javafx.beans.property.SimpleDoubleProperty;
public class HeronsFormulaExample {
    public static void main(String[] args) {
        DoubleProperty a = new SimpleDoubleProperty(0);
        DoubleProperty b = new SimpleDoubleProperty(0);
        DoubleProperty c = new SimpleDoubleProperty(0);

        DoubleBinding s = a.add(b).add(c).divide(2.0D);

        final DoubleBinding areaSquared = new When(
                    a.add(b).greaterThan(c)
                    .and(b.add(c).greaterThan(a))
                    .and(c.add(a).greaterThan(b)))
                .then(s.multiply(s.subtract(a))
                    .multiply(s.subtract(b))
                    .multiply(s.subtract(c)))
                .otherwise(0.0D);

        a.set(3);
        b.set(4);
        c.set(5);
        System.out.printf("Given sides a = %1.0f, b = %1.0f, and c = %1.0f," +
```

```
                " the area of the triangle is %3.2f\n", a.get(), b.get(), c.get(),
                Math.sqrt(areaSquared.get())));

        a.set(2);
        b.set(2);
        c.set(2);
        System.out.printf("Given sides a = %1.0f, b = %1.0f, and c = %1.0f," +
                " the area of the triangle is %3.2f\n", a.get(), b.get(), c.get(),
                Math.sqrt(areaSquared.get())));
    }
}
```

Inasmuch as there is no ready-made binding method in DoubleExpression that calculates the square root, we create a DoubleBinding for areaSquared instead. The constructor argument for When() is a BooleanBinding built out of the three conditions on a, b, and c. The argument for the then() method is a DoubleBinding that calculates the square of the area of the triangle. And because the then() argument is numeric, the otherwise() argument also has to be numeric. We choose to use 0.0D to signal that an invalid triangle is encountered.

■ **Note**   Instead of using the When() constructor, you can also use the factory method when() in the Bindings utility class to create the When object.

When we run the program in Listing 3-7, the following output is printed to the console:

```
Given sides a = 3, b = 4, and c = 5, the area of the triangle is 6.00.
Given sides a = 2, b = 2, and c = 2, the area of the triangle is 1.73.
```

If the binding defined in Listing 3-7 makes your head spin a little, you are not alone. We choose this example simply to illustrate the use of the fluent interface API offered by the When class. As a matter of fact, this example might be better served with a direct subclassing approach we first introduced in the "Understanding the Binding Interface" section.

The program in Listing 3-8 solves the same problem as Listing 3-7 by using the direct extension method.

Listing 3-8. HeronsFormulaDirectExtensionExample.java

```java
import javafx.beans.binding.DoubleBinding;
import javafx.beans.property.DoubleProperty;
import javafx.beans.property.SimpleDoubleProperty;

public class HeronsFormulaDirectExtensionExample {
    public static void main(String[] args) {
        final DoubleProperty a = new SimpleDoubleProperty(0);
        final DoubleProperty b = new SimpleDoubleProperty(0);
        final DoubleProperty c = new SimpleDoubleProperty(0);
```

```
DoubleBinding area = new DoubleBinding() {
    {
        super.bind(a, b, c);
    }
    @Override
    protected double computeValue() {
        double a0 = a.get();
        double b0 = b.get();
        double c0 = c.get();

        if ((a0 + b0 > c0) && (b0 + c0 > a0) && (c0 + a0 > b0)) {
            double s = (a0 + b0 + c0) / 2.0D;
            return Math.sqrt(s * (s - a0) * (s - b0) * (s - c0));
        } else {
            return 0.0D;
        }
    }
};

a.set(3);
b.set(4);
c.set(5);
System.out.printf("Given sides a = %1.0f, b = %1.0f, and c = %1.0f," +
        " the area of the triangle is %3.2f\n", a.get(), b.get(), c.get(),
        area.get());

a.set(2);
b.set(2);
c.set(2);
System.out.printf("Given sides a = %1.0f, b = %1.0f, and c = %1.0f," +
        " the area of the triangle is %3.2f\n", a.get(), b.get(), c.get(),
        area.get());
    }
}
```

The direct extension method is preferred for complicated expressions and for expressions that go beyond the available operators.

Now that you have mastered all the APIs in the javafx.beans, javafx.beans.binding, javafx.beans. property, and javafx.beans.value packages, you are ready to step beyond the details of the JavaFX properties and bindings framework and learn how these properties are organized into bigger components called JavaFX Beans.

Understanding the JavaFX Beans Convention

JavaFX introduces the concept of JavaFX Beans, a set of conventions that provide properties support for Java objects. In this section, we talk about the naming conventions for specifying JavaFX Beans properties, several ways of implementing JavaFX Beans properties, and finally the use of selection bindings.

The JavaFX Beans Specification

For many years Java has used the JavaBeans API to represent a property of an object. A JavaBeans property is represented by a pair of getter and setter methods. Property changes are propagated to property change listeners through the firing of property change events in the setter code.

JavaFX introduces the JavaFX Beans specification that adds properties support to Java objects through the help of the properties classes from the JavaFX properties and bindings framework.

■ **Caution**   The word *property* is used here with two distinct meanings. When we say, "JavaFX Beans properties," it should be understood to mean a higher-level concept similar to JavaBeans properties. When we say, "JavaFX properties and bindings framework properties," it should be understood to mean the various implementations of the Property or ReadOnlyProperty interfaces, such as IntegerProperty, StringProperty, and so on. JavaFX Beans properties are specified using the JavaFX properties and bindings framework properties.

Like their JavaBeans counterparts, *JavaFX Beans properties* are specified by a set of methods in a Java class. To define a JavaFX Beans property in a Java class, you provide three methods: the getter, the setter, and the property getter. For a property named height of type double, the three methods are:

```
public final double getHeight();
public final void setHeight(double h);
public DoubleProperty heightProperty();
```

The names of the getter and setter methods follow the JavaBeans convention. They are obtained by concatenating "get" and "set" with the name of the property with the first character capitalized. For boolean type properties, the getter name can also start with "is". The name of the property getter is obtained by concatenating the name of the property with "Property". To define a *read-only JavaFX Beans property*, you can either remove the setter method or change it to a private method and change the return type of the property getter to be a ReadOnlyProperty.

This specification speaks only about the interface of JavaFX Beans properties and does not impose any implementation constraints. Depending on the number of properties a JavaFX Bean may have, and the usage patterns of these properties, there are several implementation strategies. Not surprisingly, all of them use the JavaFX properties and bindings framework properties as the backing store for the values of the JavaFX Beans properties. We show you these strategies in the next two subsections.

Understanding the Eagerly Instantiated Properties Strategy

The *eagerly instantiated properties* strategy is the simplest way to implement JavaFX Beans properties. For every JavaFX Beans property you want to define in an object, you introduce a private field in the class that is of the appropriate JavaFX properties and bindings framework property type. These private fields are instantiated at bean construction time. The getter and setter methods simply call the private field's get() and set() methods. The property getter simply returns the private field itself.

The program in Listing 3-9 defines a JavaFX Bean with an int property i, a String property str, and a Color property color.

Listing 3-9. `JavaFXBeanModelExample.java`

```java
import javafx.beans.property.IntegerProperty;
import javafx.beans.property.ObjectProperty;
import javafx.beans.property.SimpleIntegerProperty;
import javafx.beans.property.SimpleObjectProperty;
import javafx.beans.property.SimpleStringProperty;
import javafx.beans.property.StringProperty;
import javafx.scene.paint.Color;

public class JavaFXBeanModelExample {
    private IntegerProperty i = new SimpleIntegerProperty(this, "i", 0);
    private StringProperty str = new SimpleStringProperty(this, "str", "Hello");
    private ObjectProperty<Color> color = new SimpleObjectProperty<Color>(this, "color",↵
 Color.BLACK);

    public final int getI() {
        return i.get();
    }

    public final void setI(int i) {
        this.i.set(i);
    }

    public IntegerProperty iProperty() {
        return i;
    }

    public final String getStr() {
        return str.get();
    }

    public final void setStr(String str) {
        this.str.set(str);
    }

    public StringProperty strProperty() {
        return str;
    }

    public final Color getColor() {
        return color.get();
    }

    public final void setColor(Color color) {
        this.color.set(color);
    }

    public ObjectProperty<Color> colorProperty() {
        return color;
    }
}
```

This is a straightforward Java class. There are only two things we want to point out in this implementation. First, the getter and setter methods are declared final by convention. Second, when the private fields are initialized, we called the simple properties constructors with the full context information, supplying them with this as the first parameter. In all of our previous examples in this chapter, we used null as the first parameter for the simple properties constructors because those properties are not part of a higher-level JavaFX Bean object.

The program in Listing 3-10 defines a view class that watches over an instance of the JavaFX Bean defined in Listing 3-9. It observes changes to the i, str, and color properties of the bean by hooking up change listeners that print out any changes to the console.

Listing 3-10. JavaFXBeanViewExample.java

```java
import javafx.beans.value.ChangeListener;
import javafx.beans.value.ObservableValue;
import javafx.scene.paint.Color;

public class JavaFXBeanViewExample {
    private JavaFXBeanModelExample model;

    public JavaFXBeanViewExample(JavaFXBeanModelExample model) {
        this.model = model;
        hookupChangeListeners();
    }

    private void hookupChangeListeners() {
        model.iProperty().addListener(new ChangeListener<Number>() {
            @Override
            public void changed(ObservableValue<? extends Number> observableValue, Number
            oldValue, Number newValue) {
                System.out.println("Property i changed: old value = " + oldValue + ", new
                value = " + newValue);
            }
        });

        model.strProperty().addListener(new ChangeListener<String>() {
            @Override
            public void changed(ObservableValue<? extends String> observableValue, String
            oldValue, String newValue) {
                System.out.println("Property str changed: old value = " + oldValue + ", new
                value = " + newValue);
            }
        });

        model.colorProperty().addListener(new ChangeListener<Color>() {
            @Override
            public void changed(ObservableValue<? extends Color> observableValue, Color
            oldValue, Color newValue) {
                System.out.println("Property color changed: old value = " + oldValue + ",
                new value = " + newValue);
            }
        });
    }
}
```

The program in Listing 3-11 defines a controller that can modify a model object.

Listing 3-11. `JavaFXBeanControllerExample.java`

```
import javafx.scene.paint.Color;

public class JavaFXBeanControllerExample {
    private JavaFXBeanModelExample model;
    private JavaFXBeanViewExample view;

    public JavaFXBeanControllerExample(JavaFXBeanModelExample model,
JavaFXBeanViewExampleÉ
 view) {
        this.model = model;
        this.view = view;
    }

    public void incrementIPropertyOnModel() {
        model.setI(model.getI() + 1);
    }

    public void changeStrPropertyOnModel() {
        final String str = model.getStr();
        if (str.equals("Hello")) {
            model.setStr("World");
        } else {
            model.setStr("Hello");
        }
    }

    public void switchColorPropertyOnModel() {
        final Color color = model.getColor();
        if (color.equals(Color.BLACK)) {
            model.setColor(Color.WHITE);
        } else {
            model.setColor(Color.BLACK);
        }
    }
}
```

Notice that this is not a full-blown controller and does not do anything with its reference to the view object. The program in Listing 3-12 provides a main program that assembles and test drives the classes in Listings 3-9 to 3-11 in a typical model–view–controller pattern.

Listing 3-12. `JavaFXbeanMainExample.java`

```java
public class JavaFXBeanMainExample {
    public static void main(String[] args) {
        JavaFXBeanModelExample model = new JavaFXBeanModelExample();
        JavaFXBeanViewExample view = new JavaFXBeanViewExample(model);
        JavaFXBeanControllerExample controller = new JavaFXBeanControllerExample(model, view);

        controller.incrementIPropertyOnModel();
        controller.changeStrPropertyOnModel();
        controller.switchColorPropertyOnModel();
        controller.incrementIPropertyOnModel();
        controller.changeStrPropertyOnModel();
        controller.switchColorPropertyOnModel();
    }
}
```

When we run the program in Listings 3-9 to 3-12, the following output is printed to the console:

```
Property i changed: old value = 0, new value = 1
Property str changed: old value = Hello, new value = World
Property color changed: old value = 0x000000ff, new value = 0xffffffff
Property i changed: old value = 1, new value = 2
Property str changed: old value = World, new value = Hello
Property color changed: old value = 0xffffffff, new value = 0x000000ff
```

Understanding the Lazily Instantiated Properties Strategy

If your JavaFX Bean has many properties, instantiating all the properties objects up front at bean creation time may be too heavy an approach. The memory for all the properties objects is truly wasted if only a few of the properties are actually used. In such situations, you can use one of several lazily instantiated properties strategies. Two typical such strategies are the *half-lazy instantiation* strategy and the *full-lazy instantiation* strategy.

In the half-lazy strategy, the property object is instantiated only if the setter is called with a value that is different from the default value, or if the property getter is called. The program in Listing 3-13 illustrates how this strategy is implemented.

Listing 3-13. `JavaFXBeanModelHalfLazyExample.java`

```java
import javafx.beans.property.SimpleStringProperty;
import javafx.beans.property.StringProperty;

public class JavaFXBeanModelHalfLazyExample {
    private static final String DEFAULT_STR = "Hello";
    private StringProperty str;

    public final String getStr() {
        if (str != null) {
            return str.get();
        } else {
```

```
            return DEFAULT_STR;
        }
    }

    public final void setStr(String str) {
        if ((this.str != null) || !(str.equals(DEFAULT_STR))) {
            strProperty().set(str);
        }
    }

    public StringProperty strProperty() {
        if (str == null) {
            str = new SimpleStringProperty(this, "str", DEFAULT_STR);
        }
        return str;
    }
}
```

In this strategy, the client code can call the getter many times without the property object being instantiated. If the property object is null, the getter simply returns the default value. As soon as the setter is called with a value that is different from the default value, it will call the property getter, which lazily instantiates the property object. The property object is also instantiated if the client code calls the property getter directly.

In the full-lazy strategy, the property object is instantiated only if the property getter is called. The getter and setter go through the property object only if it is already instantiated; otherwise, they go through a separate field.

The program in Listing 3-14 shows an example of a full-lazy property.

Listing 3-14. JavaFXBeanModelFullLazyExample.java

```java
import javafx.beans.property.SimpleStringProperty;
import javafx.beans.property.StringProperty;

public class JavaFXBeanModelFullLazyExample {
    private static final String DEFAULT_STR = "Hello";
    private StringProperty str;
    private String _str = DEFAULT_STR;

    public final String getStr() {
        if (str != null) {
            return str.get();
        } else {
            return _str;
        }
    }

    public final void setStr(String str) {
        if (this.str != null) {
            this.str.set(str);
        } else {
            _str = str;
        }
    }
```

```
    public StringProperty strProperty() {
        if (str == null) {
            str = new SimpleStringProperty(this, "str", _str);
        }
        return str;
    }
}
```

▓ **Caution** The full-lazy instantiation strategy incurs the cost of an extra field to stave off the need for property instantiation a little longer. Similarly, both the half-lazy and the full-lazy instantiation strategies incur costs of implementation complexity and runtime performance to gain the benefit of a potentially reduced runtime memory footprint. This is a classic trade-off situation in software engineering. Which strategy you choose will depend on the circumstance of your application. Our advice is to introduce optimization only if there is a need.

Using Selection Bindings

As you saw in the "Understanding the Bindings Utility Class" section, the Bindings utility class contains seven selection operators. The method signatures of these operators are:

- select(Object root, String… steps)

- selectBoolean(Object root, String… steps)

- selectDouble(Object root, String… steps)

- selectFloat(Object root, String… steps)

- selectInteger(Object root, String… steps)

- selectLong(Object root, String… steps)

- selectString(Object root, String… steps)

These selection operators allow you to create bindings that observe deeply nested JavaFX Beans properties. Suppose that you have a JavaFX bean that has a property, whose type is a JavaFX bean that has a property, whose type is a JavaFX bean that has a property, and so on. Suppose also that you are observing the root of this properties chain through an ObjectProperty. You can then create a binding that observes the deeply nested JavaFX Beans property by calling one of the select methods whose type matches the type of the deeply nested JavaFX Beans property with the ObjectProperty as the root, and the successive JavaFX Beans property names that reach into the deeply nested JavaFX Beans property as the rest of the arguments.

▓ **Note** There is another set of select methods that takes an ObservableValue as the first parameter. They were introduced in JavaFX 2.0. The set of select methods that takes an Object as the first parameter allows us to use any Java object, not merely JavaFX Beans, as the root of a selection binding.

In the following example, we use a few classes from the `javafx.scene.effect` package—Lighting and Light—to illustrate how the selection operator works. We teach you how to apply lighting to a JavaFX scene graph in a later chapter of the book. For now, our interest lies in the fact that Lighting is a JavaFX bean that has a property named light whose type is Light, and that Light is also a JavaFX bean that has a property named color whose type is Color (in `javafx.scene.paint`).

The program in Listing 3-15 illustrates how to observe the color of the light of the lighting.

Listing 3-15. SelectBindingExample.java

```java
import javafx.beans.binding.Bindings;
import javafx.beans.binding.ObjectBinding;
import javafx.beans.property.ObjectProperty;
import javafx.beans.property.SimpleObjectProperty;
import javafx.beans.value.ChangeListener;
import javafx.beans.value.ObservableValue;
import javafx.scene.effect.Light;
import javafx.scene.effect.Lighting;
import javafx.scene.paint.Color;

public class SelectBindingExample {
    public static void main(String[] args) {
        ObjectProperty<Lighting> root = new SimpleObjectProperty<>(new Lighting());
        final ObjectBinding<Color> selectBinding = Bindings.select(root, "light", "color");
        selectBinding.addListener(new ChangeListener<Color>() {
            @Override
            public void changed(ObservableValue<? extends Color> observableValue, Color
                oldValue, Color newValue) {
                System.out.println("\tThe color changed:\n\t\told color = " +
                    oldValue + ",\n\t\tnew color = " + newValue);
            }
        });

        System.out.println("firstLight is black.");
        Light firstLight = new Light.Point();
        firstLight.setColor(Color.BLACK);

        System.out.println("secondLight is white.");
        Light secondLight = new Light.Point();
        secondLight.setColor(Color.WHITE);

        System.out.println("firstLighting has firstLight.");
        Lighting firstLighting = new Lighting();
        firstLighting.setLight(firstLight);

        System.out.println("secondLighting has secondLight.");
        Lighting secondLighting = new Lighting();
        secondLighting.setLight(secondLight);

        System.out.println("Making root observe firstLighting.");
        root.set(firstLighting);
```

```
        System.out.println("Making root observe secondLighting.");
        root.set(secondLighting);

        System.out.println("Changing secondLighting's light to firstLight");
        secondLighting.setLight(firstLight);

        System.out.println("Changing firstLight's color to red");
        firstLight.setColor(Color.RED);
    }
}
```

In this example, the root is an ObjectProperty that observes Lighting objects. The binding colorBinding observes the color property of the light property of the Lighting object that is the value of root. We then created some Light and Lighting objects and changed their configuration in various ways.

When we run the program in Listing 3-15, the following output is printed to the console:

```
firstLight is black.
secondLight is white.
firstLighting has firstLight.
secondLighting has secondLight.
Making root observe firstLighting.
    The color changed:
        old color = 0xffffffff,
        new color = 0x000000ff
Making root observe secondLighting.
    The color changed:
        old color = 0x000000ff,
        new color = 0xffffffff
Changing secondLighting's light to firstLight
    The color changed:
        old color = 0xffffffff,
        new color = 0x000000ff
Changing firstLight's color to red
    The color changed:
        old color = 0x000000ff,
        new color = 0xff0000ff
```

As expected, a change event is fired for every change in the configuration of the object being observed by root, and the value of colorBinding always reflects the color of the light of the current Lighting object in root.

■ **Caution**   The JavaFX properties and bindings framework does not issue any warnings if the supplied property names do not match any property names in a JavaFX bean. It will simply have the default value for the type: null for object type, zero for numeric types, false for boolean type, and the empty string for string type.

Adapting JavaBeans Properties to JavaFX Properties

Over the many years since the JavaBeans specification was published, a lot of JavaBeans were written for various projects, products, and libraries. To better help Java developers leverage these JavaBeans, a set of adapters were provided in the `javafx.beans.properties.adapter` package to make them useful in the JavaFX world by creating a JavaFX property out of JavaBeans properties.

In this section, we first briefly review the JavaBeans specification definition of properties, bound properties, and constrained properties by way of a simple example. We then show you how to create JavaFX properties out of JavaBeans properties using the adapters.

Understanding JavaBeans Properties

JavaBeans *properties* are defined using the familiar getter and setter naming convention. A property is "read only" if only a getter is provided, and it is "read/write" if both a getter and a setter are provided. A JavaBeans event is made up of the event object, the event listener interface, and listener registration methods on the JavaBean. Two particular kinds of events are available for use by JavaBeans properties: A `PropertyChange` event can be fired when a JavaBeans property is changed; a `VetoableChange` event can also be fired when a JavaBeans property is changed; and if the listener throws a `PropertyVetoException`, the property change should not take effect. A property whose setter fires `PropertyChange` events is called a *bound property*. A property whose setter fires `VetoableChange` events is called a *constrained property*. Helper classes `PropertyChangeSupport` and `VetoableChangeSupport` allow bound properties and constrained properties to be easily defined in JavaBean classes.

Listing 3-16 defines a JavaBean `Person` with three properties: name, address, and phoneNumber. The address property is a bound property, and the phoneNumber property is a constrained property.

Listing 3-16. Person.java

```java
import java.beans.PropertyChangeListener;
import java.beans.PropertyChangeSupport;
import java.beans.PropertyVetoException;
import java.beans.VetoableChangeListener;
import java.beans.VetoableChangeSupport;

public class Person {
    private PropertyChangeSupport propertyChangeSupport;
    private VetoableChangeSupport vetoableChangeSupport;
    private String name;
    private String address;
    private String phoneNumber;

    public Person() {
        propertyChangeSupport = new PropertyChangeSupport(this);
        vetoableChangeSupport = new VetoableChangeSupport(this);
    }

    public String getName() {
        return name;
    }
```

```java
    public void setName(String name) {
        this.name = name;
    }

    public String getAddress() {
        return address;
    }

    public void setAddress(String address) {
        String oldAddress = this.address;
        this.address = address;
        propertyChangeSupport.firePropertyChange("address", oldAddress, this.address);
    }

    public String getPhoneNumber() {
        return phoneNumber;
    }

    public void setPhoneNumber(String phoneNumber) throws PropertyVetoException {
        String oldPhoneNumber = this.phoneNumber;
        vetoableChangeSupport.fireVetoableChange("phoneNumber", oldPhoneNumber,
        phoneNumber);
        this.phoneNumber = phoneNumber;
        propertyChangeSupport.firePropertyChange("phoneNumber", oldPhoneNumber, this.
        phoneNumber);
    }

    public void addPropertyChangeListener(PropertyChangeListener l) {
        propertyChangeSupport.addPropertyChangeListener(l);
    }

    public void removePropertyChangeListener(PropertyChangeListener l) {
        propertyChangeSupport.removePropertyChangeListener(l);
    }

    public PropertyChangeListener[] getPropertyChangeListeners() {
        return propertyChangeSupport.getPropertyChangeListeners();
    }

    public void addVetoableChangeListener(VetoableChangeListener l) {
        vetoableChangeSupport.addVetoableChangeListener(l);
    }

    public void removeVetoableChangeListener(VetoableChangeListener l) {
        vetoableChangeSupport.removeVetoableChangeListener(l);
    }

    public VetoableChangeListener[] getVetoableChangeListeners() {
        return vetoableChangeSupport.getVetoableChangeListeners();
    }
}
```

Understanding the JavaFX Property Adapters

The interfaces and classes in the `javafx.beans.property.adapter` package can be used to easily adapt JavaBeans properties to JavaFX properties. The `ReadOnlyJavaBeanProperty` interface is a subinterface of `ReadOnlyProperty`, and adds two methods:

```
void dispose()
void fireValueChangedEvent()
```

The `JavaBeanProperty` interface extends the `ReadOnlyJavaBeanProperty` and the `Property` interfaces. Each of these two interfaces has concrete class specializations for `Boolean`, `Integer`, `Long`, `Float`, `Double`, `Object`, and `String` types. These classes do not have public constructors. Instead, builder classes are provided to create instances of these types. We use the `JavaBeanStringProperty` class in the following example code. The same pattern applies to all other JavaFX property adapters. The `JavaBeanStringPropertyBuilder` supports the following methods:

```
public static JavaBeanStringPropertyBuilder create()
public JavaBeanStringProperty build()
public JavaBeanStringPropertyBuilder name(java.lang.String)
public JavaBeanStringPropertyBuilder bean(java.lang.Object)
public JavaBeanStringPropertyBuilder beanClass(java.lang.Class<?>)
public JavaBeanStringPropertyBuilder getter(java.lang.String)
public JavaBeanStringPropertyBuilder setter(java.lang.String)
public JavaBeanStringPropertyBuilder getter(java.lang.reflect.Method)
public JavaBeanStringPropertyBuilder setter(java.lang.reflect.Method)
```

To use the builder, start by calling its static method `create()`. Then call a chain of the methods that returns the builder itself. Finally, the `build()` method is called to create the property. For most cases, it suffices to call the `bean()` and the `name()` methods to specify the JavaBean instance and the name of the property. The `getter()` and `setter()` methods can be used to specify a getter and setter that does not follow the naming convention. The `beanClass()` method can be used to specify the JavaBean class. Setting the JavaBean class up front on the builder allows you to more efficiently create adapters for the same JavaBeans property for multiple instances of the same JavaBean class.

■ **Note**   Although the builders of the JavaFX scene, control, and so on, classes have been deprecated, the builders in the `javafx.beans.property.adapter` package have not been deprecated. They are required to generate the JavaBeans property adapters.

The program in Listing 3-17 illustrates the adaption of the three JavaBeans properties of the `Person` class into `JavaBeanStringProperty` objects.

Listing 3-17. `JavaBeanPropertiesExamples.java`

```
import javafx.beans.property.SimpleStringProperty;
import javafx.beans.property.adapter.JavaBeanStringProperty;
import javafx.beans.property.adapter.JavaBeanStringPropertyBuilder;

import java.beans.PropertyVetoException;
```

```java
public class JavaBeanPropertiesExample {
    public static void main(String[] args) throws NoSuchMethodException {
        adaptJavaBeansProperty();
        adaptBoundProperty();
        adaptConstrainedProperty();
    }

    private static void adaptJavaBeansProperty() throws NoSuchMethodException {
        Person person = new Person();
        JavaBeanStringProperty nameProperty = JavaBeanStringPropertyBuilder.create()
            .bean(person)
            .name("name")
            .build();
        nameProperty.addListener((observable, oldValue, newValue) -> {
            System.out.println("JavaFX property " + observable + " changed:");
            System.out.println("\toldValue = " + oldValue + ", newValue = " + newValue);
        });

        System.out.println("Setting name on the JavaBeans property");
        person.setName("Stephen Chin");
        System.out.println("Calling fireValueChange");
        nameProperty.fireValueChangedEvent();
        System.out.println("nameProperty.get() = " + nameProperty.get());

        System.out.println("Setting value on the JavaFX property");
        nameProperty.set("Johan Vos");
        System.out.println("person.getName() = " + person.getName());
    }

    private static void adaptBoundProperty() throws NoSuchMethodException {
        System.out.println();
        Person person = new Person();
        JavaBeanStringProperty addressProperty = JavaBeanStringPropertyBuilder.create()
            .bean(person)
            .name("address")
            .build();
        addressProperty.addListener((observable, oldValue, newValue) -> {
            System.out.println("JavaFX property " + observable + " changed:");
            System.out.println("\toldValue = " + oldValue + ", newValue = " + newValue);
        });

        System.out.println("Setting address on the JavaBeans property");
        person.setAddress("12345 Main Street");
    }

    private static void adaptConstrainedProperty() throws NoSuchMethodException {
        System.out.println();
        Person person = new Person();
        JavaBeanStringProperty phoneNumberProperty = JavaBeanStringPropertyBuilder.create()
            .bean(person)
            .name("phoneNumber")
            .build();
```

```
        phoneNumberProperty.addListener((observable, oldValue, newValue) -> {
            System.out.println("JavaFX property " + observable + " changed:");
            System.out.println("\toldValue = " + oldValue + ", newValue = " + newValue);
        });

        System.out.println("Setting phoneNumber on the JavaBeans property");
        try {
            person.setPhoneNumber("800-555-1212");
        } catch (PropertyVetoException e) {
            System.out.println("A JavaBeans property change is vetoed.");
        }

        System.out.println("Bind phoneNumberProperty to another property");
        SimpleStringProperty stringProperty = new SimpleStringProperty("866-555-1212");
        phoneNumberProperty.bind(stringProperty);

        System.out.println("Setting phoneNumber on the JavaBeans property");
        try {
            person.setPhoneNumber("888-555-1212");
        } catch (PropertyVetoException e) {
            System.out.println("A JavaBeans property change is vetoed.");
        }
        System.out.println("person.getPhoneNumber() = " + person.getPhoneNumber());
    }
}
```

In the adaptJavaBeanProperty() method, we instantiated a Person bean and adapted its name JavaBeans property into a JavaFX JavaBeanStringProperty. To help you understand when a ChangeEvent is delivered to the nameProperty, we added a ChangeListener (in the form of a lambda expression) to it. Because name is not a bound property, when we call person.setName(), the nameProperty is not aware of the change. To notify nameProperty of the change, we call its fireValueChangedEvent() method. When we call nameProperty.get(), we get the name that we have set on the person bean. Conversely, after we call nameProperty.set(), a call to person.getName() will return what we have set on nameProperty.

In the adaptBoundProperty() method, we instantiated a Person bean and adapted its address JavaBeans property into a JavaFX JavaBeanStringProperty. To help you understand when a ChangeEvent is delivered to the addressProperty, we added a ChangeListener (in the form of a lambda expression) to it. Because address is a bound property, the addressProperty is registered as a PropertyChangeListener to the person bean; therefore, when we call person.setAddress(), the addressProperty is notified immediately without us having to call the fireValuechangedEvent() method.

In the adaptConstrainedProperty() method, we instantiated a Person bean and adapted its phoneNumber JavaBeans property into a JavaBeanStringProperty. Again we added a ChangeListener to it. Because phoneNumber is a constrained property, phoneNumberProperty is capable of vetoing person.setPhoneNumber() calls. When that happens, the person.setPhoneNumber() call throws a PropertyVetoException. The phoneNumberProperty will veto such a change if it is itself bound to another JavaFX property. We call person.setPhoneNumber() twice, once before we bind phoneNumberProperty to another JavaFX property, and once after phoneNumberProperty is bound. The first call succeeds in altering the value of the phoneNumberProperty, and the second call throws a PropertyVetoException.

When we run the program in Listing 3-17, the following output is printed to the console:

```
Setting name on the JavaBeans property
Calling fireValueChange
JavaFX property StringProperty [bean: Person@776ec8df, name: name, value: Stephen Chin] changed:
        oldValue = null, newValue = Stephen Chin
nameProperty.get() = Stephen Chin
Setting value on the JavaFX property
JavaFX property StringProperty [bean: Person@776ec8df, name: name, value: Johan Vos] changed:
        oldValue = Stephen Chin, newValue = Johan Vos
person.getName() = Johan Vos

Setting address on the JavaBeans property
JavaFX property StringProperty [bean: Person@41629346, name: address, value: 12345 main
Street] changed:
        oldValue = null, newValue = 12345 main Street

Setting phoneNumber on the JavaBeans property
JavaFX property StringProperty [bean: Person@6d311334, name: phoneNumber, value: 800-555-
1212] changed:
        oldValue = null, newValue = 800-555-1212
Bind phoneNumberProperty to another property
JavaFX property StringProperty [bean: Person@6d311334, name: phoneNumber, value: 866-555-
1212] changed:
        oldValue = 800-555-1212, newValue = 866-555-1212
Setting phoneNumber on the JavaBeans property
A JavaBeans property change is vetoed.
person.getPhoneNumber() = 866-555-1212
```

Summary

In this chapter, you learned the fundamentals of the JavaFX properties and bindings framework, and the JavaFX Beans specification. You should now understand the following important principles.

- JavaFX properties and bindings are the fundamental workhorses of the framework.

- They conform to the key interfaces of the framework.

- They fire two kinds of events: an invalidation event and a change event.

- All properties and bindings provided by the framework recalculate their values lazily—only when a value is requested. To force them into eager reevaluation, a ChangeListener needs to be attached.

- New bindings are created out of existing properties and bindings in one of three ways: using the factory methods of the Bindings utility class, using the fluent interface API, or directly extending the IntegerBinding series of abstract classes.

- The JavaFX Beans specification uses three methods to define a property: the getter, the setter, and the property getter.

- JavaFX Beans properties can be implemented through the eager, half-lazy, and full-lazy strategies.

- Old-style JavaBeans properties can be adapted easily to JavaFX properties.

Resources

The following are useful resources on properties and bindings.

- Martin Fowler's write-up on fluent interface APIs: `www.martinfowler.com/bliki/FluentInterface.html`

- The Properties and Binding tutorial at Oracle's JavaFX.com: `http://docs.oracle.com/javase/8/javafx/properties-binding-tutorial/`

- Michael Heinrichs's blog includes entries on JavaFX properties and bindings: `http://blog.netopyr.com/`

CHAPTER 4

■ ■ ■

Using Scene Builder to Create a User Interface

> *Give me a lever long enough and a fulcrum on which to place it, and I shall move the world.*

> —Archimedes

In Chapter 2, you learned about the two ways of creating a JavaFX UI, programmatically and declaratively, and how to programmatically create a UI using the JavaFX APIs. You are familiar with the theater metaphor of the JavaFX UI, with the Stage representing a window in a Windows, Mac, or Linux program, or the touch screen in a mobile device, the Scene and the Nodes it contains representing the content of the UI. In this chapter, we tackle the other side of the UI story in JavaFX: the declarative creation of UIs.

At the center of this approach of UI design is the FXML file. It is an XML file format designed specifically to hold information about UI elements. It contains the "what" of the UI elements, but not the "how." This is why this method of creating JavaFX UIs is called *declarative*. At its core, FXML is a Java object serialization format that can be used for any Java classes written in a certain way, including all old-style JavaBeans. In practice, however, it is only used for specifying JavaFX UIs.

Aside from direct editing in a text editor or your favorite Java integrated development environment (IDE), FXML files can also be manipulated by a graphical tool designed for working with FXML files called JavaFX Scene Builder. JavaFX Scene Builder 1.0 was released in August 2012, and JavaFX Scene Builder 1.1 was released in September 2013. Both 1.0 and 1.1 work with JavaFX 2. JavaFX Scene Builder 2.0 was released in May 2014 and works with JavaFX 8. The JavaFX Scene Builder 2.0 code base is released as open source, and while the Oracle JavaFX team is still contributing to it, the development and release of Scene Builder is now coordinated by Gluon.

Gluon merges contributions from Oracle, Gluon engineers and community contributors, and maintains a public code repository and an issue tracker. Also, Gluon creates binary releases for Windows, Mac, and Linux. All information on Scene Builder, including how to download and install, is now maintained at http://gluonhq.com/products/scene-builder/.

JavaFX Scene Builder is a fully graphical tool that allows you to paint the screens of your UI out of a palette of available containers, controls, and other visual nodes, and lay them out by direct manipulation on the screen and modification of their properties through property editors.

FXML files are loaded into JavaFX applications by the JavaFX runtime using the FXMLLoader class. The result of loading an FXML file is always a Java object, usually a container Node such as a Group or a Pane. This object can be used as the root in a Scene, or attached to a bigger programmatically created scene graph as a node. To the rest of the JavaFX application, the nodes loaded from an FXML file are no different from programmatically constructed nodes.

J. Vos et al., *Pro JavaFX 9*, https://doi.org/10.1007/978-1-4842-3042-8_4

We present the intricately related materials about the content and format of FXML files, how they are loaded at runtime, and how they are fashioned at design time, in a spiraling progression. We start this chapter with a complete example showing how the StageCoach program in Listing 2-1 from Chapter 2 can be done using FXML. We then present the FXML loading facility in detail. We then present a series of small handcrafted FXML files that highlight all the features of the FXML file format. Once you understand the FXML file format, we show you how to create these FXML files using JavaFX Scene Builder, covering all the features of JavaFX Scene Builder 2.0.

■ **Note**   You will need to download and install Gluon's open source JavaFX Scene Builder 9.0 from `http://gluonhq.com/products/scene-builder/` to go through the examples in this chapter. We also highly recommend configuring your favorite IDE to use JavaFX Scene Builder 9.0 to edit FXML files. NetBeans and IntelliJ IDEA come bundled with JavaFX support. Eclipse users can install the e(fx)clipse plug-in. Once configured, you can right-click any FXML files in your projects in your IDE and select the "Edit with Scene Builder" context menu item. Of course, you can also use your IDE's XML file editing capabilities to edit FXML files as XML files.

Setting the Stage with FXML

The process of converting the StageCoach program in Chapter 2 from using a programmatically created UI to using a declaratively created UI is straightforward.

Creating a User Interface Graphically with JavaFX Scene Builder

We first created an FXML file that represented the root node of the scene with JavaFX Scene Builder. Figure 4-1 shows a screenshot as this UI is being created.

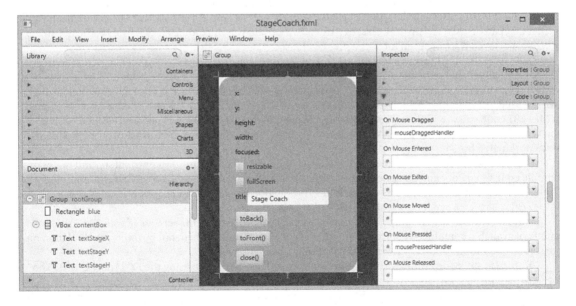

Figure 4-1. *StageCoach.fxml being created in JavaFX Scene Builder*

We will go into details of how to use JavaFX Scene Builder in the latter half of this chapter. For now, simply observe the major functional areas of the tool. In the middle is the Content panel showing the look of the UI being worked on. On the left side are the Library panel at the top, which includes all the possible nodes that can be used in the Content panel divided into neat subsets such as Containers, Controls, Shapes, Charts, and so on, and the Document panel below, which shows the scene graph that is being worked on in the Content panel as a tree structure called the Hierarchy, and the Controller that provides event handler code for the various controls in the UI. On the right side is the Inspector area that has subareas that allow you to manipulate Properties, Layout, and Code hookup of the currently selected control.

Understanding the FXML File

Listing 4-1 shows the FXML file that is saved by JavaFX Scene Builder from the UI we have created.

Listing 4-1. StageCoach.fxml

```
<?xml version="1.0" encoding="UTF-8"?>

<?import javafx.scene.control.Button?>
<?import javafx.scene.control.CheckBox?>
<?import javafx.scene.control.Label?>
<?import javafx.scene.control.TextField?>
<?import javafx.scene.Group?>
<?import javafx.scene.layout.HBox?>
<?import javafx.scene.layout.VBox?>
<?import javafx.scene.shape.Rectangle?>
<?import javafx.scene.text.Text?>
<Group fx:id="rootGroup"
       onMouseDragged="#mouseDraggedHandler"
       onMousePressed="#mousePressedHandler"
       xmlns="http://javafx.com/javafx/8"
       xmlns:fx="http://javafx.com/fxml/1"
       fx:controller="projavafx.stagecoach.ui.StageCoachController">
    <children>
      <Rectangle fx:id="blue"
                 arcHeight="50.0"
                 arcWidth="50.0"
                 fill="SKYBLUE"
                 height="350.0"
                 strokeType="INSIDE"
                 width="250.0"/>
      <VBox fx:id="contentBox"
            layoutX="30.0"
            layoutY="20.0"
            spacing="10.0">
        <children>
          <Text fx:id="textStageX"
                strokeType="OUTSIDE"
                strokeWidth="0.0"
                text="x:"
                textOrigin="TOP"/>
          <Text fx:id="textStageY"
```

```
                    layoutX="10.0"
                    layoutY="23.0"
                    strokeType="OUTSIDE"
                    strokeWidth="0.0"
                    text="y:"
                    textOrigin="TOP"/>
        <Text fx:id="textStageH"
                    layoutX="10.0"
                    layoutY="50.0"
                    strokeType="OUTSIDE"
                    strokeWidth="0.0"
                    text="height:"
                    textOrigin="TOP"/>
        <Text fx:id="textStageW"
                    layoutX="10.0"
                    layoutY="77.0"
                    strokeType="OUTSIDE"
                    strokeWidth="0.0"
                    text="width:"
                    textOrigin="TOP"/>
        <Text fx:id="textStageF"
                    layoutX="10.0"
                    layoutY="104.0"
                    strokeType="OUTSIDE"
                    strokeWidth="0.0"
                    text="focused:"
                    textOrigin="TOP"/>
        <CheckBox fx:id="checkBoxResizable"
                        mnemonicParsing="false"
                        text="resizable"/>
        <CheckBox fx:id="checkBoxFullScreen"
                        mnemonicParsing="false"
                        text="fullScreen"/>
        <HBox fx:id="titleBox">
            <children>
                <Label fx:id="titleLabel"
                        text="title"/>
                <TextField fx:id="titleTextField"
                            text="Stage Coach"/>
            </children>
        </HBox>
        <Button fx:id="toBackButton"
                    mnemonicParsing="false"
                    onAction="#toBackEventHandler"
                    text="toBack()"/>
        <Button fx:id="toFrontButton"
                    mnemonicParsing="false"
                    onAction="#toFrontEventHandler"
                    text="toFront()"/>
        <Button fx:id="closeButton"
                    mnemonicParsing="false"
                    onAction="#closeEventHandler"
```

```
                            text="close()"/>
                </children>
            </VBox>
        </children>
</Group>
```

■ **Note**   The FXML file created by JavaFX Scene Builder has longer lines. We reformatted the FXML file to fit the page of the book.

Most of this FXML file can be understood intuitively: It represents a Group holding two children, a Rectangle and a VBox. The VBox in turn holds five Text nodes, two CheckBoxes, an HBox, and three Buttons. The HBox holds a Label and a TextField. Various properties of these nodes are set to some sensible values; for example, the text on the three Buttons is set to "toBack()", "toFront()" and "close()".

Some of the constructs in this FXML file need a little bit more explanation. The XML processing instructions at the top of the file

```
<?import javafx.scene.control.Button?>
<?import javafx.scene.control.CheckBox?>
<?import javafx.scene.control.Label?>
<?import javafx.scene.control.TextField?>
<?import javafx.scene.Group?>
<?import javafx.scene.layout.HBox?>
<?import javafx.scene.layout.VBox?>
<?import javafx.scene.shape.Rectangle?>
<?import javafx.scene.text.Text?>
```

inform the consumer of this file, either JavaFX Scene Builder at design time or FXMLLoader at runtime, to import the mentioned Java classes. These have the same effect as import directives in Java source files.

Two namespace declarations are provided for the top-level element Group. JavaFX Scene Builder puts these namespaces in every FXML file it creates:

```
xmlns="http://javafx.com/javafx/8"
xmlns:fx="http://javafx.com/fxml/1"
```

■ **Caution**   The FXML file is not validated against any XML schemas. The namespaces specified here are used by the FXMLLoader, JavaFX Scene Builder, and Java IDEs such as NetBeans, Eclipse, and IntelliJ IDEA to provide assistance when editing FXML files. The actual prefix, empty string for the first namespace and "fx" for the second namespace, should not be altered.

This FXML file contains two kinds of attributes with the fx prefix, fx:controller and fx:id. The fx:controller attribute appears on the top-level element Group. It informs the JavaFX runtime that the UI designed in the current FXML file is meant to work together with a Java class called its *controller*:

```
fx:controller="projavafx.stagecoach.ui.StageCoachController"
```

The preceding attribute declares that StageCoach.fxml will work together with the Java class projavafx.stagecoach.ui.StageCoachController. The fx:id attribute can appear in every element that represents a JavaFX Node. The value of fx:id is the name of a field in the controller that represents the Node after the FXML file has been loaded. The StageCoach.fxml file declares the following fx:ids (only lines with fx:id attribute are shown):

```
<Group fx:id="rootGroup"
        <Rectangle fx:id="blue"
        <VBox fx:id="contentBox"
                <Text fx:id="textStageX"
                <Text fx:id="textStageY"
                <Text fx:id="textStageH"
                <Text fx:id="textStageW"
                <Text fx:id="textStageF"
                <CheckBox fx:id="checkBoxResizable"
                <CheckBox fx:id="checkBoxFullScreen"
                <HBox fx:id="titleBox">
                        <Label fx:id="titleLabel"
                        <TextField fx:id="titleTextField"
                <Button fx:id="toBackButton"
                <Button fx:id="toFrontButton"
                <Button fx:id="closeButton"
```

Thus after the FXMLLoader is done loading the FXML file, the top-level Group node in the FXML file can be accessed and manipulated in Java code as the rootGroup field of the StageCoachController class. In this FXML file, we assigned an fx:id to all the nodes that we create. This is done for illustration purposes only. If there is no reason to manipulate a node programmatically, such as is the case for a static label, both the fx:id attribute and the corresponding field in the controller can be omitted.

Providing programmatic access to the nodes in an FXML file is one role that the controller plays. Another role the controller plays is to provide the methods that handle user input and interaction events originating from the nodes in an FXML file. These event handlers are specified by attributes whose name begins with "on", such as onMouseDragged, onMousePressed, and onAction. They correspond to the setOnMouseDragged(), setOnMousePressed(), and setOnAction() methods in the Node classes or its subclasses. To set the event handlers to a method in the controller, use the method name preceded with a "#" character as the value of the onMouseDragged, onMousePressed, and onAction attributes. The StageCoach.fxml file declares the following event handlers (only lines with event handlers are shown):

```
<Group fx:id="rootGroup"
        onMouseDragged="#mouseDraggedHandler"
        onMousePressed="#mousePressedHandler"
                <Button fx:id="toBackButton"
                        onAction="#toBackEventHandler"
                <Button fx:id="toFrontButton"
                        onAction="#toFrontEventHandler"
                <Button fx:id="closeButton"
                        onAction="#closeEventHandler"
```

The event handler methods in the controller class should in general conform to the signature of the single method in the EventHandler<T> interface

```
void handle(T event)
```

where T is the appropriate event object, MouseEvent for the onMouseDragged and onMousePressed event handlers, and ActionEvent for the onAction event handlers. A method that does not take any arguments can also be set as event handler methods. You can use such a method if you do not plan to use the event object.

Now that we understand the FXML file, we move on to the controller class next.

Understanding the Controller

Listing 4-2 shows the controller class that works with the FXML file we created in the last subsection.

Listing 4-2. StageCoachController.java

```java
package projavafx.stagecoach.ui;

import javafx.beans.property.SimpleStringProperty;
import javafx.beans.property.StringProperty;
import javafx.event.ActionEvent;
import javafx.fxml.FXML;
import javafx.scene.control.Button;
import javafx.scene.control.CheckBox;
import javafx.scene.control.Label;
import javafx.scene.control.TextField;
import javafx.scene.input.MouseEvent;
import javafx.scene.layout.HBox;
import javafx.scene.layout.VBox;
import javafx.scene.shape.Rectangle;
import javafx.scene.text.Text;
import javafx.stage.Stage;
import javafx.stage.StageStyle;

public class StageCoachController {
    @FXML
    private Rectangle blue;

    @FXML
    private VBox contentBox;

    @FXML
    private Text textStageX;

    @FXML
    private Text textStageY;

    @FXML
    private Text textStageH;

    @FXML
    private Text textStageW;

    @FXML
    private Text textStageF;
```

```
@FXML
private CheckBox checkBoxResizable;

@FXML
private CheckBox checkBoxFullScreen;

@FXML
private HBox titleBox;

@FXML
private Label titleLabel;

@FXML
private TextField titleTextField;

@FXML
private Button toBackButton;

@FXML
private Button toFrontButton;

@FXML
private Button closeButton;

private Stage stage;
private StringProperty title = new SimpleStringProperty();
private double dragAnchorX;
private double dragAnchorY;

public void setStage(Stage stage) {
    this.stage = stage;
}

public void setupBinding(StageStyle stageStyle) {
    checkBoxResizable.setDisable(stageStyle == StageStyle.TRANSPARENT
        || stageStyle == StageStyle.UNDECORATED);
    textStageX.textProperty().bind(new SimpleStringProperty("x: ")
        .concat(stage.xProperty().asString()));
    textStageY.textProperty().bind(new SimpleStringProperty("y: ")
        .concat(stage.yProperty().asString()));
    textStageW.textProperty().bind(new SimpleStringProperty("width: ")
        .concat(stage.widthProperty().asString()));
    textStageH.textProperty().bind(new SimpleStringProperty("height: ")
        .concat(stage.heightProperty().asString()));
    textStageF.textProperty().bind(new SimpleStringProperty("focused: ")
        .concat(stage.focusedProperty().asString()));
    stage.setResizable(true);
    checkBoxResizable.selectedProperty()
        .bindBidirectional(stage.resizableProperty());
    checkBoxFullScreen.selectedProperty().addListener((ov, oldValue, newValue) ->
        stage.setFullScreen(checkBoxFullScreen.selectedProperty().getValue()));
```

```
        title.bind(titleTextField.textProperty());
        stage.titleProperty().bind(title);
        stage.initStyle(stageStyle);
    }

    @FXML
    public void toBackEventHandler(ActionEvent e) {
        stage.toBack();
    }

    @FXML
    public void toFrontEventHandler(ActionEvent e) {
        stage.toFront();
    }

    @FXML
    public void closeEventHandler(ActionEvent e) {
        stage.close();
    }

    @FXML
    public void mousePressedHandler(MouseEvent me) {
        dragAnchorX = me.getScreenX() - stage.getX();
        dragAnchorY = me.getScreenY() - stage.getY();
    }

    @FXML
    public void mouseDraggedHandler(MouseEvent me) {
        stage.setX(me.getScreenX() - dragAnchorX);
        stage.setY(me.getScreenY() - dragAnchorY);
    }
}
```

This class is extracted from the StageCoachMain class of Chapter 2, and this is the class that we specified as the controller class for the FXML file StageCoach.fxml. Indeed, it includes fields whose types and names match the fx:ids in the FXML file. It also includes methods whose names and signatures match those specified as the event handlers for the various nodes in the FXML file.

The only thing that needs some explanation is the @FXML annotation. It belongs to the javafx.fxml package. This is a marker annotation with a runtime retention that can be applied to fields and methods. When applied to a field, the @FXML annotation tells JavaFX Scene Builder the field's name can be used as the fx:id of the appropriately typed elements in an FXML file. When applied to a method, the @FXML annotation tells JavaFX Scene Builder the method's name can be used as the value of the appropriately typed event handler attributes. Fields and methods annotated with @FXML are made accessible to the FXML loading facility regardless of the modifiers. Therefore it is safe to change all the @FXML annotated fields from public to private without adversely affecting the FXML loading process.

The StageCoachController class includes matching fields for all the fx:ids declared in the FXML file. It also includes the five event handler methods to which the event handler attributes in the FXML file point. All of these fields and methods are annotated with @FXML.

The StageCoachController also includes some fields and methods that are not annotated with the @FXML annotation. These fields and methods are present in the class for other purposes. For example, the stage field, the setStage(), and the setupBindings() methods are used directly in Java code.

Understanding the FXMLLoader

Now that we understand both the FXML file and the controller class that works with the FXML file, we turn our attention to the loading of the FXML file at runtime. The FXMLLoader class in the javafx.fxml package does the bulk of the work of loading FXML files. In our example, the FXML file loading is done in the StageCoachMain class. Listing 4-3 shows the StageCoachMain class.

Listing 4-3. StageCoachMain.java

```java
package projavafx.stagecoach.ui;

import javafx.application.Application;
import javafx.fxml.FXMLLoader;
import javafx.geometry.Rectangle2D;
import javafx.scene.Group;
import javafx.scene.Scene;
import javafx.scene.paint.Color;
import javafx.stage.Screen;
import javafx.stage.Stage;
import javafx.stage.StageStyle;

import java.io.IOException;
import java.util.List;

public class StageCoachMain extends Application {
    @Override
    public void start(Stage stage) throws IOException {
        final StageStyle stageStyle = configStageStyle();

        FXMLLoader fxmlLoader = new FXMLLoader(StageCoachMain.class
            .getResource("/projavafx/stagecoach/ui/StageCoach.fxml"));
        Group rootGroup = fxmlLoader.load();

        final StageCoachController controller = fxmlLoader.getController();
        controller.setStage(stage);
        controller.setupBinding(stageStyle);

        Scene scene = new Scene(rootGroup, 250, 350);
        scene.setFill(Color.TRANSPARENT);

        stage.setScene(scene);
        stage.setOnCloseRequest(we -> System.out.println("Stage is closing"));
        stage.show();
        Rectangle2D primScreenBounds = Screen.getPrimary().getVisualBounds();
        stage.setX((primScreenBounds.getWidth() - stage.getWidth()) / 2);
        stage.setY((primScreenBounds.getHeight() - stage.getHeight()) / 4);
    }

    public static void main(String[] args) {
        launch(args);
    }
```

```
    private StageStyle configStageStyle() {
        StageStyle stageStyle = StageStyle.DECORATED;
        List<String> unnamedParams = getParameters().getUnnamed();
        if (unnamedParams.size() > 0) {
            String stageStyleParam = unnamedParams.get(0);
            if (stageStyleParam.equalsIgnoreCase("transparent")) {
                stageStyle = StageStyle.TRANSPARENT;
            } else if (stageStyleParam.equalsIgnoreCase("undecorated")) {
                stageStyle = StageStyle.UNDECORATED;
            } else if (stageStyleParam.equalsIgnoreCase("utility")) {
                stageStyle = StageStyle.UTILITY;
            }
        }
        return stageStyle;
    }
}
```

Before looking at the FXMLLoader code, let me point out that for this example, we choose to put the StageCoach.fxml file together with the StageCoachMain.java and the StageCoachController.java files. And they all reside in the projavafx/stagecoach/ui directory. That relation is preserved when we compile the source files. Therefore when we run this program, the FXML file appears as a resource /projavafx/stagecoach/ui/StageCoach.fxml in the classpath. Figure 4-2 illustrates the file layout of our example.

Figure 4-2. *The file layout of the StageCoach example*

The loading of the FXML file is performed by the following snippet of code:

```
FXMLLoader fxmlLoader = new FXMLLoader(StageCoachMain.class
    .getResource("/projavafx/stagecoach/ui/StageCoach.fxml"));
Group rootGroup = fxmlLoader.load();

final StageCoachController controller = fxmlLoader.getController();
```

Here we use the one-parameter constructor of the FXMLLoader class to construct an fxmlLoader object and pass in a URL object returned by the getResource() call on the Class object of StageCoachMain. This URL object is a jar URL or a file URL, depending on whether you run this program from a jar. We then call the load() method on the fxmlLoader object. This method reads the FXML file, parses it, instantiates all the nodes it specified, and hooks them up according to the containment relationships it specified. Because a controller is specified in the FXML file, the method also instantiates a StageCoachController instance and assigns the nodes to the fields of the controller instance according to the fx:ids. This step is usually called *injecting* the FXML nodes into the controller. The event handlers are also hooked up. The load() method returns the top-level object in the FXML file, which in our example is a Group. This returned Group object is assigned to the rootGroup variable and is used in subsequent code the same way as the programmatically created rootGroup in Chapter 2 is used. We then call the getController() method to get the controller with its node fields already injected by the FXMLLoader. This controller is assigned to the controller variable and is used in subsequent code as if we have just created it and assigned its node fields programmatically.

Now that we've finished switching the Stage Coach program from programmatic to declarative UI creation, we can run it. It behaves just like in Chapter 2. Figure 4-3 shows the program running with the transparent command-line argument.

Figure 4-3. *The Stage Coach program run with transparent command-line argument*

In this section we touched on all aspects of the FXML design-time and runtime facilities. However, we described only parts of each facility, barely enough to get our example program going. In the rest of this chapter, we study each of the facilities in detail.

Understanding the FXML Loading Facility

The FXML file loading facility is made up of two classes, an interface, an exception, and an annotation in the javafx.fxml package. The FXMLLoader is the class that does the bulk of the work, such as reading and parsing the FXML file, recognizing processing instructions in the FXML file, and responding with the necessary actions, recognizing each element and attribute of the FXML file and delegating the object creation tasks to a set of builders, creating the controller object if necessary and injecting the nodes and other objects into the controller. The JavaFXBuilderFactory is responsible for creating builders in response for FXMLLoader's requests for builders for a particular class. The Initializable interface can be implemented by controller classes to receive information from the FXMLLoader as in previous versions of JavaFX; however, this functionality has been superseded by the injection approach, so we do not discuss it. A LoadException is thrown if the FXML file contains errors that make it impossible for the FXMLLoader to construct all the objects specified in the FXML file. The @FXML annotation can be used in controller classes to mark certain fields as injection targets and certain methods as event handler candidates.

Understanding the FXMLLoader Class

The FXMLLoader class has the following public constructors:

- FXMLLoader()

- FXMLLoader(URL location)

- FXMLLoader(URL location, ResourceBundle resources)

- FXMLLoader(URL location, ResourceBundle resources, BuilderFactory builderFactory)

- FXMLLoader(URL location, ResourceBundle resources, BuilderFactory BuilderFactory builderFactory, Callback<Class<?>, Object> controllerFactory)

- FXMLLoader(Charset charset)

- FXMLLoader(URL location, ResourceBundle resources, BuilderFactory BuilderFactory builderFactory, Callback<Class<?> controllerFactory, Object>, Charset charset)

- FXMLLoader(URL location, ResourceBundle resources, BuilderFactory BuilderFactory builderFactory, Callback<Class<?>, Object> controllerFactory, Charset charset, LinkedList<FXMLLoader> loaders)

Constructors with fewer parameters delegate to constructors with more parameters, with the missing parameters filled in with default values. The location parameter is the URL of the FXML file to be loaded. It defaults to null. The resources parameter is the resource bundle to be used with the FXML file. This is necessary if internationalized strings are used in the FXML file. It defaults to null. The builderFactory parameter is the builder factory that FXMLLoader uses to get the builders of the various objects that it creates. It defaults to an instance of the JavaFXBuilderFactory. This builder factory has knowledge about all the standard JavaFX types that are likely to appear in FXML files, so a customized builder factory is rarely used. The controllerFactory is a javafx.util.CallBack that is capable of returning an instance of the controller when provided with the class of the controller. It defaults to null, in which case the FXMLLoader will instantiate the controller through reflection by calling the no-parameters constructor of the controller class. Therefore you need to supply a controllerFactory only if the controller cannot be constructed that way. The charset is used when the FXML is parsed. It defaults to UTF-8. The loaders parameter is a list of FXMLLoaders. It defaults to an empty list.

The FXMLLoader class has the following getter and setter methods that alter the states of the FXMLLoader:

- URL getLocation()

- void setLocation(URL location)

- ResourceBundle getResources()

- void setResources(ResourceBundle resources)

- ObservableMap<String, Object> getNamespace()

- <T> T getRoot()

- void setRoot(Object root)

- <T> T getController()

- void setController(Object controller)

- `BuilderFactory getBuilderFactory()`

- `void setBuilderFactory(BuilderFactory builderFactory)`

- `Callback<Class<?>, Object> getControllerFactory()`

- `void setControllerFactory(Callback<Class<?>, Object> controllerFactory)`

- `Charset getCharset()`

- `void setCharset(Charset charset)`

- `ClassLoader getClassLoader()`

- `void setClassLoader(ClassLoader classLoader)`

As you can see from this list, the `location`, `resources`, `builderFactory`, `controllerFactory`, and the charset can also be set after the `FXMLLoader` is constructed. In addition, we can get and set the `root`, `controller`, `classLoader`, and get the `namespace` of the `FXMLLoader`. The `root` is relevant only if the FXML file uses `fx:root` as its root element, in which case `setRoot()` must be called before the FXML file is loaded. We go into more detail about the usage of `fx:root` in the next section. The `controller` needs to be set before the FXML file is loaded only if the `fx:controller` attribute is not present in the top-level element in the FXML file. The `classLoader` and `namespace` are mostly used internally by the `FXMLLoader` and usually are not called by user code.

The actual loading of the FXML file happens when one of the `load()` methods is called. The `FXMLLoader` class has the following load methods:

- `<T> T load() throws IOException`

- `<T> T load(InputStream input) throws IOException`

- `static <T> T load(URL location) throws IOException`

- `static <T> T load(URL location, ResourceBundle resources) throws IOException`

- `static <T> T load(URL location, ResourceBundle resources, BuilderFactory builderFactory) throws IOException`

- `static <T> T load(URL location, ResourceBundle resources, BuilderFactory builderFactory, Callback<Class<?>, Object> controllerFactory) throws IOException`

- `static <T> T load(URL location, ResourceBundle resources, BuilderFactory builderFactory, Callback<Class<?>, Object> controllerFactory, Charset charset) throws IOException`

The `load()` method with no argument can be called on an `FXMLLoader` instance that has all the necessary fields already initialized. The `load()` method that takes an `InputStream` argument will load the FXML from the specified input. All the static `load()` methods are convenience methods that will instantiate an `FXMLLoader` with the supplied parameters and then call one of its nonstatic `load()` methods.

In our next example, we deliberately did not specify `fx:controller` in the FXML file. We also added a one-parameter constructor to the controller class. The FXML file, the controller class, and the main class are shown in Listings 4-4, 4-5, and 4-6.

Listing 4-4. FXMLLoaderExample.fxml

```xml
<?xml version="1.0" encoding="UTF-8"?>

<?import javafx.geometry.Insets?>
<?import javafx.scene.control.Button?>
<?import javafx.scene.control.TextField?>
<?import javafx.scene.layout.HBox?>
<?import javafx.scene.layout.VBox?>
<?import javafx.scene.web.WebView?>
<VBox maxHeight="-Infinity"
      maxWidth="-Infinity"
      minHeight="-Infinity"
      minWidth="-Infinity"
      prefHeight="400.0"
      prefWidth="600.0"
      spacing="10.0"
      xmlns="http://javafx.com/javafx/8"
      xmlns:fx="http://javafx.com/fxml/1">
    <children>
        <HBox spacing="10.0">
            <children>
                <TextField fx:id="address"
                           onAction="#actionHandler"
                           HBox.hgrow="ALWAYS">
                    <padding>
                        <Insets bottom="4.0" left="4.0" right="4.0" top="4.0"/>
                    </padding>
                </TextField>
                <Button fx:id="loadButton"
                        mnemonicParsing="false"
                        onAction="#actionHandler"
                        text="Load"/>
            </children>
        </HBox>
        <WebView fx:id="webView"
                 prefHeight="200.0"
                 prefWidth="200.0"
                 VBox.vgrow="ALWAYS"/>
    </children>
    <padding>
        <Insets bottom="10.0" left="10.0" right="10.0" top="10.0"/>
    </padding>
</VBox>
```

Listing 4-5. FXMLLoaderExampleController.java

```java
import javafx.event.ActionEvent;
import javafx.fxml.FXML;
import javafx.scene.control.Button;
import javafx.scene.control.TextField;
import javafx.scene.web.WebView;
```

143

```java
public class FXMLLoaderExampleController {
    @FXML
    private TextField address;

    @FXML
    private WebView webView;

    @FXML
    private Button loadButton;

    private String name;

    public FXMLLoaderExampleController(String name) {
        this.name = name;
    }

    @FXML
    public void actionHandler() {
        webView.getEngine().load(address.getText());
    }
}
```

Listing 4-6. FXMLLoaderExampleMain.java

```java
import javafx.application.Application;
import javafx.fxml.FXMLLoader;
import javafx.scene.Scene;
import javafx.scene.layout.VBox;
import javafx.stage.Stage;

public class FXMLLoaderExampleMain extends Application {
    @Override
    public void start(Stage primaryStage) throws Exception {
        FXMLLoader fxmlLoader = new FXMLLoader();
        fxmlLoader.setLocation(
            FXMLLoaderExampleMain.class.getResource("/FXMLLoaderExample.fxml"));
        fxmlLoader.setController(
            new FXMLLoaderExampleController("FXMLLoaderExampleController"));
        final VBox vBox = fxmlLoader.load();
        Scene scene = new Scene(vBox, 600, 400);
        primaryStage.setTitle("FXMLLoader Example");
        primaryStage.setScene(scene);
        primaryStage.show();
    }

    public static void main(String[] args) {
        launch(args);
    }
}
```

Because we did not specify the `fx:controller` attribute in the top-level element of the FXML file, we need to set the controller on `fxmlLoader` before loading the FXML file:

```
FXMLLoader fxmlLoader = new FXMLLoader();
fxmlLoader.setLocation(
    FXMLLoaderExampleMain.class.getResource("/FXMLLoaderExample.fxml"));
fxmlLoader.setController(
    new FXMLLoaderExampleController("FXMLLoaderExampleController"));
final VBox vBox = fxmlLoader.load();
```

If the controller is not set, a `LoaderException` will be thrown, with a message "No controller specified." This is because we did specify the controller method `actionHandler` as the action event handler for both the text field and the button. The `FXMLLoader` needs the controller to fulfill these specifications in the FXML file. Had the event handlers not been specified, the FXML file would have been loaded successfully because there is no need for a controller.

This program is a very primitive web browser with an address bar `TextField`, a load `Button`, and a `WebView`. Figure 4-4 shows the FXMLLoaderExample program at work.

Figure 4-4. *The FXMLLoaderExample program*

Our next example, ControllerFactoryExample, is nearly identical to the FXMLLoaderExample with only two differences, so we do not show the complete code here. You can find it in the code download bundle. Unlike in FXMLLoaderExample, we do specify fx:controller in the FXML file. This forces us to remove the setController() call in the main class, because otherwise we get a LoadException with a message "Controller value already specified." However, because our controller does not have a default constructor, FXMLLoader will throw a LoadException caused by its inability to instantiate the controller. This exception can be remedied by a simple controller factory that we set on the fxmlLoader:

```
fxmlLoader.setControllerFactory(
    clazz -> new ControllerFactoryExampleController("ExampleController"));
```

Here we used a simple lambda expression to implement the functional interface Callback<Class<?>, Object>, which has a single method:

```
Object call(Class<?>)
```

In our implementation we simply return an instance of ControllerFactoryExampleController.

Understanding the @FXML Annotation

We have seen two uses of the @FXML annotation. It can be applied to fields in the controller of an FXML file whose name and type match the fx:id attribute and element name of an FXML element to be injected with the node. It can be applied to void methods that take either no parameter or one parameter of type javafx.event.Event or its subtype, making them eligible for use as event handlers for elements in FXML files.

The FXMLLoader will inject its location and resources into the controller if it has the fields to receive them:

```
@FXML
private URL location;

@FXML
private ResourceBundle resources;
```

The FXMLLoader will also invoke an @FXML annotated initialization method with the following signature:

```
@FXML
public void initialize() {
    // ...
}
```

The FXMLInjectionExample in Listings 4-7, 4-8, and 4-9 illustrates how these features work. In this example, we put four Labels in a VBox in the FXML file. We inject two of the Labels into the controller. We also specify the location and resources injection fields in the controller class. Finally, in the initialize() method, we set the text of the two injected Labels to the string representations of location and resource.

Listing 4-7. FXMLInjectionExample.fxml

```
<?xml version="1.0" encoding="UTF-8"?>

<?import javafx.geometry.Insets?>
<?import javafx.scene.control.Label?>
<?import javafx.scene.layout.VBox?>
```

```
<?import javafx.scene.text.Font?>
<VBox alignment="CENTER_LEFT"
      maxHeight="-Infinity"
      maxWidth="-Infinity"
      minHeight="-Infinity"
      minWidth="-Infinity"
      prefHeight="150.0"
      prefWidth="700.0"
      spacing="10.0"
      xmlns="http://javafx.com/javafx/8"
      xmlns:fx="http://javafx.com/fxml/1"
      fx:controller="FXMLInjectionExampleController">
    <children>
        <Label text="Location:">
            <font>
                <Font name="System Bold" size="14.0"/>
            </font>
        </Label>
        <Label fx:id="locationLabel" text="[location]"/>
        <Label text="Resources:">
            <font>
                <Font name="System Bold" size="14.0"/>
            </font>
        </Label>
        <Label fx:id="resourcesLabel" text="[resources]"/>
    </children>
    <opaqueInsets>
        <Insets/>
    </opaqueInsets>
    <padding>
        <Insets bottom="10.0" left="10.0" right="10.0" top="10.0"/>
    </padding>
</VBox>
```

Listing 4-8. FXMLInjectionExampleController.java

```java
import javafx.fxml.FXML;
import javafx.scene.control.Label;

import java.net.URL;
import java.util.ResourceBundle;

public class FXMLInjectionExampleController {
    @FXML
    private Label resourcesLabel;

    @FXML
    private Label locationLabel;

    @FXML
    private URL location;
```

```
    @FXML
    private ResourceBundle resources;

    @FXML
    public void initialize() {
        locationLabel.setText(location.toString());
        resourcesLabel.setText(resources.getBaseBundleName());
    }
}
```

Listing 4-9. FXMLInjectionExampleMain.java

```
import javafx.application.Application;
import javafx.fxml.FXMLLoader;
import javafx.scene.Scene;
import javafx.scene.layout.VBox;
import javafx.stage.Stage;

import java.util.ResourceBundle;

public class FXMLInjectionExampleMain extends Application {
    @Override
    public void start(Stage primaryStage) throws Exception {
        FXMLLoader fxmlLoader = new FXMLLoader();
        fxmlLoader.setLocation(
            FXMLInjectionExampleMain.class.getResource("/FXMLInjectionExample.fxml"));
        fxmlLoader.setResources(ResourceBundle.getBundle("FXMLInjectionExample"));
        VBox vBox = fxmlLoader.load();
        Scene scene = new Scene(vBox);
        primaryStage.setTitle("FXML Injection Example");
        primaryStage.setScene(scene);
        primaryStage.show();
    }

    public static void main(String[] args) {
        launch(args);
    }
}
```

Notice that we also created an empty FXMLInjectionExample.properties file to use as the resource bundle to illustrate the injection of the resources field into the controller. We explain how to use resource bundles with FXML files in the next section. When the FXMLInjectionExample is run on our machine, the FXML Injection Example window in Figure 4-5 is displayed on the screen.

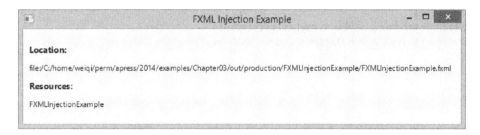

Figure 4-5. *The FXMLInjection program*

The @FXML annotation can also be used for included FXML file controller injection, and for marking controller properties of javafx.event.EventHandler type for use as event handlers in FXML files. We cover them in detail when we discuss the relevant features of the FXML file in the next section.

Exploring the Capabilities of FXML Files

In this section, we go over the features of the FXML file format. Because a major goal of the FXMLLoader is to deserialize an FXML file into Java objects, it should be no surprise that it provides facilities that help to make writing FXML files easier.

The Deserialization Power of the FXML Format

Because the features that we cover in this section have more to do with deserializing generic Java objects, we will move away from the GUI world and work with plain Java classes. We use the JavaBean defined in Listing 4-10 in our discussion. It is a made-up class meant to illustrate the different FXML features.

Listing 4-10. FXMLBasicFeaturesBean.java

```java
package projavafx.fxmlbasicfeatures;

import javafx.scene.paint.Color;

import java.util.ArrayList;
import java.util.HashMap;
import java.util.List;
import java.util.Map;

public class FXMLBasicFeaturesBean {
    private String name;
    private String address;
    private boolean flag;
    private int count;
    private Color foreground;
    private Color background;
    private Double price;
    private Double discount;
    private List<Integer> sizes;
    private Map<String, Double> profits;
```

```java
    private Long inventory;
    private List<String> products = new ArrayList<String>();
    private Map<String, String> abbreviations = new HashMap<>();

    public String getName() {
        return name;
    }

    public void setName(String name) {
        this.name = name;
    }

    public String getAddress() {
        return address;
    }

    public void setAddress(String address) {
        this.address = address;
    }

    public boolean isFlag() {
        return flag;
    }

    public void setFlag(boolean flag) {
        this.flag = flag;
    }

    public int getCount() {
        return count;
    }

    public void setCount(int count) {
        this.count = count;
    }

    public Color getForeground() {
        return foreground;
    }

    public void setForeground(Color foreground) {
        this.foreground = foreground;
    }

    public Color getBackground() {
        return background;
    }

    public void setBackground(Color background) {
        this.background = background;
    }
```

```java
public Double getPrice() {
    return price;
}

public void setPrice(Double price) {
    this.price = price;
}

public Double getDiscount() {
    return discount;
}

public void setDiscount(Double discount) {
    this.discount = discount;
}

public List<Integer> getSizes() {
    return sizes;
}

public void setSizes(List<Integer> sizes) {
    this.sizes = sizes;
}

public Map<String, Double> getProfits() {
    return profits;
}

public void setProfits(Map<String, Double> profits) {
    this.profits = profits;
}

public Long getInventory() {
    return inventory;
}

public void setInventory(Long inventory) {
    this.inventory = inventory;
}

public List<String> getProducts() {
    return products;
}

public Map<String, String> getAbbreviations() {
    return abbreviations;
}

@Override
public String toString() {
    return "FXMLBasicFeaturesBean{" +
```

```
                    "name='" + name + '\'' +
                    ",\n\taddress='" + address + '\'' +
                    ",\n\tflag=" + flag +
                    ",\n\tcount=" + count +
                    ",\n\tforeground=" + foreground +
                    ",\n\tbackground=" + background +
                    ",\n\tprice=" + price +
                    ",\n\tdiscount=" + discount +
                    ",\n\tsizes=" + sizes +
                    ",\n\tprofits=" + profits +
                    ",\n\tinventory=" + inventory +
                    ",\n\tproducts=" + products +
                    ",\n\tabbreviations=" + abbreviations +
                    '}';
    }
}
```

The FXML file in Listing 4-11 is loaded and printed out to the console in the program in Listing 4-12.

Listing 4-11. FXMLBasicFeatures.fxml

```
<?import javafx.scene.paint.Color?>
<?import projavafx.fxmlbasicfeatures.FXMLBasicFeaturesBean?>
<?import projavafx.fxmlbasicfeatures.Utilities?>
<?import java.lang.Double?>
<?import java.lang.Integer?>
<?import java.lang.Long?>
<?import java.util.HashMap?>
<?import java.lang.String?>
<FXMLBasicFeaturesBean name="John Smith"
                       flag="true"
                       count="12345"
                       xmlns:fx="http://javafx.com/fxml/1">
    <address>12345 Main St.</address>
    <foreground>#ff8800</foreground>
    <background>
        <Color red="0.0" green="1.0" blue="0.5"/>
    </background>
    <price>
        <Double fx:value="3.1415926"/>
    </price>
    <discount>
        <Utilities fx:constant="TEN_PCT"/>
    </discount>
    <sizes>
        <Utilities fx:factory="createList">
            <Integer fx:value="1"/>
            <Integer fx:value="2"/>
            <Integer fx:value="3"/>
        </Utilities>
    </sizes>
```

```
        <profits>
            <HashMap q1="1000" q2="1100" q3="1200" a4="1300"/>
        </profits>
        <fx:define>
            <Long fx:id="inv" fx:value="9765625"/>
        </fx:define>
        <inventory>
            <fx:reference source="inv"/>
        </inventory>
        <products>
            <String fx:value="widget"/>
            <String fx:value="gadget"/>
            <String fx:value="models"/>
        </products>
        <abbreviations CA="California" NY="New York" FL="Florida" MO="Missouri"/>

</FXMLBasicFeaturesBean>
```

Listing 4-12. FXMLBasicFeaturesMain.java

```java
package projavafx.fmlbasicfeatures;

import javafx.fxml.FXMLLoader;

import java.io.IOException;

public class FXMLBasicFeaturesMain {
    public static void main(String[] args) throws IOException {
        FXMLBasicFeaturesBean bean = FXMLLoader.load(
            FXMLBasicFeaturesMain.class.getResource(
                "/projavafx/fmlbasicfeatures/FXMLBasicFeatures.fxml")
        );
        System.out.println("bean = " + bean);
    }
}
```

We made use of a small utility class that contains a few constants and a factory method that creates a List<Integer>, as shown in Listing 4-13.

Listing 4-13. Utilities.java

```java
package projavafx.fmlbasicfeatures;

import java.util.ArrayList;
import java.util.List;

public class Utilities {
    public static final Double TEN_PCT = 0.1d;
    public static final Double TWENTY_PCT = 0.2d;
    public static final Double THIRTY_PCT = 0.3d;
```

```
    public static List<Integer> createList() {
        return  new ArrayList<>();
    }
}
```

The FXMLBasicFeaturesBean object is being created in the FXML file; this is indicated by the fact that the top-level element of the FXML file is FXMLBasicFeaturesBean. The name and address fields illustrate that a field can be set either as an attribute or as a subelement:

```
<FXMLBasicFeaturesBean name="John Smith"
                       flag="true"
                       count="12345"
                       xmlns:fx="http://javafx.com/fxml/1">
    <address>12345 Main St.</address>
```

The foreground and background fields illustrate two ways of setting a javafx.scene.paint.Color subelement, either through a hex string, or using a Color element (remember Color is an immutable object without a default constructor):

```
<foreground>#ff8800</foreground>
<background>
    <Color red="0.0" green="1.0" blue="0.5"/>
</background>
```

The price field illustrates a way to construct a Double object. The fx:value attribute invokes the valueOf(String) method on Double. This works on any Java class that has a factory method valueOf(String):

```
<price>
    <Double fx:value="3.1415926"/>
</price>
```

The discount field illustrates how to use a constant defined in a Java class. The fx:constant attribute accesses constant (public static final) fields of the type of its element. The following sets the discount field to Utilities.TEN_PCT, which is 0.1:

```
<discount>
    <Utilities fx:constant="TEN_PCT"/>
</discount>
```

The sizes field illustrates the use of factory methods to create objects. The fx:factory attribute invokes the specified factory method on the type of its element. In our case, it calls Utilities.createList() to create a list of Integers, which is then populated with three Integers. Notice that sizes is a read-write property. You will see an example of how a read-only list property is populated later.

```
<sizes>
    <Utilities fx:factory="createList">
        <Integer fx:value="1"/>
        <Integer fx:value="2"/>
        <Integer fx:value="3"/>
    </Utilities>
```

```
</sizes>
```

The profits field illustrates how to populate a read-write map. Here we set the profits field to a HashMap that we create with key/value pairs:

```
<profits>
    <HashMap q1="1000" q2="1100" q3="1200" a4="1300"/>
</profits>
```

The inventory field illustrates how to define an object in one place and reference it in another place. The fx:define element creates a stand-alone object that has an fx:id attribute. The fx:reference element creates a reference to an object defined elsewhere, and its source attribute points to the fx:id of a previously defined object:

```
<fx:define>
    <Long fx:id="inv" fx:value="9765625"/>
</fx:define>
<inventory>
    <fx:reference source="inv"/>
</inventory>
```

The products field illustrates how to populate a read-only list. The following fragment of FXML is equivalent to invoking bean.getProducts().addAll("widget", "gadget", "models"):

```
<products>
    <String fx:value="widget"/>
    <String fx:value="gadget"/>
    <String fx:value="models"/>
</products>
```

The abbreviations field illustrates how to populate a read-only map:

```
<abbreviations CA="California" NY="New York" FL="Florida" MO="Missouri"/>
```

When the FXMLBasicFeaturesMain program is run, the following output is printed to the console, as expected:

```
bean = FXMLBasicFeaturesBean{name='John Smith',
        address='12345 Main St.',
        flag=true,
        count=12345,
        foreground=0xff8800ff,
        background=0x00ff80ff,
        price=3.1415926,
        discount=0.1,
        sizes=[1, 2, 3],
        profits={q1=1000, q2=1100, q3=1200, a4=1300},
        inventory=9765625,
        products=[widget, gadget, models],
        abbreviations={MO=Missouri, FL=Florida, NY=New York, CA=California}}
```

Understanding Default and Static Properties

Many JavaFX classes have a default property. *Default properties* are specified with a @DefaultProperty annotation on the class. The @DefaultProperty annotation belongs to the javafx.beans package. The default property of the javafx.scene.Group class, for example, is its children property. In FXML files, when a default property is specified via a subelement, the beginning and ending tag of the default property itself can be omitted. As an example, the following snippet, which you saw in Listing 4-1.

```
<HBox fx:id="titleBox">
    <children>
        <Label fx:id="titleLabel"
               text="title"/>
        <TextField fx:id="titleTextField"
                   text="Stage Coach"/>
    </children>
</HBox>
```

can be simplified to

```
<HBox fx:id="titleBox">
    <Label fx:id="titleLabel"
           text="title"/>
    <TextField fx:id="titleTextField"
               text="Stage Coach"/>
</HBox>
```

A *static property* is a property that is set on an object not by calling a setter method on the object itself, but by calling a static method of a different class, passing both the object and the value of the property as parameters. Many of JavaFX's container Nodes have such static methods. These methods are called on a Node prior to adding it to the container to affect certain results. Static properties are represented in FXML files as attributes on the inner object (the object that is passed in as the first parameter to the static method) with a name that includes both the class name and the static method name separated by a dot. You can spot an example of a static property in Listing 4-4:

```
<WebView fx:id="webView"
         prefHeight="200.0"
         prefWidth="200.0"
         VBox.vgrow="ALWAYS"/>
```

Here we are adding a WebView to a VBox, and the VBox.vgrow attribute indicates that the FXMLLoader needs to call the following prior to adding webView to the VBox.

```
VBox.vgrow(webView, Priority.ALWAYS)
```

Static properties can appear as subelements in addition to appearing as attributes.

Understanding Attribute Resolutions and Bindings

As you have seen in earlier parts of this chapter, object properties can be represented both as attributes and as subelements. Sometimes it is as effective to model a property as a subelement or an attribute. However, the FXMLLoader will perform additional processing for attributes, making it more attractive to use attributes.

When processing attributes, the FXMLLoader will perform three kinds of attribute value resolutions and expression binding.

When an attribute's value starts with the @ character, FXMLLoader will treat the value as a location relative to the current file. This is called *location resolution*. When an attribute's value starts with a % character, FXMLLoader will treat the value as a key in a resource bundle and substitute the locale-specific value for the key. This is called *resource resolution*. When an attribute's value starts with a $ character, FXMLLoader will treat the value as a variable name, and substitute the value of the referenced variable as the value of the attribute. This is called *variable resolution*.

When an attribute's value starts with ${ and ends with }, and if the attribute represents a JavaFX property, FXMLLoader will treat the value as a binding expression, and binds the JavaFX property to the enclosed expression. This is called *expression binding*. You will learn about JavaFX properties and bindings in Chapter 3. For now simply understand that when a property is bound to an expression, every time the expression changes value, the change is reflected in the property. Supported expressions include string literals, boolean literals, numeric literals, the unary – (minus) and ! (negation) operators, the arithmetic operators (+, –, *, /, %), the logical operators (&&, ||), and the relational operators (>, >=, <, <=, ==, !=).

The ResolutionAndBindingExample, shown in Listings 4-14 to 4-19, illustrates the use of location resolution, resource resolution, and variable resolution as well as expression binding.

Listing 4-14. ResolutionAndBindingExample.fxml

```
<?xml version="1.0" encoding="UTF-8"?>

<?import javafx.geometry.Insets?>
<?import javafx.scene.control.Label?>
<?import javafx.scene.control.TextField?>
<?import javafx.scene.layout.HBox?>
<?import javafx.scene.layout.VBox?>
<?import javafx.scene.text.Font?>
<?import java.util.Date?>
<VBox id="vbox" alignment="CENTER_LEFT" maxHeight="-Infinity" maxWidth="-Infinity"
minHeight="-Infinity"
      minWidth="-Infinity" prefHeight="200.0" prefWidth="700.0" spacing="10.0"
      stylesheets="@ResolutionAndBindingExample.css" xmlns="http://javafx.com/javafx/8"
      xmlns:fx="http://javafx.com/fxml/1" fx:controller="ResolutionAndBindingController">
   <children>
      <Label text="%location">
         <font>
            <Font name="System Bold" size="14.0"/>
         </font>
      </Label>
      <Label fx:id="locationLabel" text="[location]"/>
      <Label text="%resources">
         <font>
            <Font name="System Bold" size="14.0"/>
         </font>
      </Label>
      <Label fx:id="resourcesLabel" text="[resources]"/>
      <Label text="%currentDate">
         <font>
            <Font name="System Bold" size="14.0"/>
         </font>
      </Label>
```

```
        <HBox alignment="BASELINE_LEFT" spacing="10.0">
            <children>
                <fx:define>
                    <Date fx:id="capturedDate"/>
                </fx:define>
                <Label fx:id="currentDateLabel" text="$capturedDate"/>
                <TextField fx:id="textField"/>
                <Label text="${textField.text}"/>
            </children>
        </HBox>
    </children>
    <opaqueInsets>
        <Insets/>
    </opaqueInsets>
    <padding>
        <Insets bottom="10.0" left="10.0" right="10.0" top="10.0"/>
    </padding>
</VBox>
```

Listing 4-15. ResolutionAndBindingController.java

```java
import javafx.fxml.FXML;
import javafx.scene.control.Label;

import java.net.URL;
import java.util.ResourceBundle;

public class ResolutionAndBindingController {
    @FXML
    private Label resourcesLabel;

    @FXML
    private Label locationLabel;

    @FXML
    private Label currentDateLabel;

    @FXML
    private URL location;

    @FXML
    private ResourceBundle resources;

    @FXML
    public void initialize() {
        locationLabel.setText(location.toString());
        resourcesLabel.setText(resources.getBaseBundleName() +
            " (" + resources.getLocale().getCountry() +
            ", " + resources.getLocale().getLanguage() + ")");
    }
}
```

Listing 4-16. ResolutionAndBindingExample.java

```java
import javafx.application.Application;
import javafx.fxml.FXMLLoader;
import javafx.scene.Scene;
import javafx.scene.layout.VBox;
import javafx.stage.Stage;

import java.util.ResourceBundle;

public class ResolutionAndBindingExample extends Application {
    @Override
    public void start(Stage primaryStage) throws Exception {
        FXMLLoader fxmlLoader = new FXMLLoader();
        fxmlLoader.setLocation(
            ResolutionAndBindingExample.class.getResource(
                "/ResolutionAndBindingExample.fxml"));
        fxmlLoader.setResources(
            ResourceBundle.getBundle(
                "ResolutionAndBindingExample"));
        VBox vBox = fxmlLoader.load();
        Scene scene = new Scene(vBox);
        primaryStage.setTitle("Resolution and Binding Example");
        primaryStage.setScene(scene);
        primaryStage.show();
    }

    public static void main(String[] args) {
        launch(args);
    }
}
```

Listing 4-17. ResourceAndBindingExample.properties

```
location=Location:
resources=Resources:
currentDate=CurrentDate:
```

Listing 4-18. ResolutionAndBindingExample_fr_FR.properties

```
location=Emplacement:
resources=Resources:
currentDate=Date du jour:
```

Listing 4-19. ResolutionAndBindingExample.css

```css
#vbox {
    -fx-background-color: azure ;
}
```

Location resolution is used in the FXML file to specify the location of the CSS file. The `stylesheet` attribute is set to the location "@ResolutionAndBindingExample.css":

```
<VBox id="vbox" alignment="CENTER_LEFT" maxHeight="-Infinity" maxWidth="-Infinity"
minHeight="-Infinity"
        minWidth="-Infinity" prefHeight="200.0" prefWidth="700.0" spacing="10.0"
        stylesheets="@ResolutionAndBindingExample.css" xmlns="http://javafx.com/javafx/8"
        xmlns:fx="http://javafx.com/fxml/1" fx:controller="ResolutionAndBindingController">
```

The stylesheet sets the background color of the VBox to azure. Resource resolution is used to set the text for three labels in the program:

```
<Label text="%location">
<Label text="%resources">
<Label text="%currentDate">
```

These labels will get their texts from the resource bundle that is supplied to the `FXMLLoader` before the FXML file is loaded. Both the default locale and a French locale translation of the properties file are provided. Variable resolution happens between a defined `java.util.Date` instance and a `Label`:

```
<fx:define>
    <Date fx:id="capturedDate"/>
</fx:define>
<Label fx:id="currentDateLabel" text="$capturedDate"/>
```

The defined `Date` was given the `fx:id` of `capturedDate` and the label used the variable for its text. Finally, the expression binding happens between a `TextField` and a `Label`:

```
<TextField fx:id="textField"/>
<Label text="${textField.text}"/>
```

The `TextField` was given the `fx:id` of `textField` and the label binds to the expression `textField.text`, with a result of the label mimicking what is typed in the text field. When the ResolutionAndBindingExample is run with the French locale, the Resolution and Binding Example window shown in Figure 4-6 is displayed.

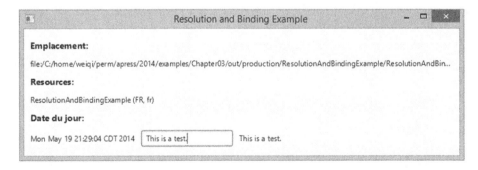

Figure 4-6. *The ResolutionAndBindingExample program*

Using Multiple FXML Files

Because the result of loading an FXML file is a JavaFX Node that can be used in a Scene, you are not limited to using only one FXML file for any Scene. You can, for example, break your scene into two or more parts and represent each part by its own FXML file. Then you can call one of the load() methods of FXMLLoader on the FXML file of each part, and assemble the resulting nodes programmatically into your scene.

The FXML file format supports another mechanism to combine separately prepared FXML files together. One FXML file can include another with an fx:include element. The fx:include element supports three attributes: the source attribute holds the location of the included FXML file; the resources attribute holds the location of the resource bundle that is used by the included FXML file; and the charset attribute holds the charset for the included FXML file. If the source attribute starts with a "/" character, it is interpreted as a path in the classpath; otherwise it is interpreted as relative to the location of the including FXML file. The resource and the charset attributes are optional. When they are not specified, their values used for loading the including FXML file are used. The builder factory and the controller factory used for loading the including FXML file are also used for loading the included FXML file.

An fx:id can be specified for an fx:include element. When an fx:id is specified, a corresponding field in the controller of the including FXML file can be specified, and the FXMLLoader will inject this field with the result of loading the included FXML file. Moreover, if the included FXML file has an fx:controller specified in its root element, that included FXML file's controller can also be injected into the including FXML file's controller, provided a properly named and typed field is available in the including file's controller to receive the injected included FXML file's controller. In the example application of this section, we use two FXML files to represent the application's UI. The including FXML file has lines like the following:

```
<BorderPane maxHeight="-Infinity"
        ...
        fx:controller="IncludeExampleTreeController">
    <fx:include fx:id="details"
               source="IncludeExampleDetail.fxml" />
```

And the included FXML has lines like the following:

```
<VBox maxHeight="-Infinity"
    ...
    fx:controller="IncludeExampleDetailController">
```

Consequently, loading the included FXML file will result in a root element of type VBox, and a controller of type IncludeExampleDetailController. The controller of the including FXML file, IncludeExampleTreeController has fields like the following:

```
@FXML
private VBox details;

@FXML
private IncludeExampleDetailController detailsController;
```

These fields will hold the loaded root and controller of the included FXML file when the including FXML file is loaded.

The complete source codes of this section's example are shown in Listings 4-20 to 4-25.

Listing 4-20. IncludeExampleTree.fxml

```xml
<?xml version="1.0" encoding="UTF-8"?>

<?import javafx.geometry.Insets?>
<?import javafx.scene.control.Label?>
<?import javafx.scene.control.TreeTableColumn?>
<?import javafx.scene.control.TreeTableView?>
<?import javafx.scene.layout.BorderPane?>
<?import javafx.scene.layout.VBox?>
<?import javafx.scene.text.Font?>
<BorderPane maxHeight="-Infinity"
            maxWidth="-Infinity"
            minHeight="-Infinity"
            minWidth="-Infinity"
            prefHeight="400.0"
            prefWidth="600.0"
            xmlns="http://javafx.com/javafx/8"
            xmlns:fx="http://javafx.com/fxml/1"
            fx:controller="IncludeExampleTreeController">
    <top>
        <Label text="Product Details"
               BorderPane.alignment="CENTER">
            <font>
                <Font name="System Bold Italic" size="36.0"/>
            </font>
        </Label>
    </top>
    <left>
        <VBox spacing="10.0">
            <children>
                <Label text="List of Products:">
                    <font>
                        <Font name="System Bold" size="12.0"/>
                    </font>
                </Label>
                <TreeTableView fx:id="treeTableView"
                               prefHeight="200.0"
                               prefWidth="200.0"
                               BorderPane.alignment="CENTER"
                               VBox.vgrow="ALWAYS">
                <columns>
                    <TreeTableColumn fx:id="category"
                                     editable="false"
                                     prefWidth="125.0"
                                     text="Category"/>
                    <TreeTableColumn fx:id="name"
                                     editable="false"
                                     prefWidth="75.0"
                                     text="Name"/>
                </columns>
```

```
                </TreeTableView>
            </children>
            <BorderPane.margin>
                <Insets/>
            </BorderPane.margin>
        </VBox>
    </left>
    <center>
        <fx:include fx:id="details"
                    source="IncludeExampleDetail.fxml"/>
    </center>
    <padding>
        <Insets bottom="10.0" left="10.0" right="10.0" top="10.0"/>
    </padding>
</BorderPane>
```

Listing 4-21. IncludeExampleDetail.fxml

```
<?xml version="1.0" encoding="UTF-8"?>

<?import javafx.geometry.Insets?>
<?import javafx.scene.control.Label?>
<?import javafx.scene.control.TextArea?>
<?import javafx.scene.layout.VBox?>
<?import javafx.scene.text.Font?>
<VBox maxHeight="-Infinity"
      maxWidth="-Infinity"
      minHeight="-Infinity"
      minWidth="-Infinity"
      prefHeight="346.0"
      prefWidth="384.0"
      spacing="10.0"
      xmlns="http://javafx.com/javafx/8"
      xmlns:fx="http://javafx.com/fxml/1"
      fx:controller="IncludeExampleDetailController">
    <children>
        <Label text="Category:">
            <font>
                <Font name="System Bold" size="12.0"/>
            </font>
        </Label>
        <Label fx:id="category" text="[Category]"/>
        <Label text="Name:">
            <font>
                <Font name="System Bold" size="12.0"/>
            </font>
        </Label>
        <Label fx:id="name" text="[Name]"/>
        <Label text="Description:">
            <font>
```

```
                    <Font name="System Bold" size="12.0"/>
                </font>
            </Label>
            <TextArea fx:id="description"
                        prefHeight="200.0"
                        prefWidth="200.0"
                        VBox.vgrow="ALWAYS"/>
        </children>
        <padding>
            <Insets bottom="10.0" left="20.0" right="10.0" top="30.0"/>
        </padding>
</VBox>
```

Listing 4-22. IncludeExampleTreeController.java

```java
import javafx.beans.property.ReadOnlyStringWrapper;
import javafx.fxml.FXML;
import javafx.scene.control.TreeItem;
import javafx.scene.control.TreeTableColumn;
import javafx.scene.control.TreeTableView;
import javafx.scene.layout.VBox;

public class IncludeExampleTreeController {
    @FXML
    private TreeTableView<Product> treeTableView;

    @FXML
    private TreeTableColumn<Product, String> category;

    @FXML
    private TreeTableColumn<Product, String> name;

    @FXML
    private VBox details;

    @FXML
    private IncludeExampleDetailController detailsController;

    @FXML
    public void initialize() {
        Product[] products = new Product[101];
        for (int i = 0; i <= 100; i++) {
            products[i] = new Product();
            products[i].setCategory("Category" + (i / 10));
            products[i].setName("Name" + i);
            products[i].setDescription("Description" + i);
        }
        TreeItem<Product> root = new TreeItem<>(products[100]);
        root.setExpanded(true);
        for (int i = 0; i < 10; i++) {
            TreeItem<Product> firstLevel =
                new TreeItem<>(products[i * 10]);
```

```
            firstLevel.setExpanded(true);
            for (int j = 1; j < 10; j++) {
                TreeItem<Product> secondLevel =
                    new TreeItem<>(products[i * 10 + j]);
                secondLevel.setExpanded(true);
                firstLevel.getChildren().add(secondLevel);
            }
            root.getChildren().add(firstLevel);
        }

        category.setCellValueFactory(param ->
            new ReadOnlyStringWrapper(param.getValue().getValue().getCategory()));
        name.setCellValueFactory(param ->
            new ReadOnlyStringWrapper(param.getValue().getValue().getName()));

        treeTableView.setRoot(root);

        treeTableView.getSelectionModel().selectedItemProperty()
            .addListener((observable, oldValue, newValue) -> {
                Product product = null;
                if (newValue != null) {
                    product = newValue.getValue();
                }
                detailsController.setProduct(product);
            });
    }
}
```

Listing 4-23. IncludeExampleDetailController.java

```
import javafx.beans.value.ChangeListener;
import javafx.fxml.FXML;
import javafx.scene.control.Label;
import javafx.scene.control.TextArea;

public class IncludeExampleDetailController {
    @FXML
    private Label category;

    @FXML
    private Label name;

    @FXML
    private TextArea description;

    private Product product;
    private ChangeListener<String> listener;

    public void setProduct(Product product) {
        if (this.product != null) {
            unhookListener();
        }
```

```
            this.product = product;
            hookTo(product);
        }

    private void unhookListener() {
        description.textProperty().removeListener(listener);
    }

    private void hookTo(Product product) {
        if (product == null) {
            category.setText("");
            name.setText("");
            description.setText("");
            listener = null;
        } else {
            category.setText(product.getCategory());
            name.setText(product.getName());
            description.setText(product.getDescription());
            listener = (observable, oldValue, newValue) ->
                product.setDescription(newValue);
            description.textProperty().addListener(listener);
        }
    }
}
```

Listing 4-24. IncludeExample.java

```
import javafx.application.Application;
import javafx.fxml.FXMLLoader;
import javafx.scene.Scene;
import javafx.scene.layout.BorderPane;
import javafx.stage.Stage;

public class IncludeExample extends Application {
    @Override
    public void start(Stage primaryStage) throws Exception {
        FXMLLoader fxmlLoader = new FXMLLoader();
        fxmlLoader.setLocation(
            IncludeExample.class.getResource("IncludeExampleTree.fxml"));
        final BorderPane borderPane = fxmlLoader.load();
        Scene scene = new Scene(borderPane, 600, 400);
        primaryStage.setTitle("Include Example");
        primaryStage.setScene(scene);
        primaryStage.show();
    }

    public static void main(String[] args) {
        launch(args);
    }
}
```

166

Listing 4-25. `Product.java`

```java
public class Product {
    private String category;
    private String name;
    private String description;

    public String getCategory() {
        return category;
    }

    public void setCategory(String category) {
        this.category = category;
    }

    public String getDescription() {
        return description;
    }

    public void setDescription(String description) {
        this.description = description;
    }

    public String getName() {
        return name;
    }

    public void setName(String name) {
        this.name = name;
    }
}
```

In this IncludeExample program, we build up the UI in two FXML files, each one backed by its own controller. The UI features a `TreeTableView` on the left side, and some `Label`s and a `TextArea` on the right side. The `TreeTableView` is loaded with dummy `Product` data. When a row in the left `TreeTableView` is selected, the corresponding `Product` is shown on the right side. You can edit the `Product`'s description field using the `TextArea` on the right side. As you navigate away from an old row to a new row on the left side, the `Product` on the right side reflects the change. However, all the changes that you made to previously displayed `Product`s are retained in the model. When you navigate back to a modified `Product`, your changes will be shown again. The `TreeTableView` class is covered in more detail in Chapter 6.

We used a `ChangeListener<String>` that is attached to the `TextField`'s `textProperty` to synchronize the text in the `TextField` and the `description` in the `Product`. JavaFX properties and change listeners are part of the JavaFX Properties and Bindings API. We cover this API in the next chapter.

When the IncludeExample is run, the Include Example window shown in Figure 4-7 is displayed.

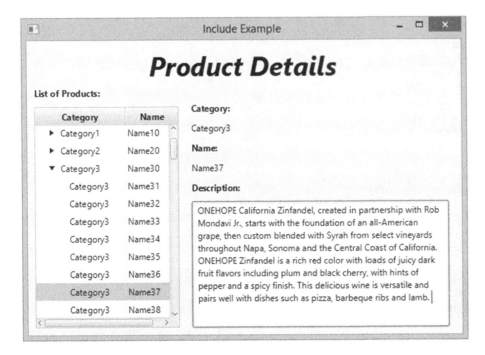

Figure 4-7. *The IncludeExample program*

Creating Custom Components Using fx:root

The `fx:include` element allows us to attach one FXML file into another FXML file. Similarly, the `fx:root` element allows us to attach an FXML file to a Node that is provided in code. The `fx:root` element must be the top-level element in an FXML file. It must be supplied with a `type` attribute, which determines the type of the Node that needs to be created in code to load this FXML file.

In its simplest form, you can change any one of the earlier FXML files' top-level element from

```
<SomeType ...
```

to

```
<fx:root type="some.package.SomeType" ...
```

and instantiate SomeType in code and set it as the root in the FXMLLoader before loading the FXML file, like the following:

```
SomeType someType = new SomeType();
fxmlLoader.setRoot(someType);
fxmlLoader.load();
```

The next example goes one step further. It defines a class that extends the `fx:root` type of the FXML file, and serves as both the root and the controller of the FXML file. It loads the FXML file in its constructor, and uses the `initialize()` method to set up the desired relationships between the nodes that are constructed in the FXML file. This class can then be used as if it is a native JavaFX node. Classes that are constructed this way are called *custom components*.

The custom component we define here is a simple *composite* custom component, meaning that it is composed of several nodes that together fulfill some business requirement. The custom component we create in this example is called ProdId. It's designed to help with data entry of product ID that must have the form "A-123456" where there is only one character before the dash, and it must be "A" or "B" or "C." There could be up to six characters after the dash. This program is shown in Listings 4-26 to 4-28.

Listing 4-26. `ProdId.fxml`

```xml
<?xml version="1.0" encoding="UTF-8"?>

<?import javafx.scene.control.Label?>
<?import javafx.scene.control.TextField?>
<fx:root type="javafx.scene.layout.HBox"
         alignment="BASELINE_LEFT"
         maxHeight="-Infinity"
         maxWidth="-Infinity"
         minHeight="-Infinity"
         minWidth="-Infinity"
         xmlns="http://javafx.com/javafx/8"
         xmlns:fx="http://javafx.com/fxml/1">
    <children>
        <TextField fx:id="prefix" prefColumnCount="1"/>
        <Label text="-"/>
        <TextField fx:id="prodCode" prefColumnCount="6"/>
    </children>
</fx:root>
```

Listing 4-27. `ProdId.java`

```java
package projavafx.customcomponent;

import javafx.beans.property.SimpleStringProperty;
import javafx.beans.property.StringProperty;
import javafx.fxml.FXML;
import javafx.fxml.FXMLLoader;
import javafx.scene.control.TextField;
import javafx.scene.layout.HBox;

import java.io.IOException;

public class ProdId extends HBox {

    @FXML
    private TextField prefix;

    @FXML
    private TextField prodCode;

    private StringProperty prodId = new SimpleStringProperty();
```

```java
    public ProdId() throws IOException {
        FXMLLoader fxmlLoader = new FXMLLoader(ProdId.class.getResource("ProdId.fxml"));
        fxmlLoader.setRoot(this);
        fxmlLoader.setController(this);
        fxmlLoader.load();
    }

    @FXML
    public void initialize() {
        prefix.textProperty().addListener((observable, oldValue, newValue) -> {
            switch (newValue) {
                case "A":
                case "B":
                case "C":
                    prodCode.requestFocus();
                    break;
                default:
                    prefix.setText("");
            }
        });
        prodCode.textProperty().addListener((observable, oldValue, newValue) -> {
            if (newValue.length() > 6) {
                prodCode.setText(newValue.substring(0, 6));
            } else if (newValue.length() == 0) {
                prefix.requestFocus();
            }
        });
        prodId.bind(prefix.textProperty().concat("-").concat(prodCode.textProperty()));
    }

    public String getProdId() {
        return prodId.get();
    }

    public StringProperty prodIdProperty() {
        return prodId;
    }

    public void setProdId(String prodId) {
        this.prodId.set(prodId);
    }
}
```

Listing 4-28. CustomComponent.java

```java
package projavafx.customcomponent;

import javafx.application.Application;
import javafx.geometry.Insets;
import javafx.geometry.Pos;
import javafx.scene.Scene;
import javafx.scene.control.Label;
```

```java
import javafx.scene.layout.HBox;
import javafx.scene.layout.VBox;
import javafx.scene.text.Font;
import javafx.stage.Stage;

public class CustomComponent extends Application {
    @Override
    public void start(Stage primaryStage) throws Exception {
        VBox vBox = new VBox(10);
        vBox.setPadding(new Insets(10, 10, 10, 10));
        vBox.setAlignment(Pos.BASELINE_CENTER);

        final Label prodIdLabel = new Label("Enter Product Id:");
        final ProdId prodId = new ProdId();

        final Label label = new Label();
        label.setFont(Font.font(48));
        label.textProperty().bind(prodId.prodIdProperty());

        HBox hBox = new HBox(10);
        hBox.setPadding(new Insets(10, 10, 10, 10));
        hBox.setAlignment(Pos.BASELINE_LEFT);
        hBox.getChildren().addAll(prodIdLabel, prodId);

        vBox.getChildren().addAll(hBox, label);
        Scene scene = new Scene(vBox);
        primaryStage.setTitle("Custom Component Example");
        primaryStage.setScene(scene);
        primaryStage.show();
    }

    public static void main(String[] args) {
        launch(args);
    }
}
```

Notice that in the main program CustomComponent class, we did not load any FXML files. We simply instantiated ProdId, and proceed to use it as if it is a native JavaFX node. The FXML file simply put two TextFields and a Label in an HBox type fx:root. No fx:controller is set because we want to set it in the constructor of the ProdId class. In addition to the two injected TextFields, we have another StringProperty field called prodId, for which we defined a getter getProdId(), a setter setProdId(), and a property getter prodIdProperty().

```java
private StringProperty prodId = new SimpleStringProperty();

public String getProdId() {
    return prodId.get();
}

public StringProperty prodIdProperty() {
    return prodId;
}
```

```
public void setProdId(String prodId) {
    this.prodId.set(prodId);
}
```

The validation requirement and the convenience functionality are in the initialize() method, which will be called by the FXMLLoader when it has finished loading the FXML file. We hooked up ChangeListeners to the textProperty of the two TextFields, and allow only valid changes to occur. We also move the cursor to prodCode when the prefix is filled with the correct data. Likewise, when we back off from the prodCode field, the cursor will naturally jump to the prefix text field.

```
@FXML
public void initialize() {
    prefix.textProperty().addListener((observable, oldValue, newValue) -> {
        switch (newValue) {
            case "A":
            case "B":
            case "C":
                prodCode.requestFocus();
                break;
            default:
                prefix.setText("");
        }
    });
    prodCode.textProperty().addListener((observable, oldValue, newValue) -> {
        if (newValue.length() > 6) {
            prodCode.setText(newValue.substring(0, 6));
        } else if (newValue.length() == 0) {
            prefix.requestFocus();
        }
    });
    prodId.bind(prefix.textProperty().concat("-").concat(prodCode.textProperty()));
}
```

When the CustomComponent program is run, the Custom Component Example window shown in Figure 4-8 is displayed.

Figure 4-8. *The CustomComponent program*

Event Handling Using Scripting or Controller Properties

In the last section, we introduced you to using a method of the controller as an event handler for a node in an FXML file. JavaFX allows two more ways to set up event handlers in FXML files. One way is to use scripting. Any JSR-223 compatible `javax.script`-based scripting engine can be used. The language to be used for scripting must be specified at the top of the FXML file. To use the Nashorn JavaScript engine that ships with Oracle JDK 8, the following processing instruction must be present at the top of the FXML file:

```
<?language javascript?>
```

The `fx:script` element is used to introduce scripts. Both inline scripts and external file scripts are supported. The following is an inline script:

```
<fx:script>
    function actionHandler(event) {
        webView.getEngine().load(address.getText());
    }
</fx:script>
```

The external script takes the following form:

```
<fx:script source="myscript.js"/>
```

Any node in the FXML file that has an `fx:id` can be accessed from the scripting environment by their `fx:id` names. If the FXML file has a controller, then the controller is available as a variable named `controller`. Variables declared in `fx:script` sections are also available for use as variables in attributes in the rest of the FXML file. To use the `actionHandler(event)` function defined in the `fx:script` section as an event handler, it can be specified as follows:

```
<TextField fx:id="address"
           onAction="actionHandler(event)"
```

▨ **Caution**   You can use either a function that takes no argument if your event handler does not need to inspect the event object, or a function that takes one argument as the value of the event handler attribute, such as `onAction`. If you call a function with one argument, then you must pass the system-provided event variable into it.

The ScriptingExample in Listings 4-29 and 4-30 illustrates event handling using scripting.

Listing 4-29. `ScriptingExample.fxml`

```
<?xml version="1.0" encoding="UTF-8"?>

<?language javascript?>

<?import javafx.geometry.Insets?>
<?import javafx.scene.control.Button?>
<?import javafx.scene.control.TextField?>
<?import javafx.scene.layout.HBox?>
```

```
<?import javafx.scene.layout.VBox?>
<?import javafx.scene.web.WebView?>
<VBox maxHeight="-Infinity"
      maxWidth="-Infinity"
      minHeight="-Infinity"
      minWidth="-Infinity"
      prefHeight="400.0"
      prefWidth="600.0"
      spacing="10.0"
      xmlns="http://javafx.com/javafx/8"
      xmlns:fx="http://javafx.com/fxml/1">
    <fx:script>
        function actionHandler(event) {
            webView.getEngine().load(address.getText());
        }
        </fx:script>
    <children>
        <HBox spacing="10.0">
            <children>
                <TextField fx:id="address"
                           onAction="actionHandler(event)"
                           HBox.hgrow="ALWAYS">
                    <padding>
                        <Insets bottom="4.0" left="4.0" right="4.0" top="4.0"/>
                    </padding>
                </TextField>
                <Button fx:id="loadButton"
                        mnemonicParsing="false"
                        onAction="actionHandler(event)"
                        text="Load"/>
            </children>
        </HBox>
        <WebView fx:id="webView"
                 prefHeight="200.0"
                 prefWidth="200.0"
                 VBox.vgrow="ALWAYS"/>
    </children>
    <padding>
        <Insets bottom="10.0" left="10.0" right="10.0" top="10.0"/>
    </padding>
</VBox>
```

Listing 4-30. ScriptingExample.java

```
import javafx.application.Application;
import javafx.fxml.FXMLLoader;
import javafx.scene.Scene;
import javafx.scene.layout.VBox;
import javafx.stage.Stage;
```

```
public class ScriptingExample extends Application {
    @Override
    public void start(Stage primaryStage) throws Exception {
        FXMLLoader fxmlLoader = new FXMLLoader();
        fxmlLoader.setLocation(
            ScriptingExample.class.getResource("/ScriptingExample.fxml"));
        final VBox vBox = fxmlLoader.load();
        Scene scene = new Scene(vBox, 600, 400);
        primaryStage.setTitle("Scripting Example");
        primaryStage.setScene(scene);
        primaryStage.show();
    }

    public static void main(String[] args) {
        launch(args);
    }
}
```

When the ScriptingExample is run, the Scripting Example window very similar to Figure 4-4 is displayed.

You can also specify an event handler with the variable syntax:

```
<TextField fx:id="address"
        onAction="$controller.actionHandler"
```

This will set the `actionHandler` property from the controller as the event handler of the `onActionEvent`. In the controller, the `actionHandler` property should have the correct event handler type. For the `onAction` event, the property should be like the following:

```
@FXML
public EventHandler<ActionEvent> getActionHandler() {
    return event -> {
        // handle the event
    };
}
```

Now that we have a thorough understanding of the FXML file format, we can effectively take advantage of the GUI editing convenience in creating FXML files.

Using JavaFX Scene Builder

In the previous sections, you learned the fundamentals of the FXML file format. That knowledge should come in very handy when trying to use and comprehend the JavaFX Scene Builder tool. In this last section of the chapter, we dive into the usages of the JavaFX Scene Builder.

Because laying out a UI is a highly subjective, sometimes artistic endeavor, a lot depends on the application at hand and the design sensibilities of the UI and user experience teams. We do not pretend to know the best ways of doing UI design. So in this section, we give you a guided tour of the JavaFX Scene Builder 2.0 itself, point out to you the various parts of the UI designer, and discuss how to turn the knobs and switch the gears to achieve a desired result.

Overview of JavaFX Scene Builder

When you start JavaFX Scene Builder, the screen looks like Figure 4-9.

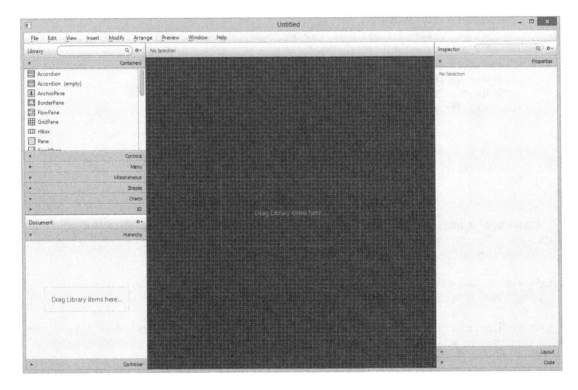

Figure 4-9. *The JavaFX Scene Builder program*

When first started, the JavaFX Scene Builder UI has a menu bar at the top, two accordion containers named Library and Document on the left side of the screen, a Content panel in the middle of the screen, and an accordion container named Inspector on the right of the screen.

Understanding the Menu Bar and Items

There are nine menus in JavaFX Scene Builder. Let's examine them one by one.

The File menu is shown in Figure 4-10.

Figure 4-10. *The File menu*

The New, Open, Save, Save As, Revert to Saved, Reveal in Explorer (or Finder, or Desktop), Close Window, and Exit menu items do pretty much what you think they should do. The New from Template menu item creates a new FXML file from an existing template. The list of templates is shown in Figure 4-11.

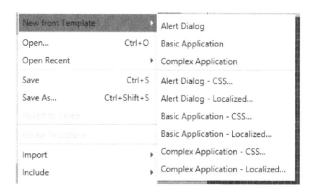

Figure 4-11. *The templates*

The Import menu item allows you to copy the content of another FXML file into the current FXML file. It also allows you to add image and media files to the current FXML file. Such imported files are wrapped in an `ImageView` or `MediaView` node. The Include menu item allows you to add an `fx:include` element into the current FXML file. The Close Window menu item closes the FXML file being edited in the current window. The Preferences menu item allows you to set certain preferences that control how JavaFX Scene Builder looks. The Quit menu item allows you to exit the JavaFX Scene Builder application entirely. It will ask you to save any unsaved files before shutting the application down.

The Edit menu is shown in Figure 4-12.

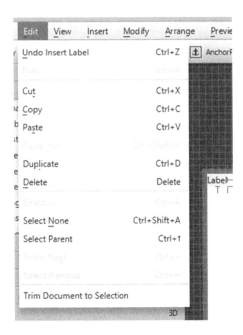

Figure 4-12. *The Edit menu*

The Undo, Redo, Cut, Copy, Paste, Paste Into, Duplicate, Delete, Select All, Select None, Select Parent, Select Next, and Select Previous menu items all perform their normal duties. The Trim Document to Selection menu item deletes everything that is not selected.

The View menu is shown in Figure 4-13.

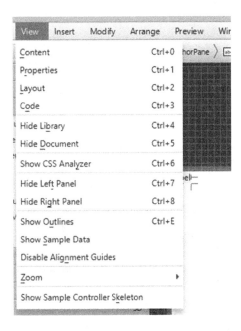

Figure 4-13. *The View menu*

The Content menu item puts the focus on the Content panel in the middle of the screen. The Properties, Layout, and Code menu items put the focus on the Property, Layout, or Code sections in the Inspector panel on the right side of the screen. The Hide Library command hides the Library panel on the top of the left side of the screen. The menu item will change to Show Library once the Library is hidden. The Hide Document menu item does the same to the Document panel on the bottom of the left side of the screen. The Show CSS Analyzer menu item shows the CSS Analyzer, which is initially not shown. The Hide Left Panel and Hide Right Panel menu items hide the left panel (the Library panel and the Document panel) or the Right panel (the Inspector panel). The Show Outlines menu item shows the outlines of the items. The Show Sample Data menu item will show sample data for `TreeView`, `TableView`, and `TreeTableView` nodes to help you visualize the node at work. The sample data are not saved with the FXML file. The Disable Alignment Guides menu item disables the alignment guidelines that are shown when you move a node around in a container in the Content panel. These alignment guidelines help you to position the nodes in the right spot on the screen. The Zoom menu item allows you to change the magnification rate of the Content panel. The Show Sample Controller Skeleton menu item will open a dialog box showing a skeleton controller class declaration based on the controller setting made in the Document panel and the `fx:id`s declared for the nodes in the FXML file.

Figure 4-14 shows the JavaFX Scene Builder screen with the CSS Analyzer shown.

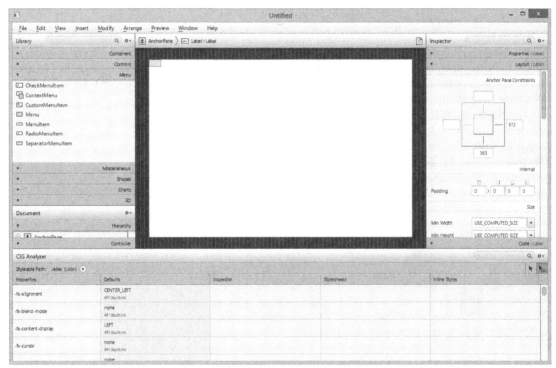

Figure 4-14. *The JavaFX Scene Builder screen with the CSS Analyzer shown*

The Insert menu is shown in Figure 4-15.

Figure 4-15. *The Insert menu*

The Insert menu contains submenus and menu items that allow you to insert different kinds of nodes into the Content panel. The submenus and their menu items represent the same hierarchy as in the Library panel. They include the Containers, Controls, Menu, Miscellaneous, Shapes, Charts, and 3D categories. We cover these nodes in more detail in subsequent chapters.

The Modify menu is shown in Figure 4-16.

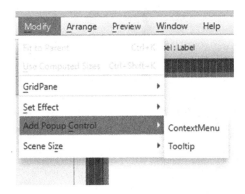

Figure 4-16. *The Modify menu*

The Fit to Parent menu item will expand the selected node to fill an AnchorPane container and anchor the node to the parent on all sides. The Use Computed Sizes menu item will resize the selected element to USE_COMPUTED_SIZE. The GridPane submenu contains items that work with the GridPane container. The Set Effect submenu contains items for each effect that can be set on the current node. The Add Popup Control allows you to add a ContextMenu or a Tooltip to the selected node. The Scene Size submenu allows you to change the size of the scene to some popular sizes, including 320×240 (QVGA), 640×480 (VGA), 1280×800, and 1920×1080.

The Arrange menu is shown in Figure 4-17.

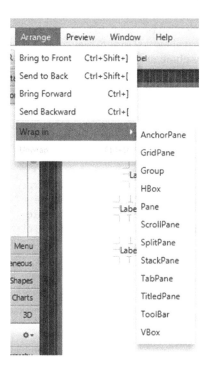

Figure 4-17. *The Arrange menu*

The Bring to Front, Send to Back, Bring Forward, and Send Backward menu items move the selected node to the front, back, up, or down the z-order of overlapping nodes. The Wrap in submenu contains items for each container type and allows you to wrap a group of selected nodes into the container. For example, you can choose to wrap two adjacent Labels into an HBox. The Unwrap menu item removes the container from the selected node.

The Preview menu is shown in Figure 4-18.

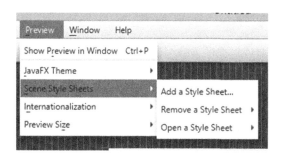

Figure 4-18. *The Preview menu*

The Show Preview in Window menu item allows you to preview the scene in a live window to see how it works in real life. This is the most useful menu item because you will be using it many times. The JavaFX Theme submenu contains various themes that you can preview the scene with. The Scene Style Sheets submenu contains items that allow you to add, remove, or edit a style sheet that is applied to the scene during the preview. The Internationalization submenu contains items that allow you to add, remove, or edit a resource bundle that is used during the preview. The Preview Size submenu contains items for the preferred screen size during the preview.

The Window menu allows you to switch between multiple FXML files that are being edited at the same time.

The Help menu shows the online help and the about box for JavaFX Scene Builder.

Understanding the Library Panel

The Library panel lives in the top portion of the left panel, and can be hidden using the View ➤ Hide Library menu item. It holds the containers and nodes that you can use to build a UI. Figure 4-19 shows the Library panel with its Containers drawer open, showing some of the containers. You can click the other drawers to see what they contain. Figure 4-20 shows the Library panel with its Controls drawer open, showing some of the controls.

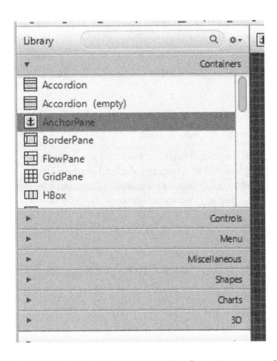

Figure 4-19. *The Library panel with its Containers drawer open*

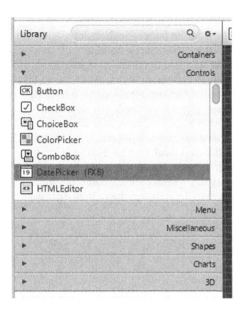

Figure 4-20. *The Library panel with its Controls drawer open*

There is a search box at the top of the Library panel. You can type in the name of a container or a control or something that belongs to one of the other drawers into the search box. As you type, the Library panel will change its display from the accordion arrangement to a single list with all the nodes whose names match the name entered in the search box. This allows you to find a node by name quickly without having to go through the drawers one by one. Figure 4-21 shows the Library panel in search mode. To exit search mode, simply click the x mark on the right end of the search box.

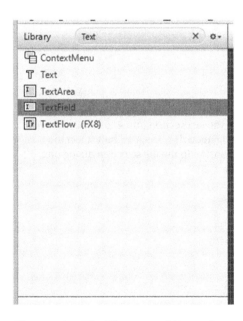

Figure 4-21. *The Library panel in search mode*

Once a container or a node is found, you can drag it to the Content panel, drag it to the Hierarchy tree in the Document panel, or double-click it. Bringing containers to the Content panel and then populating the containers with controls and other nodes is how you build up a UI in the JavaFX Scene Builder.

To the right of the search box is a menu button that contains several menu items and a submenu that alters the Library panel's behavior. Figure 4-22 shows what is available in this menu button. The View as List menu item changes the Library panel from displaying its nodes in several sections into displaying its nodes all together without sections. The View as Sections changes the Library panel from displaying its nodes in one list into displaying its nodes in several sections. The Import JAR/FXML File menu item allows you to import an external jar file or FXML file into JavaFX Scene Builder as a custom component. The Import Selection menu item allows you to import the currently selected nodes into JavaFX Scene Builder as custom components. The Custom Library Folder submenu contains two menu items. The Reveal in Explorer menu item opens the folder that holds the custom components in the operating system's File Explorer (or Finder), allowing you to remove any imported custom libraries. The Show JAR Analysis Report menu item displays a report showing JavaFX Scene Builder's assessment of the imported jar files.

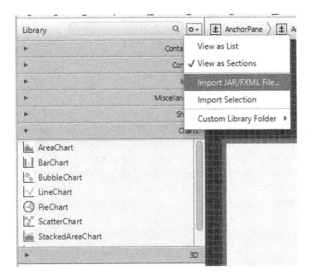

Figure 4-22. *The Library panel with its menu open*

To illustrate the importing of a custom component into JavaFX Scene Builder, we package the class files and the FXML file from the CustomComponent example from the last section into a CustomComponent.jar file. We then invoke the Import JAR/FXML File menu item, navigate to the directory, and select the CustomComponent.jar file to import. As soon as we click the Open button in the file selection dialog box, JavaFX Scene Builder opens the Import dialog box, shown in Figure 4-23.

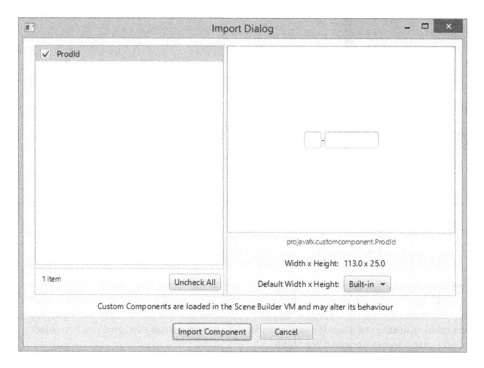

Figure 4-23. *The Import dialog for importing* `CustomComponent.jar`

We can examine each custom component included in the jar file by clicking the custom component name in the list on the left. Information about the selected custom component, including a visual representation of the custom component, is displayed on the right side of the screen. We can select which custom components to import by selecting the check box by the name of the component. We then click the Import Component button to finish the importing process. After importing, the ProdId custom component shows up in the Library panel's Custom section, and can be added to any further UIs that are built.

Understanding the Document Panel

The Document panel lives in the bottom portion of the left panel, and can be hidden using the View ➤ Hide Document menu item. It holds two sections. The Hierarchy section displays a tree view of all the nodes that are added to the Content panel, organized by the containment relationship. Because the layout of the nodes in the Content panel might make it tricky to select a node from the Content panel, it might be easier to make the selection in the Hierarchy section in the Document panel.

Figure 4-24 shows the Hierarchy section of the Document panel for the FXML file in the FXMLLoaderExample in Listing 4-4. You can see the expanded node tree with the WebView node selected.

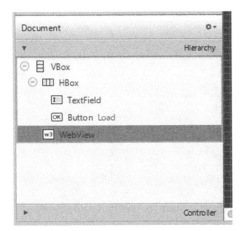

Figure 4-24. *The Hierarchy section of the Document panel for* `FXMLLoaderExample.fxml`

The Controller section displays information about the controller of the FXML file. Figure 4-25 shows the Controller section of the Document panel for the FXML file in the FXMLInjectionExample in Listing 4-7. You can set the name of the controller class in this section. You can also choose to use the `fx:root` construct for the FXML file in this section. You also see a list of nodes with `fx:ids` that are already set, and you can select the nodes by clicking on the row in the Assigned fx:id table.

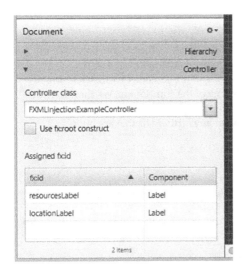

Figure 4-25. *The Controller section of the Document panel for* `FXMLInjectionExample.fxml`

There is a menu button in the top right corner of the Document panel. It contains a Hierarchy Displays submenu that has three menu items, as shown in Figure 4-26. The Info menu item causes the Hierarchy section to display each node with its general information, usually what is also displayed in the Content panel for the same node. The fx:id menu item causes the Hierarchy section to display each node with its fx:id if it has been set. The Node Id menu item causes the Hierarchy section to display each node with its node ID if it has been set. The node ID is used by CSS to find the node and to manipulate the node's styles.

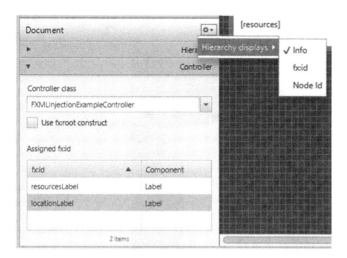

Figure 4-26. *The Document panel with its menu open*

Understanding the Content Panel

The Content panel is where the UI is composed. You first drag a container to the Content panel. You then drag other nodes to the Content panel and position then onto the container node. As you drag your nodes, red guidelines will appear as the node you drag reaches certain alignment and spacing positions. With the help of these guidelines, you should be able to create visually pleasing UIs.

Above the Content panel, there is a bread-crumb bar that shows the path of the selected node in the content area. This allows you to easily navigate to the containing nodes of the currently selected node. JavaFX Scene Builder will display warning and error messages in this bar when the situation arises.

One handy feature of JavaFX Scene Builder is that when you have several nodes selected, you can go to the context menu by right-clicking the selected nodes, choosing the Wrap in submenu, and then selecting one of the container types. You can also Unwrap a node this way, removing any containers that contain the node.

Figure 4-27 shows the `IncludeExampleTree.fxml` file from Listing 4-20 being edited in JavaFX Scene Builder.

Figure 4-27. The `IncludeExampleTree.fxml` file being edited in JavaFX Scene Builder

Understanding the Inspector Panel

The Inspector panel lives in the right panel and can be hidden using the View ➤ Hide Right Panel menu item. It contains the Properties, Layout, and Code sections. The Properties section lists all the generic properties of the selected node in the Content panel. You can set the properties by changing the values shown here. You can also change a property back to its default value by invoking the small menu button to the right of the property. You can set the node ID in the ID property editor in the Properties section. Figure 4-28 shows the Properties section of the Inspector panel.

Figure 4-28. *The Properties section of the Inspector panel*

The Layout section lists all layout-related properties of the currently selected node. Figure 4-29 shows the Layout section of the Inspector panel.

Figure 4-29. *The Layout section of the Inspector panel*

The Code section lists all the event handlers the selected node in the Content panel could have. It also allows you to set the fx:id for the selected node. You can hook up the event handlers in the Code section in any way you want, but the most convenient way of providing event handlers is to set them to properly signatured methods in the controller. Figure 4-30 shows the Code section of the Inspector panel.

Figure 4-30. *The Code section of the Inspector panel*

Summary

In this chapter, you learned the declarative way of creating a UI in JavaFX. You learned the following important tools and information:

- FXML files are the carriers of declarative UI information, and are central assets of JavaFX projects.

- FXML files are loaded into JavaFX applications by `FXMLLoader`. The result of the loading is a node that can be incorporated into a `Scene`.

- FXML files can have a companion controller class that performs programmatical functions, such as event handling, at runtime on behalf of the nodes declared in the FXML file.

- FXML files can be edited easily in your favorite Java IDEs with smart suggestions and completions.

- FXML files can also be edited in Gluon Scene Builder 9.0, an open source tool for editing FXML files.

- The JavaFX Scene Builder is a highly productive tool for specifying JavaFX UIs. You can add containers, controls, and other JavaFX nodes into the content of an FXML file.

- You can set up a controller and define the `fx:id`s of the various nodes in the scene.

- You can organize the hierarchical information in an FXML file by manipulating the containers, controls, and other nodes in the Hierarchy section of the Document panel.

- You can manipulate the attributes of nodes in an FXML file by using the Properties, Layout, and Code sections in the Inspector panel.

- You can visually compose your UI in the Content panel.

- You can analyze the CSS of the UI with the CSS Analyzer.

Resources

- The Gluon Scene Builder information site:

  `http://gluonhq.com/products/scene-builder`

- Jasper Pott's blog post announcing the release of JavaFX Scene Builder 2.0: `http://fxexperience.com/2014/05/announcing-scenebuilder-2-0/`

- A nine-minute video showing JavaFX Scene Builder 2.0's capabilities (accompanies Jasper Pott's announcement): `https://www.youtube.com/watch?v=ijOHwRAlCmo&feature=youtu.be`

- The e(fx)clipse Eclipse plug-in to provide JavaFX support for Eclipse IDEs: `www.eclipse.org/efxclipse/install.html`

CHAPTER 5

Collections and Concurrency

> *When you know a thing, to hold that you know it; and when you do not know a thing, to allow that you do not know it—this is knowledge.*
>
> —Confucius

After the fast-paced exploration of JavaFX UI controls in Chapter 4, we refocus our attention on some of the lower level facilities of JavaFX in this chapter.

Recall that in Chapter 4 you learned about the Observable interface and one of its subinterfaces ObservableValue. In this chapter, we examine four other subinterfaces of Observable—ObservableList, ObservableMap, ObservableSet, and ObservableArray—rounding out the story of the Observable family of interfaces and classes.

We then cover concurrency in JavaFX. We explain the JavaFX threading model, pointing out the most important threads present in a JavaFX application. We look at the rules that you must follow to ensure your JavaFX application is responsive to user inputs and not locked up by event handlers that take too long to execute. We also show you how the javafx.concurrent framework can be used to offload long-running routines to background threads.

We conclude this chapter with examples that show how a JavaFX scene graph can be embedded into a Swing application using JFXPanel, how it can be embedded into an SWT application using FXCanvas, paying attention to how to make the JavaFX event thread play nicely with the Swing event dispatching thread, and how Swing components can be embedded into a JavaFX scene using SwingNode.

Understanding Observable Collections and Arrays

As we saw in Chapter 4, the Observable interface has five direct subinterfaces—the ObservableValue interface, the ObservableList interface, the ObservableMap interface, the ObservableSet interface, and the ObservableArray interface. We learned that the ObservableValue interface plays a central role in the JavaFX Properties and Bindings framework.

The ObservableList, ObservableMap, ObservableSet, and ObservableArray interfaces reside in the javafx.collections package, and are referred to as the JavaFX observable collections and arrays. In addition to extending the Observable interface, ObservableList, ObservableMap, and ObservableSet also extend the java.util.List, java.util.Map, and java.util.Set interfaces, respectively, making them genuine collections in the eyes of the Java collections framework. You can call all the Java collections framework methods you are familiar with on objects of these interfaces and expect exactly the same results. What the JavaFX observable collections and arrays provide in addition to the stock Java collections framework are notifications to registered listeners. Because they are Observables, you can register InvalidationListeners with the JavaFX observable collections objects and be notified when the content of the observable collections and arrays becomes invalid.

Each of the JavaFX observable collections and arrays interfaces supports a change event that conveys more detailed information of the change. We examine the JavaFX observable collections and arrays and the change events that they support in the following sections.

Understanding ObservableList

Figure 5-1 is a UML diagram showing the ObservableList and supporting interfaces.

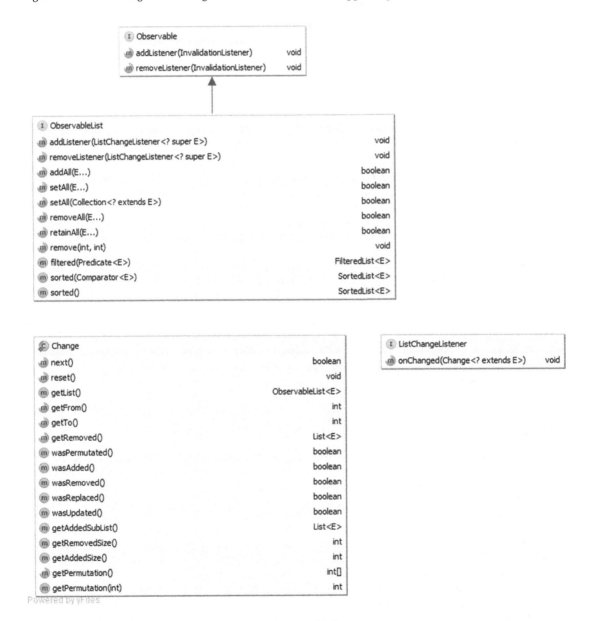

Figure 5-1. *Key interfaces that support the JavaFX observable list*

To prevent clutter, we omitted the java.util.List interface from the diagram in Figure 5-1. The java.util.List interface is the other super interface of ObservableList. The following two methods on the ObservableList interface allow you to register and unregister ListChangeListeners:

- addListener(ListChangeListener<? super E> listener)

- removeListener(ListChangeListener<? super E> listener)

The following additional methods on ObservableList make working with the interface easier:

- addAll(E... elements)

- setAll(E... elements)

- setAll(Collection<? extends E> col)

- removeAll(E... elements)

- retainAll(E... elements)

- remove(int from, int to)

- filtered(Predicate<E>)

- sorted(Comparator<E>)

- sorted()

The filtered() and the two sorted() methods return a FilteredList or a SortedList that wraps the ObservableList. When the original ObservableList is mutated, the wrapper FilteredList and SortedList reflect the changes.

The ListChangeListener interface has only one method: onChange(ListChangeListener.Change<? extends E> change). This method is called back when the content of the ObservableList is manipulated. Notice that this method's parameter type is the nested class Change that is declared in the ListChangeListener interface. We show you how to use the ListChangeListener.Change class in the next subsection. For now, we look at a simple example in Listing 5-1 illustrating the firing of invalidation and list change events when an ObservableList is manipulated.

Listing 5-1. ObservableListExample.java

```java
package com.projavafx.collections;

import javafx.beans.Observable;
import javafx.collections.FXCollections;
import javafx.collections.ObservableList;

import java.util.Arrays;
import java.util.Iterator;
import java.util.List;

import static javafx.collections.ListChangeListener.Change;

public class ObservableListExample {
    public static void main(String[] args) {
        ObservableList<String> strings = FXCollections.observableArrayList();
```

```java
        strings.addListener((Observable observable) -> {
            System.out.println("\tlist invalidated");
        });

        strings.addListener((Change<? extends String> change) -> {
            System.out.println("\tstrings = " + change.getList());
        });

        System.out.println("Calling add(\"First\"): ");
        strings.add("First");

        System.out.println("Calling add(0, \"Zeroth\"): ");
        strings.add(0, "Zeroth");

        System.out.println("Calling addAll(\"Second\", \"Third\"): ");
        strings.addAll("Second", "Third");

        System.out.println("Calling set(1, \"New First\"): ");
        strings.set(1, "New First");

        final List<String> list = Arrays.asList("Second_1", "Second_2");
        System.out.println("Calling addAll(3, list): ");
        strings.addAll(3, list);

        System.out.println("Calling remove(2, 4): ");
        strings.remove(2, 4);

        final Iterator<String> iterator = strings.iterator();
        while (iterator.hasNext()) {
            final String next = iterator.next();
            if (next.contains("t")) {
                System.out.println("Calling remove() on iterator: ");
                iterator.remove();
            }
        }

        System.out.println("Calling removeAll(\"Third\", \"Fourth\"): ");
        strings.removeAll("Third", "Fourth");
    }
}
```

Unlike the Java collections framework, where the public API contains both the interfaces, such as List, Map, and Set, and concrete implementations of the interfaces that you can instantiate, such as ArrayList, HashMap, and HashSet, the JavaFX observable collections framework provides only the interfaces ObservableList, ObservableMap, ObservableSet, and ObservableArray. The concrete implementation classes are not public, but you have to use the utility class FXCollections to obtain an object of a JavaFX observable collections and arrays. In Listing 5-1, we obtain an ObservableList<String> object by calling a factory method on FXCollections:

```java
ObservableList<String> strings = FXCollections.observableArrayList();
```

We then hooked an InvalidationListener and a ListChangeListener to the observable list. Because both listeners have a one-argument method and are added using addListener(), we have to specify the parameter type in the lambda expressions. The invalidation listener simply prints out a message every time it's called. The list change listener prints out the content of the observable list. The rest of the program simply manipulates the content of the observable list in various ways: by calling methods on the java.util. List interface, by calling some of the new convenience methods added to ObservableList, and by calling the remove() method on an Iterator obtained from the observable list.

When we run the program in Listing 5-1, the following output is printed to the console:

```
Calling add("First"):
        list invalidated
        strings = [First]
Calling add(0, "Zeroth"):
        list invalidated
        strings = [Zeroth, First]
Calling addAll("Second", "Third"):
        list invalidated
        strings = [Zeroth, First, Second, Third]
Calling set(1, "New First"):
        list invalidated
        strings = [Zeroth, New First, Second, Third]
Calling addAll(3, list):
        list invalidated
        strings = [Zeroth, New First, Second, Second_1, Second_2, Third]
Calling remove(2, 4):
        list invalidated
        strings = [Zeroth, New First, Second_2, Third]
Calling remove() on iterator:
        list invalidated
        strings = [New First, Second_2, Third]
Calling remove() on iterator:
        list invalidated
        strings = [Second_2, Third]
Calling removeAll("Third", "Fourth"):
        list invalidated
        strings = [Second_2]
```

Indeed, every call that we made in the code to change the content of the observable list triggered a callback on both the invalidation listener and the list change listener.

If an instance of an invalidation listener or a list change listener has already been added as a listener to an observable list, all subsequent addListener() calls with that instance as an argument are ignored. Of course, you can add as many distinct invalidation listeners and list change listeners as you like to an observable list.

Handling Change Events in ListChangeListener

In this section, we take a closer look at the `ListChangeListener.Change` class and discuss how the `onChange()` callback method should handle the list change event.

As we saw in the preceding section, for an `ObservableList` obtained by calling `FXCollections.observableArrayList()`, each mutator call—that is, each call to a single method that changes the content of the observable list—generates a list change event delivered to each registered observer. The event object, an instance of a class that implements the `ListChangeListener.Change` interface, can be thought of as representing one or more discrete changes, each of which is of one of four kinds: elements added, elements removed, elements replaced, or elements permuted. The `ListChangeListener.Change` class provides the following methods that allow you to get at this detailed information about the change:

- `boolean next()`

- `void reset()`

- `boolean wasAdded()`

- `boolean wasRemoved()`

- `boolean wasReplaced()`

- `boolean wasPermutated()`

- `int getFrom()`

- `int getTo()`

- `int getAddedSize()`

- `List<E> getAddedSublist()`

- `int getRemovedSize()`

- `List<E> getRemoved()`

- `int getPermutation(int i)`

- `ObservableList<E> getList()`

The `next()` and `reset()` methods control a cursor that iterates through all the discrete changes in the event object. On entry to the `onChange()` method of `ListChangeListener`, the cursor is positioned before the first discrete change. You must call the `next()` method to move the cursor to the first discrete change. Succeeding calls to the `next()` method will move the cursor to the remaining discrete changes. If the next discrete change is reached, the return value will be `true`. If the cursor is already on the last discrete change, the return value will be `false`. Once the cursor is positioned on a valid discrete change, the `wasAdded()`, `wasRemoved()`, `wasReplaced()`, and `wasPermutated()` methods can be called to determine the kind of change the discrete change represents.

■ **Caution** The `wasAdded()`, `wasRemoved()`, `wasReplaced()`, and `wasPermutated()` methods are not orthogonal. A discrete change is a replacement only if it is both an addition and a removal. The proper order for testing the kind of a discrete change is to first determine whether it is a permutation or a replacement and then to determine whether it is an addition or a removal.

Once you have determined the kind of discrete change, you can call the other methods to get more information about it. For addition, the getFrom() method returns the index in the observable list where new elements were added; the getTo() method returns the index of the element that is one past the end of the added elements; the getAddedSize() method returns the number of elements that were added; and the getAddedSublist() method returns a List<E> that contains the added elements. For removal, the getFrom() and getTo() methods both return the index in the observable list where elements were removed; the getRemovedSize() method returns the number of elements that were removed; and the getRemoved() method returns a List<E> that contains the removed elements. For replacement, both the methods that are relevant for addition and the methods that are relevant for removal should be examined, because a replacement can be seen as a removal followed by an addition at the same index. For permutation, the getPermutation(int i) method returns the index of an element in the observable list after the permutation whose index in the observable list before the permutation was i. In all situations, the getList() method always returns the underlying observable list.

In the example shown in Listing 5-2, we perform various list manipulations after attaching a ListChangeListener to an ObservableList. The implementation of ListChangeListener, called MyListener, includes a pretty printer for the ListChangeListener.Change object, and prints out the list change event object when an event is fired.

Listing 5-2. ListChangeEventExample.java

```java
package com.projavafx.collections;

import javafx.collections.FXCollections;
import javafx.collections.ListChangeListener;
import javafx.collections.ObservableList;

public class ListChangeEventExample {
    public static void main(String[] args) {
        ObservableList<String> strings = FXCollections.observableArrayList();
        strings.addListener(new MyListener());

        System.out.println("Calling addAll(\"Zero\", \"One\", \"Two\", \"Three\"): ");
        strings.addAll("Zero", "One", "Two", "Three");

        System.out.println("Calling FXCollections.sort(strings): ");
        FXCollections.sort(strings);

        System.out.println("Calling set(1, \"Three_1\"): ");
        strings.set(1, "Three_1");

        System.out.println("Calling setAll(\"One_1\", \"Three_1\", \"Two_1\", \"Zero_1\"): ");
        strings.setAll("One_1", "Three_1", "Two_1", "Zero_1");

        System.out.println("Calling removeAll(\"One_1\", \"Two_1\", \"Zero_1\"): ");
        strings.removeAll("One_1", "Two_1", "Zero_1");
    }

    private static class MyListener implements ListChangeListener<String> {
        @Override
        public void onChanged(Change<? extends String> change) {
            System.out.println("\tlist = " + change.getList());
            System.out.println(prettyPrint(change));
        }
```

```java
    private String prettyPrint(Change<? extends String> change) {
        StringBuilder sb = new StringBuilder("\tChange event data:\n");
        int i = 0;
        while (change.next()) {
            sb.append("\t\tcursor = ")
                .append(i++)
                .append("\n");

            final String kind =
                change.wasPermutated() ? "permutated" :
                    change.wasReplaced() ? "replaced" :
                        change.wasRemoved() ? "removed" :
                            change.wasAdded() ? "added" : "none";

            sb.append("\t\tKind of change: ")
                .append(kind)
                .append("\n");

            sb.append("\t\tAffected range: [")
                .append(change.getFrom())
                .append(", ")
                .append(change.getTo())
                .append("]\n");

            if (kind.equals("added") || kind.equals("replaced")) {
                sb.append("\t\tAdded size: ")
                    .append(change.getAddedSize())
                    .append("\n");
                sb.append("\t\tAdded sublist: ")
                    .append(change.getAddedSubList())
                    .append("\n");
            }

            if (kind.equals("removed") || kind.equals("replaced")) {
                sb.append("\t\tRemoved size: ")
                    .append(change.getRemovedSize())
                    .append("\n");
                sb.append("\t\tRemoved: ")
                    .append(change.getRemoved())
                    .append("\n");
            }

            if (kind.equals("permutated")) {
                StringBuilder permutationStringBuilder = new StringBuilder("[");
                for (int k = change.getFrom(); k < change.getTo(); k++) {
                    permutationStringBuilder.append(k)
                        .append("->")
                        .append(change.getPermutation(k));
                    if (k < change.getTo() - 1) {
                        permutationStringBuilder.append(", ");
                    }
```

```
            }
            permutationStringBuilder.append("]");
            String permutation = permutationStringBuilder.toString();
            sb.append("\t\tPermutation: ").append(permutation).append("\n");
        }
    }
    return sb.toString();
}
}
}
```

In the preceding example, we triggered the four kinds of discrete changes in an observable list. Because no methods on an ObservableList will trigger a permutation event, we used the sort() utility method from the FXCollections class to effect a permutation. We have more to say about FXCollections in a later section. We triggered the replace event twice, once with set(), and once with setAll(). The nice thing about setAll() is that it effectively does a clear() and an addAll() in one operation and generates only one change event.

When we run the program in Listing 5-2, the following output is printed to the console:

```
Calling addAll("Zero", "One", "Two", "Three"):
        list = [Zero, One, Two, Three]
        Change event data:
                cursor = 0
                Kind of change: added
                Affected range: [0, 4]
                Added size: 4
                Added sublist: [Zero, One, Two, Three]

Calling FXCollections.sort(strings):
        list = [One, Three, Two, Zero]
        Change event data:
                cursor = 0
                Kind of change: permutated
                Affected range: [0, 4]
                Permutation: [0->3, 1->0, 2->2, 3->1]

Calling set(1, "Three_1"):
        list = [One, Three_1, Two, Zero]
        Change event data:
                cursor = 0
                Kind of change: replaced
                Affected range: [1, 2]
                Added size: 1
                Added sublist: [Three_1]
                Removed size: 1
                Removed: [Three]

Calling setAll("One_1", "Three_1", "Two_1", "Zero_1"):
        list = [One_1, Three_1, Two_1, Zero_1]
        Change event data:
                cursor = 0
```

```
                   Kind of change: replaced
                   Affected range: [0, 4]
                   Added size: 4
                   Added sublist: [One_1, Three_1, Two_1, Zero_1]
                   Removed size: 4
                   Removed: [One, Three_1, Two, Zero]

Calling removeAll("One_1", "Two_1", "Zero_1"):
        list = [Three_1]
        Change event data:
                   cursor = 0
                   Kind of change: removed
                   Affected range: [0, 0]
                   Removed size: 1
                   Removed: [One_1]
                   cursor = 1
                   Kind of change: removed
                   Affected range: [1, 1]
                   Removed size: 2
                   Removed: [Two_1, Zero_1]
```

In all but the removeAll() call, the list change event object contains only one discrete change. The reason that the removeAll() call generates a list change event that contains two discrete changes is that the three elements that we wish to remove fall in two disjoint ranges in the list.

In the majority of use cases where we care about list change events, you don't necessarily need to distinguish the kinds of discrete changes. Sometimes you simply want to do something to all added and removed elements. In such a case, your ListChangeListener method can be as simple as the following.

```
@Override
public void onChanged(Change<? extends Foo> change) {
    while (change.next()) {
        for (Foo foo : change.getAddedSubList()) {
            // starting up
        }
        for (Foo foo : change.getRemoved()) {
            // cleaning up
        }
    }
}
```

Understanding ObservableMap

Although ObservableMap appears equivalent to ObservableList in the JavaFX observable collections framework hierarchy, it is actually not as sophisticated as ObservableList. Figure 5-2 is a UML diagram showing the ObservableMap and supporting interfaces.

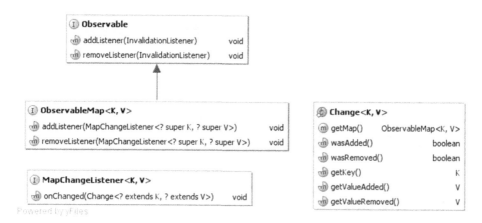

Figure 5-2. *Key interfaces that support the JavaFX observable map*

To prevent clutter, we omitted the java.util.Map interface from the diagram in Figure 5-2. The java.util.Map interface is the other super interface of ObservableMap. The following methods on the ObservableMap interface allow you to register and unregister MapChangeListeners:

- addListener(MapChangeListener<? super K, ? super V> listener)

- addListener(MapChangeListener<? super K, ? super V> listener)

There are no additional convenience methods on ObservableMap.

The MapChangeListener interface has only one method: onChange(MapChangeListener.Change<? extends K, ? extends V> change). This method is called back when the content of the ObservableMap is manipulated. Notice that this method's parameter type is the nested class Change that is declared in the MapChangeListener interface. Unlike the ListChangeListener.Change class, the MapChangeListener. Change class is geared toward reporting the change of a single key in a map. If a method call on ObservableMap affects multiple keys, as many map change events as the number of affected keys will be fired.

The MapChangeListener.Change class provides the following methods for you to inspect the changes made to a key.

- boolean wasAdded()returns true if a new value was added for the key.

- boolean wasRemoved()returns true if an old value was removed from the key.

- K getKey()returns the affected key.

- V getValueAdded()returns the value that was added for the key.

- V getValueRemoved()returns the value that was removed for the key. (Note that a put() call with an existing key will cause the old value to be removed.)

- ObservableMap<K, V> getMap()

In the example in Listing 5-3, we perform various map manipulations after attaching a MapChangeListener to an ObservableMap. The implementation of MapChangeListener, called MyListener, includes a pretty printer for the MapChangeListener.Change object, and prints out the map change event object when an event is fired.

Listing 5-3. MapChangeEventExample.java

```java
package com.projavafx.collections;

import javafx.collections.FXCollections;
import javafx.collections.MapChangeListener;
import javafx.collections.ObservableMap;

import java.util.HashMap;
import java.util.Iterator;
import java.util.Map;

public class MapChangeEventExample {
    public static void main(String[] args) {
        ObservableMap<String, Integer> map = FXCollections.observableHashMap();
        map.addListener(new MyListener());

        System.out.println("Calling put(\"First\", 1): ");
        map.put("First", 1);

        System.out.println("Calling put(\"First\", 100): ");
        map.put("First", 100);

        Map<String, Integer> anotherMap = new HashMap<>();
        anotherMap.put("Second", 2);
        anotherMap.put("Third", 3);
        System.out.println("Calling putAll(anotherMap): ");
        map.putAll(anotherMap);

        final Iterator<Map.Entry<String, Integer>> entryIterator = map.entrySet().
        iterator();
        while (entryIterator.hasNext()) {
            final Map.Entry<String, Integer> next = entryIterator.next();
            if (next.getKey().equals("Second")) {
                System.out.println("Calling remove on entryIterator: ");
                entryIterator.remove();
            }
        }

        final Iterator<Integer> valueIterator = map.values().iterator();
        while (valueIterator.hasNext()) {
            final Integer next = valueIterator.next();
            if (next == 3) {
                System.out.println("Calling remove on valueIterator: ");
                valueIterator.remove();
            }
        }
    }
}
```

```
    private static class MyListener implements MapChangeListener<String, Integer> {
        @Override
        public void onChanged(Change<? extends String, ? extends Integer> change) {
            System.out.println("\tmap = " + change.getMap());
            System.out.println(prettyPrint(change));
        }

        private String prettyPrint(Change<? extends String, ? extends Integer> change) {
            StringBuilder sb = new StringBuilder("\tChange event data:\n");
            sb.append("\t\tWas added: ").append(change.wasAdded()).append("\n");
            sb.append("\t\tWas removed: ").append(change.wasRemoved()).append("\n");
            sb.append("\t\tKey: ").append(change.getKey()).append("\n");
            sb.append("\t\tValue added: ").append(change.getValueAdded()).append("\n");
            sb.append("\t\tValue removed: ").append(change.getValueRemoved()).append("\n");
            return sb.toString();
        }
    }
}
```

When we run the program in Listing 5-3, the following output is printed to the console:

```
Calling put("First", 1):
        map = {First=1}
        Change event data:
                Was added: true
                Was removed: false
                Key: First
                Value added: 1
                Value removed: null

Calling put("First", 100):
        map = {First=100}
        Change event data:
                Was added: true
                Was removed: true
                Key: First
                Value added: 100
                Value removed: 1
Calling putAll(anotherMap):
        map = {Second=2, First=100}
        Change event data:
                Was added: true
                Was removed: false
                Key: Second
                Value added: 2
                Value removed: null

        map = {Second=2, Third=3, First=100}
        Change event data:
                Was added: true
                Was removed: false
```

```
                Key: Third
                Value added: 3
                Value removed: null
Calling remove on entryIterator:
        map = {Third=3, First=100}
        Change event data:
                Was added: false
                Was removed: true
                Key: Second
                Value added: null
                Value removed: 2

Calling remove on valueIterator:
        map = {First=100}
        Change event data:
                Was added: false
                Was removed: true
                Key: Third
                Value added: null
                Value removed: 3
```

In the preceding example, notice that the putAll() call generated two map change events because the other map contains two keys.

Understanding ObservableSet

The ObservableSet interface is similar to the ObservableMap interface in that its SetChangeListener.Change object tracks a single element. Figure 5-3 is a UML diagram showing the ObservableSet and supporting interfaces.

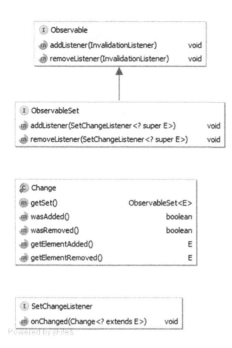

Figure 5-3. *Key interfaces that support the JavaFX observable set*

To prevent clutter, we omitted the `java.util.Set` interface from the diagram in Figure 5-3. The `java.util.Set` interface is the other super interface of `ObservableSet`. The following methods on the `ObservableSet` interface allow you to register and unregister `SetChangeListener`s:

- `addListener(SetChangeListener<? super E> listener)`

- `addListener(SetChangeListener<? super E> listener)`

There are no additional convenience methods on `ObservableSet`.

The `SetChangeListener` interface has only one method: `onChange(SetChangeListener.Change<? extends E> change)`. This method is called back when the content of the `ObservableSet` is manipulated. Notice that this method's parameter type is the nested class `Change` that is declared in the `SetChangeListener` interface. The `SetChangeListener.Change` class is geared toward reporting the change of a single element in a set. If a method call on `ObservableSet` affects multiple elements, as many set change events as the number of affected elements will be fired.

The `SetChangeListener.Change` class provides the following methods for you to inspect the changes made to an element.

- `boolean wasAdded()` returns `true` if a new element was added to the set.

- `boolean wasRemoved()` returns `true` if an element was removed from the set.

- `E getElementAdded()` returns the element that was added to the set.

- `E getElementRemoved()` returns the element that was removed from the set.

- `ObservableSet<E> getSet()`

In the example in Listing 5-4, we perform various set manipulations after attaching a SetChangeListener to an ObservableSet. The implementation of SetChangeListener, called MyListener, includes a pretty printer for the SetChangeListener.Change object, and prints out the set change event object when an event is fired.

Listing 5-4. SetChangeEventExample.java

```java
package com.projavafx.collections;

import javafx.collections.FXCollections;
import javafx.collections.ObservableSet;
import javafx.collections.SetChangeListener;

import java.util.Arrays;

public class SetChangeEventExample {
    public static void main(String[] args) {
        ObservableSet<String> set = FXCollections.observableSet();
        set.addListener(new MyListener());

        System.out.println("Calling add(\"First\"): ");
        set.add("First");

        System.out.println("Calling addAll(Arrays.asList(\"Second\", \"Third\")): ");
        set.addAll(Arrays.asList("Second", "Third"));

        System.out.println("Calling remove(\"Third\"): ");
        set.remove("Third");
    }

    private static class MyListener implements SetChangeListener<String> {
        @Override
        public void onChanged(Change<? extends String> change) {
            System.out.println("\tset = " + change.getSet());
            System.out.println(prettyPrint(change));
        }

        private String prettyPrint(Change<? extends String> change) {
            StringBuilder sb = new StringBuilder("\tChange event data:\n");
            sb.append("\t\tWas added: ").append(change.wasAdded()).append("\n");
            sb.append("\t\tWas removed: ").append(change.wasRemoved()).append("\n");
            sb.append("\t\tElement added: ").append(change.getElementAdded()).append("\n");
            sb.append("\t\tElement removed: ").append(change.getElementRemoved()).
            append("\n");
            return sb.toString();
        }
    }
}
```

When we run the program in Listing 5-4, the following output is printed to the console:

```
Calling add("First"):
        set = [First]
        Change event data:
                Was added: true
                Was removed: false
                Element added: First
                Element removed: null

Calling addAll(Arrays.asList("Second", "Third")):
        set = [Second, First]
        Change event data:
                Was added: true
                Was removed: false
                Element added: Second
                Element removed: null

        set = [Second, First, Third]
        Change event data:
                Was added: true
                Was removed: false
                Element added: Third
                Element removed: null

Calling remove("Third"):
        set = [Second, First]
        Change event data:
                Was added: false
                Was removed: true
                Element added: null
                Element removed: Third
```

In the preceding example, notice that the addAll() call generated two set change events because the list that was added to the observable set contains two elements.

Understanding ObservableArrays

The ObservableArray interface is introduced for situations where a list of primitive int or float values needs to be observed but the overhead of boxing and unboxing of the primitive values every time they are added or removed from the list is unacceptable for performance reasons. Implementations of ObservableArray and its two subinterfaces, ObservableIntegerArray and ObservableFloatArray, are expected to use primitive arrays as the backing stores of their content. The JavaFX 3D API makes use of ObservableArray, ObservableIntegerArray, and ObservableFloatArray. Figure 5-4 is a UML diagram showing the ObservableArray and supporting interfaces.

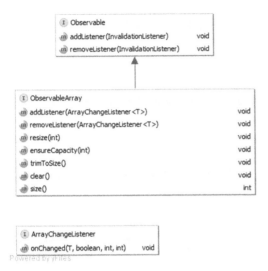

Figure 5-4. *Key interfaces that support the JavaFX observable array*

Unlike for the ObservableList, ObservableMap, and ObservableSet interfaces, the ObservableArray interface does not implement any Java collections framework interfaces. The following methods on the ObservableArray interface allow you to register and unregister ArrayChangeListeners:

- addListener(ArrayChangeListener<T> listener)

- removeListener(ArrayChangeListener<T> listener)

The following additional methods on ObservableArray give you control of the underlying primitive arrays:

- resize(int size)

- ensureCapacity(int capacity)

- trimToSize()

- clear()

- size()

These methods deal with the capacity and size of an ObservableArray. The *capacity* is the length of the underlying primitive array. The *size* is the number of elements that actually contain application data. The capacity is always greater than or equal to the size. The ensureCapacity() method allocates a new underlying primitive array if the length of the current underlying primitive array is less than the desired new capacity. The resize() method changes the size of ObservableArray. If the new size is greater than the current capacity, the capacity is increased. If the new size is greater than the current size, the additional elements are filled with zero. If the new size is less than the current size, resize() does not actually shrink the array, but the "lost" elements are filled with zero. The trimToSize() method replaces the underlying primitive array with one whose length is the same as the size of the ObservableArray. The clear() method resizes the ObservableArray to size zero. The size() method returns the current size of the ObservableArray.

The ArrayChangeListener interface has only one method: onChanged(T observableArray, boolean sizeChanged, int from, int to). Notice that instead of passing a Change object to the onChange() method, as is done in ListChangeListener, MapChangeListener, and SetChangeListener, ArrayChangeListener passes characteristics of the change directly as parameters. The first parameter is

210

the ObservableArray itself. The sizeChanged parameter will be true if the size of the observable array has changed. The from and to parameters mark the range of the changed elements, inclusive on the from end, and exclusive on the to end.

The ObservableIntegerArray and ObservableFloatArray interfaces have methods that manipulate the data in a type-specific way. We list the methods of ObservableIntegerArray (methods of ObservableFloatArray are similar):

- `copyTo(int srcIndex, int[] dest, int destIndex, int length)`
- `copyTo(int srcIndex, ObservableIntegerArray dest, int destIndex, int length)`
- `int get(int index)`
- `addAll(int... elements)`
- `addAll(ObservableIntegerArray src)`
- `addAll(int[] src, int srcIndex, int length)`
- `addAll(ObservableIntegerArray src, int srcIndex, int length)`
- `setAll(int... elements)`
- `setAll(int[] src, int srcIndex, int length)`
- `setAll(ObservableIntegerArray src)`
- `setAll(ObservableIntegerArray src, int srcIndex, int length)`
- `set(int destIndex, int[] src, int srcIndex, int length)`
- `set(int destIndex, ObservableIntegerArray src, int srcIndex, int length)`
- `set(int index, int value)`
- `int[] toArray(int[] dest)`
- `int[] toArray(int srcIndex, int[] dest, int length)`

The addAll() methods append to the ObservableIntegerArray. The setAll() methods replace the content of the ObservableIntegerArray. The sources to these two sets of methods can be a vararg array of ints, an ObservableIntegerArray, an int array with a starting index and a length, or an ObservableIntegerArray with a starting index and a length. The get() method returns the value at the specified index. The set() methods replace a portion of the ObservableIntegerArray with new values starting at the index specified in the first parameter. The replacement data can be a single int value, an int array with a starting index and a length, or an ObservableIntegerArray with a starting index and a length. If there is not enough room in the original ObservableIntegerArray to accommodate the replacement data, an ArrayIndexOutOfBoundsException is thrown. The copyTo() methods copy a portion of the ObservableIntegerArray starting at the specified srcIndex into a destination int array or ObservableIntegerArray starting at the specified destIndex. The length parameter dictates the length of the portion copied. If there are not enough elements in the source ObservableIntegerArray to form a portion of the specified length, or if there is not enough room in the destination to accommodate the copied portion, an ArrayIndexOutOfBoundsException is thrown. The toArray() methods copy the content of the ObservableIntegerArray into an int array. If the dest parameter is not null and has enough room, it is filled and returned; otherwise, a new int array is allocated, filled, and returned. In the form where the srcIndex and length are specified, if there are not enough elements in the ObservableIntegerArray, an ArrayIndexOutOfBoundsException is thrown.

In the example shown in Listing 5-5, we perform various array manipulations after attaching an ArrayChangeListener to an ObservableIntegerArray. We print out the parameters passed to the onChange() method when an event is fired.

Listing 5-5. ArrayChangeEventExample.java

```java
package com.projavafx.collections;

import javafx.collections.FXCollections;
import javafx.collections.ObservableIntegerArray;

public class ArrayChangeEventExample {
    public static void main(String[] args) {
        final ObservableIntegerArray ints = FXCollections.observableIntegerArray(10, 20);
        ints.addListener((array, sizeChanged, from, to) -> {
            StringBuilder sb = new StringBuilder("\tObservable Array = ").append(array).
            append("\n")
                .append("\t\tsizeChanged = ").append(sizeChanged).append("\n")
                .append("\t\tfrom = ").append(from).append("\n")
                .append("\t\tto = ").append(to).append("\n");
            System.out.println(sb.toString());
        });

        ints.ensureCapacity(20);

        System.out.println("Calling addAll(30, 40):");
        ints.addAll(30, 40);

        final int[] src = {50, 60, 70};
        System.out.println("Calling addAll(src, 1, 2):");
        ints.addAll(src, 1, 2);

        System.out.println("Calling set(0, src, 0, 1):");
        ints.set(0, src, 0, 1);

        System.out.println("Calling setAll(src):");
        ints.setAll(src);

        ints.trimToSize();

        final ObservableIntegerArray ints2 = FXCollections.observableIntegerArray();
        ints2.resize(ints.size());

        System.out.println("Calling copyTo(0, ints2, 0, ints.size()):");
        ints.copyTo(0, ints2, 0, ints.size());

        System.out.println("\tDestination = " + ints2);
    }
}
```

When we run the program in Listing 5-5, the following output is printed to the console:

```
Calling addAll(30, 40):
        Observable Array = [10, 20, 30, 40]
                sizeChanged = true
                from = 2
                to = 4

Calling addAll(src, 1, 2):
        Observable Array = [10, 20, 30, 40, 60, 70]
                sizeChanged = true
                from = 4
                to = 6

Calling set(0, src, 0, 1):
        Observable Array = [50, 20, 30, 40, 60, 70]
                sizeChanged = false
                from = 0
                to = 1

Calling setAll(src):
        Observable Array = [50, 60, 70]
                sizeChanged = true
                from = 0
                to = 3

Calling copyTo(0, ints2, 0, ints.size()):
        Destination = [50, 60, 70]
```

Using Factory and Utility Methods from FXCollections

The FXCollections class plays a similar role in the JavaFX observable collections and arrays framework that the java.util.Collections class plays in the Java collections framework. The FXCollections class contains the following factory methods for ObservableList:

- ObservableList<E> observableList(List<E> list)

- ObservableList<E> observableList(List<E> list, Callback<E, Observable[]> extractor);

- ObservableList<E> observableArrayList()

- ObservableList<E> observableArrayList(Callback<E, Observable[]> extractor);

- ObservableList<E> observableArrayList(E... items)

- ObservableList<E> observableArrayList(Collection<? extends E> col)

- ObservableList<E> concat(ObservableList<E>... lists)

- ObservableList<E> unmodifiableObservableList(ObservableList<E> list)

- `ObservableList<E> checkedObservableList(ObservableList<E> list, Class<E> type)`

- `ObservableList<E> synchronizedObservableList(ObservableList<E> list)`

- `ObservableList<E> emptyObservableList()`

- `ObservableList<E> singletonObservableList(E e)`

It contains the following factory methods for `ObservableMap`:

- `ObservableMap<K, V> observableMap(Map<K, V> map)`

- `ObservableMap<K, V> unmodifiableObservableMap(ObservableMap<K, V> map)`

- `ObservableMap<K, V> checkedObservableMap(ObservableMap<K, V> map, Class<K> keyType, Class<V> valType)`

- `ObservableMap<K, V> synchronizedObservableMap(ObservableMap<K, V> map)`

- `ObservableMap<K, V> emptyObservableMap();`

- `ObservableMap<K, V> observableHashMap()`

It contains the following factory methods for `ObservableSet`:

- `ObservableSet<E> observableSet(Set<E> set)`

- `ObservableSet<E> observableSet(E...)`

- `ObservableSet<E> unmodifiableObservableSet(ObservableSet<E> set)`

- `ObservableSet<E> checkedObservableSet(ObservableSet<E> set, Class<E> type)`

- `ObservableSet<E> synchronizedObservableSet(ObservableSet<E>)`

- `ObservableSet<E> emptyObservableSet()`

It contains the following factory methods for `ObservableIntegerArray` and `ObservableFloatArray`:

- `ObservableIntegerArray observableIntegerArray()`

- `ObservableIntegerArray observableIntegerArray(int...)`

- `ObservableIntegerArray observableIntegerArray(ObservableIntegerArray)`

- `ObservableFloatArray observableFloatArray()`

- `ObservableFloatArray observableFloatArray(float...)`

- `ObservableFloatArray observableFloatArray(ObservableFloatArray)`

It also contains nine utility methods that are parallels of methods with the same name in `java.util.Collections`. They all act on `ObservableList` objects. And they differ from their `java.util.Collections` counterparts in that when they act on an `ObservableList`, care is taken to generate only one list change event, whereas their `java.util.Collections` counterpart would have generated more than one list change event.

- `void copy(ObservableList<? super T> dest, java.util.List<? extends T> src)`

- `void fill(ObservableList<? super T> list, T obj)`

- `boolean replaceAll(ObservableList<T> list, T oldVal, T newVal)`

- void reverse(ObservableList list)

- void rotate(ObservableList list, int distance)

- void shuffle(ObservableList<?> list)

- void shuffle(ObservableList list, java.util.Random rnd)

- void sort(ObservableList<T> list)

- void sort(ObservableList<T> list, java.util.Comparator<? super T> c)

We illustrate the effects of these utility methods in Listing 5-6.

Listing 5-6. FXCollectionsExample.java

```java
package com.projavafx.collections;

import javafx.collections.FXCollections;
import javafx.collections.ListChangeListener;
import javafx.collections.ObservableList;

import java.util.Arrays;
import java.util.Comparator;
import java.util.Random;

public class FXCollectionsExample {
    public static void main(String[] args) {
        ObservableList<String> strings = FXCollections.observableArrayList();
        strings.addListener(new MyListener());

        System.out.println("Calling addAll(\"Zero\", \"One\", \"Two\", \"Three\"): ");
        strings.addAll("Zero", "One", "Two", "Three");

        System.out.println("Calling copy: ");
        FXCollections.copy(strings, Arrays.asList("Four", "Five"));

        System.out.println("Calling replaceAll: ");
        FXCollections.replaceAll(strings, "Two", "Two_1");

        System.out.println("Calling reverse: ");
        FXCollections.reverse(strings);

        System.out.println("Calling rotate(strings, 2): ");
        FXCollections.rotate(strings, 2);

        System.out.println("Calling shuffle(strings): ");
        FXCollections.shuffle(strings);

        System.out.println("Calling shuffle(strings, new Random(OL)): ");
        FXCollections.shuffle(strings, new Random(OL));

        System.out.println("Calling sort(strings): ");
        FXCollections.sort(strings);
```

```
        System.out.println("Calling sort(strings, c) with custom comparator: ");
        FXCollections.sort(strings, new Comparator<String>() {
            @Override
            public int compare(String lhs, String rhs) {
                // Reverse the order
                return rhs.compareTo(lhs);
            }
        });

        System.out.println("Calling fill(strings, \"Ten\"): ");
        FXCollections.fill(strings, "Ten");
    }

    // We omitted the nested class MyListener, which is the same as in Listing 5-2
}
```

When we run the program in Listing 5-6, the following output is printed to the console:

```
Calling addAll("Zero", "One", "Two", "Three"):
        list = [Zero, One, Two, Three]
        Change event data:
                cursor = 0
                Kind of change: added
                Affected range: [0, 4]
                Added size: 4
                Added sublist: [Zero, One, Two, Three]

Calling copy:
        list = [Four, Five, Two, Three]
        Change event data:
                cursor = 0
                Kind of change: replaced
                Affected range: [0, 4]
                Added size: 4
                Added sublist: [Four, Five, Two, Three]
                Removed size: 4
                Removed: [Zero, One, Two, Three]

Calling replaceAll:
        list = [Four, Five, Two_1, Three]
        Change event data:
                cursor = 0
                Kind of change: replaced
                Affected range: [0, 4]
                Added size: 4
                Added sublist: [Four, Five, Two_1, Three]
                Removed size: 4
                Removed: [Four, Five, Two, Three]

Calling reverse:
        list = [Three, Two_1, Five, Four]
```

```
        Change event data:
                cursor = 0
                Kind of change: replaced
                Affected range: [0, 4]
                Added size: 4
                Added sublist: [Three, Two_1, Five, Four]
                Removed size: 4
                Removed: [Four, Five, Two_1, Three]

Calling rotate(strings, 2):
        list = [Five, Four, Three, Two_1]
        Change event data:
                cursor = 0
                Kind of change: replaced
                Affected range: [0, 4]
                Added size: 4
                Added sublist: [Five, Four, Three, Two_1]
                Removed size: 4
                Removed: [Three, Two_1, Five, Four]

Calling shuffle(strings):
        list = [Three, Four, Two_1, Five]
        Change event data:
                cursor = 0
                Kind of change: replaced
                Affected range: [0, 4]
                Added size: 4
                Added sublist: [Three, Four, Two_1, Five]
                Removed size: 4
                Removed: [Five, Four, Three, Two_1]

Calling shuffle(strings, new Random(0L)):
        list = [Five, Three, Four, Two_1]
        Change event data:
                cursor = 0
                Kind of change: replaced
                Affected range: [0, 4]
                Added size: 4
                Added sublist: [Five, Three, Four, Two_1]
                Removed size: 4
                Removed: [Three, Four, Two_1, Five]
Calling sort(strings):
        list = [Five, Four, Three, Two_1]
        Change event data:
                cursor = 0
                Kind of change: permutated
                Affected range: [0, 4]
                Permutation: [0->0, 1->2, 2->1, 3->3]
Calling sort(strings, c) with custom comparator:
        list = [Two_1, Three, Four, Five]
        Change event data:
```

217

```
                cursor = 0
                Kind of change: permutated
                Affected range: [0, 4]
                Permutation: [0->3, 1->2, 2->1, 3->0]
Calling fill(strings, "Ten"):
        list = [Ten, Ten, Ten, Ten]
        Change event data:
                cursor = 0
                Kind of change: replaced
                Affected range: [0, 4]
                Added size: 4
                Added sublist: [Ten, Ten, Ten, Ten]
                Removed size: 4
                Removed: [Two_1, Three, Four, Five]
```

Notice that each invocation of a utility method in FXCollections generated exactly one list change event.

Using the JavaFX Concurrency Framework

It is common knowledge nowadays that almost all GUI platforms use a single-threaded event dispatching model. JavaFX is no exception, and indeed all UI events in JavaFX are processed in the *JavaFX Application Thread*. However, with multicore desktop machines becoming common in recent years (e.g., this chapter was written on a quad-core PC), it is natural for the designers of JavaFX to take advantage of the full power of the hardware by leveraging the excellent concurrency support of the Java programming language.

In this section, we examine important threads that are present in all JavaFX applications. We explain the role they play in the overall scheme of JavaFX applications. We then turn our attention to the JavaFX Application Thread, explaining why executing long-running code in the JavaFX Application Thread makes your application appear to hang. Finally, we look at the javafx.concurrent framework and show you how to use it to execute long-running code in a worker thread off the JavaFX Application Thread and communicate the result back to the JavaFX Application Thread to update the GUI states.

■ **Note**   If you are familiar with Swing programming, the JavaFX Application Thread is similar to Swing's Event Dispatcher Thread (EDT), usually with the name AWT-EventQueue-0.

Identifying the Threads in a JavaFX Application

The program in Listing 5-7 creates a simple JavaFX GUI with a ListView, a TextArea and a Button, and populates the ListView with the names of all live threads of the application. When you select an item from the ListView, that thread's stack trace is displayed in the TextArea. The original list of threads and stack traces is populated as the application is starting up. You can update the list of threads and stack traces by clicking the Update button.

Listing 5-7. JavaFXThreadsExample.java

```java
package com.projavafx.collections;

import javafx.application.Application;
import javafx.beans.value.ChangeListener;
import javafx.beans.value.ObservableValue;
import javafx.collections.FXCollections;
import javafx.collections.ObservableList;
import javafx.event.ActionEvent;
import javafx.event.EventHandler;
import javafx.geometry.Insets;
import javafx.scene.Scene;
import javafx.scene.control.Button;
import javafx.scene.control.ListView;
import javafx.scene.control.TextArea;
import javafx.scene.layout.VBox;
import javafx.stage.Stage;

import java.util.Map;

public class JavaFXThreadsExample extends Application
    implements EventHandler<ActionEvent>, ChangeListener<Number> {

    private Model model;
    private View view;

    public static void main(String[] args) {
        launch(args);
    }

    public JavaFXThreadsExample() {
        model = new Model();
    }

    @Override
    public void start(Stage stage) throws Exception {
        view = new View(model);
        hookupEvents();
        stage.setTitle("JavaFX Threads Information");
        stage.setScene(view.scene);
        stage.show();
    }

    private void hookupEvents() {
        view.updateButton.setOnAction(this);
        view.threadNames.getSelectionModel().selectedIndexProperty().addListener(this);
    }

    @Override
    public void changed(ObservableValue<? extends Number> observableValue,
                        Number oldValue, Number newValue) {
```

```java
            int index = (Integer) newValue;
            if (index >= 0) {
                view.stackTrace.setText(model.stackTraces.get(index));
            }
        }
    }

    @Override
    public void handle(ActionEvent actionEvent) {
        model.update();
    }

    public static class Model {
        public ObservableList<String> threadNames;
        public ObservableList<String> stackTraces;

        public Model() {
            threadNames = FXCollections.observableArrayList();
            stackTraces = FXCollections.observableArrayList();
            update();
        }

        public void update() {
            threadNames.clear();
            stackTraces.clear();
            final Map<Thread, StackTraceElement[]> map = Thread.getAllStackTraces();
            for (Map.Entry<Thread, StackTraceElement[]> entry : map.entrySet()) {
                threadNames.add("\"" + entry.getKey().getName() + "\"");
                stackTraces.add(formatStackTrace(entry.getValue()));
            }
        }

        private String formatStackTrace(StackTraceElement[] value) {
            StringBuilder sb = new StringBuilder("StackTrace: \n");
            for (StackTraceElement stackTraceElement : value) {
                sb.append("    at ").append(stackTraceElement.toString()).append("\n");
            }
            return sb.toString();
        }
    }

    private static class View {
        public ListView<String> threadNames;
        public TextArea stackTrace;
        public Button updateButton;
        public Scene scene;
```

```
        private View(Model model) {
            threadNames = new ListView<>(model.threadNames);
            stackTrace = new TextArea();
            updateButton = new Button("Update");
            VBox vBox = new VBox(10, threadNames, stackTrace, updateButton);
            vBox.setPadding(new Insets(10, 10, 10, 10));
            scene = new Scene(vBox, 440, 640);
        }
    }
}
```

This is a pretty minimal JavaFX GUI application. Before letting you run this program, we point out several features of the program. First of all, make a mental note of the main() method:

```
public static void main(String[] args) {
    launch(args);
}
```

You have seen this method several times already. This stylized main() method always appears in a class that extends the javafx.application.Application class. There is an overloaded version of the Application.launch() method that takes a Class object as the first parameter that can be called from other classes:

```
launch(Class<? Extends Application> appClass, String[] args)
```

Therefore, you can move the main() method to another class:

```
public class Main {
    public static void main(String[] args) {
        Application.launch(JavaFXThreadsExample.class, args);
    }
}
```

to achieve the same result.

Next, notice that the nested class Model builds up its data model, which consists of a list of all live threads and the stack traces of each thread, in its update() method:

```
public void update() {
    threadNames.clear();
    stackTraces.clear();
    final Map<Thread, StackTraceElement[]> map = Thread.getAllStackTraces();
    for (Map.Entry<Thread, StackTraceElement[]> entry : map.entrySet()) {
        threadNames.add("\"" + entry.getKey().getName() + "\"");
        stackTraces.add(formatStackTrace(entry.getValue()));
    }
}
```

This method is called once in the constructor of Model, which is called from the constructor of the JavaFXThreadsExample, and once from the event handler of the Update button.

When we run the program in Listing 5-7, the GUI in Figure 5-5 is displayed on the screen. You can explore the threads in this JavaFX program by clicking on each thread name in the list and seeing the stack trace for that thread in the text area. Here are some interesting observations:

- The "main" thread's call stack includes a call to com.sun.javafx.application. LauncherImpl.launchApplication().

- The "JavaFX-Launcher" thread's call stack includes a call to com.sun.javafx. application.PlatformImpl.runAndWait(). This puts code, including the invocation of the constructor, on the JavaFX Application Thread.

- The "JavaFX Application Thread" thread's call stack includes the native com. sun.glass.ui.win.WinApplication._runLoop()method on a Windows box, and something similar on Mac or Linux boxes.

- The "QuantumRenderer-0" thread's call stack includes the com.sun.javafx. tk.quantum.QuantumRenderer$PipelineRunnable.run()method.

Now when you click the Update button and examine the call stack for the "JavaFX Application Thread" thread, you will discover that the event handler of the Update button is executed on the JavaFX Application Thread.

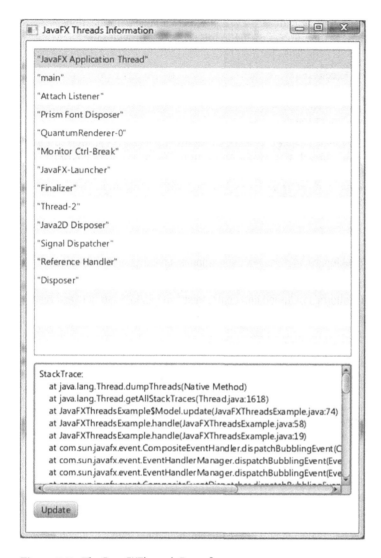

Figure 5-5. The JavaFXThreadsExample program

This little experiment reveals some of the architectural elements of the JavaFX runtime system. Although parts of this information include implementation details represented by, appropriately, classes in the com.sun hierarchy (therefore not to be used in code of normal JavaFX applications), it is nevertheless beneficial to have some knowledge of how the internals work.

■ **Caution**   In the discussion that follows, we mention Java classes in packages with names that begin with com.sun. These classes are implementation details of the JavaFX runtime system and are not meant to be used in normal JavaFX applications. They might change in future releases of JavaFX.

The javafx.application.Application class provides life-cycle support for JavaFX applications. In addition to the two static launch() methods we mentioned earlier in this section, it provides the following life-cycle methods.

- public void init() throws Exception

- public abstract void start(Stage stage) throws Exception

- public void stop() throws Exception

The init() method is called in the "JavaFX-Launcher" thread. The constructor, start(), and stop() methods are called in the JavaFX Application Thread. The JavaFX Application Thread is part of the *Glass Windowing Toolkit* in the com.sun.glass package hierarchy. JavaFX events are processed on the JavaFX Application Thread. All live scene manipulation must be performed in the JavaFX Application Thread. Nodes that are not attached to a live scene can be created and manipulated in other threads until they are attached to a live scene.

■ **Note**   The role the Glass Windowing Toolkit plays in a JavaFX application is similar to that of the AWT in Swing applications. It provides drawing surfaces and input events from the native platform. Unlike in AWT, where the EDT is different from the native platform's UI thread and communication has to occur between them, the JavaFX Application Thread in the Glass Windowing Toolkit uses the native platform's UI thread directly.

The owner of the "QuantumRenderer-0" thread is the *Quantum Toolkit* that lives in the com.sun.javafx.tk.quantum package hierarchy. This thread is responsible for rendering the JavaFX scene graph using the *Prism Graphics Engine* in the com.sun.prism package hierarchy. Prism will use a fully accelerated rendering path if the graphics hardware is supported by JavaFX. Prism will fall back to the Java2D rendering path if the graphics hardware is not supported by JavaFX. The Quantum Toolkit is also responsible for coordinating the activities of the event thread and the rendering thread. It does the coordination using pulse events.

■ **Note**   A *pulse event* is an event that is put on the queue for the JavaFX application thread. When it is processed, it synchronizes the state of the elements of the scene graph down the rendering layer. Pulse events are scheduled if the states of the scene graph change, either through running animation or by modifying the scene graph directly. Pulse events are throttled at 60 frames per second.

Had the JavaFXThreadsExample program included media playing, another thread named "JFXMedia Player EventQueueThread" would have shown up on the list. This thread is responsible for synchronizing the latest frame through the scene graph by using the JavaFX application thread.

Fixing Unresponsive UIs

Event handlers execute on the JavaFX application thread, thus if an event handler takes too long to finish its work, the whole UI will become unresponsive because any subsequent user actions will simply queue up and won't be handled until the long-running event handler is done.

We illustrate this in Listing 5-8.

Listing 5-8. `UnresponsiveUIExample.java`

```java
package com.projavafx.collections;

import javafx.application.Application;
import javafx.beans.property.ObjectProperty;
import javafx.beans.property.SimpleObjectProperty;
import javafx.geometry.Insets;
import javafx.geometry.Pos;
import javafx.scene.Scene;
import javafx.scene.control.Button;
import javafx.scene.layout.BorderPane;
import javafx.scene.layout.HBox;
import javafx.scene.paint.Color;
import javafx.scene.paint.Paint;
import javafx.scene.shape.Rectangle;
import javafx.stage.Stage;

public class UnresponsiveUIExample extends Application {
    private Model model;
    private View view;

    public static void main(String[] args) {
        launch(args);
    }

    public UnresponsiveUIExample() {
        model = new Model();
    }

    @Override
    public void start(Stage stage) throws Exception {
        view = new View(model);
        hookupEvents();
        stage.setTitle("Unresponsive UI Example");
        stage.setScene(view.scene);
        stage.show();
    }

    private void hookupEvents() {
        view.changeFillButton.setOnAction(actionEvent -> {
            final Paint fillPaint = model.getFillPaint();
            if (fillPaint.equals(Color.LIGHTGRAY)) {
                model.setFillPaint(Color.GRAY);
            } else {
                model.setFillPaint(Color.LIGHTGRAY);
            }
```

```java
            // Bad code, this will cause the UI to be unresponsive
            try {
                Thread.sleep(Long.MAX_VALUE);
            } catch (InterruptedException e) {
                // TODO properly handle interruption
            }
        });

        view.changeStrokeButton.setOnAction(actionEvent -> {
            final Paint strokePaint = model.getStrokePaint();
            if (strokePaint.equals(Color.DARKGRAY)) {
                model.setStrokePaint(Color.BLACK);
            } else {
                model.setStrokePaint(Color.DARKGRAY);
            }
        });
    }

    private static class Model {
        private ObjectProperty<Paint> fillPaint = new SimpleObjectProperty<>();
        private ObjectProperty<Paint> strokePaint = new SimpleObjectProperty<>();

        private Model() {
            fillPaint.set(Color.LIGHTGRAY);
            strokePaint.set(Color.DARKGRAY);
        }

        final public Paint getFillPaint() {
            return fillPaint.get();
        }

        final public void setFillPaint(Paint value) {
            this.fillPaint.set(value);
        }

        final public Paint getStrokePaint() {
            return strokePaint.get();
        }

        final public void setStrokePaint(Paint value) {
            this.strokePaint.set(value);
        }

        final public ObjectProperty<Paint> fillPaintProperty() {
            return fillPaint;
        }

        final public ObjectProperty<Paint> strokePaintProperty() {
            return strokePaint;
        }
    }
```

```
private static class View {
    public Rectangle rectangle;
    public Button changeFillButton;
    public Button changeStrokeButton;
    public HBox buttonHBox;
    public Scene scene;

    private View(Model model) {
        rectangle = new Rectangle(200, 200);
        rectangle.setStrokeWidth(10);
        rectangle.fillProperty().bind(model.fillPaintProperty());
        rectangle.strokeProperty().bind(model.strokePaintProperty());

        changeFillButton = new Button("Change Fill");
        changeStrokeButton = new Button("Change Stroke");

        buttonHBox = new HBox(10, changeFillButton, changeStrokeButton);
        buttonHBox.setPadding(new Insets(10, 10, 10, 10));
        buttonHBox.setAlignment(Pos.CENTER);

        BorderPane root = new BorderPane(rectangle, null, null, buttonHBox, null);
        root.setPadding(new Insets(10, 10, 10, 10));

        scene = new Scene(root);
    }
}
}
```

This class stands up a simple UI with a rectangle with a pronounced Color.DARKGRAY stroke and a Color.LIGHTGRAY fill in the center of a BorderPane, and two buttons at the bottom labeled Change Fill and Change Stroke. The Change Fill button is supposed to toggle the fill of the rectangle between Color. LIGHTGRAY and Color.GRAY. The Change Stroke button is supposed to toggle the stroke of the rectangle between Color.DARKGRAY and Color.BLACK. When we run the program in Listing 5-8, the GUI in Figure 5-6 is displayed on the screen.

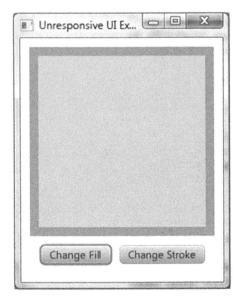

Figure 5-6. *The* UnresponsiveUIExample *program*

However, this program has a bug in the event handler of the Change Fill button:

```
@Override
public void handle(ActionEvent actionEvent) {
    final Paint fillPaint = model.getFillPaint();
    if (fillPaint.equals(Color.LIGHTGRAY)) {
        model.setFillPaint(Color.GRAY);
    } else {
        model.setFillPaint(Color.LIGHTGRAY);
    }
    // Bad code, this will cause the UI to be unresponsive
    try {
        Thread.sleep(Long.MAX_VALUE);
    } catch (InterruptedException e) {
        // TODO properly handle interruption
    }
}
```

The Thread.sleep(Long.MAX_VALUE) simulates code that takes a long time to execute. In real-life applications, this might be a database call, a web service call, or a piece of complicated code. As a result, if you click the Change Fill button, the color change is not seen in the rectangle. What is worse, the whole UI appears to be locked up: The Change Fill and Change Stroke buttons stop working; the close window button that is provided by the operating system will not have the desired effect. The operating system might also mark the program as Not Responding, and the only way to stop the program is to use the operating system's forced kill functionality.

To fix problems like this, we need to offload long-running code to worker threads and communicate the result of the long computation back to the JavaFX application thread to update the states of the UI so that the user can see the result. Depending on when you learned your Java, your answer to the first question of offloading code to worker threads might be different. If you are a longtime Java programmer your instinctive reaction might be to instantiate a Runnable, wrap it in a Thread, and call `start()` on it. If you started with Java after Java 5 and learned the `java.util.concurrent` hierarchy of classes, your reaction might be to stand up a `java.util.concurrent.ExecutorService` and submit `java.util.concurrent.FutureTasks` to it. JavaFX includes a worker threading framework based on the latter approach in the `javafx.concurrent` package.

We examine the interfaces and classes in this framework in the next few sections, but before we do that we use the Runnable and Thread approach to offload computation to a worker thread. Our intention here is to highlight the answer to the second question of how to cause code to be run on the JavaFX application thread from a worker thread. The complete corrected program can be found in `ResponsiveUIExample.java`. Here is the new code for the event handler of the Change Fill button:

```java
view.changeFillButton.setOnAction(actionEvent -> {
    final Paint fillPaint = model.getFillPaint();
    if (fillPaint.equals(Color.LIGHTGRAY)) {
        model.setFillPaint(Color.GRAY);
    } else {
        model.setFillPaint(Color.LIGHTGRAY);
    }
    Runnable task = () -> {
        try {
            Thread.sleep(3000);
            Platform.runLater(() -> {
                final Rectangle rect = view.rectangle;
                double newArcSize =
                    rect.getArcHeight() < 20 ? 30 : 0;
                rect.setArcWidth(newArcSize);
                rect.setArcHeight(newArcSize);
            });
        } catch (InterruptedException e) {
            // TODO properly handle interruption
        }
    };
    new Thread(task).start();
});
```

We have replaced the long sleep with code that executes in a worker thread. After sleeping for three seconds, the worker thread calls the `runLater()` method of the `javafx.application.Platform` class, passing it another Runnable that toggles the rounded corners of the rectangle. Because the long-running computation is done in a worker thread, the event handler is not blocking the JavaFX application thread. The change of fill is now reflected immediately in the UI. Because the `Platform.runLater()` call causes the Runnable to be executed on the JavaFX application thread, the change to the rounded corners is reflected in the UI after three seconds. The reason we have to execute the Runnable on the JavaFX application thread is that it modifies the state of a live scene.

The Platform class includes the following other helpful utility methods:

- `public static boolean isFxApplicationThread()` returns true if it is executed on the JavaFX application thread and false otherwise.

- `public static boolean isSupported(ConditionalFeature)` tests whether the execution environment supports a ConditionalFeature. Testable ConditionalFeatures include GRAPHICS, CONTROLS, MEDIA, WEB, SWT, SWING, FXML, SCENE3D, EFFECT, SHAPE_CLIP, INPUT_METHOD, TRANSPARENT_WINDOW, UNIFIED_WINDOW, TWO_LEVEL_FOCUS, VIRTUAL_KEYBOARD, INPUT_TOUCH, INPUT_MULTITOUCH, and INPUT_POINTER.

- public static void exit(), if called after the application's start() method has been called, causes the application's stop() method to be executed on the JavaFX application thread before the JavaFX application thread and other JavaFX platform threads are taken down. If the application's start() method has not been called yet, the application's stop() method may not be called.

- public static boolean isImplicitExit() and public static void setImplicitExit(boolean) tests and sets the implicit exit flag. When this flag is true, the JavaFX runtime will shut down when the last application window is closed; otherwise, you have to explicitly call Platform.exit() to shut down the JavaFX runtime. The default value of this flag is true.

■ **Note**　If you are familiar with Swing programming, you should see the similarity between JavaFX's Platform.runLater() and Swing's EventQueue.invokeLater(), or SwingUtilities.invokeLater().

Now that we have solved our problem with Runnable and Thread and Platform.runLater(), it is time to see how we can use JavaFX's built-in worker threading framework to solve the problem in a more flexible and elegant way.

Understanding the javafx.concurrent Framework

The JavaFX worker threading framework in the javafx.concurrent package combines the versatility and flexibility of the Java concurrency framework introduced in Java 5 with the convenience of the JavaFX properties and bindings framework to produce an easy-to-use toolset that is aware of the JavaFX application threading rules and also very easy to use. It consists of one interface, Worker, and three abstract base classes—Task<V>, Service<V>, and ScheduledService<V>—that implement the interface.

Understanding the Worker Interface

The Worker interface specifies a JavaFX bean with nine read-only properties, one method named cancel(), and a state model and state transition rules. A Worker represents a unit of work that runs in one or more background threads yet has some of its internal states safely observable to the JavaFX application thread. The nine read-only properties are as follows.

- title is a String property that represents the title of the task.

- message is a String property that represents a more detailed message as the task progresses.

- running is a boolean property that is true only when the Worker is in the Worker.State.SCHEDULED or Worker.State.RUNNING state.

- state is an Object property that represents the Worker.State of the task.

- totalWork is a double property that represents the total amount of work of the task. Its value is -1.0 when the total amount of work is not known.

- workDone is a double property that represents the amount of work that has been done so far in the task. Its value is -1.0 or a number between 0 and totalWork.

- progress is a double property that represents the percentage of the total work that has been done so far in the task. Its value is –1.0 or the ratio between workDone and totalWork.

- value is an Object property that represents the output of the task. Its value is non-null only when the task has finished successfully, that is, has reached the Worker.State.SUCCEEDED state.

- exception is an Object property that represents a Throwable that the implementation of the task has thrown to the JavaFX worker threading framework. Its value is non-null only when the task is in the Worker.State.FAILED state.

The preceding properties are meant to be accessed from the JavaFX application thread. It is safe to bind scene graph properties to them because the invalidation events and change events of these properties are fired on the JavaFX application thread. It is helpful to think of the properties through an imaginary task progress message box that you see in many GUI applications. They usually have a title, a progress bar indicating the percentage of the work that has been done, and a message telling the user how many items it has processed already and how many more to go. All of these properties are set by the JavaFX worker threading framework itself or by the actual implementation of the task.

The running, state, value, and exception properties are controlled by the framework and no user intervention is needed for them to be observed in the JavaFX application thread. When the framework wants to change these properties, it does the heavy lifting of making sure that the change is done on the JavaFX application thread. The title, message, totalWork, workDone, and progress properties are updatable by the implementation code of the task by calling framework-provided protected methods that guarantee the change is done on the JavaFX application thread.

Worker.State is a nested enum that defines the following six states of a Worker:

- READY (initial state)

- SCHEDULED (transitional state)

- RUNNING (transitional state)

- SUCCEEDED (terminal state)

- CANCELLED (terminal state)

- FAILED (terminal state)

The cancel() method will transition the Worker to the CANCELLED state if it is not already in the SUCCEEDED or FAILED state.

Now that you are familiar with the properties and states of the Worker interface, you can proceed to learn the three abstract classes in the JavaFX worker threading framework that implements this interface, Task<V> and Service<V>, and ScheduledService<V>.

Understanding the Task<V> Abstract Class

The Task<V> abstract class is an implementation of the Worker interface that is meant to be used for one-shot tasks. Once its state progresses to SUCCEEDED or FAILED or CANCELLED, it will stay in the terminal state forever. The Task<V> abstract class extends the FutureTask<V> class, and as a consequence supports the Runnable, Future<V>, and RunnableFuture<V> interfaces as well as the Worker interface. The Future<V>, RunnableFuture<V>, and FutureTask<V> interfaces and class are part of the java.util.concurrent package. Because of this heritage, a Task<V> object can be used in various ways that befit its parent class. However, for typical JavaFX usage, it is enough to use just the methods in the Task<V> class itself, a list of which can be found in the Javadoc for the class. The following is a list of these methods, excluding the read-only properties that were discussed in the preceding section:

- `protected abstract V call() throws Exception`
- `public final boolean cancel()`
- `public boolean cancel(boolean mayInterruptIfRunning)`
- `protected void updateTitle(String title)`
- `protected void updateMessage(String message)`
- `protected void updateProgress(long workDone, long totalWork)`
- `protected void updateProgress(double workDone, double totalWork)`
- `protected void updateValue(V)`

The `Task<V>` abstract class implements the `javafx.event.EventTarget` interface. The events it supports are represented by the `WorkerStateEvent` class. There is a `WorkerStateEvent` for each of the five `Worker.States`. The events are fired when the `Task<V>` transitions into a state. There are five object properties of type `EventHandler<WorkerStateEvent>` as well as five protected methods in `Task<V>`. These event handlers and protected methods are called when the corresponding event is fired:

- `onScheduled` property
- `onRunning` property
- `onSucceeded` property
- `onCancelled` property
- `onFailed` property
- `protected void scheduled()`
- `protected void running()`
- `protected void succeeded()`
- `protected void cancelled()`
- `protected void failed()`

Extensions of `Task<V>` must override the protected abstract `call()` method to perform the actual work. The implementation of the `call()` method may call the protected methods `updateTitle()`, `updateMessage()`, `updateProgress()`, and `updateValue()` to publish its internal state to the JavaFX application thread. The implementation has total control of what the title and message of the task should be. For the `updateProgress()` call that takes two longs, the `workDone` and `totalWork` must either both be −1, indicating indeterminate progress, or satisfy the relations `workDone >= 0` and `workDone <= totalWork`, resulting in a progress value of between `0.0` and `1.0` (0% to 100%).

■ **Caution**   The `updateProgress()` API will throw an exception if `workDone > totalWork`, or if one of them is `<-1`. However, it allows you to pass in `(0, 0)`, resulting in a progress of NaN.

The two `cancel()` methods can be called from any thread, and will move the task to the CANCELLED state if it is not already in the SUCCEEDED or FAILED state. If either `cancel()` method is called before the task is run, it will move to the CANCELLED state and will never be run. The two cancel() methods differ only if the task is in the RUNNING state, and only in their treatment of the running thread. If cancel(true) is called, the thread will receive an interrupt. For this interrupt to have the desired effect of causing the task to finish processing quickly, the implementation of the call() method has to be coded in a way that will detect the interrupt and skip any further processing. The no-argument cancel() method simply forwards to cancel(true).

Listing 5-9 illustrates the creation of a Task, starting it, and observing the properties of the task from a simple GUI that displays all nine of the properties.

Listing 5-9. WorkerAndTaskExample.java

```java
package com.projavafx.collections;

import javafx.application.Application;
import javafx.beans.binding.Bindings;
import javafx.beans.property.ReadOnlyObjectProperty;
import javafx.concurrent.Task;
import javafx.concurrent.Worker;
import javafx.geometry.HPos;
import javafx.geometry.Insets;
import javafx.geometry.Pos;
import javafx.scene.Scene;
import javafx.scene.control.Button;
import javafx.scene.control.Label;
import javafx.scene.control.ProgressBar;
import javafx.scene.layout.BorderPane;
import javafx.scene.layout.ColumnConstraints;
import javafx.scene.layout.GridPane;
import javafx.scene.layout.HBox;
import javafx.stage.Stage;

import java.util.concurrent.atomic.AtomicBoolean;

public class WorkerAndTaskExample extends Application {
    private Model model;
    private View view;

    public static void main(String[] args) {
        launch(args);
    }

    public WorkerAndTaskExample() {
        model = new Model();
    }

    @Override
    public void start(Stage stage) throws Exception {
        view = new View(model);
        hookupEvents();
        stage.setTitle("Worker and Task Example");
        stage.setScene(view.scene);
        stage.show();
    }
```

```java
    private void hookupEvents() {
        view.startButton.setOnAction(actionEvent -> {
            new Thread((Runnable) model.worker).start();
        });
        view.cancelButton.setOnAction(actionEvent -> {
            model.worker.cancel();
        });
        view.exceptionButton.setOnAction(actionEvent -> {
            model.shouldThrow.getAndSet(true);
        });
    }

    private static class Model {
        public Worker<String> worker;
        public AtomicBoolean shouldThrow = new AtomicBoolean(false);

        private Model() {
            worker = new Task<String>() {
                @Override
                protected String call() throws Exception {
                    updateTitle("Example Task");
                    updateMessage("Starting...");
                    final int total = 250;
                    updateProgress(0, total);
                    for (int i = 1; i <= total; i++) {
                        if (isCancelled()) {
                            updateValue("Canceled at " + System.currentTimeMillis());
                            return null; // ignored
                        }
                        try {
                            Thread.sleep(20);
                        } catch (InterruptedException e) {
                            updateValue("Canceled at " + System.currentTimeMillis());
                            return null; // ignored                             }
                        if (shouldThrow.get()) {
                            throw new RuntimeException("Exception thrown at " + System.
                            currentTimeMillis());
                        }
                        updateTitle("Example Task (" + i + ")");
                        updateMessage("Processed " + i + " of " + total + " items.");
                        updateProgress(i, total);
                    }
                    return "Completed at " + System.currentTimeMillis();
                }

                @Override
                protected void scheduled() {
                    System.out.println("The task is scheduled.");
                }
```

```
                @Override
                protected void running() {
                    System.out.println("The task is running.");
                }
            };
            ((Task<String>) worker).setOnSucceeded(event -> {
                System.out.println("The task succeeded.");
            });
            ((Task<String>) worker).setOnCancelled(event -> {
                System.out.println("The task is canceled.");
            });
            ((Task<String>) worker).setOnFailed(event -> {
                System.out.println("The task failed.");
            });
        }
    }

    private static class View {
        public ProgressBar progressBar;

        public Label title;
        public Label message;
        public Label running;
        public Label state;
        public Label totalWork;
        public Label workDone;
        public Label progress;
        public Label value;
        public Label exception;

        public Button startButton;
        public Button cancelButton;
        public Button exceptionButton;

        public Scene scene;

        private View(final Model model) {
            progressBar = new ProgressBar();
            progressBar.setMinWidth(250);

            title = new Label();
            message = new Label();
            running = new Label();
            state = new Label();
            totalWork = new Label();
            workDone = new Label();
            progress = new Label();
            value = new Label();
            exception = new Label();

            startButton = new Button("Start");
            cancelButton = new Button("Cancel");
            exceptionButton = new Button("Exception");
```

```java
final ReadOnlyObjectProperty<Worker.State> stateProperty =
    model.worker.stateProperty();

progressBar.progressProperty().bind(model.worker.progressProperty());

title.textProperty().bind(
    model.worker.titleProperty());
message.textProperty().bind(
    model.worker.messageProperty());
running.textProperty().bind(
    Bindings.format("%s", model.worker.runningProperty()));
state.textProperty().bind(
    Bindings.format("%s", stateProperty));
totalWork.textProperty().bind(
    model.worker.totalWorkProperty().asString());
workDone.textProperty().bind(
    model.worker.workDoneProperty().asString());
progress.textProperty().bind(
    Bindings.format("%5.2f%%", model.worker.progressProperty().multiply(100)));
value.textProperty().bind(
    model.worker.valueProperty());
exception.textProperty().bind(Bindings.createStringBinding(() -> {
    final Throwable exception = model.worker.getException();
    if (exception == null) return "";
    return exception.getMessage();
}, model.worker.exceptionProperty()));

startButton.disableProperty().bind(
    stateProperty.isNotEqualTo(Worker.State.READY));
cancelButton.disableProperty().bind(
    stateProperty.isNotEqualTo(Worker.State.RUNNING));
exceptionButton.disableProperty().bind(
    stateProperty.isNotEqualTo(Worker.State.RUNNING));

HBox topPane = new HBox(10, progressBar);
topPane.setAlignment(Pos.CENTER);
topPane.setPadding(new Insets(10, 10, 10, 10));

ColumnConstraints constraints1 = new ColumnConstraints();
constraints1.setHalignment(HPos.CENTER);
constraints1.setMinWidth(65);

ColumnConstraints constraints2 = new ColumnConstraints();
constraints2.setHalignment(HPos.LEFT);
constraints2.setMinWidth(200);

GridPane centerPane = new GridPane();
centerPane.setHgap(10);
centerPane.setVgap(10);
centerPane.setPadding(new Insets(10, 10, 10, 10));
centerPane.getColumnConstraints()
    .addAll(constraints1, constraints2);
```

```
            centerPane.add(new Label("Title:"), 0, 0);
            centerPane.add(new Label("Message:"), 0, 1);
            centerPane.add(new Label("Running:"), 0, 2);
            centerPane.add(new Label("State:"), 0, 3);
            centerPane.add(new Label("Total Work:"), 0, 4);
            centerPane.add(new Label("Work Done:"), 0, 5);
            centerPane.add(new Label("Progress:"), 0, 6);
            centerPane.add(new Label("Value:"), 0, 7);
            centerPane.add(new Label("Exception:"), 0, 8);

            centerPane.add(title, 1, 0);
            centerPane.add(message, 1, 1);
            centerPane.add(running, 1, 2);
            centerPane.add(state, 1, 3);
            centerPane.add(totalWork, 1, 4);
            centerPane.add(workDone, 1, 5);
            centerPane.add(progress, 1, 6);
            centerPane.add(value, 1, 7);
            centerPane.add(exception, 1, 8);

            HBox buttonPane = new HBox(10,
                startButton, cancelButton, exceptionButton);
            buttonPane.setPadding(new Insets(10, 10, 10, 10));
            buttonPane.setAlignment(Pos.CENTER);

            BorderPane root = new BorderPane(centerPane,
                topPane, null, buttonPane, null);
            scene = new Scene(root);
        }
    }
}
```

The Model nested class for this program holds a worker field of type Worker, and a shouldThrow field of type AtomicBoolean. The worker field is initialized to an instance of an anonymous subclass of Task<String> that implements its call() method by simulating the processing of 250 items at a 20-milliseconds-per-item pace. It updates the properties of the task at the beginning of the call and in each iteration of the loop. It handles cancellation in two places. It checks the isCancelled() flag at the top of each iteration, and it also checks the isCancelled() flag in the InterruptedException handler of the Thread.sleep() call. If the task is cancelled, it calls the updateValue(), and gets out of the loop and returns quickly. The return value is ignored by the framework. The shouldThrow field is controlled by the View to communicate to the task that it should throw an exception.

The View nested class of this program creates a simple UI that has a ProgressBar at the top, a set of Labels at the center that display the various properties of the worker, and three buttons at the bottom. The contents of the Labels are bound to the various properties of the worker. The disable properties of the buttons are also bound to the state property of the worker so that only the relevant buttons are enabled at any time. For example, the Start button is enabled when the program starts but becomes disabled after it is pressed and the task execution begins. Similarly, the Cancel and Exception buttons are enabled only if the task is running.

When we run the program in Listing 5-9, the GUI in Figure 5-7 is displayed on the screen.

Figure 5-7. *The WorkerAndTaskExample program after starting up*

Notice that the progress bar is in an indeterminate state. The values of Title, Message, Value, and Exception are empty. The value of Running is false. The value of State is READY, the values of Total Work and Work Done are –1.0, and Progress displays –100%. The Start button is enabled, whereas the Cancel and Exception buttons are disabled.

After the Start button is clicked, the task starts to execute and the GUI automatically reflects the values of the properties as the task progresses. Figure 5-8 is a screenshot of the application at this stage. Notice that the progress bar is in a determinate state and reflects the progress of the task. The values of Title and Message reflect what is set to these properties in the implementation of the call() method in the task. The value of Running is true. The value of State is RUNNING, and the values of Total Work, Work Done, and Progress reflect the current state of the executing task: 156 of 250 items done. The Value and the Exception fields are empty because neither a value nor an exception is available from the task. The Start button is disabled now. The Cancel and Exception buttons are enabled, indicating that we may attempt to cancel the task or force an exception to be thrown from the task at this moment.

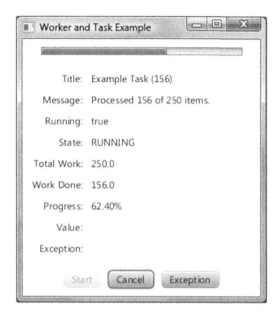

Figure 5-8. *The* `WorkerAndTaskExample` *program while a task is in progress*

When the task finishes normally, we arrive at the screenshot in Figure 5-9. Notice that the progress bar is at 100.00%. The Title, Message, Total Work, Work Done, and Progress fields all have values that reflect the fact that the task has finished processing all 250 items. The Running value is false. The State is SUCCEEDED, and the Value field now contains the return value from the `call()` method.

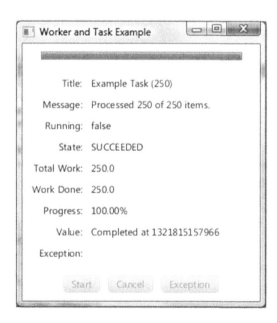

Figure 5-9. *The* `WorkerAndTaskExample` *program after the task succeeded*

If, instead of letting the task finish normally, we click the Cancel button, the task will finish immediately and the screenshot in Figure 5-10 results. Notice that the State field has the value CANCELLED now. The Value field contains the string we passed to the updateValue() method when the task was cancelled. When we detect that the task is cancelled, we have two choices of exiting from the method body. In the program in Listing 5-7, we chose to update the Value and return from the method. We could also have chosen to exit from the method body by throwing a RuntimeException. Had we made that choice, the screenshot would have an empty Value field but with a nonempty Exception field. The state of the worker would have been CANCELLED either way.

■ **Caution**   When you return normally in response to cancellation, a bug in the current implementation of Task causes an IllegalStateException to be recorded as the exception of the Task. This will be fixed in the next release.

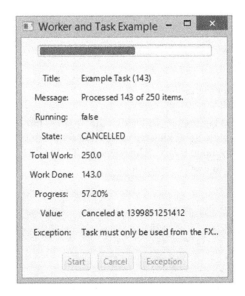

Figure 5-10. *The WorkerAndTaskExample program after the task has been cancelled*

The final screenshot, Figure 5-11, shows what happens when the Exception button is clicked when the task is executing. We simulate an exception in the task by setting an AtomicBoolean flag from the JavaFX application, which the task then picks up in the worker thread and throws the exception. Notice that the status field has the value FAILED now. The Value field is empty because the task did not complete successfully. The Exception field is filled with the message of the RuntimeException that we threw.

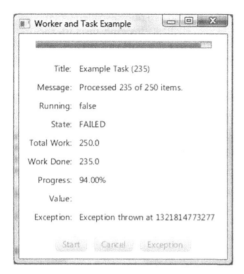

Figure 5-11. *The* `WorkerAndTaskExample` *program after the task threw an exception*

We overrode the `scheduled()` and `running()` methods in the anonymous extension of `Task`, and set up event handlers for the succeeded, cancelled, and failed events, in the `Model` class. You should see these events being logged to the console as you work through the scenarios.

▪ **Note**　The `Task<V>` class defines one-shot tasks that are executed once and never run again. You have to restart the `WorkerAndTaskExample` program after each run of the task.

Understanding the Service<V> Abstract Class

The `Service<V>` abstract class is an implementation of the `Worker` interface that is meant to be reused. It extends `Worker`'s state model by allowing its state to be reset to `Worker.State.READY`. The `Service<V>` abstract class does not extend any class and implements the `Worker` and `EventTarget` interfaces. In addition to the nine read-only properties of the `Worker` interface, `Service<V>` has an additional read write property of type `Executor` called executor. It also has the event handler properties and the protected event callback methods just like the `Task` class. The following is a list of the rest of the `Service<V>` methods:

- `protected abstract Task<V> createTask()`
- `public void start()`
- `public void reset()`
- `public void restart()`
- `public boolean cancel()`

Extensions of `Service<V>` must override the protected abstract `createTask()` method to generate a freshly created `Task`. The `start()` method can only be called when the `Service<V>` object is in the `Worker.State.READY` state. It calls `createTask()` to obtain a freshly minted `Task`, and asks the executor property for an `Executor`. If the executor property is not set, it creates its own `Executor`. It binds the `Service<V>` object's nine `Worker` properties to that of the `Task`'s. It then transitions the `Task` to the `Worker.State.`

241

SCHEDULED state, and executes the Task on the Executor. The reset() method can only be called when the Service<V>'s state is not Worker.State.SCHEDULED or Worker.State.RUNNING. It simply unbinds the nine Service<V> properties from that of the underlying Task and resets their values to fresh startup values: Worker.State.READY for the state property, and null or "" or false or –1 for the other properties. The restart() method simply cancels the currently executing Task, if any, and then does a reset() followed by a start(). The cancel() method will cancel the currently executing Task, if any; otherwise, it will transition the Service<V> to the Worker.State.CANCELLED state.

Listing 5-10 illustrates using an instance of an anonymous subclass of the Service<V> abstract class to execute Tasks repeatedly in its own Executor.

Listing 5-10. ServiceExample.java

```
package com.projavafx.collections;

import javafx.application.Application;
import javafx.beans.binding.Bindings;
import javafx.beans.property.IntegerProperty;
import javafx.beans.property.ReadOnlyObjectProperty;
import javafx.beans.property.SimpleIntegerProperty;
import javafx.concurrent.Service;
import javafx.concurrent.Task;
import javafx.concurrent.Worker;
import javafx.geometry.HPos;
import javafx.geometry.Insets;
import javafx.geometry.Pos;
import javafx.scene.Scene;
import javafx.scene.control.Button;
import javafx.scene.control.Label;
import javafx.scene.control.ProgressBar;
import javafx.scene.control.TextField;
import javafx.scene.layout.BorderPane;
import javafx.scene.layout.ColumnConstraints;
import javafx.scene.layout.GridPane;
import javafx.scene.layout.HBox;
import javafx.stage.Stage;

import java.util.concurrent.atomic.AtomicBoolean;

public class ServiceExample extends Application {
    private Model model;
    private View view;

    public static void main(String[] args) {
        launch(args);
    }

    public ServiceExample() {
        model = new Model();
    }

    @Override
    public void start(Stage stage) throws Exception {
```

```java
            view = new View(model);
            hookupEvents();
            stage.setTitle("Service Example");
            stage.setScene(view.scene);
            stage.show();
        }

        private void hookupEvents() {
            view.startButton.setOnAction(actionEvent -> {
                model.shouldThrow.getAndSet(false);
                ((Service) model.worker).restart();
            });
            view.cancelButton.setOnAction(actionEvent -> {
                model.worker.cancel();
            });
            view.exceptionButton.setOnAction(actionEvent -> {
                model.shouldThrow.getAndSet(true);
            });
        }

        private static class Model {
            public Worker<String> worker;
            public AtomicBoolean shouldThrow = new AtomicBoolean(false);
            public IntegerProperty numberOfItems = new SimpleIntegerProperty(250);

            private Model() {
                worker = new Service<String>() {
                    @Override
                    protected Task createTask() {
                        return new Task<String>() {
                            @Override
                            protected String call() throws Exception {
                                updateTitle("Example Service");
                                updateMessage("Starting...");
                                final int total = numberOfItems.get();
                                updateProgress(0, total);
                                for (int i = 1; i <= total; i++) {
                                    if (isCancelled()) {
                                        updateValue("Canceled at " + System.currentTimeMillis());
                                        return null; // ignored
                                    }
                                    try {
                                        Thread.sleep(20);
                                    } catch (InterruptedException e) {
                                        if (isCancelled()) {
                                            updateValue("Canceled at " + System.currentTimeMillis());
                                            return null; // ignored
                                        }
                                    }
                                    if (shouldThrow.get()) {
                                        throw new RuntimeException("Exception thrown at " +
                                            System.currentTimeMillis());
```

```
                            }
                            updateTitle("Example Service (" + i + ")");
                            updateMessage("Processed " + i + " of " + total + " items.");
                            updateProgress(i, total);
                        }
                        return "Completed at " + System.currentTimeMillis();
                    }
                };
            }
        };
    }
}

    private static class View {
        public ProgressBar progressBar;

        public Label title;
        public Label message;
        public Label running;
        public Label state;
        public Label totalWork;
        public Label workDone;
        public Label progress;
        public Label value;
        public Label exception;

        public TextField numberOfItems;
        public Button startButton;
        public Button cancelButton;
        public Button exceptionButton;

        public Scene scene;

        private View(final Model model) {
            progressBar = new ProgressBar();
            progressBar.setMinWidth(250);

            title = new Label();
            message = new Label();
            running = new Label();
            state = new Label();
            totalWork = new Label();
            workDone = new Label();
            progress = new Label();
            value = new Label();
            exception = new Label();
            numberOfItems = new TextField();
            numberOfItems.setMaxWidth(40);

            startButton = new Button("Start");
            cancelButton = new Button("Cancel");
```

```
exceptionButton = new Button("Exception");

final ReadOnlyObjectProperty<Worker.State> stateProperty =
    model.worker.stateProperty();

progressBar.progressProperty().bind(model.worker.progressProperty());

title.textProperty().bind(
    model.worker.titleProperty());
message.textProperty().bind(
    model.worker.messageProperty());
running.textProperty().bind(
    Bindings.format("%s", model.worker.runningProperty()));
state.textProperty().bind(
    Bindings.format("%s", stateProperty));
totalWork.textProperty().bind(
    model.worker.totalWorkProperty().asString());
workDone.textProperty().bind(
    model.worker.workDoneProperty().asString());
progress.textProperty().bind(
    Bindings.format("%5.2f%%", model.worker.progressProperty().multiply(100)));
value.textProperty().bind(
    model.worker.valueProperty());
exception.textProperty().bind(Bindings.createStringBinding(() -> {
    final Throwable exception = model.worker.getException();
    if (exception == null) return "";
    return exception.getMessage();
}, model.worker.exceptionProperty()));

model.numberOfItems.bind(Bindings.createIntegerBinding(() -> {
    final String text = numberOfItems.getText();
    int n = 250;
    try {
        n = Integer.parseInt(text);
    } catch (NumberFormatException e) {
    }
    return n;
}, numberOfItems.textProperty()));

startButton.disableProperty().bind(
    stateProperty.isEqualTo(Worker.State.RUNNING));
cancelButton.disableProperty().bind(
    stateProperty.isNotEqualTo(Worker.State.RUNNING));
exceptionButton.disableProperty().bind(
    stateProperty.isNotEqualTo(Worker.State.RUNNING));

HBox topPane = new HBox(10, progressBar);
topPane.setPadding(new Insets(10, 10, 10, 10));
topPane.setAlignment(Pos.CENTER);
```

245

```
        ColumnConstraints constraints1 = new ColumnConstraints();
        constraints1.setHalignment(HPos.RIGHT);
        constraints1.setMinWidth(65);
        ColumnConstraints constraints2 = new ColumnConstraints();
        constraints2.setHalignment(HPos.LEFT);
        constraints2.setMinWidth(200);

        GridPane centerPane = new GridPane();
        centerPane.setHgap(10);
        centerPane.setVgap(10);
        centerPane.setPadding(new Insets(10, 10, 10, 10));
        centerPane.getColumnConstraints().addAll(constraints1, constraints2);
        centerPane.add(new Label("Title:"), 0, 0);
        centerPane.add(new Label("Message:"), 0, 1);
        centerPane.add(new Label("Running:"), 0, 2);
        centerPane.add(new Label("State:"), 0, 3);
        centerPane.add(new Label("Total Work:"), 0, 4);
        centerPane.add(new Label("Work Done:"), 0, 5);
        centerPane.add(new Label("Progress:"), 0, 6);
        centerPane.add(new Label("Value:"), 0, 7);
        centerPane.add(new Label("Exception:"), 0, 8);

        centerPane.add(title, 1, 0);
        centerPane.add(message, 1, 1);
        centerPane.add(running, 1, 2);
        centerPane.add(state, 1, 3);
        centerPane.add(totalWork, 1, 4);
        centerPane.add(workDone, 1, 5);
        centerPane.add(progress, 1, 6);
        centerPane.add(value, 1, 7);
        centerPane.add(exception, 1, 8);

        HBox buttonPane = new HBox(10,
            new Label("Process"), numberOfItems, new Label("items"),
            startButton, cancelButton, exceptionButton);
        buttonPane.setPadding(new Insets(10, 10, 10, 10));
        buttonPane.setAlignment(Pos.CENTER);

        BorderPane root = new BorderPane(centerPane, topPane, null, buttonPane, null);
        scene = new Scene(root);
    }
  }
}
```

The preceding program is derived from the WorkerAndTaskExample class that we studied in the previous section. The Model nested class for this program holds a worker field of type Worker, a shouldThrow field of type AtomicBoolean, and a numberOfItems field of type IntegerProperty. The worker field is initialized to an instance of an anonymous subclass of Service<String> that implements its createTask() method to return a Task<String> with a call() method that is implemented almost exactly like the Task<String> implementation in the last section, except that instead of always processing 250 items, it picks up the number of items to process from the numberOfItems property from the Model class.

The View nested class of this program creates a UI that is almost identical to that in the previous section but with some additional controls in the button panel. One of the controls added to the button panel is a TextField named numberOfItems. The model's numberOfItems IntegerProperty is bound to an IntegerBinding created with the textProperty() of the view's numberOfItems field. This effectively controls the number of items each newly created Task will process. The Start button is disabled only if the service is in the Worker.State.RUNNING state. Therefore, you can click the Start button after a task has finished.

The action handler of the Start button now resets the shouldThrow flag to false and calls restart() of the service.

The screenshots in Figures 5-12 to 5-16 are taken with the ServiceExample program under situations similar to those for the screenshots in Figures 5-7 to 5-11 for the WorkerAndTaskExample program.

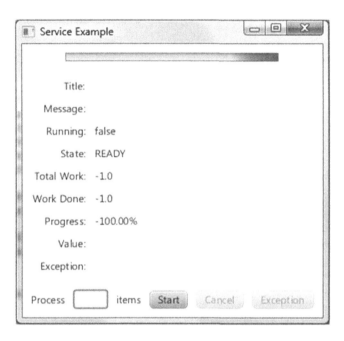

Figure 5-12. *The ServiceExample program after starting up*

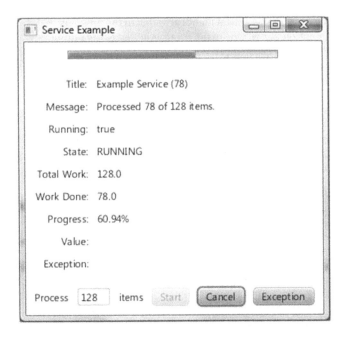

Figure 5-13. *The ServiceExample program while a task is in progress*

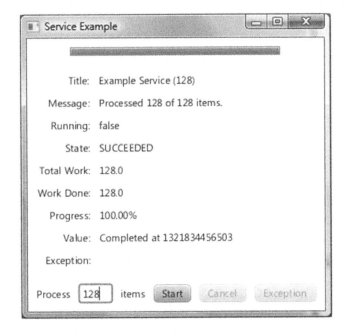

Figure 5-14. *The ServiceExample program after the task succeeded*

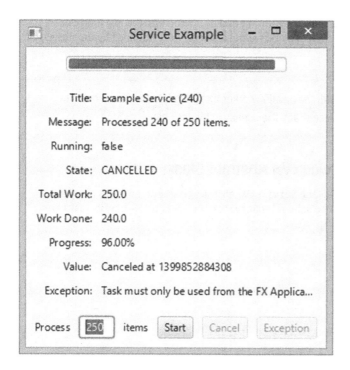

Figure 5-15. *The* ServiceExample *program after the task has been cancelled*

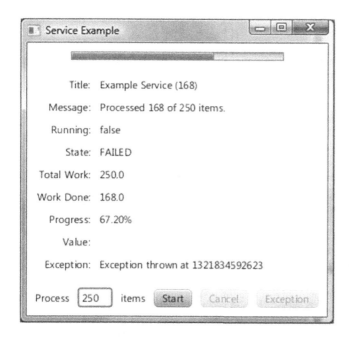

Figure 5-16. *The* ServiceExample *program after the task threw an exception*

As you can see from the preceding screenshots, the number that is entered into the text field does indeed influence the number of items processed in each run of the service, as is evidenced by the messages reflected in the UI in the screenshots.

■ **Caution**   Because the task that is started with the JavaFX worker threading framework executes in background threads, it is very important not to access any live scenes in the task code.

Understanding the ScheduledService<V> Abstract Class

The ScheduledService<V> abstract class extends the Service<V> abstract class, and provides repeated executions of the tasks created by the service. The ScheduledService<V> class controls how its tasks are repeated through the following properties:

- delay
- period
- backOffStrategy
- restartOnFailure
- maximumFailureCount
- currentFailureCount
- cumulativePeriod
- maximumCumulativePeriod
- lastValue

The delay property controls how much time must elapse after the start() call on the scheduled service before the task starts to run. The period property controls how much time must elapse after one run of the task before the next run of the task can start. The period measures the differences between the start of one run and the start of the next run. The delay and period are object properties of type Duration. If no failure condition occurs while the task is executing, the ScheduledService will keep on repeating the task indefinitely.

If a failure condition occurs while the task is executing, what happens next is controlled by the restartOnFailure property. If this property is false, the ScheduledService will remain in the FAILED state and nothing more will happen. If the restartOnFailure property is true, the ScheduledService will rerun the task again. The rerunning of failed tasks is controlled by the backOffStrategy, maximumFailureCount, and maximumCumulativePeriod properties. The back off strategy is simply a lambda expression that takes the ScheduledService as an argument and returns a Duration, which is set as the value of the cumulativePeriod property. The rerunning of the task will start when the elapsed time since the start of the last failed run of the task reaches cumulativePeriod. In addition to cumulativePeriod, the ScheduledService also keeps track of the currentFailureCount property, which is the number of consecutive failed runs in the current sequence of failed runs. If the rerunning of the task is successful, ScheduledService will go back to its normal behavior of running the task in period time intervals; otherwise (that is, if the rerun failed again), ScheduledService will ask the backOffStrategy for a new cumulativePeriod, and rerun again. If the currentFailureCount reaches maximumFailureCount, or if the cumulativePeriod becomes greater than or equal to the maximumCumulativePeriod, the ScheduledService will go into the FAILED state and nothing more will happen.

Three back off strategies are provided. They are constants in ScheduledService. The LINEAR_BACKOFF_ STRATEGY returns ever longer Durations that grow linearly. The EXPONENTIAL_BACKOFF_STRATEGY returns ever longer Durations that grow exponentially. The LOGARITHMIC_BACKOFF_STRATEGY returns ever longer Durations that grow logarithmically. You can easily define your own back off strategies.

You can reset and restart a ScheduledService by calling reset() and start() methods.

Mixing JavaFX with Other GUI Toolkits

Having examined the threading paradigm of the JavaFX runtime and ways to execute code from the JavaFX application thread, we now look at how to make JavaFX coexist with some other GUI toolkits. JavaFX provides classes and frameworks that make it possible to mix JavaFX with Swing or SWT. You can embed a JavaFX scene in a Swing application. You can embed a JavaFX scene in a SWT application. And you can embed Swing components in a JavaFX application.

Embedding JavaFX Scenes in Swing Applications

JavaFX supports embedding a JavaFX scene into a Swing application through the javafx.embed.swing package of classes. This is a pretty small package that includes one public class for embedding JavaFX scenes into Swing—JFXPanel—and another class—SwingNode—for embedding Swing components into JavaFX applications. The JFXPanel class extends javax.swing.JComponent, and as such can be placed in a Swing program just as any other Swing component. JFXPanel can also host a JavaFX scene, and as such can add a JavaFX scene to a Swing program.

However, this Swing program with a JavaFX scene embedded in it needs both the Swing runtime to make its Swing portion function correctly, and the JavaFX runtime to make the JavaFX portion function correctly. Therefore, it has both the Swing Event Dispatching Thread (EDT) and the JavaFX Application Thread. The JFXPanel class does a two-way translation of all the user events between Swing and JavaFX.

Just as JavaFX has the rule that requires all access to live scenes to be done in the JavaFX Application Thread, Swing has the rule that requires all access to Swing GUIs to be done in the EDT. You still need to jump the thread if you want to alter a Swing component from a JavaFX event handler or vice versa. The proper way to execute a piece of code on the JavaFX Application Thread, as we saw earlier, is to use Platform.runLater(). The proper way to execute a piece of code on the Swing EDT is to use EventQueue. invokeLater().

In this section, we convert a pure Swing program into a Swing and JavaFX hybrid program. We start off with the Swing program in Listing 5-11, which is very similar to the ResponsiveUIExample program.

Listing 5-11. NoJavaFXSceneInSwingExample.java

```
package com.projavafx.collections;

import javax.swing.*;
import java.awt.*;
import java.awt.event.ActionEvent;
import java.awt.event.ActionListener;

public class NoJavaFXSceneInSwingExample {
    public static void main(final String[] args) {
        EventQueue.invokeLater(new Runnable() {
```

```java
            @Override
            public void run() {
                swingMain(args);
            }
        });
    }
    private static void swingMain(String[] args) {
        Model model = new Model();
        View view = new View(model);
        Controller controller = new Controller(model, view);
        controller.mainLoop();
    }

    private static class Model {
        public Color fillColor = Color.LIGHT_GRAY;
        public Color strokeColor = Color.DARK_GRAY;
    }

    private static class View {
        public JFrame frame;
        public JComponent canvas;
        public JButton changeFillButton;
        public JButton changeStrokeButton;

        private View(final Model model) {
            frame = new JFrame("No JavaFX in Swing Example");
            canvas = new JComponent() {
                @Override
                public void paint(Graphics g) {
                    g.setColor(model.strokeColor);
                    g.fillRect(0, 0, 200, 200);
                    g.setColor(model.fillColor);
                    g.fillRect(10, 10, 180, 180);
                }

                @Override
                public Dimension getPreferredSize() {
                    return new Dimension(200, 200);
                }
            };
            FlowLayout canvasPanelLayout = new FlowLayout(FlowLayout.CENTER, 10, 10);
            JPanel canvasPanel = new JPanel(canvasPanelLayout);
            canvasPanel.add(canvas);

            changeFillButton = new JButton("Change Fill");
            changeStrokeButton = new JButton("Change Stroke");
            FlowLayout buttonPanelLayout = new FlowLayout(FlowLayout.CENTER, 10, 10);
            JPanel buttonPanel = new JPanel(buttonPanelLayout);
            buttonPanel.add(changeFillButton);
            buttonPanel.add(changeStrokeButton);
```

```
            frame.add(canvasPanel, BorderLayout.CENTER);
            frame.add(buttonPanel, BorderLayout.SOUTH);
            frame.setDefaultCloseOperation(JFrame.EXIT_ON_CLOSE);
            frame.setLocationByPlatform(true);
            frame.pack();
        }
    }
    private static class Controller {
        private View view;

        private Controller(final Model model, final View view) {
            this.view = view;
            this.view.changeFillButton.addActionListener(new ActionListener() {
                @Override
                public void actionPerformed(ActionEvent e) {
                    if (model.fillColor.equals(Color.LIGHT_GRAY)) {
                        model.fillColor = Color.GRAY;
                    } else {
                        model.fillColor = Color.LIGHT_GRAY;
                    }
                    view.canvas.repaint();
                }
            });
            this.view.changeStrokeButton.addActionListener(new ActionListener() {
                @Override
                public void actionPerformed(ActionEvent e) {
                    if (model.strokeColor.equals(Color.DARK_GRAY)) {
                        model.strokeColor = Color.BLACK;
                    } else {
                        model.strokeColor = Color.DARK_GRAY;
                    }
                    view.canvas.repaint();
                }
            });
        }

        public void mainLoop() {
            view.frame.setVisible(true);
        }
    }
}
```

When the program in Listing 5-11 is run, the UI in Figure 5-17 is displayed. It is a JFrame holding three Swing components, a JComponent with overridden paint() and getPreferredSize() methods that makes it look like the rectangle we saw in the earlier program, and two JButtons that will change the fill and the stroke of the rectangle.

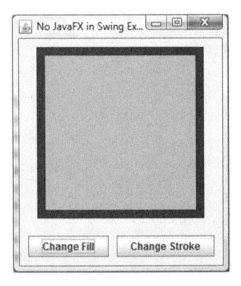

Figure 5-17. *The NoJavaFXSceneInSwingExample program*

Inasmuch as the custom-painted JComponent in NoJavaFXSceneInSwingExample is hard to maintain over the long run, we replace it with the JavaFX Rectangle. This is done by replacing the Swing code with the equivalent JFXPanel code. This is the Swing code:

```
canvas = new JComponent() {
    @Override
    public void paint(Graphics g) {
        g.setColor(model.strokeColor);
        g.fillRect(0, 0, 200, 200);
        g.setColor(model.fillColor);
        g.fillRect(10, 10, 180, 180);
    }

    @Override
    public Dimension getPreferredSize() {
        return new Dimension(200, 200);
    }
};
```

And here is the JFXPanel code:

```
canvas = new JFXPanel();
canvas.setPreferredSize(new Dimension(210, 210));
Platform.runLater(new Runnable() {
    @Override
    public void run() {
        final Rectangle rectangle = new Rectangle(200, 200);
        rectangle.setStrokeWidth(10);
        rectangle.fillProperty().bind(model.fillProperty());
        rectangle.strokeProperty().bind(model.strokeProperty());
```

```
        final VBox vBox = new VBox(rectangle);
        final Scene scene = new Scene(vBox);
        canvas.setScene(scene);
    }
});
```

The JFXPanel constructor bootstraps the JavaFX runtime system. We set the preferred size to the JFXPanel for it to be laid out correctly in Swing containers. We then constructed the scene graph on the JavaFX application thread and bound it to the model, which we changed into a JavaFX bean. Another set of changes that need to be made are in the ActionListeners of the two JButtons. Modifying the model triggers a change to the JavaFX rectangle, so the following code needs to be run on the JavaFX application thread:

```
this.view.changeFillButton.addActionListener(e -> {
    Platform.runLater(() -> {
        final Paint fillPaint = model.getFill();
        if (fillPaint.equals(Color.LIGHTGRAY)) {
            model.setFill(Color.GRAY);
        } else {
            model.setFill(Color.LIGHTGRAY);
        }
    });
});
```

The completed Swing JavaFX hybrid program is shown in Listing 5-12.

Listing 5-12. JavaFXSceneInSwingExample.java

```
package com.projavafx.collections;

import javafx.application.Platform;
import javafx.beans.property.ObjectProperty;
import javafx.beans.property.SimpleObjectProperty;
import javafx.embed.swing.JFXPanel;
import javafx.scene.Scene;
import javafx.scene.layout.VBox;
import javafx.scene.paint.Color;
import javafx.scene.paint.Paint;
import javafx.scene.shape.Rectangle;

import javax.swing.*;
import java.awt.*;

public class JavaFXSceneInSwingExample {
    public static void main(final String[] args) {
        EventQueue.invokeLater(() -> {
            swingMain(args);
        });
    }

    private static void swingMain(String[] args) {
        Model model = new Model();
        View view = new View(model);
```

```
        Controller controller = new Controller(model, view);
        controller.mainLoop();
    }

    private static class Model {
        private ObjectProperty<Color> fill = new SimpleObjectProperty<>(Color.LIGHTGRAY);
        private ObjectProperty<Color> stroke = new SimpleObjectProperty<>(Color.DARKGRAY);

        public final Color getFill() {
            return fill.get();
        }

        public final void setFill(Color value) {
            this.fill.set(value);
        }

        public final Color getStroke() {
            return stroke.get();
        }

        public final void setStroke(Color value) {
            this.stroke.set(value);
        }

        public final ObjectProperty<Color> fillProperty() {
            return fill;
        }

        public final ObjectProperty<Color> strokeProperty() {
            return stroke;
        }
    }

    private static class View {
        public JFrame frame;
        public JFXPanel canvas;
        public JButton changeFillButton;
        public JButton changeStrokeButton;

        private View(final Model model) {
            frame = new JFrame("JavaFX in Swing Example");
            canvas = new JFXPanel();
            canvas.setPreferredSize(new Dimension(210, 210));
            Platform.runLater(new Runnable() {
                @Override
                public void run() {
                    final Rectangle rectangle = new Rectangle(200, 200);
                    rectangle.setStrokeWidth(10);
                    rectangle.fillProperty().bind(model.fillProperty());
                    rectangle.strokeProperty().bind(model.strokeProperty());
                    final VBox vBox = new VBox(rectangle);
```

```java
            final Scene scene = new Scene(vBox);
            canvas.setScene(scene);
        }
    });
    FlowLayout canvasPanelLayout = new FlowLayout(FlowLayout.CENTER, 10, 10);
    JPanel canvasPanel = new JPanel(canvasPanelLayout);
    canvasPanel.add(canvas);

    changeFillButton = new JButton("Change Fill");
    changeStrokeButton = new JButton("Change Stroke");
    FlowLayout buttonPanelLayout = new FlowLayout(FlowLayout.CENTER, 10, 10);
    JPanel buttonPanel = new JPanel(buttonPanelLayout);
    buttonPanel.add(changeFillButton);
    buttonPanel.add(changeStrokeButton);

    frame.add(canvasPanel, BorderLayout.CENTER);
    frame.add(buttonPanel, BorderLayout.SOUTH);
    frame.setDefaultCloseOperation(JFrame.EXIT_ON_CLOSE);
    frame.setLocationByPlatform(true);
    frame.pack();
    }
}

private static class Controller {
    private View view;

    private Controller(final Model model, final View view) {
        this.view = view;
        this.view.changeFillButton.addActionListener(e -> {
            Platform.runLater(() -> {
                final Paint fillPaint = model.getFill();
                if (fillPaint.equals(Color.LIGHTGRAY)) {
                    model.setFill(Color.GRAY);
                } else {
                    model.setFill(Color.LIGHTGRAY);
                }
            });
        });
        this.view.changeStrokeButton.addActionListener(e -> {
            Platform.runLater(() -> {
                final Paint strokePaint = model.getStroke();
                if (strokePaint.equals(Color.DARKGRAY)) {
                    model.setStroke(Color.BLACK);
                } else {
                    model.setStroke(Color.DARKGRAY);
                }
            });
        });
    }
```

```
        public void mainLoop() {
            view.frame.setVisible(true);
        }
    }
}
```

When the program in Listing 5-12 is run, the GUI in Figure 5-18 is displayed. You can't tell from the screenshot, but the rectangle in the center of the JFrame is a JavaFX rectangle.

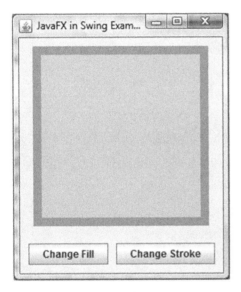

Figure 5-18. *The JavaFXSceneInSwingExample program*

Embedding JavaFX Scenes in SWT Applications

JavaFX is capable of embedding a JavaFX scene into an SWT application through the javafx.embed.swt package of classes. It contains two public classes, FXCanvas and SWTFXUtils. The FXCanvas class extends org.eclipse.swt.widgets.Canvas, and can be placed in an SWT program just like any other SWT widget. FXCanvas can also host a JavaFX scene, and can add a JavaFX scene to an SWT program.

Because both SWT and JavaFX use the native platform's UI thread as their own event dispatching thread, the SWT UI thread (where a Display object is instantiated and where the main loop is started and where all other UI widgets must be created and accessed) and the JavaFX application thread are one and the same. Therefore, there is no need to use Platform.runLater() or its SWT equivalent display.asyncExec() in your SWT and JavaFX event handlers.

The SWT program in Listing 5-13 is an SWT port of the Swing program in Listing 5-11.

■ **Note** You need to add the jar file that contains the SWT classes to your classpath to compile the programs in Listings 5-13 and 5-14. On our development machine, the SWT jar is located in %ECLIPSE_HOME%\plugins\ org.eclipse.swt.win32.win32.x86_64_3.102.1.v20140206-1358.jar, where %ECLIPSE_HOME% is an Eclipse (Kepler SR2) installation directory.

Listing 5-13. `NoJavaFXSceneInSWTExample.java`

```java
import org.eclipse.swt.SWT;
import org.eclipse.swt.events.MouseEvent;
import org.eclipse.swt.events.MouseMoveListener;
import org.eclipse.swt.events.MouseTrackAdapter;
import org.eclipse.swt.events.PaintEvent;
import org.eclipse.swt.events.PaintListener;
import org.eclipse.swt.events.SelectionAdapter;
import org.eclipse.swt.events.SelectionEvent;
import org.eclipse.swt.graphics.Color;
import org.eclipse.swt.graphics.GC;
import org.eclipse.swt.graphics.RGB;
import org.eclipse.swt.layout.RowData;
import org.eclipse.swt.layout.RowLayout;
import org.eclipse.swt.widgets.Button;
import org.eclipse.swt.widgets.Canvas;
import org.eclipse.swt.widgets.Composite;
import org.eclipse.swt.widgets.Display;
import org.eclipse.swt.widgets.Label;
import org.eclipse.swt.widgets.Shell;

public class NoJavaFXSceneInSWTExample {
    public static void main(final String[] args) {
        Model model = new Model();
        View view = new View(model);
        Controller controller = new Controller(model, view);
        controller.mainLoop();
    }

    private static class Model {
        public static final RGB LIGHT_GRAY = new RGB(0xd3, 0xd3, 0xd3);
        public static final RGB GRAY = new RGB(0x80, 0x80, 0x80);
        public static final RGB DARK_GRAY = new RGB(0xa9, 0xa9, 0xa9);
        public static final RGB BLACK = new RGB(0x0, 0x0, 0x0);
        public RGB fillColor = LIGHT_GRAY;
        public RGB strokeColor = DARK_GRAY;
    }

    private static class View {
        public Display display;
        public Shell frame;
        public Canvas canvas;
        public Button changeFillButton;
        public Button changeStrokeButton;
        public Label mouseLocation;
        public boolean mouseInCanvas;

        private View(final Model model) {
            this.display = new Display();
            frame = new Shell(display);
            frame.setText("No JavaFX in SWT Example");
```

259

```
        RowLayout frameLayout = new RowLayout(SWT.VERTICAL);
        frameLayout.spacing = 10;
        frameLayout.center = true;
        frame.setLayout(frameLayout);

        Composite canvasPanel = new Composite(frame, SWT.NONE);
        RowLayout canvasPanelLayout = new RowLayout(SWT.VERTICAL);
        canvasPanelLayout.spacing = 10;
        canvasPanel.setLayout(canvasPanelLayout);

        canvas = new Canvas(canvasPanel, SWT.NONE);
        canvas.setLayoutData(new RowData(200, 200));
        canvas.addPaintListener(new PaintListener() {
            @Override
            public void paintControl(PaintEvent paintEvent) {
                final GC gc = paintEvent.gc;
                final Color strokeColor = new Color(display, model.strokeColor);
                gc.setBackground(strokeColor);
                gc.fillRectangle(0, 0, 200, 200);
                final Color fillColor = new Color(display, model.fillColor);
                gc.setBackground(fillColor);
                gc.fillRectangle(10, 10, 180, 180);
                strokeColor.dispose();
                fillColor.dispose();
            }
        });

        Composite buttonPanel = new Composite(frame, SWT.NONE);
        RowLayout buttonPanelLayout = new RowLayout(SWT.HORIZONTAL);
        buttonPanelLayout.spacing = 10;
        buttonPanelLayout.center = true;
        buttonPanel.setLayout(buttonPanelLayout);

        changeFillButton = new Button(buttonPanel, SWT.NONE);
        changeFillButton.setText("Change Fill");
        changeStrokeButton = new Button(buttonPanel, SWT.NONE);
        changeStrokeButton.setText("Change Stroke");
        mouseLocation = new Label(buttonPanel, SWT.NONE);
        mouseLocation.setLayoutData(new RowData(50, 15));

        frame.pack();
    }
}

private static class Controller {
    private View view;

    private Controller(final Model model, final View view) {
        this.view = view;
        view.changeFillButton.addSelectionListener(new SelectionAdapter() {
            @Override
```

```java
            public void widgetSelected(SelectionEvent e) {
                if (model.fillColor.equals(model.LIGHT_GRAY)) {
                    model.fillColor = model.GRAY;
                } else {
                    model.fillColor = model.LIGHT_GRAY;
                }
                view.canvas.redraw();
            }
        });
        view.changeStrokeButton.addSelectionListener(new SelectionAdapter() {
            @Override
            public void widgetSelected(SelectionEvent e) {
                if (model.strokeColor.equals(model.DARK_GRAY)) {
                    model.strokeColor = model.BLACK;
                } else {
                    model.strokeColor = model.DARK_GRAY;
                }
                view.canvas.redraw();
            }
        });
        view.canvas.addMouseMoveListener(new MouseMoveListener() {
            @Override
            public void mouseMove(MouseEvent mouseEvent) {
                if (view.mouseInCanvas) {
                    view.mouseLocation.setText("(" + mouseEvent.x + ",
                    " + mouseEvent.y + ")");
                }
            }
        });
        this.view.canvas.addMouseTrackListener(new MouseTrackAdapter() {
            @Override
            public void mouseEnter(MouseEvent e) {
                view.mouseInCanvas = true;
            }

            @Override
            public void mouseExit(MouseEvent e) {
                view.mouseInCanvas = false;
                view.mouseLocation.setText("");
            }
        });

    }

    public void mainLoop() {
        view.frame.open();
        while (!view.frame.isDisposed()) {
            if (!view.display.readAndDispatch()) {
                view.display.sleep();
            }
        }
```

```
            view.display.dispose();
        }
    }
}
```

When the program in Listing 5-13 is run, the UI in Figure 5-19 is displayed. It is an SWT Shell holding four SWT widgets, a Canvas with a PaintListener that makes it look like the rectangle we saw earlier, two Buttons that will change the fill and the stroke of the rectangle, and a Label widget that will show the location of the mouse pointer when the mouse is inside the rectangle.

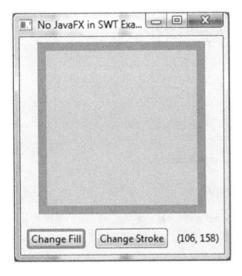

Figure 5-19. *The NoJavaFXSceneInSWTExample program*

As we did with the Swing example, we replace the custom painted Canvas widget in the program NoJavaFXSceneInSWTExample with a JavaFX Rectangle. This is done by replacing the SWT code with the equivalent FXCanvas code. The following is the SWT code:

```
canvas = new Canvas(canvasPanel, SWT.NONE);
canvas.setLayoutData(new RowData(200, 200));
canvas.addPaintListener(new PaintListener() {
    @Override
    public void paintControl(PaintEvent paintEvent) {
        final GC gc = paintEvent.gc;
        final Color strokeColor = new Color(display, model.strokeColor);
        gc.setBackground(strokeColor);
        gc.fillRectangle(0, 0, 200, 200);
        final Color fillColor = new Color(display, model.fillColor);
        gc.setBackground(fillColor);
        gc.fillRectangle(10, 10, 180, 180);
        strokeColor.dispose();
        fillColor.dispose();
    }
});
```

And here is the FXCanvas code:

```
canvas = new FXCanvas(canvasPanel, SWT.NONE);
rectangle = new Rectangle(200, 200);
rectangle.setStrokeWidth(10);
VBox vBox = new VBox(rectangle);
Scene scene = new Scene(vBox, 210, 210);
canvas.setScene(scene);
rectangle.fillProperty().bind(model.fillProperty());
rectangle.strokeProperty().bind(model.strokeProperty());
```

We also changed the model into a JavaFX bean. The event listeners are changed in a natural way. The complete SWT JavaFX hybrid program is shown in Listing 5-14.

Listing 5-14. `JavaFXSceneInSWTExample.java`

```
package com.projavafx.collections;

import javafx.beans.property.ObjectProperty;
import javafx.beans.property.SimpleObjectProperty;
import javafx.embed.swt.FXCanvas;
import javafx.event.EventHandler;
import javafx.scene.Scene;
import javafx.scene.input.MouseEvent;
import javafx.scene.layout.VBox;
import javafx.scene.paint.Color;
import javafx.scene.paint.Paint;
import javafx.scene.shape.Rectangle;
import org.eclipse.swt.SWT;
import org.eclipse.swt.events.SelectionAdapter;
import org.eclipse.swt.events.SelectionEvent;
import org.eclipse.swt.layout.RowData;
import org.eclipse.swt.layout.RowLayout;
import org.eclipse.swt.widgets.Button;
import org.eclipse.swt.widgets.Composite;
import org.eclipse.swt.widgets.Display;
import org.eclipse.swt.widgets.Label;
import org.eclipse.swt.widgets.Shell;

public class JavaFXSceneInSWTExample {
    public static void main(final String[] args) {
        Model model = new Model();
        View view = new View(model);
        Controller controller = new Controller(model, view);
        controller.mainLoop();
    }

    private static class Model {
        private ObjectProperty<Color> fill = new SimpleObjectProperty<>(Color.LIGHTGRAY);
        private ObjectProperty<Color> stroke = new SimpleObjectProperty<>(Color.DARKGRAY);
```

```java
        public Color getFill() {
            return fill.get();
        }

        public void setFill(Color value) {
            this.fill.set(value);
        }

        public Color getStroke() {
            return stroke.get();
        }

        public void setStroke(Color value) {
            this.stroke.set(value);
        }

        public ObjectProperty<Color> fillProperty() {
            return fill;
        }

        public ObjectProperty<Color> strokeProperty() {
            return stroke;
        }
    }

    private static class View {
        public Display display;
        public Shell frame;
        public FXCanvas canvas;
        public Button changeFillButton;
        public Button changeStrokeButton;
        public Label mouseLocation;
        public boolean mouseInCanvas;
        public Rectangle rectangle;

        private View(final Model model) {
            this.display = new Display();
            frame = new Shell(display);
            frame.setText("JavaFX in SWT Example");
            RowLayout frameLayout = new RowLayout(SWT.VERTICAL);
            frameLayout.spacing = 10;
            frameLayout.center = true;
            frame.setLayout(frameLayout);

            Composite canvasPanel = new Composite(frame, SWT.NONE);
            RowLayout canvasPanelLayout = new RowLayout(SWT.VERTICAL);
            canvasPanelLayout.spacing = 10;
            canvasPanel.setLayout(canvasPanelLayout);
            canvas = new FXCanvas(canvasPanel, SWT.NONE);
            rectangle = new Rectangle(200, 200);
            rectangle.setStrokeWidth(10);
```

```
        VBox vBox = new VBox(rectangle);
        Scene scene = new Scene(vBox, 210, 210);
        canvas.setScene(scene);
        rectangle.fillProperty().bind(model.fillProperty());
        rectangle.strokeProperty().bind(model.strokeProperty());

        Composite buttonPanel = new Composite(frame, SWT.NONE);
        RowLayout buttonPanelLayout = new RowLayout(SWT.HORIZONTAL);
        buttonPanelLayout.spacing = 10;
        buttonPanelLayout.center = true;
        buttonPanel.setLayout(buttonPanelLayout);

        changeFillButton = new Button(buttonPanel, SWT.NONE);
        changeFillButton.setText("Change Fill");
        changeStrokeButton = new Button(buttonPanel, SWT.NONE);
        changeStrokeButton.setText("Change Stroke");
        mouseLocation = new Label(buttonPanel, SWT.NONE);
        mouseLocation.setLayoutData(new RowData(50, 15));

        frame.pack();
    }
}

private static class Controller {
    private View view;

    private Controller(final Model model, final View view) {
        this.view = view;
        view.changeFillButton.addSelectionListener(new SelectionAdapter() {
            @Override
            public void widgetSelected(SelectionEvent e) {
                final Paint fillPaint = model.getFill();
                if (fillPaint.equals(Color.LIGHTGRAY)) {
                    model.setFill(Color.GRAY);
                } else {
                    model.setFill(Color.LIGHTGRAY);
                }
            }
        });
        view.changeStrokeButton.addSelectionListener(new SelectionAdapter() {
            @Override
            public void widgetSelected(SelectionEvent e) {
                final Paint strokePaint = model.getStroke();
                if (strokePaint.equals(Color.DARKGRAY)) {
                    model.setStroke(Color.BLACK);
                } else {
                    model.setStroke(Color.DARKGRAY);
                }
            }
        });
        view.rectangle.setOnMouseEntered(new EventHandler<MouseEvent>() {
```

```
                @Override
                public void handle(MouseEvent mouseEvent) {
                    view.mouseInCanvas = true;
                }
            });
            view.rectangle.setOnMouseExited(new EventHandler<MouseEvent>() {
                @Override
                public void handle(final MouseEvent mouseEvent) {
                    view.mouseInCanvas = false;
                    view.mouseLocation.setText("");
                }
            });
            view.rectangle.setOnMouseMoved(new EventHandler<MouseEvent>() {
                @Override
                public void handle(final MouseEvent mouseEvent) {
                    if (view.mouseInCanvas) {
                        view.mouseLocation.setText("(" + (int) mouseEvent.getSceneX() + ",
                        " + (int) mouseEvent.getSceneY() + ")");
                    }
                }
            });
        }

    public void mainLoop() {
        view.frame.open();
        while (!view.frame.isDisposed()) {
            if (!view.display.readAndDispatch()) view.display.sleep();
        }
        view.display.dispose();
    }
  }
}
```

When the program in Listing 5-14 is run, the GUI in Figure 5-20 is displayed. The rectangle in the center of the SWT Shell is a JavaFX rectangle.

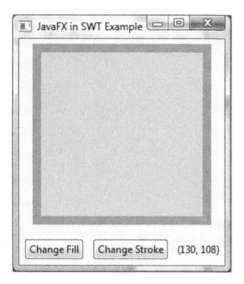

Figure 5-20. *The JavaFXSceneInSWTExample program*

Embedding Swing Components in JavaFX Applications

The SwingNode class in the javafx.embed.swing package is a JavaFX Node that can host a Swing JComponent, and therefore allows you to embed a Swing component in your JavaFX application. This gives legacy Swing applications a piecemeal way of migrating to JavaFX. Aside from the default constructor, the only other public methods designed for use by application developers are a pair of getter and setter methods for the embedded JComponent:

- public void setContent(JComponent)
- public JComponent getContent()

When a SwingNode that contains a JComponent is attached to a live JavaFX scene, the SwingNode class takes care of forwarding all JavaFX input and focus events to the embedded JComponent. Only lightweight Swing components are allowed to be embedded in JavaFX applications. Just like in the case for a JavaFX scene embedded in a Swing application, the presence of the two event dispatching threads in a JavaFX application with an embedded Swing component, the JavaFX Application Thread and the Swing EDT, warrants our attention. In particular, the requirement of performing JavaFX live scene manipulation in the JavaFX Application Thread and the requirement of performing Swing UI manipulations in the Swing EDT should be honored. In practical terms, this means that if you want to manipulate the Swing UI in a JavaFX event handler, you should send it to the Swing EDT with EventQueue.invokeLater(); and if you want to manipulate JavaFX Nodes in a Swing event listener method, you should send it to the JavaFX Application Thread with Platform.runLater().

In this section, we turn the sample program that we have been using for this chapter into a JavaFX application with an embedded custom Swing component. The custom Swing component is a simple subclass of JComponent that draws a rectangle with a thick border in two different colors.

```
private static class MyRectangle extends JComponent {
    private final Model model;

    public MyRectangle(Model model) {
        this.model = model;
    }
```

```java
    @Override
    public void paint(Graphics g) {
        g.setColor(model.getStrokeColor());
        g.fillRect(0, 0, 200, 200);
        g.setColor(model.getFillColor());
        g.fillRect(10, 10, 180, 180);
    }

    @Override
    public Dimension getMaximumSize() {
        return new Dimension(200, 200);
    }
}
```

The current implementation of SwingNode lacks the ability to respond well to its JavaFX container Nodes layout requests. We extend it so that the layout of the application is improved:

```java
private static class MySwingNode extends SwingNode {
    @Override
    public double minWidth(double height) {
        return 250;
    }

    @Override
    public double minHeight(double width) {
        return 200;
    }
}
```

When the two JavaFX buttons are clicked, we invoke code that alters the state of the Swing component MyRectangle in a Runnable represented as a lambda expression through EventQueue.invokeLater():

```java
view.changeFillButton.setOnAction(actionEvent -> {
    EventQueue.invokeLater(() -> {
        final java.awt.Color fillColor = model.getFillColor();
        if (fillColor.equals(java.awt.Color.LIGHT_GRAY)) {
            model.setFillColor(java.awt.Color.GRAY);
        } else {
            model.setFillColor(java.awt.Color.LIGHT_GRAY);
        }
        view.canvas.repaint();
    });
});
```

■ **Note**   The repaint() method is actually one of the rare Swing UI methods that can be called from any thread, not just the Swing EDT. Our use of EventQueue.invokeLater() is for illustration purposes only.

CHAPTER 5 ■ COLLECTIONS AND CONCURRENCY

When the mouse hovers over the MyRectangle, we update a JavaFX Label by updating a StringProperty named mouseLocation in our Model class that the textProperty of the Label binds to:

```
canvas.addMouseMotionListener(new MouseMotionListener() {
    @Override
    public void mouseDragged(MouseEvent e) {
    }

    @Override
    public void mouseMoved(MouseEvent e) {
        Platform.runLater(() -> {
            model.setMouseLocation("(" + e.getX() + ", " + e.getY() + ")");
        });
    }
});
swingNode.setContent(canvas);
```

The complete Swing component in JavaFX example application is shown in Listing 5-15.

Listing 5-15. SwingComponentInJavaFXExample.java

```
package com.projavafx.collections;

import javafx.application.Application;
import javafx.application.Platform;
import javafx.beans.property.SimpleStringProperty;
import javafx.beans.property.StringProperty;
import javafx.embed.swing.SwingNode;
import javafx.geometry.Insets;
import javafx.geometry.Pos;
import javafx.scene.Scene;
import javafx.scene.control.Button;
import javafx.scene.control.Label;
import javafx.scene.layout.HBox;
import javafx.scene.layout.VBox;
import javafx.stage.Stage;

import javax.swing.*;
import java.awt.*;
import java.awt.event.MouseAdapter;
import java.awt.event.MouseEvent;
import java.awt.event.MouseMotionListener;

public class SwingComponentInJavaFXExample extends Application {
    private Model model;
    private View view;

    public static void main(String[] args) {
        launch(args);
    }
```

```java
public SwingComponentInJavaFXExample() {
    model = new Model();
}

@Override
public void start(Stage stage) throws Exception {
    view = new View(model);
    hookupEvents();
    stage.setTitle("Swing in JavaFX Example");
    stage.setScene(view.scene);
    stage.show();
}

private void hookupEvents() {
    view.changeFillButton.setOnAction(actionEvent -> {
        EventQueue.invokeLater(() -> {
            final java.awt.Color fillColor = model.getFillColor();
            if (fillColor.equals(java.awt.Color.LIGHT_GRAY)) {
                model.setFillColor(java.awt.Color.GRAY);
            } else {
                model.setFillColor(java.awt.Color.LIGHT_GRAY);
            }
            view.canvas.repaint();
        });
    });

    view.changeStrokeButton.setOnAction(actionEvent -> {
        EventQueue.invokeLater(() -> {
            final java.awt.Color strokeColor = model.getStrokeColor();
            if (strokeColor.equals(java.awt.Color.GRAY)) {
                model.setStrokeColor(java.awt.Color.BLACK);
            } else {
                model.setStrokeColor(java.awt.Color.GRAY);
            }
            view.canvas.repaint();
        });
    });
}

private static class Model {
    private java.awt.Color fillColor;
    private java.awt.Color strokeColor;
    final private StringProperty mouseLocation = new SimpleStringProperty(this,
    "mouseLocation", "");

    private Model() {
        fillColor = java.awt.Color.LIGHT_GRAY;
        strokeColor = java.awt.Color.GRAY;
    }
```

```java
    public java.awt.Color getFillColor() {
        return fillColor;
    }

    public void setFillColor(java.awt.Color fillColor) {
        this.fillColor = fillColor;
    }

    public java.awt.Color getStrokeColor() {
        return strokeColor;
    }

    public void setStrokeColor(java.awt.Color strokeColor) {
        this.strokeColor = strokeColor;
    }

    public final void setMouseLocation(String mouseLocation) {
        this.mouseLocation.set(mouseLocation);
    }

    public final StringProperty mouseLocationProperty() {
        return mouseLocation;
    }
}

private static class View {
    public JComponent canvas;
    public Button changeFillButton;
    public Button changeStrokeButton;
    public Label mouseLocation;
    public HBox buttonHBox;
    public Scene scene;

    private View(Model model) {
        SwingNode swingNode = new MySwingNode();

        EventQueue.invokeLater(() -> {
            canvas = new MyRectangle(model);
            canvas.addMouseListener(new MouseAdapter() {
                @Override
                public void mouseExited(MouseEvent e) {
                    Platform.runLater(() -> {
                        model.setMouseLocation("");
                    });
                }
            });
            canvas.addMouseMotionListener(new MouseMotionListener() {
                @Override
                public void mouseDragged(MouseEvent e) {
                }
```

```
                @Override
                public void mouseMoved(MouseEvent e) {
                    Platform.runLater(() -> {
                        model.setMouseLocation("(" + e.getX() + ", " + e.getY() + ")");
                    });
                }
            });
            swingNode.setContent(canvas);
        });

        changeFillButton = new Button("Change Fill");
        changeStrokeButton = new Button("Change Stroke");
        mouseLocation = new Label("(100, 100)");
        mouseLocation.setPrefSize(60, 15);
        mouseLocation.textProperty().bind(model.mouseLocationProperty());

        buttonHBox = new HBox(10, changeFillButton, changeStrokeButton, mouseLocation);
        buttonHBox.setPadding(new Insets(10, 0, 10, 0));
        buttonHBox.setAlignment(Pos.CENTER);

        VBox root = new VBox(10, swingNode, buttonHBox);
        root.setPadding(new Insets(10, 10, 10, 10));

        scene = new Scene(root);
    }
}

private static class MySwingNode extends SwingNode {
    @Override
    public double minWidth(double height) {
        return 250;
    }

    @Override
    public double minHeight(double width) {
        return 200;
    }
}

private static class MyRectangle extends JComponent {
    private final Model model;

    public MyRectangle(Model model) {
        this.model = model;
    }

    @Override
    public void paint(Graphics g) {
        g.setColor(model.getStrokeColor());
        g.fillRect(0, 0, 200, 200);
        g.setColor(model.getFillColor());
```

```
            g.fillRect(10, 10, 180, 180);
        }

        @Override
        public Dimension getMaximumSize() {
            return new Dimension(200, 200);
        }
    }
}
```

When the program in Listing 5-15 is run, the GUI in Figure 5-21 is displayed. The rectangle in the center of the JavaFX application is a Swing `JComponent`.

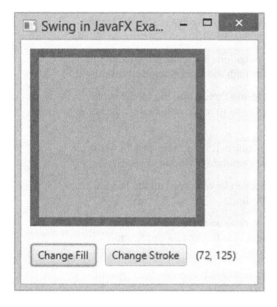

Figure 5-21. *The* `SwingComponentInJavaFXExample` *program*

■ **Tip**   In case you are wondering if there is a way to embed an SWT widget into a JavaFX application, the answer is no. The reason is that SWT widgets are heavyweight components and thus harder to integrate into a lightweight GUI toolkit like JavaFX.

Summary

In this chapter, we looked at JavaFX observable collections, the JavaFX worker threading framework, embedding a JavaFX scene in Swing and SWT applications, and embedding Swing components in JavaFX applications to help you understand the following principles and techniques.

- JavaFX supports observable collections and arrays: `ObservableList`, `ObservableMap`, `ObservableSet`, and `ObservableArray`, with subinterfaces `ObservableIntegerArray` and `ObservableFloatArray`.

- `ObservableList` fires Change events through `ListChangeListener`. `ListChangeListener.Change` may contain one or more discrete changes.

- `ObservableMap` fires Change events through `MapChangeListener`. `MapChangeListener.Change` represents the change of only one key.

- `ObservableSet` fires Change events through `SetChangeListener`. `SetChangeListener.Change` represents the change of only one element.

- `ObservableArray` and its subinterfaces fire change events through `ArrayChangeListener`.

- The `FXCollections` class contains factory methods to create observable collections and arrays, and utility methods to work on them.

- The main event processing thread in JavaFX applications is the JavaFX application thread. All access to live scenes must be done through the JavaFX application thread.

- Other important threads such as the prism rendering thread and the media event thread collaborate with the JavaFX application thread to make graphics rendering and media playback possible.

- Long-running computations on the JavaFX application thread make JavaFX GUIs unresponsive. They should be farmed out to background, or worker, threads.

- The `Worker` interface defines nine properties that can be observed on the JavaFX application thread. It also defines a `cancel()` method.

- `Task<V>` defines a one-time task for offloading work to background, or worker, threads and communicates the results or exceptions to the JavaFX application thread.

- `Service<V>` defines a reusable mechanism for creating and running background tasks.

- `ScheduledService<V>` defines a reusable mechanism for creating and running background tasks in a recurring fashion.

- The `JFXPanel` class is a `JComponent` that can put a JavaFX scene into a Swing application.

- In a Swing JavaFX hybrid program, use `Platform.runLater()` in Swing event listeners to access the JavaFX scene, and use `EventQueue.invokeLater()` or `SwingUtilities.invokeLater()` in JavaFX event handlers to access Swing widgets.

- The `FXCanvas` class is an SWT widget that can put a JavaFX scene into an SWT application.

- In an SWT JavaFX hybrid program, the SWT UI thread and the JavaFX application thread are one and the same.

- The `SwingNode` class is a JavaFX Node that can put a Swing component into a JavaFX application.

Resources

Here are some useful resources for understanding this chapter's material:

- The original JavaFX worker threading framework write-up on FX Experience:
  http://fxexperience.com/2011/07/worker-threading-in-javafx-2-0/

- The original JavaFX and SWT interoperability write-up on FX Experience:
  http://fxexperience.com/2011/12/swt-interop/

CHAPTER 6

▓ ▓ ▓

Creating Charts in JavaFX

Any sufficiently advanced technology is indistinguishable from magic.

—Arthur C. Clarke

Reporting is an important aspect in many business applications. The JavaFX platform contains an API for creating charts. Because a Chart is basically a Node, integrating charts with other parts of a JavaFX application is straightforward. As a consequence, reporting is an integral part of the typical JavaFX business application.

Designing an API is often a compromise among a number of requirements. Two of the most common requirements are "make it easy" and "make it easy to extend." The JavaFX Chart API fulfills both of these. The Chart API contains a number of methods that allow developers to change the look and feel as well as the data of the chart, making it a flexible API that can be easily extended. The default values for the settings are very reasonable, though, and make it easy to integrate a chart with a custom application, with only a few lines of code.

The JavaFX Chart API in JavaFX 9 has eight concrete implementations that are ready to be used by developers. Apart from those, developers can add their own implementations by extending one of the abstract classes.

Structure of the JavaFX Chart API

Different types of charts exist, and there are a number of ways to categorize them. The JavaFX Chart API distinguishes between two-axis charts and charts without an axis. The JavaFX 9 release contains one implementation of a no-axis chart, which is the PieChart. There are a number of two-axis charts, which all extend the abstract XYChart class, as shown in Figure 6-1.

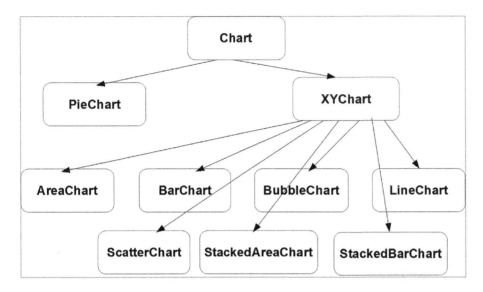

Figure 6-1. *Overview of the charts in the JavaFX Chart API*

The abstract Chart class defines the setup for all charts. Basically, a chart consists of three parts: the title, legend, and content. The content is specific for each implementation of the chart, but the legend and the title concepts are similar across the implementations. Therefore, the Chart class has a number of properties with corresponding getter and setter methods that allow the manipulation of those concepts. The Javadoc of the Chart class mentions the following properties.

```
BooleanProperty animated
ObjectProperty<Node> legend
BooleanProperty legendVisible
ObjectProperty<Side> legendSide
StringProperty title
ObjectProperty<Side> titleSide
```

We use some of these properties in the upcoming examples, but we also show that even without setting values for these properties, the Chart API allows you to create nice charts.

Because Chart extends Region, Parent, and Node, all of the properties and methods available on these classes can be used on a Chart as well. One of the benefits is that the same CSS styling techniques that are used to add style information to JavaFX Nodes also apply to JavaFX charts.

The *JavaFX CSS Reference Guide*, available at http://download.java.net/jdk8/jfxdocs/ javafx/ scene/doc-files/cssref.html, contains an overview of CSS properties that can be altered by designers and developers. By default, the modena style sheet that comes with the JavaFX 9 runtime is used to skin JavaFX charts. For more information on using CSS styles in JavaFX charts, refer to the Oracle chart tutorial at http://docs.oracle.com/javase/8/javafx/user-interface-tutorial/css-styles.htm.

Using the JavaFX PieChart

A `PieChart` renders information in a typical pie structure, where the sizes of the slices are proportional to the values of the data. Before diving into the details, we show a small application that renders a `PieChart`.

The Simple Example

Our example shows the "market share" of a number of programming languages, based on the TIOBE index in April 2017. The TIOBE Programming Community Index is available at `https://www.tiobe.com/tiobe-index`, and it provides an indication of the popularity of programming languages based on search engine traffic. A screenshot of the ranking in April 2017 is shown in Figure 6-2.

Apr 2017	Apr 2016	Change	Programming Language	Ratings	Change
1	1		Java	15.568%	-5.28%
2	2		C	6.966%	-6.94%
3	3		C++	4.554%	-1.36%
4	4		C#	3.579%	-0.22%
5	5		Python	3.457%	+0.13%
6	6		PHP	3.376%	+0.38%
7	10	⌃	Visual Basic .NET	3.251%	+0.98%
8	7	⌄	JavaScript	2.851%	+0.28%
9	11	⌃	Delphi/Object Pascal	2.816%	+0.60%
10	8	⌄	Perl	2.413%	-0.11%
11	9	⌄	Ruby	2.310%	-0.04%
12	15	⌃	Swift	2.287%	+0.81%
13	12	⌄	Assembly language	2.168%	-0.03%
14	13	⌄	Objective-C	2.163%	+0.45%
15	18	⌃	R	2.138%	+0.87%
16	14	⌄	Visual Basic	2.058%	+0.45%
17	16	⌄	MATLAB	2.045%	+0.70%
18	44	⌃⌃	Go	1.974%	+1.73%
19	24	⌃⌃	Scratch	1.668%	+0.86%
20	17	⌄	PL/SQL	1.619%	+0.30%

Figure 6-2. *Screenshot of the TIOBE index in April 2017, taken from* `www.tiobe.com/tiobe-index`

■ **Note**   The algorithm used by TIOBE is described at `https://www.tiobe.com/tiobe-index/programming-languages-definition/`. The scientific value of the numbers is out of scope for our examples.

Listing 6-1 contains the code for the example.

Listing 6-1. Rendering the TIOBE Index in a PieChart

```java
package com.projavafx.charts ;

import javafx.application.Application;
import javafx.collections.FXCollections;
import javafx.collections.ObservableList;
import javafx.scene.Scene;
import javafx.scene.chart.PieChart;
import javafx.scene.layout.StackPane;
import javafx.stage.Stage;

public class ChartApp1 extends Application {

    @Override
    public void start(Stage primaryStage) {
        PieChart pieChart = new PieChart();
        pieChart.setData(getChartData());

        primaryStage.setTitle("PieChart");
        StackPane root = new StackPane();
        root.getChildren().add(pieChart);
        primaryStage.setScene(new Scene(root, 400, 250));
        primaryStage.show();
    }

    private ObservableList<PieChart.Data> getChartData() {
        ObservableList<PieChart.Data> answer = FXCollections.observableArrayList();
                answer.addAll(new PieChart.Data("java", 15.57),
                new PieChart.Data("C", 6.97),
                new PieChart.Data("C++", 4.55),
                new PieChart.Data("C#", 3.58),
                new PieChart.Data("Python", 3.45),
                new PieChart.Data("PHP", 3.38),
                new PieChart.Data("Visual Basic .NET", 3.25));
        return answer;
    }
}
```

The result of running this example is shown in Figure 6-3.

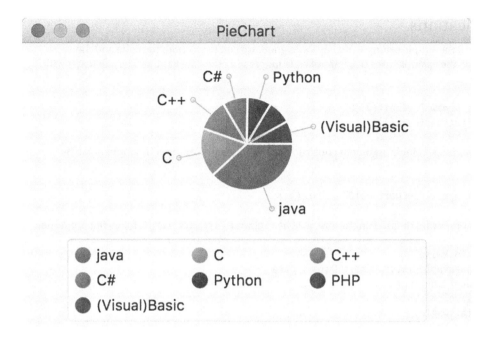

Figure 6-3. *Rendering the TIOBE index in a* `PieChart`

With only a limited amount of code, we can render data in a `PieChart`. Before we make modifications to this example, we explain the different parts.

The code required for setting up the application, the stage, and the scene is covered in Chapter 1. A `PieChart` extends a `Node`, so we can easily add it to the scene graph. The first two lines of code in the start method create the `PieChart`, and add the required data to it:

```
PieChart pieChart = new PieChart();
pieChart.setData(getChartData());
```

The data, which are of type `ObservableList<PieChart.Data>` are obtained from the `getChartData()` method and for our example, it contains static data. As the return type of the `getChartData()` method specifies, the returned data are an `ObservableList` of `PieChart.Data`.

An instance of `PieChart.Data`, which is a nested class of `PieChart`, contains the information required to draw one slice of the pie. `PieChart.Data` has a constructor that takes the name of the slice and its value:

```
PieChart.Data(String name, double value)
```

We use this constructor to create data elements containing the name of a programming language and its score in the TIOBE index.

```
new PieChart.Data("java", 15.57)
```

We then add those elements to the ObservableList<PieChart.Data> we need to return.

Some Modifications

Although the result of the simple example already looks good, we can tweak both the code and the rendering. First of all, the example uses two lines of code for creating the PieChart and populating it with data:

```
PieChart pieChart = new PieChart();
pieChart.setData(getChartData());
```

Because PieChart has a single argument constructor as well, the preceding code snippets can be replaced as follows.

```
PieChart pieChart = new PieChart(getChartData());
```

Apart from the properties defined on the abstract Chart class, a PieChart has the following properties.

```
BooleanProperty clockwise
ObjectProperty<ObservableList<PieChart.Data>> data
DoubleProperty labelLineLength
BooleanProperty labelsVisible
DoubleProperty startAngle
```

We covered the data property in the previous section. Some of the other properties are demonstrated in the next code snippet. Listing 6-2 contains a modified version of the start() method.

Listing 6-2. Modified Version of the PieChart Example

```java
public void start(Stage primaryStage) {
  PieChart pieChart = new PieChart();
  pieChart.setData(getChartData());
  pieChart.setTitle("Tiobe index");
  pieChart.setLegendSide(Side.LEFT);
  pieChart.setClockwise(false);
  pieChart.setLabelsVisible(false);

  primaryStage.setTitle("PieChart");

  StackPane root = new StackPane();
  root.getChildren().add(pieChart);
  primaryStage.setScene(new Scene(root, 400, 250));
  primaryStage.show();
}
```

Because we used the Side.LEFT field in the new code, we have to import the Side class in our application as well. This is done by adding the following line in the import block of the code.

```
import javafx.geometry.Side
```

Running this modified version results in the modified output shown in Figure 6-4.

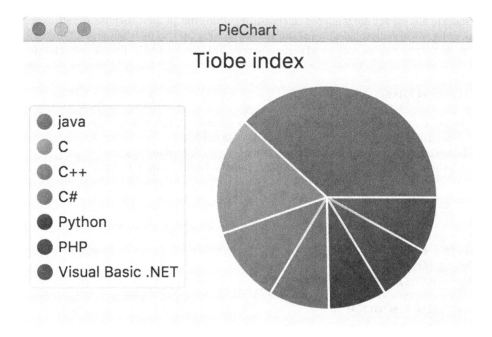

Figure 6-4. *The output of the modified PieChart example*

Changing a few lines of code results in output that looks very different. We go over the changes we made in a bit more detail. First, we added a title to the chart. That was done using the call

```
pieChart.setTitle("Tiobe index");
```

We could also have used the `titleProperty`:

```
pieChart.titleProperty().set("Tiobe index");
```

Both approaches result in the same output.

■ **Note**   The upcoming modifications could also be done using the same patterns. We only document the approach with setter methods, but it is easy to replace this with a property-based approach.

The next line of code in our modified example changes the location of the legend:

```
pieChart.setLegendSide(Side.LEFT);
```

When the `legendSide` is not specified, the legend is shown at the default location, which is below the chart. The `title` and the `legendSide` are both properties that belong to the abstract `Chart` class. As a consequence, they can be set on any chart. The next line in our modified example modifies a property that is specific to a `PieChart`:

```
pieChart.setClockwise(false);
```

By default, the slices in a PieChart are rendered clockwise. By setting this property to false, the slices are rendered counterclockwise. We also disabled showing the labels in the PieChart. The labels are still shown in the legend, but they do not point to the individual slices anymore. This is achieved by the following line of code:

```
pieChart.setLabelsVisible(false);
```

All layout changes so far are done programmatically. It is also possible, and often recommended, to style applications in general and charts in particular using a CSS style sheet.

We remove the layout changes from the Java code and add a style sheet containing some layout instructions. Listing 6-3 shows the modified code of the start() method and Listing 6-4 contains the style sheet we added.

Listing 6-3. Remove Programmatic Layout Instructions

```java
public void start(Stage primaryStage) {
    PieChart pieChart = new PieChart();
    pieChart.setData(getChartData());
     pieChart.titleProperty().set("Tiobe index");

    primaryStage.setTitle("PieChart");
    StackPane root = new StackPane();
    root.getChildren().add(pieChart);
    Scene scene = new Scene (root, 400, 250);
    scene.getStylesheets().add("/chartappstyle.css");
    primaryStage.setScene(scene);
    primaryStage.show();
}
```

Listing 6-4. Style Sheet for PieChart Example

```css
.chart {
    -fx-clockwise: false;
    -fx-pie-label-visible: true;
    -fx-label-line-length: 5;
    -fx-start-angle: 90;
    -fx-legend-side: right;
}

.chart-pie-label {
    -fx-font-size:9px;

}
.chart-content {
    -fx-padding:1;
}

.default-color0.chart-pie {
    -fx-pie-color:blue;
}
```

```
.chart-legend {
    -fx-background-color: #f0e68c;
    -fx-border-color: #696969;
    -fx-border-width:1;
}
```

Running this code results in the output shown in Figure 6-5.

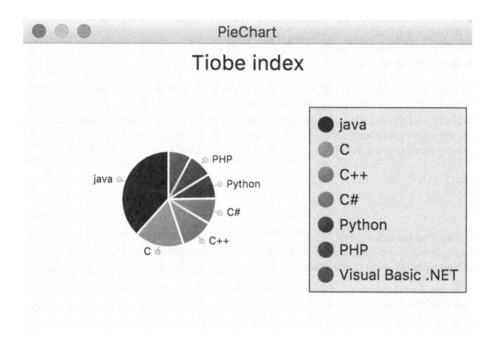

Figure 6-5. *Using CSS to style the PieChart*

We now go over the changes we made. Before we go over the individual changes in detail, we show how we include the CSS with our application. This is achieved by adding the style sheet to the scene, which is done as follows.

```
scene.getStylesheets().add("/chartappstyle.css");
```

The file containing the style sheet, `chartappstyle.css`, must be in the classpath when the application is running.

In Listing 6-2, we set the clockwise configuration using

```
pieChart.setClockwise(false)
```

We removed that line from the code in Listing 6-3, and instead defined the `-fx-clockwise` property on the chart class in the style sheet:

```
.chart {
    -fx-clockwise: false;
    -fx-pie-label-visible: true;
```

```
    -fx-label-line-length: 5;
    -fx-start-angle: 90;
    -fx-legend-side: right;
}
```

In that same `.chart` class definition, we make the labels on the pie visible by setting the `-fx-pie-label-visible` property to true, and we specify the length of the lines for each label to be 5.

Also, we rotate the whole pie by 90 degrees, which is achieved by defining the `-fx-start-angle` property. The labels are now defined in the style sheet, and we remove the corresponding definition from the code by omitting the following line.

```
pieChart.setLabelsVisible(false)
```

To make sure the legend will appear at the right side of the chart, we specify the `-fx-legend-side` property.

By default, a `PieChart` uses the default colors defined in the caspian style sheet. The first slice is filled with `default-color0`, the second slice with `default-color1`, and so on. The easiest way to change the color of the different slices is by overriding the definitions of the default color. In our style sheet, this is done by

```
.default-color0.chart-pie {
    -fx-pie-color: blue;
}
```

The same can be done for the other slices.

If you run the example without the other parts of the CSS, you would notice the chart itself is rather small, and the size of the labels takes too much space. Therefore, we modify the font size of the labels as follows:

```
.chart-pie-label {
    -fx-font-size:9px;
}
```

Also, we decrease the padding in the chart area:

```
.chart-content {
    -fx-padding:1;
}
```

Finally, we change the background and the stroke of the legend. This is achieved by overriding the `chart-legend` class as follows.

```
.chart-legend {
    -fx-background-color: #f0e68c;
    -fx-border-color: #696969;
    -fx-border-width:1;
}
```

Again, we refer the reader to `http://docs.oracle.com/javase/9/javafx/user-interface-tutorial/css-styles.htm` [TODO: FINAL LINK] for more information about using CSS with JavaFX charts.

Using the XYChart

The XYChart class is an abstract class with seven direct known subclasses. The difference between these classes and the PieChart class is that an XYChart has two axes and an optional alternativeColumn or alternativeRow. This translates to the following list of additional properties on an XYChart.

```
BooleanProperty alternativeColumnFillVisible
BooleanProperty alternativeRowFillVisible
ObjectProperty<ObservableList<XYChart.Series<X,Y>>> data
BooleanProperty horizontalGridLinesVisible
BooleanProperty horizontalZeroLineVisible
BooleanProperty verticalGridLinesVisible
BooleanProperty verticalZeroLineVisible
```

Data in an XYChart are ordered in series. How these series are rendered is specific to the implementation of the subclass of XYChart. In general, a single element in a series contains a number of pairs. The following examples use a hypothetical projection of market share of three programming languages in the future. We start with the TIOBE index for Java, C, and C++ in 2017, and add random values (between –2 and +2) to them for each year until 2020. The resulting (year, number) pairs for Java constitute the Java Series, and the same holds for C and C++. As a result, we have three series, each containing 10 pairs.

A major difference between a PieChart and an XYChart is the presence of an x axis and a y axis in the XYChart. These axes are required when creating an XYChart, as can be observed from the following constructor.

```
XYChart (Axis<X> xAxis, Axis<Y> yAxis)
```

The Axis class is an abstract class extending Region (hence also extending Parent and Node) with two subclasses: CategoryAxis and ValueAxis. The CategoryAxis is used to render labels that are in the String format, as can be observed from the class definition:

```
public class CategoryAxis extends Axis<java.lang.String>
```

The ValueAxis is used to render data entries that represent a Number. It is an abstract class itself, defined as follows.

```
public abstract class ValueAxis <T extends java.lang.Number> extends Axis<T>
```

The ValueAxis class has one concrete subclass, which is the NumberAxis:

```
public final class NumberAxis extends ValueAxis<java.lang.Number>
```

The differences between those Axis classes will become clear throughout the examples. We now show some examples of the different XYChart implementations, starting with the ScatterChart. Some features common to all XYCharts are also explained in the section on ScatterChart.

■ **Note**   Because the Axis classes extend Region, they allow for applying the same CSS elements as any other Regions. This allows for highly customized Axis instances.

Using the ScatterChart

An instance of the ScatterChart class is used to render data where each data item is represented as a symbol in a two-dimensional area. As mentioned in the previous section, we will render a chart containing three series of data, representing the hypothetical evolution of the TIOBE index for Java, C, and C++. We first show the code of a naive implementation, and refine that to something more useful.

A Simple Implementation

A first implementation of our application using a ScatterChart is shown in Listing 6-5.

Listing 6-5. First Implementation of Rendering Data in a ScatterChart

```
package com.projavafx ;

import javafx.application.Application;
import javafx.collections.FXCollections;
import javafx.collections.ObservableList;
import javafx.scene.Scene;
import javafx.scene.chart.NumberAxis;
import javafx.scene.chart.ScatterChart;
import javafx.scene.chart.XYChart;
import javafx.scene.chart.XYChart.Series;
import javafx.scene.layout.StackPane;
import javafx.stage.Stage;

public class ChartApp3 extends Application {

    public static void main(String[] args) {
        launch(args);
    }

    @Override
    public void start(Stage primaryStage) {
        NumberAxis xAxis = new NumberAxis();
        NumberAxis yAxis = new NumberAxis();
        ScatterChart scatterChart = new ScatterChart(xAxis, yAxis);
        scatterChart.setData(getChartData());
        primaryStage.setTitle("ScatterChart");

        StackPane root = new StackPane();
        root.getChildren().add(scatterChart);
        primaryStage.setScene(new Scene(root, 400, 250));
        primaryStage.show();
    }

    private ObservableList<XYChart.Series<Integer, Double>> getChartData() {
        double javaValue = 15.57;
        double cValue = 6.97;
        double cppValue = 4.55;
```

```
ObservableList<XYChart.Series<Integer, Double>> answer = FXCollections.
observableArrayList();
Series<Integer, Double> java = new Series<>();
Series<Integer, Double> c = new Series<>();
Series<Integer, Double> cpp = new Series<>();
for (int i = 2017; i < 2027; i++) {
    java.getData().add(new XYChart.Data(i, javaValue));
    javaValue = javaValue + 4 * Math.random() - 2;
    c.getData().add(new XYChart.Data(i, cValue));
    cValue = cValue + Math.random() - .5;
    cpp.getData().add(new XYChart.Data(i, cppValue));
    cppValue = cppValue + 4 * Math.random() - 2;
}
answer.addAll(java, c, cpp);
return answer;
    }
}
```

Executing this application results in a graph similar to the image shown in Figure 6-6.

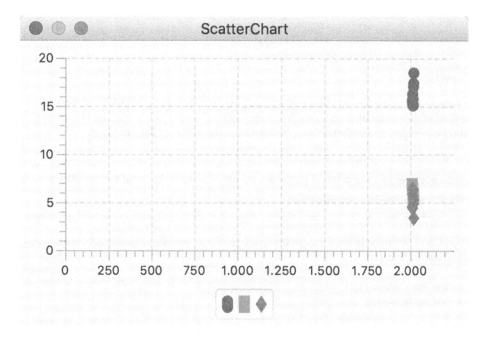

Figure 6-6. *The result of the naive implementation of the ScatterChart*

Although the chart shows the required information, it is not very readable. We add a number of enhancements, but first let's have a deeper look at the different parts of the code.

Similar to the PieChart example, we created a separate method for obtaining the data. One of the reasons for this is that in real-world applications, it is unlikely to have static data. By isolating the data retrieval in a separate method, it becomes easier to change the way data are obtained.

A single data point is defined by an instance of XYChart.Data<Integer, Double>, created with the constructor XYChart.Data(Integer i, Double d) where the parameters have the following definitions.

```
i: Integer, representing a specific year (between 2017 and 2026)
d: Double, representing the hypothetical TIOBE index for the particular series in the year
specified by I
```

The local variables javaValue, cValue, and cppValue are used for keeping track of the scores for the different programming languages. They are initialized with the real values from 2017. Each year, an individual score is incremented or decremented by a random value between –2 and +2. Data points are stacked into a series. In our examples, we have three series each containing 10 instances of XYChart.Data<Integer, Double>. Those series are of type XYChart.Series<Integer, Double>.

The data entries are added to the respective series by calling

```
java.getData().add (...)
c.getData().add(...)
```

and

```
cpp.getData().add(...)
```

Finally, all series are added to the ObservableList<XYChart.Series<Integer, Double>> and returned.

The start() method of the application contains the functionality required for creating and rendering the ScatterChart, and for populating it with the data obtained from the getChartData method.

■ **Note** As discussed earlier, we can use different patterns here with PieChart. We used the JavaBeans pattern in the examples, but we could also use properties.

To create a ScatterChart, we need to create an xAxis and a yAxis. In our first simple implementation, we use two instances of NumberAxis for this:

```
NumberAxis xAxis = new NumberAxis();
NumberAxis yAxis = new NumberAxis();
```

Apart from calling the following ScatterChart constructor, there is nothing different in this method than in the case of the PieChart.

```
ScatterChart scatterChart = new ScatterChart(xAxis, yAxis);
```

Improving the Simple Implementation

One of the first observations when looking at Figure 6-5 is that all data plots in a series are almost rendered on top of each other. The reason for this is clear: the x-Axis starts at 0 and ends at 2250. By default, the NumberAxis determines its range automatically. We can overrule this behavior by setting the autoRanging property to false, and by providing values for the lowerBound and the upperBound. If we replace the constructor for the xAxis in the original example by the following code snippet,

```
NumberAxis xAxis = new NumberAxis();
xAxis.setAutoRanging(false);
xAxis.setLowerBound(2017);
xAxis.setUpperBound(2027);
```

the resulting output will look similar to that shown in Figure 6-7.

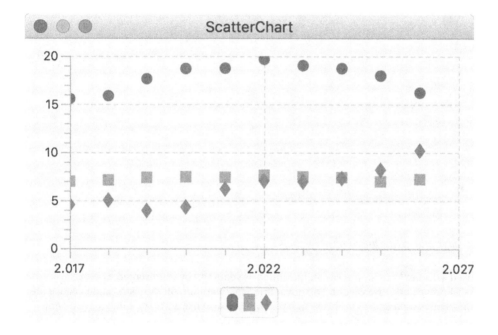

Figure 6-7. *Defining the behavior of the xAxis*

Next, we want to add a title to the chart, and we want to have names near the symbols in the legend node. Adding a title to the chart is no different from adding a title to the PieChart and is achieved by the code:

```
scatterChart.setTitle("Speculations");
```

By adding a name to the three instances of XYChart.Series, we add labels to the symbols in the legend node. The relevant part of the getChartData method becomes

```
Series<Integer, Double> java = new Series<>();
Series<Integer, Double> c = new Series<>();
Series<Integer, Double> cpp = new Series<>();
```

291

```
java.setName("java");
c.setName("C");
cpp.setName("C++");
```

Running the application again after applying both changes results in output similar to that shown in Figure 6-8.

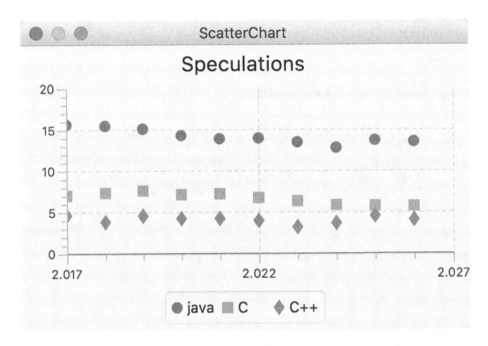

Figure 6-8. *ScatterChart with a title and named symbols*

Until now, we used a NumberAxis for the xAxis. Inasmuch as years can be represented as Number instances, that works. However, because we don't do any numerical operation on the years, and because the distance between consecutive data entries is always one year, we can also use a String value to represent this information.

We now modify the code to work with a CategoryAxis for the xAxis. Changing the xAxis from a NumberAxis to a CategoryAxis also implies that the getChartData() method should return an instance of ObservableList<XYChart.Series<String, Double>> and that implies that the different elements in a single Series should have the type XYChart.Data<String, Double>.

In Listing 6-6, the original code has been modified to use the CategoryAxis.

Listing 6-6. Using CategoryAxis Instead of NumberAxis for the xAxis

```
package projavafx ;

import javafx.application.Application;
import javafx.collections.FXCollections;
import javafx.collections.ObservableList;
import javafx.scene.Scene;
import javafx.scene.chart.CategoryAxis;
```

```java
import javafx.scene.chart.NumberAxis;
import javafx.scene.chart.ScatterChart;
import javafx.scene.chart.XYChart;
import javafx.scene.chart.XYChart.Series;
import javafx.scene.layout.StackPane;
import javafx.stage.Stage;

public class ChartApp7 extends Application {

    public static void main(String[] args) {
        launch(args);
    }

    @Override
    public void start(Stage primaryStage) {
        CategoryAxis xAxis = new CategoryAxis();
        NumberAxis yAxis = new NumberAxis();
        ScatterChart scatterChart = new ScatterChart(xAxis, yAxis);
        scatterChart.setData(getChartData());
        scatterChart.setTitle("speculations");
        primaryStage.setTitle("ScatterChart example");

        StackPane root = new StackPane();
        root.getChildren().add(scatterChart);
        primaryStage.setScene(new Scene(root, 400, 250));
        primaryStage.show();
    }

    private ObservableList<XYChart.Series<String, Double>> getChartData() {
        double javaValue = 15.57;
        double cValue = 6.97;
        double cppValue = 4.55;
        ObservableList<XYChart.Series<String, Double>> answer = FXCollections.
        observableArrayList();
        Series<String, Double> java = new Series<>();
        Series<String, Double> c = new Series<>();
        Series<String, Double> cpp = new Series<>();
        java.setName("java");
        c.setName("C");
        cpp.setName("C++");

        for (int i = 2017; i < 2027; i++) {
            java.getData().add(new XYChart.Data(Integer.toString(i), javaValue));
            javaValue = javaValue + 4 * Math.random() - .2;
            c.getData().add(new XYChart.Data(Integer.toString(i), cValue));
            cValue = cValue + 4 * Math.random() - 2;
            cpp.getData().add(new XYChart.Data(Integer.toString(i), cppValue));
            cppValue = cppValue + 4 * Math.random() - 2;
        }
```

```
        answer.addAll(java, c, cpp);
        return answer;
    }
}
```

Running the modified application results in output similar to Figure 6-9.

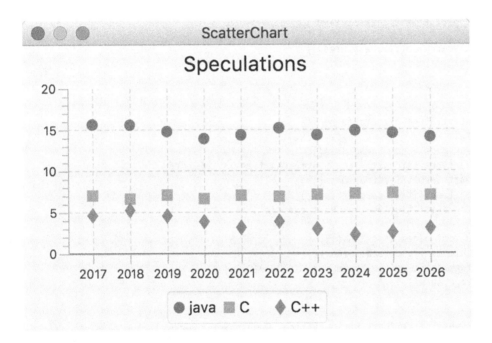

Figure 6-9. *Using a ScatterChart with a CategoryAxis on the xAxis*

Using the LineChart

The example in the previous section resulted in data entries being represented by single dots or symbols. Often, it is desirable to have the dots connected by a line because this helps in seeing trends. The JavaFX LineChart is well suited for this.

The API for the LineChart has many methods in common with the API for the ScatterChart. In fact, we can reuse most of the code in Listing 6-6, and just replace the ScatterChart occurrences with LineChart and the import for javafx.scene.chart.ScatterChart with javafx.scene.chart.LineChart. The data stay exactly the same, so we only show the new start() method in Listing 6-7.

Listing 6-7. Using a LineChart Instead of a ScatterChart

```
public void start(Stage primaryStage) {
    CategoryAxis xAxis = new CategoryAxis();
    NumberAxis yAxis = new NumberAxis();
    LineChart lineChart = new LineChart(xAxis, yAxis);
    lineChart.setData(getChartData());
    lineChart.setTitle("speculations");
    primaryStage.setTitle("LineChart example");
```

```
    StackPane root = new StackPane();
    root.getChildren().add(lineChart);
    primaryStage.setScene(new Scene(root, 400, 250));
    primaryStage.show();
}
```

Running this application gives output like that shown in Figure 6-10.

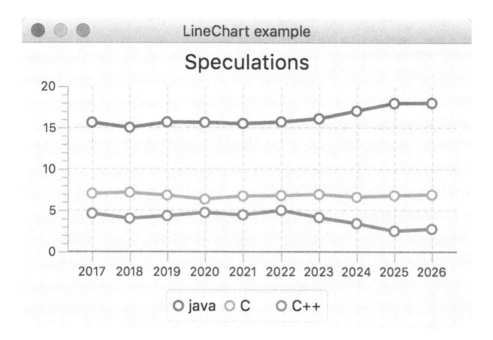

Figure 6-10. *Using a LineChart for displaying trends*

Most of the functionality available for the ScatterChart is also available for the LineChart. Changing the location of the legend, adding or removing a title, and using a NumberAxis instead of a CategoryAxis are possible using the LineChart.

Using the BarChart

A BarChart is capable of rendering the same data as a ScatterChart and a LineChart, but it looks different. In a BarChart, the focus is often more on showing the relative differences between the different series for a given category. In our case, that means that we focus on the differences between the values for Java, C, and C++.

Again, we do not need to modify the method that returns our data. Indeed, a BarChart requires a CategoryAxis for its xAxis, and we already modified the getChartData() method to return an ObservableList containing XYChart.Series<String, double>. Starting from Listing 6-6, we change only the occurrences of ScatterChart to BarChart and we obtain Listing 6-8.

Listing 6-8. Using a BarChart Instead of a ScatterChart

```
public void start(Stage primaryStage) {
    CategoryAxis xAxis = new CategoryAxis();
    NumberAxis yAxis = new NumberAxis();
    BarChart barChart = new BarChart(xAxis, yAxis);
    barChart.setData(getChartData());
    barChart.setTitle("speculations");
    primaryStage.setTitle("BarChart example");

    StackPane root = new StackPane();
    root.getChildren().add(barChart);
    primaryStage.setScene(new Scene(root, 400, 250));
    primaryStage.show();
}
```

Once we replace the import for javafx.scene.chart.ScatterChart with one for javafx.scene.chart. BarChart, we can build the application and run it. The result is a BarChart similar to that shown in Figure 6-11.

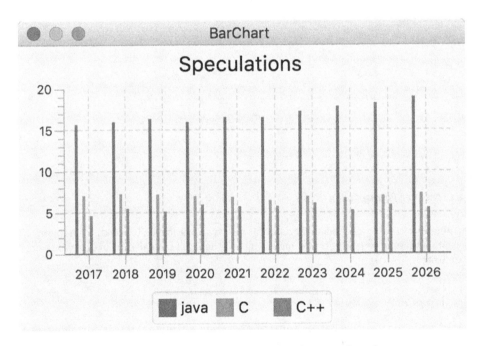

Figure 6-11. *Using BarChart for highlighting differences between the values*

Although the result indeed shows the differences between the values for each year, it is not very clear because the bars are rather small. With a total scene width at 400 pixels, there is not much space to render large bars. However, the BarChart API contains methods to define the inner gap between bars and the gap between categories. In our case, we want a smaller gap between the bars, for example, one pixel. This is done by calling

```
barChart.setBarGap(1);
```

Adding this single line of code to the start method and rerunning the application results in the output shown in Figure 6-12.

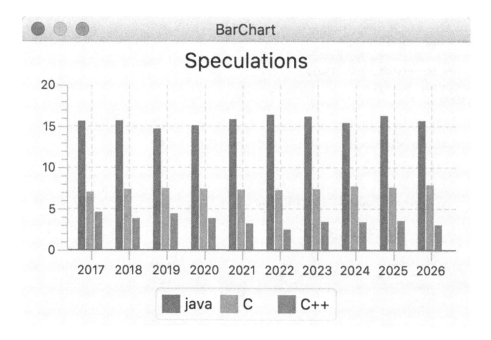

Figure 6-12. *Setting the gap between bars to one pixel*

Clearly, this one line of code leads to a huge difference in readability.

Using the StackedBarChart

The StackedBarChart was added in JavaFX 2.1. The StackedBarChart displays data in bars just like the BarChart, but instead of rendering bars in the same category next to each other, the StackedBarChart shows the bars within the same category on top of each other. This often makes it easier to inspect totals.

Typically, categories correspond with the common key values in the data series. As a consequence, in our example the different years (2017, 2018, ... 2026) can be considered as categories. We can add these categories to the xAxis, as follows:

```
IntStream.range(2017,2026).forEach(t -> xAxis.getCategories().add(String.valueOf(t)));
```

Apart from this, the only code change is replacing the BarChart with the StackedBarChart in code and in the import statement. This leads to the code snippet in Listing 6-9.

Listing 6-9. Using a StackedBarChart Instead of a ScatterChart

```
public void start(Stage primaryStage) {
    CategoryAxis xAxis = new CategoryAxis();
    IntStream.range(2017,2026).forEach(t -> xAxis.getCategories().add(String.valueOf(t)));
    NumberAxis yAxis = new NumberAxis();
    StackedBarChart stackedBarChart = new StackedBarChart(xAxis, yAxis, getChartData());
    stackedBarChart.setTitle("speculations");
    primaryStage.setTitle("StackedBarChart example");

    StackPane root = new StackPane();
    root.getChildren().add(stackedBarChart);
    Scene scene = new Scene(root, 400, 250);
    primaryStage.setScene(scene);
    primaryStage.show();
}
```

Running the application now produces output like that shown in Figure 6-13.

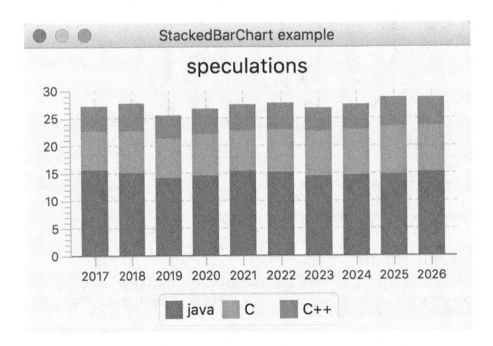

Figure 6-13. *Rendering stacked bar chart plots using StackedBarChart*

Using the AreaChart

In some cases, it makes sense to fill the area under the line connecting the dots. Although the same data are rendered as in the case of a LineChart, the result looks different. Listing 6-10 contains the modified start() method that uses an AreaChart instead of the original ScatterChart. As in the previous modifications, we didn't change the getChartData() method.

Listing 6-10. Using an AreaChart Instead of a ScatterChart

```
public void start(Stage primaryStage) {
    CategoryAxis xAxis = new CategoryAxis();
    NumberAxis yAxis = new NumberAxis();
    AreaChart areaChart = new AreaChart(xAxis, yAxis);
    areaChart.setData(getChartData());
    areaChart.setTitle("speculations");
    primaryStage.setTitle("AreaChart example");
    StackPane root = new StackPane();
    root.getChildren().add(areaChart);
    primaryStage.setScene(new Scene(root, 400, 250));
    primaryStage.show();
}
```

Running this application results in output like that shown in Figure 6-14.

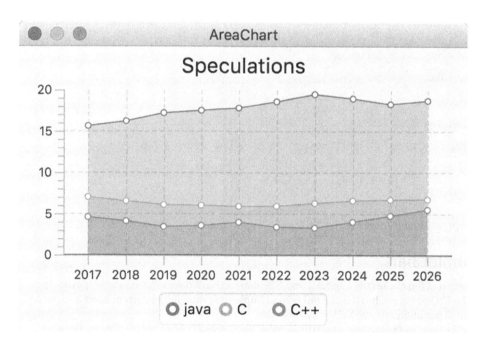

Figure 6-14. *Rendering area plots using AreaChart*

Using the StackedAreaChart

The StackedAreaChart is to the AreaChart what the StackedBarChart is to the BarChart. Rather than showing individual areas, the StackedAreaChart always shows the sum of the values in a specific category.

Changing an AreaChart into a StackedAreaChart only requires the change of one line of code and the appropriate import statement.

```
AreaChart areaChart = new AreaChart(xAxis, yAxis);
```

must be replaced with

```
StackedAreaChart areaChart = new StackedAreaChart(xAxis, yAxis);
```

Applying this change and running the application results in a graph like the one in Figure 6-15.

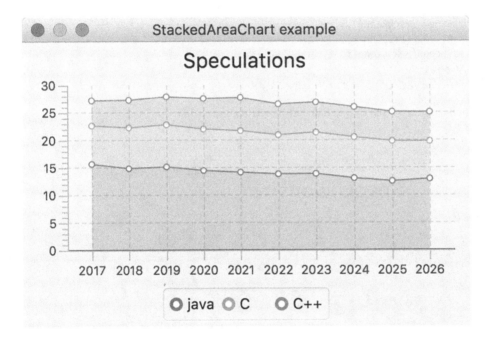

Figure 6-15. *Rendering area plots using* AreaChart

Using the BubbleChart

The last implementation of the XYChart is a special one. The BubbleChart does not contain properties that are not already on the XYChart class, but it is the only direct implementation in the current JavaFX Chart API that uses the additional parameter on the XYChart.Data class.

We first modify the code in Listing 6-6 to use the BubbleChart instead of the ScatterChart. Because by default, bubbles are stretched when the span on the xAxis is much different from the span on the yAxis, we do not use years, but a tenth of a year as the value on the xAxis. Doing so, we have a span of 100 units on the xAxis (10 years) compared with a span of about 30 units on the yAxis. This is also more or less the ratio between the width and the height of our chart. As a consequence, the bubbles are relatively circular.

Listing 6-11 contains the code for rendering a BubbleChart.

Listing 6-11. Using the BubbleChart

```java
package com.projavafx.charts;

import javafx.application.Application;
import javafx.collections.FXCollections;
import javafx.collections.ObservableList;
import javafx.scene.Scene;
import javafx.scene.chart.*;
import javafx.scene.chart.XYChart.Series;
import javafx.scene.layout.StackPane;
import javafx.stage.Stage;
import javafx.util.StringConverter;

public class ChartApp14 extends Application {

    public static void main(String[] args) {
        launch(args);
    }

    @Override
    public void start(Stage primaryStage) {
        NumberAxis xAxis = new NumberAxis();
        NumberAxis yAxis = new NumberAxis();
        yAxis.setAutoRanging(false);
        yAxis.setLowerBound(0);
        yAxis.setUpperBound(30);
        xAxis.setAutoRanging(false);
        xAxis.setAutoRanging(false);
        xAxis.setLowerBound(20170);
        xAxis.setUpperBound(20261);
        xAxis.setTickUnit(10);
        xAxis.setTickLabelFormatter(new StringConverter<Number>() {

            @Override
            public String toString(Number n) {
                return String.valueOf(n.intValue() / 10);
            }

            @Override
            public Number fromString(String s) {
                return Integer.valueOf(s) * 10;
            }
        });
        BubbleChart bubbleChart = new BubbleChart(xAxis, yAxis);
        bubbleChart.setData(getChartData());
        bubbleChart.setTitle("Speculations");
        primaryStage.setTitle("BubbleChart example");

        StackPane root = new StackPane();
        root.getChildren().add(bubbleChart);
```

```
        primaryStage.setScene(new Scene(root, 400, 250));
        primaryStage.show();
    }

    private ObservableList<XYChart.Series<Integer, Double>> getChartData() {
        double javaValue = 15.57;
        double cValue = 6.97;
        double cppValue = 4.55;
        ObservableList<XYChart.Series<Integer, Double>> answer = FXCollections.
        observableArrayList();
        Series<Integer, Double> java = new Series<>();
        Series<Integer, Double> c = new Series<>();
        Series<Integer, Double> cpp = new Series<>();
        java.setName("java");
        c.setName("C");
        cpp.setName("C++");
        for (int i = 20170; i < 20260; i = i + 10) {
            double diff = Math.random();
            java.getData().add(new XYChart.Data(i, javaValue));
            javaValue = Math.max(javaValue + 2 * diff - 1, 0);
            diff = Math.random();
            c.getData().add(new XYChart.Data(i, cValue));
            cValue = Math.max(cValue + 2 * diff - 1, 0);
            diff = Math.random();
            cpp.getData().add(new XYChart.Data(i, cppValue));
            cppValue = Math.max(cppValue + 2 * diff - 1, 0);
        }
        answer.addAll(java, c, cpp);
        return answer;
    }

}
```

The xAxis ranges from 201670 to 20261, but of course we want to show the years at the axis. This can be achieved by calling

```
xAxis.setTickLabelFormatter(new StringConverter<Number>() {
 ...
}
```

where the StringConverter we supply converts the numbers we use (e.g., 20210) to Strings (e.g., 2021) and vice versa. Doing so, we are able to use whatever quantity we want for calculating the bubbles and still have a nice way of formatting the labels. Running this example results in the chart shown in Figure 6-16.

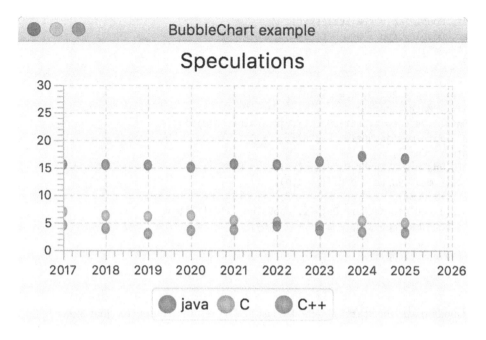

Figure 6-16. *Using a BubbleChart with fixed radius*

Until now, we didn't leverage the three-argument constructor of XYChart.Data. Apart from the two-argument constructor that we are already familiar with,

XYChart.Data (X xValue, Y yValue)

XYChart.Data also has a three-argument constructor:

XYChart.Data (X xValue, Y yValue, Object extraValue)

The extraValue argument can be of any type. This allows for developers to implement their own subclasses of XYChart that take advantage of additional information that can be enclosed inside a single data element. The BubbleChart implementation uses this extraValue for deciding how large the bubbles should be rendered.

We now modify the getChartData() method to use the three-argument constructor. The xValue and yValue parameters are still the same as in the previous listing, but we now add a third parameter that indicates an upcoming trend. The larger this parameter is, the bigger the rise in the next year. The smaller the parameter is, the bigger the drop in the next year. The modified getChartData() method is shown in Listing 6-12.

Listing 6-12. *Using a Three-Argument Constructor for XYChart.Data Instances*

```
private ObservableList<XYChart.Series<Integer, Double>> getChartData() {
    double javaValue = 15.57;
    double cValue = 6.97;
    double cppValue = 4.55;
    ObservableList<XYChart.Series<Integer, Double>> answer = FXCollections.
    observableArrayList();
    Series<Integer, Double> java = new Series<>();
```

303

```
Series<Integer, Double> c = new Series<>();
Series<Integer, Double> cpp = new Series<>();
java.setName("java");
c.setName("C");
cpp.setName("C++");
for (int i = 20170; i < 20270; i =  i+10) {
    double diff = Math.random();
    java.getData().add(new XYChart.Data(i, javaValue, 2*diff));
    javaValue = Math.max(javaValue + 2*diff - 1,0);
    diff = Math.random();
    c.getData().add(new XYChart.Data(i, cValue,2* diff));
    cValue = Math.max(cValue + 2*diff - 1,0);
    diff = Math.random();
    cpp.getData().add(new XYChart.Data(i, cppValue, 2*diff));
    cppValue = Math.max(cppValue + 2*diff - 1,0);
}
answer.addAll(java, c, cpp);
return answer;
}
```

Integrating this method with the start() method in Listing 6-11 results in output like that shown in Figure 6-17.

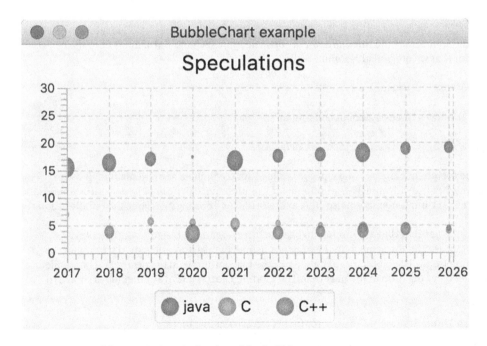

Figure 6-17. *Adding variations in the size of the Bubbles*

Summary

The JavaFX Chart API provides a number of ready-to-use implementations for different chart types. Each of these implementations serves a different purpose, and it is up to the developer to choose the most appropriate Chart.

Modifying a Chart and tuning it for a specific application can be done by applying CSS rules or by using Chart-specific methods or properties.

In case you need a more customized Chart, you can extend the abstract Chart class and take advantage of the existing properties on that class, or you can extend the abstract XYChart class if your chart requires two axes.

Resources

For more information on the JavaFX Chart API, consult the following resources:

- http://docs.oracle.com/javase/8/javafx/user-interface-tutorial/charts.htm

- http://docs.oracle.com/javase/8/javafx/user-interface-tutorial/css-styles.htm

CHAPTER 7

■ ■ ■

Connecting to Enterprise Services

An expert is a man who has made all the mistakes which can be made, in a narrow field.

—Niels Bohr

Client applications can be very exciting, but more often than not they don't live in an isolated environment. A typical client application somehow exchanges data and functionality with other applications, with back-end components and with cloud environments. This adds new requirements to the development of client applications.

So far, we've explained how the JavaFX platform can be used both for rendering information and for interactively manipulating data. In this chapter, we provide a brief overview of the options available for integrating JavaFX applications with enterprise systems, and then continue with some specific examples of that process.

Our examples are constructed to demonstrate how easily a JavaFX application can access a REST resource and then translate the response (from either JSON or XML format) into a format understandable by JavaFX controls. As our example external data source, the Stack Exchange APIs are ideal, as they are publicly available, easy to understand, and widely used on the Internet.

Front-End and Back-End Platforms

JavaFX is often considered a front-end platform. Although that statement does not do justice to the APIs in the JavaFX platform that are not related to a UI, it is true that most JavaFX applications focus on the rich and interactive visualization of "content."

One of the great things about Java is the fact that a single language can be used within a wide range of devices, desktops, and servers. The same Java language that creates the core of JavaFX is also the fundamental core of the Java Platform, Enterprise Edition (Java EE).

The Java platform is the number one development platform for enterprise applications. The combination of the JavaFX platform providing a rich and interactive UI with enterprise applications running on the Java platform creates huge possibilities. To achieve this, JavaFX applications and Java enterprise applications must be exchanging data. Exchanging data can happen in a number of ways, and depending on the requirements (from the front end as well as from the back end); one way might be more suited than another.

Basically, there are two different approaches:

- The JavaFX application can leverage the fact that it runs on the same infrastructure as typical enterprise applications, and can deeply integrate with these enterprise components. This is illustrated in Figure 7-1.

- JavaFX applications live in a relatively simple Java platform, and exchange data with enterprise servers using standard protocols that are already supported by Java enterprise components. This is shown in Figure 7-2.

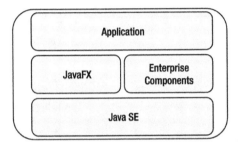

Figure 7-1. *JavaFX and enterprise components on a single system*

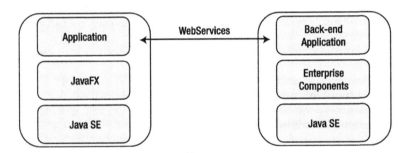

Figure 7-2. *JavaFX application communicates with enterprise components on a remote server*

The first approach is mentioned and briefly touched on, but the focus of this chapter is on the second approach, where the JavaFX client communicates with Java enterprise components on a remote server.

There is no such thing as the best approach, as it really depends on the environment and the use case. A typical Java client application runs on hardware with fewer capabilities than today's back-end server and cloud environments, and in that case the first approach is not recommended. However, there are clearly cases where resources (CPU, clustering, scalability) are widely available on client systems, and in that case this approach can definitely be considered.

It should also be stressed here that as long as a standard, well-defined protocol (e.g., SOAP/REST) is used, it is very possible to connect a JavaFX application to a non-Java back-end application. The decoupling between client and server indeed allows for different programming languages to be used on the client and on the server.

Merging JavaFX and Java Enterprise Modules in the Same Environment

JavaFX 9 is built on top of the Java Platform, Standard Edition. As a consequence, all functionality provided by this platform can be leveraged in JavaFX 9. Two of the most popular Java Enterprise frameworks—the Java Platform, Enterprise Edition and the Spring Framework—are also built on top of the Java Platform, Standard Edition. As a consequence, JavaFX applications can live in the same environment as applications using the Java Platform, Enterprise Edition, or applications built with the Spring Framework.

The JavaFX developer can thus use his or her favorite enterprise tools to create applications. There are a number of advantages in doing so. Enterprise components offer tools that allow developers to focus on a specific domain layer, while shielding them from, for example, database resources and transactions.

Java is a popular platform in the enterprise environment, and a number of enterprise components and libraries have been developed by companies, organizations, and individuals.

The Java Platform, Enterprise Edition, is defined by specifications that are standardized via the Java Community Process (JCP) program. For the different constituting parts, individual Java Specification Requests (JSRs) are filed.

Most of these individual JSRs are implemented by a number of companies, and implementations are often grouped into a product. Typical enterprise frameworks implement one or more JSRs, and they might include additional product-specific functionality.

Among the most popular implementations of some or all of these specifications, we count Tomcat/TomEE, Hibernate, JBoss/WildFly, GlassFish, Payara, WebLogic, and WebSphere. A number of products implement all JSRs, and those products are then called implementations of the Java Platform, Enterprise Edition, often referred to as Java EE platforms or application servers.

The other popular Java Enterprise Framework, the Spring Framework, contains implementations for many of the JSRs that are defined in the Java Platform, Enterprise Edition, and it adds more specific components and APIs.

Technically, there are no restrictions in the JavaFX platform that prevent Java enterprise components from being used. It is very well possible to run a Java Enterprise Application Server on a client system, or to execute Spring Framework applications on the same client system. The applications that leverage either the Java Enterprise Application Servers or the Spring Framework can also contain JavaFX code.

However, enterprise development differs from client development in a number of ways:

- Enterprise infrastructure is shifting toward the cloud. Specific tasks (e.g., storage, mail, etc.) are outsourced to components in a "cloud" that offer specific functionality. Enterprise servers are often located in a cloud environment, allowing fast and seamless interaction with cloud components.

- In terms of resource requirements, enterprise systems focus on computing resources (CPU, cache, and memory) where desktop computers and laptops focus instead on visual resources (e.g., graphical hardware acceleration).

- Startup time is hardly an issue in servers, but is critical in many desktop applications. Also, servers are supposed to be up and running 24/7, which is not the case with most clients.

- Deployment and life cycle management are often specific to a server product or a client product. Upgrading servers or server software is often a tedious process. Downtime has to be minimized because client applications might have open connections to the server. Deploying a client application can happen in a number of ways, such as via stand-alone, self-contained applications or Java Network Launch Protocol (JNLP).

- Enterprise development uses a number of patterns (e.g., Inversion of Control, container-based initialization) that can be useful in client development, but that often require a different architecture than traditional clients.

Using JavaFX to Call Remote (Web) Services

Enterprise components are often accessed via web resources. Some specifications clearly describe how web-based frameworks should interact with enterprise components for rendering information. However, there are other specifications that allow enterprise components (written in Java or in another language) to be accessed from non-web resources as well. Because those specifications allow for a decoupling between enterprise development and any other development, they have been defined by a number of stakeholders.

In 1998, Simple Object Access Protocol (SOAP) was invented by Microsoft and subsequently used as *the* exchange format between Java applications and .NET applications. SOAP is based on XML, and the current version 1.2 became a W3C recommendation in 2003. Java provides a number of tools that allow developers to exchange data with SOAP.

Although powerful and relatively readable, SOAP is often considered to be rather verbose. With the rise of mashups and simple services offering specific functionality, a new architectural style emerged: the representational state transfer (REST). REST allows server and client developers to exchange data in a loosely coupled and more streamlined way, where the protocol can be XML, JSON, Atom, or any other format.

In the next section, we will show a number of examples that are using REST APIs to establish a communication between JavaFX client applications and server or cloud components. While this approach will show how data is transmitted, it still requires some boiler plate code. Following this section, we will talk about frameworks that make the connection to enterprise components even more transparent to the JavaFX developer.

REST

Plenty of resources and documentation about REST and REST-based web services can be found on the Internet. REST-based web services expose a number of URIs that can be accessed using the HTTP protocol. Typically, different HTTP `request` methods (get, post, put, delete) are used to indicate different operations on resources.

REST-based web services can be accessed using standard HTTP technologies, and the Java platform comes with a number of APIs (mainly in `java.io` and `java.net`) that facilitate access to REST-based web services.

One of the major advantages of JavaFX being written on top of the Java Platform, Standard Edition 9, is the ability to use all of these APIs in JavaFX applications. This is what we do in the first examples in this chapter. We show how we can use Java APIs for consuming REST-based web services and how we can integrate the result in a JavaFX application.

Next, we show how to leverage the JavaFX APIs to avoid common pitfalls (e.g., unresponsive applications, no dynamic update, etc.). Finally, we give a brief overview of third-party libraries that make it easy for JavaFX developers to access REST-based web services.

Setting up the Application

First of all, we create the framework for our samples. We will use the APIs provided by Stack Exchange. The Stack Exchange network is a cluster of forums, each in a specific domain, where questions and answers are combined in such a way that the "best" answers from the most trusted users bubble to the top. Java developers are probably familiar with Stack Overflow, which was the first site in Stack Exchange and provides an incredible number of questions and related answers for IT-related issues.

The REST APIs provided by Stack Exchange are very well described at `https://api.stackexchange.com`. It is not our goal to explore all the possibilities offered by Stack Exchange and the corresponding APIs, so the interested reader is referred to the documentation available on the web site.

In the samples in this chapter, we want to visualize the author of a question, the title of the question, and the day the question was asked.

Initially, we represent a question by a Java object with getters and setters. This is shown in Listing 7-1.

Listing 7-1. Question Class

```java
package projavafx;

public class Question {

    private String owner;
    private String question;
    private long timestamp;

    public Question () {
    }
    public Question (String o, String q, long t) {
        this.owner = o;
        this.question = q;
        this.timestamp = t;
    }

    public String getOwner() {
        return owner;
    }

    public void setOwner(String owner) {
        this.owner = owner;
    }

    public String getQuestion() {
        return question;
    }

    public void setQuestion(String question) {
        this.question = question;
    }

    public long getTimestamp() {
        return timestamp;
    }
```

```
    public void setTimestamp(long timestamp) {
        this.timestamp = timestamp;
    }

}
```

Our Question class has two constructors. The zero-arg constructor is needed in one of the following examples and we come back to this later. The constructor that takes three arguments is used for convenience in other examples.

In Listing 7-2, we show how to display questions. In this first example, the questions are not obtained via the Stack Exchange API, but they are hard-coded in the example.

Listing 7-2. Framework for Rendering Questions in a ListView

```
package projavafx;

import javafx.application.Application;
import javafx.collections.FXCollections;
import javafx.collections.ObservableList;
import javafx.scene.Scene;
import javafx.scene.control.ListView;
import javafx.scene.layout.StackPane;
import javafx.stage.Stage;

public class StackOverflowApp1 extends Application {

    public static void main(String[] args) {
        launch(args);
    }

    @Override
    public void start(Stage primaryStage) {
        ListView<Question> listView = new ListView<>();
        listView.setItems(getObservableList());
        StackPane root = new StackPane();
        root.getChildren().add(listView);

        Scene scene = new Scene(root, 500, 300);
        primaryStage.setTitle("StackOverflow List");
        primaryStage.setScene(scene);
        primaryStage.show();
    }

    ObservableList<Question> getObservableList() {
        ObservableList<Question> answer = FXCollections.observableArrayList();
        long now = System.currentTimeMillis();
        long yesterday = now - 1000 * 60 * 60 * 24;
        Question q1 = new Question("James", "How can I call a REST service?", now);
        Question q2 = new Question("Stephen", "Does JavaFX work on Android?", yesterday);
```

```
        answer.addAll(q1, q2);
        return answer;
    }

}
```

If you have read the previous chapters, this code does not contain anything new. We create a ListView, add it to a StackPane, create a Scene, and render the Stage.

The ListView is populated with an ObservableList containing Questions. This ObservableList is obtained by calling the getObservableList() method. In the following samples, we modify this method and show how to retrieve Questions from the Stack Exchange API.

■ **Note** The getObservableList returns an ObservableList. The ListView automatically observes this ObservableList. As a consequence, changes in the ObservableList are immediately rendered in the ListView control. In a later sample, we leverage this functionality.

Running this example results in the window shown in Figure 7-3.

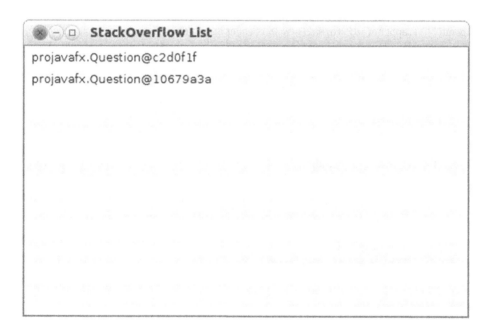

Figure 7-3. *The result of the first example*

The resulting window contains a ListView with two entries. Those entries correspond to the two questions that are created in the getObservableList() method at the bottom of Listing 7-2.

The information about the questions that is shown in the window is not very useful. Indeed, we told the ListView that it should display some instances of Question, but we did not tell how those should be displayed. The latter can be achieved by specifying a CellFactory. In this chapter, our goal is not to create a fancy UI; rather, we want to show how to retrieve data and render these data in the UI. Hence, we briefly show how the developer can alter the visualization of data by using the CellFactory concept. For an overview of the UI controls that we use in our examples (ListView and TableView), refer to Chapter 6.

In Listing 7-3, we create a QuestionCell class that extends ListCell and defines how to lay out a cell.

Listing 7-3. Define QuestionCell

```java
package projavafx;

import java.text.SimpleDateFormat;
import java.util.Date;
import javafx.scene.control.ListCell;

public class QuestionCell extends ListCell<Question> {

    static final SimpleDateFormat sdf = new SimpleDateFormat ("dd-MM-YY");
    @Override
    protected void updateItem(Question question, boolean empty){
        super.updateItem(question, empty);
        if (empty) {
            setText("");
        } else {
            StringBuilder sb= new StringBuilder();
            sb.append("[").append(sdf.format(new Date(question.getTimestamp()))).append("]")
                    .append(" ").append(question.getOwner()+": "+question.getQuestion());
            setText(sb.toString());
        }
    }
}
```

When a cell item has to be updated, we tell it to show some text containing the timestamp between square brackets, followed by the author and the title of the question. Next, the ListView needs to be told that it should render QuestionCells. We do this by calling the ListView.setCellFactory() method and provide a lambda expression that creates a new QuestionCell when called. In Listing 7-4, we show the modified version of the start method of our StackOverflowApplication.

Listing 7-4. Use CellFactory on the ListView

```java
public void start(Stage primaryStage) {
    ListView<Question> listView = new ListView<>();
    listView.setItems(getObservableList());
    listView.setCellFactory(l -> new QuestionCell());
    StackPane root = new StackPane();
    root.getChildren().add(listView);

    Scene scene = new Scene(root, 500, 300);

    primaryStage.setTitle("StackOverflow List");
    primaryStage.setScene(scene);
    primaryStage.show();
}
```

If we now run the application, the output appears as in Figure 7-4.

Figure 7-4. *The result of adding a* QuestionCell

For every question that is in the items of the ListView, the output is now what we expected it to be. We can do a lot more with CellFactories (e.g., we can use graphics instead of just text), but that is beyond the scope of this chapter.

We now replace the hard-coded questions with real information obtained via the Stack Exchange API.

Using the Stack Exchange API

The Stack Exchange network (http://stackexchange.com) allows third-party developers to browse and access questions and answers using a REST-based interface. Stack Exchange maintains a number of REST-based APIs, but for our examples we limit ourselves to the Stack Exchange Search API. More information on this API is at http://api.stackexchange.com/docs.

The resource URL—the endpoint for the REST service—is very simple:

http://api.stackexchange.com/2.2/search

A number of query parameters can be supplied here. We will only use two parameters, and the interested reader is referred to the Stack Exchange documentation for information about the other parameters.

- site: Specify the domain you want to search, in our case this is "stackoverflow".

- tagged: A semicolon delimited list of tags. We want to search all questions tagged with "javafx".

Combining both parameters leads to the following REST call:

```
http://api.stackexchange.com/2.2/search?tagged=javafx&site=stackoverflow
```

When executing this REST call in a browser, or using a command tool (e.g., cURL), the result is something like the JSON-text in Listing 7-5.

Listing 7-5. JSON Response Obtained from the Stack Exchange Search API

```
{
  "items": [
    {
      "tags": [
        "java",
        "sorting",
        "javafx",
        "tableview"
      ],
      "owner": {
        "reputation": 132,
        "user_id": 578518,
        "user_type": "registered",
        "accept_rate": 84,
        "profile_image": "https://www.gravatar.com/avatar/bdbee99c377a7063b24e09e7121fb1ab?
        s=128&d=identicon&r=PG",
        "display_name": "Rps",
        "link": "http://stackoverflow.com/users/578518/rps"
      },
      "is_answered": false,
      "view_count": 7,
      "answer_count": 1,
      "score": 0,
      "last_activity_date": 1397845222,
      "creation_date": 1397844823,
      "last_edit_date": 1397845143,
      "question_id": 23159737,
      "link": "http://stackoverflow.com/questions/23159737/javafx-tableview-ordered-by-date",
      "title": "javafx Tableview ordered by date"
    },

...
,"has_more":true
,"quota_max":300,
"quota_remaining":290
}
```

The Stack Exchange API only provides JSON-based responses. A number of web services deliver information in XML, and others provide both JSON and XML. Because we want to show how to process XML responses as well, we create our own XML-based output for the Stack Exchange REST Service. Rather than calling an external REST endpoint, this XML response will be obtained by reading a local file.

Our self-defined XML response is shown in Listing 7-6.

Listing 7-6. Artificial XML Response Obtained from the Stack Exchange Search API

```
<?xml version="1.0" encoding="UTF-8"?>

<items>

  <item>

    <tags>

      <tag>java</tag>

      <tag>sorting</tag>

      <tag>javafx</tag>

      <tag>tableview</tag>

    </tags>

    <owner>Rps</owner>

    <creation_date>1397844823</creation_date>

    <title>javafx Tableview ordered by date</title>

  <item>

</items>
```

Although the data in the JSON response contain the same information as the data in the XML response, the format is, of course, very different. JSON and XML are both widely used on the Internet, and a large number of web services offer responses in both formats.

Depending on the use case and the developer, one format might be preferred over the other. In general, JavaFX applications should be able to work with both formats, because they have to connect with third-party data, and the JavaFX developer cannot always influence the data format used by the back end.

■ **Note**   Many applications allow a number of formats, and by specifying the HTTP "Accept" Header, the client can choose between the different formats.

In the next example, we show how to retrieve and parse the JSON response used in the Stack Exchange Search API.

JSON Response Format

JSON is a very popular format on the Internet, especially in web applications where incoming data are parsed with JavaScript. JSON data are rather compact and more or less human readable.

A number of tools exist in Java for reading and writing JSON data. As of June 2013, when Java Enterprise Edition 7 was released, there is a standard specification in Java that describes how to read and write JSON data. This Java specification is defined as JSR 353, and more information can be obtained at www.jcp.org/en/jsr/detail?id=353.

JSR 353 only defines a specification, and an implementation is still needed to do the actual work. In our examples, we will use JSONP, which is the Reference Implementation of JSR 353. This Reference Implementation can be found at https://jsonp.java.net/. Readers are encouraged to try out their favorite implementation of JSR 353, though.

Although JSR 353 is a specification that is part of the Java Enterprise Edition umbrella, the reference implementation also works in a Java Standard Edition environment. There are no external dependencies.

We now replace the hard-coded list containing two fake questions with real questions obtained via the Stack Exchange REST API. We keep the existing code, but we modify the getObservableList() method as shown in Listing 7-7.

Listing 7-7. Obtain Questions via the Stack Exchange REST API, JSON Format, and Parse the JSON

```
ObservableList<Question> getObservableList() throws IOException {
    String url = "http://api.stackexchange.com/2.2/search?tagged=javafx&site=stackoverflow";
    URL host = new URL(url);
    JsonReader jr = Json.createReader(new GZIPInputStream(host.openConnection().
    getInputStream()));

    JsonObject jsonObject = jr.readObject();
    JsonArray jsonArray = jsonObject.getJsonArray("items");
    ObservableList<Question> answer = FXCollections.observableArrayList();

    jsonArray.iterator().forEachRemaining((JsonValue e) -> {
        JsonObject obj = (JsonObject) e;
        JsonString name = obj.getJsonObject("owner").getJsonString("display_name");
        JsonString quest = obj.getJsonString("title");
        JsonNumber jsonNumber = obj.getJsonNumber("creation_date");
        Question q = new Question(name.getString(), quest.getString(), jsonNumber.
        longValue() * 1000);
        answer.add(q);
    });
    return answer;
}
```

Before we dive into the code, we show the result of the modified application in Figure 7-5.

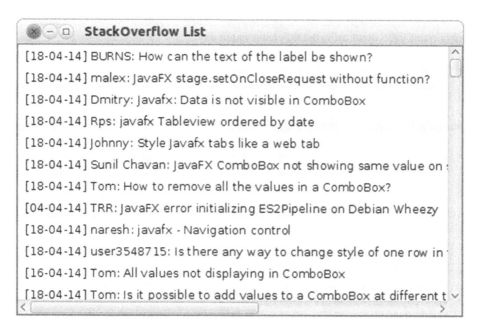

Figure 7-5. *The result of the* StackOverflowApplication *retrieving JSON data*

The code in Listing 7-7 can be divided into four parts:

1. Call the REST endpoint.

2. Obtain the raw JSON data.

3. Convert each item into a question.

4. Add the Questions to the result.

Calling the REST endpoint is very straightforward:

```
String url = "http://api.stackexchange.com/2.2/search?tagged=javafx&site=stackoverflow";
URL host = new URL(url);
JsonReader jr = Json.createReader(new GZIPInputStream(host.openConnection().
getInputStream()));
```

First, we create a URL object that refers to the desired location. Next, we open the connection to the location. Because Stack Exchange is sending its data as zipped data, we open a GZIPInputStream using the InputStream obtained from the connection. We pass this GZIPInputStream as the InputStream argument in the Json.createReader() method.

We now have a JSON reader that consumes the data we want to have. Extracting Java objects from this JSON reader manually requires specific code for a specific case.

■ **Note**   We could also have used a JSON parser instead of a JSON reader. It is not our intention to deliver an exhaustive JSON parsing guide. We only try to show how JSON data can be converted into Java objects for our specific use case. You can easily find a number of tutorials on JSON on the Internet.

In Listing 7-5, we observe that the questions are in an array named items, starting with the left square bracket ([). We can obtain this JSON array using the following statement:

```
JsonArray jsonArray = jsonObject.getJsonArray("items");
```

Next, we need to iterate over all these elements. For every item we encounter, we want to create a Question instance.

Iterating over the array elements can be done using

```
jsonArray.iterator().forEachRemaining((JsonValue e) -> {
    ...
}
```

To create a Question instance, we need to obtain the name of the author, the title, and the creation date of the question. The Java JSON API provides a standard way for doing this:

```
JsonObject obj = (JsonObject) e;
JsonString name = obj.getJsonObject("owner").getJsonString("display_name");
JsonString quest = obj.getJsonString("title");
JsonNumber jsonNumber = obj.getJsonNumber("creation_date");
```

Finally, we need to create a Question instance based on this information, and add it to the ObservableList instance we will return:

```
Question q = new Question(name.getString(), quest.getString(), jsonNumber.longValue() *
1000);
answer.add(q);
```

This example shows that it is very easy to retrieve and read JSON data obtained from a REST endpoint, and convert the result into a ListView. In the next section, we demonstrate a similar process for XML responses.

XML Response Format

The XML format is widely used in the Java platform. As a consequence, standardization of XML-based operations in Java happened years ago. There are a number of XML tools built into the Java Platform, Standard Edition, and we can use these APIs and tools in JavaFX without any external dependency. In this section, we first use a DOM processor for parsing the XML response that we artificially built. Next, we use the JAXB standard to automatically obtain Java objects.

Changing our application from JSON input to XML input requires only the getObservableList method to be changed. The new implementation is shown in Listing 7-8.

Listing 7-8. Obtaining Questions from the XML-Based Response

```
ObservableList<Question> getObservableList() throws IOException,
ParserConfigurationException, SAXException {
        ObservableList<Question> answer = FXCollections.observableArrayList();
        InputStream inputStream = this.getClass().getResourceAsStream("/stackoverflow.xml");
        DocumentBuilderFactory dbf = DocumentBuilderFactory.newInstance();
        DocumentBuilder db = dbf.newDocumentBuilder();
        Document doc = db.parse(inputStream);
```

```java
NodeList questionNodes = doc.getElementsByTagName("item");
int count = questionNodes.getLength();
for (int i = 0; i < count; i++) {
    Question question = new Question();
    Element questionNode = (Element) questionNodes.item(i);

    NodeList childNodes = questionNode.getChildNodes();
    int cnt2 = childNodes.getLength();
    for (int j = 0; j < cnt2; j++) {
        Node me = childNodes.item(j);
        String nodeName = me.getNodeName();
        if ("creation_date".equals(nodeName)) {
            question.setTimestamp(Long.parseLong(me.getTextContent()));
        }
        if ("owner".equals(nodeName)) {
            question.setOwner(me.getTextContent());
        }
        if ("title".equals(nodeName)) {
            question.setQuestion(me.getTextContent());
        }
    }
    answer.add(question);
}
return answer;

}
```

Again, the goal of this section is not to give a comprehensive overview of the DOM APIs. There are a large number of resources available on the Internet that provide information about XML in general, or DOM in particular.

To be able to compile the code in Listing 7-8, the following import statements had to be added.

```java
import javax.xml.parsers.DocumentBuilder;
import javax.xml.parsers.DocumentBuilderFactory;
import javax.xml.parsers.ParserConfigurationException;
import org.w3c.dom.Document;
import org.w3c.dom.Node;
import org.w3c.dom.NodeList;
import org.xml.sax.SAXException;
```

Before we go into detail about the code, we show the output of this example in Figure 7-6.

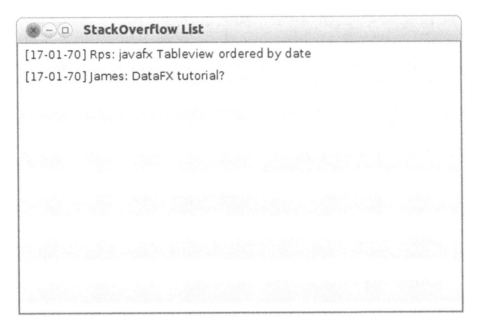

Figure 7-6. *The result of the question application using XML response*

The code in Listing 7-8 shows some similarities to the code in Listing 7-7. In both cases, we process data available in a text format (JSON or XML) and convert the data into Question instances. In Listing 7-8, the DOM approach is used to inspect the received response.

An org.w3c.dom.Document instance is obtained using the following code.

```
InputStream inputStream = this.getClass().getResourceAsStream("/stackoverflow.xml");
DocumentBuilderFactory dbf = DocumentBuilderFactory.newInstance();
DocumentBuilder db = dbf.newDocumentBuilder();
Document doc = db.parse(inputStream);
```

In this case, we create a Document based on an InputStream. The InputStream is obtained from the artificially created file. We can also create an InputStream from a URLConnection, and pass this InputStream to the db.parse() method. Even easier, the DocumentBuilder.parse method also accepts a String parameter that contains the URL of a REST endpoint.

This shows that although we are using a static file containing questions in this case, we can easily use the same code when using a real REST endpoint.

The resulting Document can now be queried. From the XML response shown in Listing 7-6, we learn that the individual questions are enclosed in XML elements named "item". We use the following to obtain a list of those XML elements.

```
NodeList questionNodes = doc.getElementsByTagName("item");
```

We then iterate over this list, and obtain the question-specific fields by inspecting the childNodes in the respective XML elements. Finally, we add the resulting question to the ObservableList of Question objects named answer.

This approach is rather simple, but we still have to do some manual XML parsing. Although this allows for flexibility, parsing becomes harder and more error prone with increasing complexity of the data structure.

Fortunately, the Java Standard Edition APIs contain tools for converting XML directly into Java objects. The specification for these APIs is defined by the JAXB standard, and is available in the javax.xml.bind package. The process of converting XML data into Java objects is called unmarshalling.

We now modify our example and make it use a mix of DOM parsing and JAXB unmarshalling. Again, we only change the getObservableList() method. The modified implementation is shown in Listing 7-9.

Listing 7-9. Combining XML Parsing and JAXB

```
ObservableList<Question> getObservableList() throws IOException,
ParserConfigurationException, SAXException {
    ObservableList<Question> answer = FXCollections.observableArrayList();
     InputStream inputStream = this.getClass().getResourceAsStream("/stackoverflow.xml");
    DocumentBuilderFactory dbf = DocumentBuilderFactory.newInstance();
    DocumentBuilder db = dbf.newDocumentBuilder();
    Document doc = db.parse(inputStream);
    NodeList questionNodes = doc.getElementsByTagName("item");
    int count = questionNodes.getLength();
    for (int i = 0; i < count; i++) {
        Element questionNode = (Element) questionNodes.item(i);
        DOMSource source = new DOMSource(questionNode);
        final Question question = (Question) JAXB.unmarshal(source, Question.class);

        answer.add(question);
    }
    return answer;

}
```

The only difference between this approach and the approach used in Listing 7-8 is the parsing of the individual questions. Instead of using DOM parsing for obtaining the specific fields of the individual questions, we use the unmarshal method in JAXB. The JAXB specifications allow for lots of flexibility and configuration, and the JAXB.unmarshal method is only a convenience method. However, in many cases, this method is sufficient. The JAXB.unmarshal method takes two parameters: the input source and the class that is the result of the conversion.

We want to convert the XML source into instances of our Question class, but how does the JAXB framework know how to map the fields? In many cases, the mapping is straightforward and does not require changes to existing code, but in other cases, the mapping is a bit more complex. Good enough, a whole package with annotations exists that we can use to help JAXB determine the conversion between XML and the Java object.

To make the code in Listing 7-9 work, we made some minor modifications to the Question class. The new code for the Question class is shown in Listing 7-10.

Listing 7-10. Question Class with JAXB Annotations

```java
package projavafx;

import javax.xml.bind.annotation.XmlAccessType;
import javax.xml.bind.annotation.XmlAccessorType;
import javax.xml.bind.annotation.XmlElement;

@XmlAccessorType(XmlAccessType.FIELD)
public class Question {

    private String owner;
    @XmlElement(name = "title")
    private String question;
    @XmlElement(name = "creation_date")
    private long timestamp;

    public Question(String o, String q, long t) {
        this.owner = o;
        this.question = q;
        this.timestamp = t;
    }

    public Question() {
    }

    /**
     * @return the owner
     */
    public String getOwner() {
        return owner;
    }

    /**
     * @param owner the owner to set
     */
    public void setOwner(String owner) {
        this.owner = owner;
    }

    /**
     * @return the question
     */
    public String getQuestion() {
        return question;
    }

    /**
     * @param question the question to set
     */
    public void setQuestion(String question) {
        this.question = question;
    }
```

```
/**
 * @return the timestamp
 */
public long getTimestamp() {
    return timestamp;
}

/**
 * @param timestamp the timestamp to set
 */
public void setTimestamp(long timestamp) {
    this.timestamp = timestamp;
}

}
```

We added three annotations to the original Question class. First, we annotated the class itself with

```
@XmlAccessorType(XmlAccessType.FIELD)
```

This annotation tells the JAXB framework to map XML data on the fields of this class, as opposed to on the JavaBean properties (getter/setter methods) of this class. The second and third annotations are added to the question field and the timeStamp field:

```
@XmlElement(name = "title")
private String question;
@XmlElement(name = "creation_date")
private long timestamp;
```

This indicates that the question field corresponds to an XML element named "title" and that the timestamp field corresponds to an XML element named "creation_date". Indeed, if we look at Listing 7-6, it shows that the question is in an element with the name "title" and that the timestamp is in an element with the name "creation_date". We have to instruct the JAXB runtime to map this element with our timestamp field, and this is what we do with the @XmlElement annotation.

Using the JAXB annotations made it easy to convert the XML question elements into individual Question instances, but we still had some manual XML processing in our main class. However, we can completely remove the manual XMLParsing and convert the whole XML response into a Java object. Doing so, the getObservableList() method becomes very simple, as shown in Listing 7-11.

Listing 7-11. Parsing Incoming XML Data Using JAXB

```
ObservableList<Question> getObservableList() {
    InputStream inputStream = this.getClass().getResourceAsStream("/stackoverflow.xml");
    QuestionResponse response = JAXB.unmarshal(inputStream, QuestionResponse.class);
    return FXCollections.observableArrayList(response.getItem());
}
```

In this example, we use JAXB to convert the XML response into an instance of QuestionResponse, and the questions are then obtained via this QuestionResponse instance. Note that we convert the questions from a regular List object into an ObservableList object, as required by the method signature. We later show an example where we don't have to do that additional conversion.

The QuestionResponse class has two goals: map the XML response onto a Java object and make the question items available as a List of Question instances. This is achieved by the code in Listing 7-12.

Listing 7-12. QuestionResponse Class, Enabling Conversion Between XML Response and Java Objects

```java
package projavafx;

import java.util.List;
import javax.xml.bind.annotation.XmlAccessType;
import javax.xml.bind.annotation.XmlAccessorType;
import javax.xml.bind.annotation.XmlRootElement;

@XmlRootElement(name="items")
@XmlAccessorType(XmlAccessType.FIELD)
public class QuestionResponse {

    private List<Question> questions;

    public List<Question> getQuestions() {
        return questions;
    }

    public void setQuestions(List<Question> questions) {
        this.questions = questions;
    }
}
```

The QuestionResponse class itself has two annotations. We've already discussed the following:

```java
@XmlAccessorType(XmlAccessType.FIELD)
```

This annotation indicates that this class corresponds to a root object in the XML structure, with the name "items".

```java
@XmlRootElement(name="items")
```

This indeed corresponds to the syntax of the XML response we created in Listing 7-6.

The previous examples show how existing technologies available in the Java 2 Platform, Standard Edition, can be used to obtain data from web services and inject these data in JavaFX controls. We now modify the example code to take advantage of some specific features of the JavaFX platform.

Asynchronous Processing

A major problem with the examples so far is that they block the UI during the process of data retrieval and parsing. In many real-world situations, this is unacceptable. Calls to external web services might take longer than expected due to network or server issues. Even when the external calls are fast, a temporarily unresponsive UI decreases the overall quality of the application.

Fortunately, the JavaFX platform allows for concurrency and asynchronous tasks. The concepts of Task, Worker, and Service were discussed in Chapter 7. In this section, we show how to leverage the javafx. concurrent package when accessing web services. We also leverage the fact that the ListView watches the ObservableList that contains its items.

The basic idea is that, when creating the ListView, we immediately return an empty ObservableList, while retrieving the data in a background thread. Once we retrieve and parse the data, we add it to the ObservableList and the result will immediately be visible in the ListView.

The main class for this example is shown in Listing 7-13. We started with the code in Listing 7-7, where we obtained the questions in JSON format using a REST request to the Stack Exchange API. With some minor modifications, we could use the XML response as well, though.

Listing 7-13. Use a Background Thread for Retrieving Question ListView

```
package projavafx;

import java.io.IOException;
import javafx.application.Application;
import static javafx.application.Application.launch;
import javafx.beans.InvalidationListener;
import javafx.beans.Observable;
import javafx.collections.FXCollections;
import javafx.collections.ObservableList;
import javafx.concurrent.Service;
import javafx.concurrent.Worker;
import javafx.scene.Scene;
import javafx.scene.control.ListView;
import javafx.scene.layout.StackPane;
import javafx.stage.Stage;

public class StackOverflow4 extends Application {

    @Override
    public void start(Stage primaryStage) throws IOException {
        ListView<Question> listView = new ListView<>();
        listView.setItems(getObservableList());
        listView.setCellFactory(l -> new QuestionCell());
        StackPane root = new StackPane();
        root.getChildren().add(listView);

        Scene scene = new Scene(root, 500, 300);

        primaryStage.setTitle("StackOverflow List");
        primaryStage.setScene(scene);
        primaryStage.show();
        System.out.println (« Done with the setup ») ;
    }

    ObservableList<Question> getObservableList() throws IOException {
        String url = "http://api.stackexchange.com/2.2/search?order=desc&sort=activity&
        tagged=javafx&site=stackoverflow";
        Service<ObservableList<Question>> service = new QuestionRetrievalService(url);

        ObservableList<Question> answer = FXCollections.observableArrayList();
        service.stateProperty().addListener(new InvalidationListener() {
```

```
                @Override
                public void invalidated(Observable observable) {
                    System.out.println("value is now "+service.getState());
                    if (service.getState().equals(Worker.State.SUCCEEDED)) {
                        answer.addAll(service.getValue());
                    }
                }
            });
        System.out.println("START SERVICE = "+service.getTitle());
        service.start();
        return answer;
    }


    /**
     * @param args the command line arguments
     */
    public static void main(String[] args) {
        launch(args);
    }
}
```

The main method is not different from the previous example, apart from the addition of a System.out log message that will print a message when we are done with the setup.

The getObservableList method will first create an instance of ObservableList, and this instance is returned on method completion. Initially, this instance will be an empty list. In this method, an instance of QuestionRetrievalService is created and the location of the REST endpoint is passed in the constructor. The QuestionRetrievalService, which extends javafx.concurrent.Service, is started, and we listen for changes in the State of the Service. When the state of the Service changes to State.SUCCEEDED, we add the retrieved questions to the ObservableList. Note that on every state change in the instance of the QuestionRetrievalService, we log a message to System.out.

We now take a closer look at the QuestionRetrievalService to understand how it starts a new thread, and how it makes sure that the retrieved questions are added to the ListView control using the JavaFX thread. The code of the QuestionRetrievalService is shown in Listing 7-14.

Listing 7-14. QuestionRetrievalService

```
package projavafx;

import java.net.URL;
import java.util.zip.GZIPInputStream;
import javafx.collections.FXCollections;
import javafx.collections.ObservableList;
import javafx.concurrent.Service;
import javafx.concurrent.Task;
import javax.json.Json;
import javax.json.JsonArray;
import javax.json.JsonNumber;
import javax.json.JsonObject;
import javax.json.JsonReader;
import javax.json.JsonString;
import javax.json.JsonValue;
```

```
public class QuestionRetrievalService extends Service<ObservableList<Question>> {

    private String loc;

    public QuestionRetrievalService(String loc) {
        this.loc = loc;
    }

    @Override
    protected Task<ObservableList<Question>> createTask() {
        return new Task<ObservableList<Question>>() {

            @Override
            protected ObservableList<Question> call() throws Exception {
                URL host = new URL(loc);
                JsonReader jr = Json.createReader(new GZIPInputStream(host.openConnection().
                getInputStream()));

                JsonObject jsonObject = jr.readObject();
                JsonArray jsonArray = jsonObject.getJsonArray("items");
                ObservableList<Question> answer = FXCollections.observableArrayList();

                jsonArray.iterator().forEachRemaining((JsonValue e) -> {
                    JsonObject obj = (JsonObject) e;
                    JsonString name = obj.getJsonObject("owner").getJsonString("display_
                    name");
                    JsonString quest = obj.getJsonString("title");
                    JsonNumber jsonNumber = obj.getJsonNumber("creation_date");
                    Question q = new Question(name.getString(), quest.getString(),
                    jsonNumber.longValue() * 1000);
                    System.out.println("Adding question "+q);
                    answer.add(q);
                });
                return answer;
            }
        };
    }

}
```

The QuestionRetrievalService extends Service and thus has to implement a createTask method. When the Service is started, this task is executed in a separate thread. The createTask method on the QuestionRetrievalService creates a new Task and returns it. The signature of this method,

```
Task<ObservableList<Question>> createTask(),
```

ensures that the Task creates an ObservableList of questions. The generic type parameter ObservableList <Question> is the same as the type parameter in the declaration of the Service. As a consequence, the getValue() method of the Service will also return an ObservableList of Questions.

Indeed, the following code snippet states that the questionRetrievalService.getValue() should return an ObservableList<Question>.

```
ObservableList<Question> answer = FXCollections.observableArrayList();
...
    if (now == State.SUCCEEDED) {
        answer.addAll(service.getValue());
    }
```

The Task instance that we created in the QuestionRetrievalService has to implement the call method. This method is actually doing what the getObservableList method in the previous examples was doing: retrieving the data and parsing them.

Although the real work in a Service (the Task created by createTask) is done in a background thread, all methods on the Service, including the getValue() call, should be accessed from the JavaFX thread. The internal implementation makes sure that all changes to the available properties in the Service are executed on the JavaFX Application Thread.

Running the example gives the exact same visual output as running the previous example. However, we added some System.out messages for clarity. If we run the example, the following messages can be seen on the console.

```
State of service is READY
State of service is SCHEDULED
Done with the setup
State of service is RUNNING
Adding question projavafx.Question@482fb3d5
...
Adding question projavafx.Question@2d622bf7
State of service is SUCCEEDED
```

This shows that the getObservableList method returns before the questions are obtained and added to the list.

■ **Note**   In theory, you could notice a different behavior inasmuch as the background thread might be completed before the other initialization has been done. In practice, however, this behavior is unlikely when network calls are involved.

Converting Web Services Data to TableView

So far, all our examples showed questions in a ListView. The ListView is an easy and powerful JavaFX control, however, there are other controls that are in some cases more suitable to render information.

We can show the Question data in a TableView as well, and that is what we do in this section. The retrieval and parsing of the data stay the same as in the previous example. However, we now use a TableView to render the data, and we have to define which columns we want to see. For each column, we have to specify the origination of the data. The code in Listing 7-15 shows the start method used in the example.

Listing 7-15. The Start Method in the Application Rendering Questions in a TableView

```
@Override
public void start(Stage primaryStage) throws IOException {
    TableView<Question> tableView = new TableView<>();
    tableView.setItems(getObservableList());
    TableColumn<Question, String> dateColumn = new TableColumn<>("Date");
```

```
TableColumn<Question, String> ownerColumn = new TableColumn<>("Owner");
TableColumn<Question, String> questionColumn = new TableColumn<>("Question");
dateColumn.setCellValueFactory((CellDataFeatures<Question, String> cdf) -> {
    Question q = cdf.getValue();
    return new SimpleStringProperty(getTimeStampString(q.getTimestamp()));
});
ownerColumn.setCellValueFactory((CellDataFeatures<Question, String> cdf) -> {
    Question q = cdf.getValue();
    return new SimpleStringProperty(q.getOwner());
});
questionColumn.setCellValueFactory((CellDataFeatures<Question, String> cdf) -> {
    Question q = cdf.getValue();
    return new SimpleStringProperty(q.getQuestion());
});
questionColumn.setPrefWidth(350);
tableView.getColumns().addAll(dateColumn, ownerColumn, questionColumn);
StackPane root = new StackPane();
root.getChildren().add(tableView);

Scene scene = new Scene(root, 500, 300);

primaryStage.setTitle("StackOverflow Table");
primaryStage.setScene(scene);
primaryStage.show();
}
```

Clearly, this example requires more code than the example showing a ListView. Setting up a table is slightly more complex, due to the different columns that are involved. There is not much difference between setting the contents of the ListView and setting the contents of the TableView. This is achieved doing

```
tableView.setItems(getObservableList());
```

where the getObservableList() method is the same implementation as in the previous example. Note that we could also use the convenient constructor

```
TableView<Question> tableView = new TableView<>(getObservableList());
```

When using a TableView, we have to define a number of TableColumns. This is done in the following code snippet.

```
TableColumn<Question, String> dateColumn = new TableColumn<>("Date");
TableColumn<Question, String> ownerColumn = new TableColumn<>("Owner");
TableColumn<Question, String> questionColumn = new TableColumn<>("Question");
```

Using the TableColumn constructor, we create one TableColumn with title "Date," one with title "Owner," and a third one titled "Question." The Generics <Question, String> indicate that each entry in a row represents a Question, and the individual cells in the specified column are of type String.

Next, the instances of TableColumn that we created need to know what data they should render. This is done using CellFactories, as shown in the following snippet.

```
dateColumn.setCellValueFactory((CellDataFeatures<Question, String> cdf) -> {
    Question q = cdf.getValue();
    return new SimpleStringProperty(getTimeStampString(q.getTimestamp())));
});
```

A detailed description of the setCellValueFactory method is beyond the scope of this chapter. The reader is encouraged to have a look at the Javadoc of the TableView and TableColumn classes while working with tables. The Javadoc explains that we have to specify a Callback class with a call method that returns an ObservableValue containing the content of the specific cell. Fortunately, we can use a lambda expression for this.

The question we are displaying in this row can be obtained via the CellDataFeatures instance that is passed as the single parameter in this lambda expression. Because we want to show the timestamp, we return a SimpleStringProperty whose content is set to the timestamp of the specified Question.

The same technique has to be used for the other TableColumns (containing the owner and the question contained within the applicable Question object).

Finally, we have to add the columns to the TableView:

```
tableView.getColumns().addAll(dateColumn, ownerColumn, questionColumn);
```

Running this example results in the visual output shown in Figure 7-7.

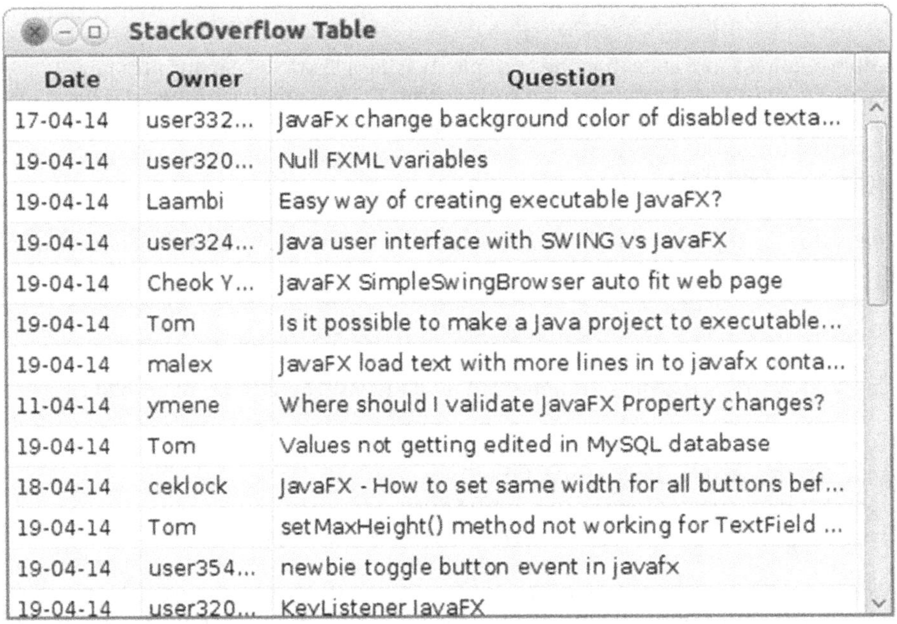

Date	Owner	Question
17-04-14	user332...	JavaFx change background color of disabled texta...
19-04-14	user320...	Null FXML variables
19-04-14	Laambi	Easy way of creating executable JavaFX?
19-04-14	user324...	Java user interface with SWING vs JavaFX
19-04-14	Cheok Y...	JavaFX SimpleSwingBrowser auto fit web page
19-04-14	Tom	Is it possible to make a Java project to executable...
19-04-14	malex	JavaFX load text with more lines in to javafx conta...
11-04-14	ymene	Where should I validate JavaFX Property changes?
19-04-14	Tom	Values not getting edited in MySQL database
18-04-14	ceklock	JavaFX - How to set same width for all buttons bef...
19-04-14	Tom	setMaxHeight() method not working for TextField ...
19-04-14	user354...	newbie toggle button event in javafx
19-04-14	user320...	KeyListener JavaFX

StackOverflow Table

Figure 7-7. *Using a TableView for rendering questions*

This sample requires lots of boilerplate code for a simple table, but fortunately the JavaFX platform contains a way to reduce the amount of code. Manually setting the CellValueFactory instances for each column is cumbersome, but we can use another method for doing this, by using JavaFX properties. Listing 7-16 contains a modified version of the start method of the main class, where we leverage the JavaFX properties concept.

Listing 7-16. Rendering Data in Columns Based on JavaFX Properties

```
@Override
public void start(Stage primaryStage) throws IOException {
    TableView<Question> tableView = new TableView<>();
    tableView.setItems(getObservableList());
    TableColumn<Question, String> dateColumn = new TableColumn<>("Date");
    TableColumn<Question, String> ownerColumn = new TableColumn<>("Owner");
    TableColumn<Question, String> questionColumn = new TableColumn<>("Question");
    dateColumn.setCellValueFactory(new PropertyValueFactory<>("timestampString"));
    ownerColumn.setCellValueFactory(new PropertyValueFactory<>("owner"));
    questionColumn.setCellValueFactory(new PropertyValueFactory<>("question"));
    questionColumn.setPrefWidth(350);
    tableView.getColumns().addAll(dateColumn, ownerColumn, questionColumn);
    StackPane root = new StackPane();
    root.getChildren().add(tableView);

    Scene scene = new Scene(root, 500, 300);

    primaryStage.setTitle("StackOverflow Table");
    primaryStage.setScene(scene);
    primaryStage.show();
}
```

This code is clearly shorter than the code in the previous sample. We actually replaced

```
dateColumn.setCellValueFactory((CellDataFeatures<Question, String> cdf) -> {
    Question q = cdf.getValue();
    return new SimpleStringProperty(getTimeStampString(q.getTimestamp()));
});
```

by

```
dateColumn.setCellValueFactory(new PropertyValueFactory<>("timestampString"));
```

The same holds for the ownerColumn and the questionColumn.

We are using instances of javafx.scene.control.cell.PropertyValueFactory<S,T>(String name) for defining what specific data should be rendered in which cell.

The PropertyValueFactory searches for a JavaFX property with the specified name and returns the ObservableValue of this property when called. In case no property with such a name can be found, the Javadoc says the following:

> *In this example, the "firstName" string is used as a reference to an assumed firstNameProperty() method in the Person class type (which is the class type of the TableView items list). Additionally, this method must return a Property instance. If a method meeting these requirements is found, then the TableCell is populated with this ObservableValue. In addition, the TableView will automatically add an observer to the returned value, such that any changes fired will be observed by the TableView, resulting in the cell immediately updating.*

> *If no method matching this pattern exists, there is fall-through support for attempting to call get<property>() or is<property>() (that is, getFirstName() or isFirstName() in the preceding example). If a method matching this pattern exists, the value returned from this method is wrapped in a ReadOnlyObjectWrapper and returned to the TableCell. However, in this situation, this means that the TableCell will not be able to observe the ObservableValue for changes (as is the case in the first approach).*

From this, it is clear that JavaFX properties are the preferred way for rendering information in a TableView. So far, we used the POJO Question class with JavaBean getter and setter methods as the value object for being displayed in both a ListView and a TableView.

Although the preceding example also works without using JavaFX properties, as stated by the Javadoc, we now modify the Question class to use a JavaFX property for the owner information. The timeStamp and the text fields could have been modified to use JavaFX properties as well, but the mixed example shows that the fall-through scenario described in the Javadoc really works. The modified Question class is shown in Listing 7-17.

Listing 7-17. Implementation of Question Class Using JavaFX Properties for the Author Field

```
package projavafx;

import java.text.SimpleDateFormat;
import java.util.Date;
import javafx.beans.property.SimpleStringProperty;
import javafx.beans.property.StringProperty;
import javax.xml.bind.annotation.XmlAccessType;
import javax.xml.bind.annotation.XmlAccessorType;

@XmlAccessorType(XmlAccessType.PROPERTY)
public class Question {

    static final SimpleDateFormat sdf = new SimpleDateFormat ("dd-MM-YY");

    private StringProperty ownerProperty = new SimpleStringProperty();
    private String question;
    private long timestamp;
```

```java
    public Question (String o, String q, long t) {
        this.ownerProperty.set(o);
        this.question = q;
        this.timestamp = t;
    }

    public String getOwner() {
        return ownerProperty.get();
    }

    public void setOwner(String owner) {
        this.ownerProperty.set(owner);
    }

    public String getQuestion() {
        return question;
    }

    public void setQuestion(String question) {
        this.question = question;
    }

    public long getTimestamp() {
        return timestamp;
    }

    public void setTimestamp(long timestamp) {
        this.timestamp = timestamp;
    }

    public String getTimestampString() {
        return sdf.format(new Date(timestamp));
    }

}
```

There are a few things to note about this implementation. The ownerProperty follows the standard JavaFX convention, as explained in Chapter 3.

Apart from the introduction of JavaFX properties, there is another major change in the implementation of the Question class. The class is now annotated with

```java
@XmlAccessorType(XmlAccessType.PROPERTY)
```

The reason for this is that when doing so, the setter methods will be called by the JAXB.unmarshal method when it creates an instance of the Question with some specific information. Now that we are using JavaFX properties instead of primitive types, this is required. The JAXB framework could easily assign the value of the XML element "owner" to the owner String field, but it cannot assign a value to a JavaFX Property object by default.

By using XmlAccessType.PROPERTY, the setOwner(String v) method will be called by the JAXB framework, supplying the value of the XML element to the setOwner method. The implementation of this method

```
ownerProperty.set(owner);
```

will then update the JavaFX property that is subsequently being used by the TableColumn and the TableView.

The other important change in the Question implementation is that we added a method

```
String getTimestampString()
```

This method will return the timestamp in a human-readable format. You might have noticed in Listing 7-16 that we set the CellValueFactory for the dateColumn to a PropertyValueFactory that points to "timestampString" rather than "timeStamp":

```
dateColumn.setCellValueFactory(new PropertyValueFactory<>("timestampString"));
```

The reason for this is that the getTimestamp() method returns a long, whereas we prefer to visualize the timestamp in a more readable format. By adding a getTimestampString() method and pointing the CellValueFactory to this method, the content of the cells in this column will be readable time indications.

The examples we have shown so far in this chapter demonstrate that the Java Platform, Standard Edition, already contains a number of APIs that are very useful when accessing web services. We also showed how to use the JavaFX Concurrent Framework, the ObservableList pattern, JavaFX properties, and the PropertyValueFactory class to enhance the flow between calling the web service and rendering the data in the JavaFX controls.

Although there is no rocket science involved in the examples, additional requirements will make things more complex, and more boilerplate code will be required. Fortunately, a number of initiatives have already popped up in the JavaFX community, with the goal of making our lives easier.

Using External Libraries

All our examples so far did not require any additional external library. The Java Platform, Standard Edition, and the JavaFX platform offer a great environment that can be used for accessing web services. In this section, we use two external libraries and show how they make accessing web services easier.

Gluon Connect

The previous editions of this book mentioned DataFX as an external library that provides a JavaFX API for connecting to remove endpoints. The development of the DataFX data services has since merged into the development of Gluon Connect.

Gluon Connect is an open-source, BSD licensed framework, managed by Gluon. The Gluon Connect product is described at http://gluonhq.com/products/mobile/connect and the code is available at Bitbucket (https://bitucket.org/gluon-oss/gluon-connect).

According to Bitbucket: "Gluon Connect is a client-side library that simplifies binding your data from any source and format to your JavaFX UI controls. It works by retrieving data from a data source and converting that data from a specific format into JavaFX observable lists and observable objects that can be used directly in JavaFX UI controls. It is designed to allow developers to easily add support for custom data sources and data formats."

A major advantage of Gluon Connect is that it is also supported on mobile platforms. We will talk about JavaFX on mobile in the next chapter.

In the next example, we integrate Gluon Connect with our Stack Exchange example. Once again, the only change is in the getObservableList method, but for clarity, we show the whole main class in Listing 7-18.

Listing 7-18. Obtaining Questions Using Gluon Connect

```java
import java.io.IOException;
import javafx.application.Application;
import static javafx.application.Application.launch;
import javafx.collections.ObservableList;
import javafx.concurrent.Worker;
import javafx.scene.Scene;
import javafx.scene.control.ListView;
import javafx.scene.layout.StackPane;
import javafx.stage.Stage;
import org.datafx.provider.ListDataProvider;
import org.datafx.provider.ListDataProviderBuilder;
import org.datafx.io.RestSource;
import org.datafx.io.RestSourceBuilder;
import org.datafx.io.converter.InputStreamConverter;
import org.datafx.io.converter.JsonConverter;

public class StackOverflowGluonConnect extends Application {

    @Override
    public void start(Stage primaryStage) throws IOException {
        ListView<Question> listView = new ListView<>();
        listView.setItems(getObservableList());
        listView.setCellFactory(l -> new QuestionCell());
        StackPane root = new StackPane();
        root.getChildren().add(listView);

        Scene scene = new Scene(root, 500, 300);

        primaryStage.setTitle("StackOverflow List");
        primaryStage.setScene(scene);
        primaryStage.show();
        System.out.println ("Done with the setup");
    }

    ObservableList<Question> getObservableList() throws IOException {
        InputStreamConverter converter = new JsonConverter("item", Question.class);

        RestSource restSource = RestSourceBuilder.create()
                .converter(converter)
                .host("http://api.stackexchange.com")
                .path("2.2").path("search")
                .queryParam("order", "desc")
                .queryParam("sort", "activity")
                .queryParam("tagged", "javafx")
                .queryParam("site", "stackoverflow").build();
```

```
        ListDataProvider<Question> ldp = ListDataProviderBuilder.create()
                .dataReader(restSource)
                .build();
        Worker<ObservableList<Question>> retrieve = ldp.retrieve();
        return retrieve.getValue();
    }

public static void main(String[] args) {
        launch(args);
    }
}
```

The relevant part, the implementation of the getObservableList method, is very simple.

We first create a RestClient, using the builder pattern. We supply information on the REST endpoint, by adding the request method, the hostname, and the path. Query parameters are supplied by calling the queryParam() method for each query parameter that needs to be used in the query.

Next, we call a convenience method on the DataProvider and ask it to retrieve the list that belongs to the RestClient we just created. We supply the target class for the different entities we expect in this list. Doing so, the DataProvider will try to map the incoming data to the target we specified. Gluon Connect will recognize JSON and XML-formatted data, and it can handle zipped InputStreams.

The latter is required in the Stack Overflow samples, as the Stack Overflow endpoint returns its data in a compressed format. It would require lots of boilerplate code to do a manual check to see if data is compressed or not.

The result of the call to DataProvider.retrieveList is an instance of GluonObservableList, a class that extends the standard JavaFX ObservableList. The GluonObservableList adds a few properties to the ObservableList that make it more suited in the particular area of remote data retrieval. For example, there is a state property that can have one of the following values:

- READY

- RUNNING

- FAILED

- SUCCEEDED

- REMOVED

In case the retrieval of data fails, the state property is set to FAILED. Another property, the exception property, will then contain the wrapped exception that indicates why the data retrieval has failed.

Calling the DataProvider.retrieveList method starts an asynchronous Service. Instead of waiting for the result, we can immediately return the result object to our visual controls. The Gluon Connect framework will update the result object while it reads and parses incoming data. For large chunks of data, this is very useful, because this approach allows developers to render parts of the data while other parts are still coming in or are still being processed.

Gluon Connect is an Open-Source framework, licensed under the business-friendly BSD license, so you are free to use it in both open-source as well as proprietary (commercial) software. It already contains a number of enhancements that remove boilerplate code, and that make it more suitable for client-to-server communication.

With Gluon Connect, you can easily retrieve data from a variety of sources, including files and REST endpoints.

Gluon also provides a commercial extension to this. Gluon CloudLink, which can be found at https://gluonhq.com/products/cloudlink, allows developers to synchronize both data and functionality between JavaFX client applications and a number of cloud providers and backend services. The Data Service component in Gluon CloudLink allows for real-time, bidirectional synchronization of content. Doing so, a Java Enterprise developer can modify a Java class in some backend code, and the result will be immediately visible in a UI component on the JavaFX client.

Gluon Connect contains support for Gluon CloudLink, and the APIs that you used in the previous example can be reused in case the data comes via Gluon CloudLink.

JAX-RS

The release of Java Enterprise Edition 7 includes the release of JAX-RS 2.0. This specification not only defines how Java developers can provide REST endpoints, but also how Java code can consume REST endpoints.

In the next example, we modify the QuestionRetrievalService of Listing 7-14 to use the JAX-RS API. This is shown in Listing 7-19.

Listing 7-19. Using JAX-RS for Retrieving Questions

```
package projavafx.jerseystackoverflow;

import javafx.collections.FXCollections;
import javafx.collections.ObservableList;
import javafx.concurrent.Service;
import javafx.concurrent.Task;
import javax.ws.rs.client.Client;
import javax.ws.rs.client.ClientBuilder;
import javax.ws.rs.client.WebTarget;
import javax.ws.rs.core.MediaType;

public class QuestionRetrievalService extends Service<ObservableList<Question>> {

    private String loc;
    private String path;
    private String search;

    public QuestionRetrievalService(String loc, String path, String search) {
        this.loc = loc;
        this.path = path;
        this.search = search;
    }

    @Override
    protected Task<ObservableList<Question>> createTask() {
        return new Task<ObservableList<Question>>() {
            @Override
            protected ObservableList<Question> call() throws Exception {
                Client client = ClientBuilder.newClient();
                WebTarget target = client.target(loc).path(path).queryParam("tagged",
                search).queryParam("site", "stackoverflow");
```

```
                QuestionResponse response = target.request(MediaType.APPLICATION_JSON).
                get(QuestionResponse.class);
                return FXCollections.observableArrayList(response.getItem());


            }
        };
    }

}
```

To show one of the nice tools of JAX-RS, we slightly modified the constructor of the QuestionRetrievalService to take three parameters:

```
public QuestionRetrievalService(String host, String path, String search);
```

This is because JAX-RS allows us to use the `Builder` pattern to construct REST resources, allowing a distinction among hostname, path, query parameters, and others.

As a consequence, we have to make a slight modification in Listing 7-13:

```
String url = "http://api.stackexchange.com/2.2/search?order=desc&sort=activity&tagged=javafx
&site=stackoverflow";
Service<ObservableList<Question>> service = new QuestionRetrievalService(url);
```

is replaced by

```
String url = "http://api.stackexchange.com/";
String path = "2.2/search";
String search = "javafx";
Service<ObservableList<Question>> service = new QuestionRetrievalService(url, path, search);
```

The hostname, path, and search parameter are used to create a JAX-RS `WebTarget`:

```
Client client = ClientBuilder.newClient();
WebTarget target = client.target(loc).path(path).queryParam("tagged", search)
        .queryParam("site", "stackoverflow");
```

On this `WebResource`, we can call the request method to execute the request, followed by the `get(Class clazz)` method, and supply a class parameter. The result of the REST call will then be parsed into an instance of the supplied class, which is also what we did using JAXB in our example in Listing 7-11.

```
QuestionResponse response = target.request(MediaType.APPLICATION_JSON).get(QuestionResponse.
class);
```

The response now contains a list of questions, and we can use the exact same code as in Listing 7-4 to render the questions.

Summary

In this chapter, we explained briefly two options for integrating JavaFX applications and enterprise applications. We demonstrated a number of techniques for retrieving data available via web services, and also showed how to render the data in typical JavaFX controls such as ListView and TableView.

We used a third-party tool that facilitates the process of retrieving, parsing, and rendering data. We demonstrated some JavaFX-specific issues related to remote web services (i.e., updating the UI should happen on the JavaFX application thread).

It is important to realize that the decoupling between JavaFX client applications and web services allows for a large degree of freedom. There are different tools and techniques for dealing with web services, and developers are encouraged to use their favorite tools in their JavaFX application.

Index

Get the eBook for only $5!

Why limit yourself?

With most of our titles available in both PDF and ePUB format, you can access your content wherever and however you wish—on your PC, phone, tablet, or reader.

Since you've purchased this print book, we are happy to offer you the eBook for just $5.

To learn more, go to http://www.apress.com/companion or contact support@apress.com.

Apress®

Printed in the United States
By Bookmasters